RED DREAMS, WHITE NIGHTMARES

Red Dreams, White Nightmares

PAN-INDIAN ALLIANCES IN THE
ANGLO-AMERICAN MIND, 1763–1815

ROBERT M. OWENS

UNIVERSITY OF OKLAHOMA PRESS : NORMAN

Also by Robert M. Owens

Mr. Jefferson's Hammer: William Henry Harrison and the Origins of American Indian Policy (Norman, Okla., 2007)

Library of Congress Cataloging-in-Publication Data

Owens, Robert M. (Robert Martin), 1974–
  Red dreams, white nightmares : pan-Indian alliances in the Anglo-American mind, 1763–1815 / Robert M. Owens. — First edition.
      pages   cm.
  Includes bibliographical references and index.
  ISBN 978-0-8061-4646-1 (hardcover) ISBN 978-0-8061-9112-6 (paperback)
  Indians of North America—Wars, 1815. 2. Indians of North America—
    Government relations. 3. Indians of North America—Ethnic identity.   I. Title.
    II. Title: Pan-Indian alliances in the Anglo-American mind, 1763–1815.
    E81.O84 2015
    323.1197—dc23   2014029839

The paper in this book meets the guidelines for permanence and durability of the Committee on Production Guidelines for Book Longevity of the Council on Library Resources, Inc. ∞

Copyright © 2015 by the University of Oklahoma Press, Norman, Publishing Division of the University. Paperback published 2022. Manufactured in the U.S.A.

All rights reserved. No part of this publication may be reproduced, stored in a retrieval system, or transmitted, in any form or by any means, electronic, mechanical, photocopying, recording, or otherwise—except as permitted under Section 107 or 108 of the United States Copyright Act—without the prior permission of the University of Oklahoma Press.

To my parents

Contents

List of Illustrations		ix
Acknowledgments		xi
Introduction		3
Part I	Tenuous Empire	17
	1. Pontiac and Pan-Indianism	19
	2. Dueling Diplomacies	31
	3. Stuart Besieged	43
	4. Dunmore's Fleeting Victory	49
	5. Revolution and Realignment	59
Part II	Pan-Indianism and Policy	71
	6. Britain's Pan-Indian Gamble	73
	7. A New Nation with Old Fears	85
	8. The Talented Mr. McGillivray	99
	9. Ohio Confederates Triumphant	107
	10. Henry Knox's Nightmare	117
	11. Bowles, Part One	137
	12. Pan-Indianism Crests	149
	13. The Fear Remains the Same	165
Part III	Paternalism vs. Pan-Indianism	173
	14. Bowles, Part Two	175
	15. Indians and the Jeffersonian Mind	181

16. Fear's Resurgence	191
17. Death by the River's Side	201
18. Bleeding Pan-Indianism	215
19. Mistimed Alliance	223
Epilogue: A Second Tecumseh?	235
Notes	245
Bibliography	281
Index	297

Illustrations

FIGURES

1. Sir William Johnson	129
2. William Augustus Bowles	130
3. Henry Knox	131
4. Tecumseh	132
5. Horseshoe Bend	133
6. William Weatherford Surrendering to Andrew Jackson	134
7. Black Hawk	135
8. Osceola	136

MAP

Key peoples, towns, and battles, 1763–1815	15

Acknowledgments

This project began in the summer of 2001. While researching my dissertation, I was fortunate enough to be working in the National Archives in Washington, D.C., and more fortunate still to have an exceedingly well-trained temporary research assistant, my chum Dr. Michael Conlin. While we were poring over microfilm trying to find letters about the American war against Indians in the Ohio country in the 1790s, Mike found a fascinating letter from 1792, wherein Secretary of War Henry Knox detailed his agitation at reports of Creek Indians paddling their canoes north to meet with the Ohio confederation. I quickly realized that while historians almost universally discussed Indian wars north and south of the Ohio as discrete events, for Knox and his contemporaries they were anything but. I had a new obsession for the next decade.

This would prove to be a massive project, taking me from Jackson, Mississippi, to Edinburgh, Scotland, and many places in between. I accrued many debts of kindness along the way. While I always enjoy working in archives and chatting with archivists and librarians, there are some I need to thank in particular. Mr. Clinton Bagley was my cordial host when I visited the Mississippi Department of Archives, and he maintained his delta gentility even after I repeatedly called him "Clayton." Thanks also to Brian Dunnigan, Deirdre, Barbara, Clayton, Val, and Janet for helping make my stay at the Clements Library in Ann Arbor so productive. I thoroughly enjoyed my time in the Historical Society of Pennsylvania—special thanks to Amanda and Steve. And my stay in Ottawa while working at the Library and Archives of Canada was thoroughly delightful. Anyone who has worked at the American Philosophical Society Library or the National Archives of Britain would agree that their collections and staff make for some of the most wonderfully professional and efficient research experiences imaginable. Special thanks to Holly Sinco; although I did not find a great deal at the Florida State Archives, she kindly mailed me my Mac power cord when I foolishly left it there in a rush to get to St. Augustine. Thanks to Dr. John Hoffmann at the Illinois History Room in Urbana (sorry I monopolized the copier for so long).

It is a great privilege to work with graduate students, bandying ideas and swapping research stories. I am particularly grateful to Mr. Dan Papsdorf and Mr. Jason Herbert, with whom I had many fruitful and pleasant discussions concerning sources for the Southeastern Indians. Thanks are due as well to Mr. Hugo Marquez, whose assistance in translating Spanish documents probably cut two years off this project. Thanks to my francophone colleague Dr. Robin Henry, who kindly reassured me that my translation of a French document was not especially terrible.

Being an academic historian can get to be a rather expensive habit. I am indebted to the Fairmount College of Liberal Arts and Sciences at Wichita State University for providing two summer grants for this project, allowing me to spend a month each in Great Britain and North Carolina (the barbecue was noticeably better in the latter). That North Carolina trip was also facilitated by an Archie K. Davis grant from the North Caroliniana Society. In terms of moral support, I would be remiss if I did not thank my colleagues here, particularly Dr. Helen Hundley.

David Nichols and Mike Conlin both read parts of early drafts of this book, and helped it considerably. I must also thank the anonymous referees for the University of Oklahoma Press. Thanks to Emily Jerman Schuster and Helen C. Meyers for overseeing the final polishing of the manuscript. The most profound gratitude is due my editor, Alessandra Jacobi Tamulevich, who also shepherded my first book to publication. Alessandra believed in this project when many others did not.

RED DREAMS, WHITE NIGHTMARES

Introduction

Henry Knox did not rattle easily; yet on April 21, 1792, he fretted. Certainly this arose from no lack of courage. As a younger man he had stood in a Trenton street and directed near-point-blank cannon fire to support his friend George Washington's stunning victory. Metaphorically, Knox had continued in that role throughout the 1780s and 1790s. As America's first true secretary of war,[1] Knox had to marshal all of his considerable abilities to forge a credible force for the cash-strapped nation. He had to maintain, or even bolster, the United States' territorial integrity, while avoiding a major armed confrontation. He faced tremendous difficulties. Knox had tried to recruit an army from a nation that, so far, had been distinguished largely by its rebellious independence and suspicion of standing armies, not to mention the considerable sectional tension between Americans in the East and West. Meanwhile, European powers prowled at the nation's borders like hungry wolves. Under the circumstances, Knox had performed most ably. Yet now he received from the West reports of the most distressing nature.

Intelligence indicated that headmen of the Creek Nation—the most numerous and (for the United States) most worrisome of the Southern Indian nations—were on the move, canoeing up the Tennessee River. They sought to confer with the Ohio Valley tribes that were currently in a state of war with the United States, particularly the Shawnees. The conclusion proved as terrifying as it was obvious: an attempted pan-Indian confederacy of Northern and Southern tribes, which would set the backcountry settlements ablaze and push American territorial ambitions back across the Appalachian Mountains. If this plan were successful, the result would be nothing less than socioeconomic and military disaster for the young United

States, and perhaps even the beginning of the country's demise. Knox noted, with his classic gift for understatement, that this Creek mission could "lead to the most pernicious effects."[2]

Perhaps Knox knew, or even sensed, that he was not the first administrator to grapple with such a problem. Many of his British opponents in the Revolutionary War had first cut their North American teeth on Indian affairs, often with results just as mixed as Knox's. All had acted their parts in the confounding play in which Knox was now the headliner: Sir Thomas Gage had been commander-in-chief of British forces in North America from 1763 to 1775 as well as royal governor of Knox's native Massachusetts; Sir William Johnson, the legendary Mohawk land baron, had been superintendent of Northern Indian Affairs; John Stuart had played Johnson's southern counterpart; and Indian agents on the ground had included George Croghan and Alexander Cameron. Like Knox, these men had seen the threat of pan-Indian alliance as ever present and had, as Knox would, engaged in tactics, both sound and desperate, to avoid the catastrophic results of a "general Indian war." Anglo-American officials repeatedly fought actual Indian wars north of the Ohio River while preoccupied with the threat of another one to the south.

Pan-Indianism can be a tricky term. Of relatively recent origin, it usually refers to late-nineteenth- and twentieth-century efforts to foster Indian unity, especially regarding efforts to protect native spiritual practices, such as the use of peyote.[3] Indeed, one of the great ironies of the colonization of Native America is that it has actually fostered far greater unity among Indian peoples than existed previously. This book's use of the term is more in line with that of Gregory Dowd and others.[4] It is, one should admit, a term of scholarly convenience, not unlike *Anglo-American*, which this book also employs. Pan-Indianism, in the context of the eighteenth and nineteenth centuries, refers to efforts by Native Americans (and encouraged or scuttled by outsiders depending on the situation) to establish broad, multitribal military coalitions.

Pan-Indian efforts would seek to bring peoples, often longtime enemies, together across regional or even continental distances. For this book's purposes, pan-Indian efforts are primarily those seeking to bring about an alliance between Native peoples from both north and south of the Ohio River. While an "Indian war" was typically a source of great dread for Europeans and Euro-Americans, the real horror was that of a "general

INTRODUCTION 5

Indian war"—a broad war against a great many different Indian peoples. By the time of Pontiac's War, the most terrifying prospect for most colonists and officials was such a war involving the fierce peoples of the Ohio Valley fighting alongside their more numerous cousins to the south.

Coalition and *alliance* are terms used interchangeably here largely to avoid excessive repetition. Strictly speaking, a coalition is a *temporary* alliance, but as George Washington himself noted, what alliance is not temporary? *Confederacy* implies a stronger political connection. It is probably proper to refer to the Great Lakes/Ohio Indians as having formed a confederacy in the 1790s to oppose American land hunger, yet it would seem a stretch to refer to a confederacy of Northern and Southern Indians, despite the ambitions of Tecumseh and the Prophet.

This is a story about fear. Recent psychological scholarship on fear tells us that "fear is a normal human emotional reaction—it is a built-in survival mechanism [and] a reaction to danger that involves both the mind and the body. . . . Fear can be individual or collective." Collective fears can often express themselves on a national level, and be far out of proportion to the actual danger; for example, contemporary American fear of terrorism. While fear serves an essential purpose—"informing us that we are in danger"—it can also become troublesome, even dangerous. Humans' ability to associate various stimuli can lead to patterns in our thinking and behavior. People are highly susceptible to such patterned thinking, or even stereotyping. "Because of our ability to associate, fear is considered to be an important factor in the development of problematic interpersonal patterns."[5]

Hypervigilance, a "narrowed down perceptual field, [and a] limited consideration of alternatives" are all classic symptoms of fear—the "fight or flight" response. While psychologists try to characterize fears as either "rational or irrational," at times "this distinction may . . . be difficult to uphold."[6] Fear of Indian attacks, as old as colonization itself, easily proliferated in the minds of Europeans and colonists in North America. Generations of children, reared on blood-curdling stories of brutal warfare with the Indians, were most likely preconditioned to such fear. Actually witnessing such attacks, or hearing secondhand accounts, would have only amplified such terror. Conditioning and other learned reactions to such stimuli—"modeling" the behavior of Indian warfare survivors—would have a lifetime impact; they could easily pass these fears on to their children and grandchildren. "Many people 'inherit,' so to say, fears of their parents about which they learn as children from their parents. . . . This kind of learning is often called 'warning.' Fears acquired in that way are maintained often because we do not get a chance to test them. Some of the learning may be based on misunderstanding or lack of information."[7]

It would seem that much of the popular imagery of the frontier worldview—the mindset of hardy "pioneers" who "won the West"—could be explained through a psychology of fear. Seeing one's environment as inherently hostile, having disdain for help from others, seeing outsiders as untrustworthy, and expecting the worst possible scenario are all typical symptoms of chronic fear.[8]

Indian attacks constituted perhaps the most universal fear for Americans in the Colonial, Revolutionary, and Early Republican eras. Yet especially in the Southern colonies, slave uprisings proved a close second. It appears, moreover, that as the plausibility of general Indian war declined, Southerners' terror of insurrection grew correspondingly. Possibly it was this fear of the *other*, in addition to simple economic ambition and greed, that helped drive Anglo-Americans to build the American empire at the expense of perceived outsiders. The widespread notion of American exceptionalism brought, as its corollary, a concept of outsiders as ill-intentioned others who were beyond trust and had to be dealt with.

From 1763 to 1815, fear drove Anglo-American policies regarding Indians and black slaves. As historian Gordon Wood has shown, European and colonial consciousness in the eighteenth century tended toward an abiding belief in conspiracies. Paradoxically, the Age of Enlightenment, which championed human agency and reason, encouraged a widespread belief that all happenings, including catastrophic misfortunes, resulted from someone's design. In an age when educated people felt all things were knowable, events that seemed beyond understanding or explanation were attributed to some secret conspiracy. Rather than a symptom of unreasoning paranoia, this preoccupation with plots was quite common among the most rational, educated minds of the day.[9] Wood and his advisor Bernard Bailyn have demonstrated how the leaders of the American Revolution could assume that they were combating a "Nasty Plot" by British leaders to enslave them. Jill Lepore, with equal skill and insight, has illuminated how such conspiratorial thinking led panic-stricken New Yorkers to execute dozens of people, mostly slaves, for an alleged plot to burn

INTRODUCTION   7

the city in 1741.¹⁰ These common fears of eighteenth-century Anglo-Americans coincided with their greatest nightmares, the threats of "general Indian war" and slave rebellion.

The fine historiography of Indian wars and Indian coalitions east of the Mississippi includes Gregory Evans Dowd's *A Spirited Resistance*, which examines pan-Indian efforts and the religious means used therein. Also, Richard White's *The Middle Ground* explores a host of issues concerning the Great Lakes/Ohio region, including efforts to form Indian alliances. Michael N. McConnell's *A Country Between* looks at the mid-eighteenth-century Ohio Valley peoples and their efforts to build coalitions to resist encroachment. The thorny issue of "Indian-hating" has been addressed by David A. Nichols in *Red Gentlemen, White Savages*, Patrick Griffin in *American Leviathan*, and Peter Silver in *Our Savage Neighbors*. This is not to mention the general works of Bernard Sheehan, Anthony F. C. Wallace, Francis Paul Prucha, and Reginald Horsman. Yet none of these works fully addresses the link between Anglo-Americans' fears of Indians, especially the dread of broad Indian alliances, and its influence on European and American Indian policy. Further, with the exception of Dowd, they tend to look at issues on either side of the Ohio as distinct, rather than related, phenomena. One goal of this work is to demonstrate how inextricable Indian affairs in the North were from those in the South.¹¹

Although slavery was certainly present in the Northern colonies and later states, it proved a great complicating factor in the South, especially regarding security fears, from at least the early eighteenth century. Recent discussions of the role of emancipation efforts during the Revolutionary and Early National periods include Jim Piecuch's *Three Peoples, One King*; Douglas Egerton's *Death or Liberty*; Alan Taylor's *The Internal Enemy*; David Geggus's *The Impact of the Haitian Revolution on the Atlantic World*; and Nathaniel Millett's *The Maroons of Prospect Bluff*.¹² The historiography demonstrates what generations of scholars tried to forget, or at least downplay: African Americans' agency in the cause of their freedom was seen as an existential threat to the slaveholding South, and both bondmen and foreign rivals were keen to use that fear to their advantage. At times, despite great efforts on the part of whites, blacks and Indians did find common cause. As with Indian coalitions, a small dose of real slave conspiracy could inflame the minds of whites, and inspire those of blacks, for decades.

We often think of the conspiratorial mindset only in regard to American Revolutionary leaders. The scholarship demonstrates, however, that leaders in Great Britain, as well as ordinary Americans, proved equally susceptible to the idea of secret cabals controlling events with malevolent intent. The Enlightenment expectation of discovering the answers to every question could lead rational men and women to conclude that obscure happenings (or unaccountable reversals), by their very opacity, grew from conspiracy. For the devout, an older but equally powerful force of malevolence—Satan—explained such inexplicable events.[13]

In studying North America, we have often attributed European and Anglo-American policies toward the natives as springing from greed and ignorance, or simple "Indian-hating." Certainly there is ample evidence for all of these sources of fear, yet it greatly oversimplifies the matter. Indian-hating was a real phenomenon, but historians have neglected the connection between hatred and its close cousin fear. As the historiography of Indian affairs has moved on from the nineteenth century's racialized depictions of Indians—think of the works of Francis Parkman or Theodore Roosevelt—scholars have adopted far more nuanced, less ethnocentric arguments. Empathy and understanding have been desperately needed. Yet fear was a central motivating factor for frontiersmen and government officials in forming repugnant ideas about blacks, Indians, and their allies. If we remove from our analysis the terror that eighteenth- and nineteenth-century whites felt regarding Indian wars and slave revolts, we effectively dehumanize them as badly as Parkman dehumanized his Indian foils. The terror felt toward Indians—and toward pan-Indian confederacies that represented Indians in their most terrifying form—was real, and would continue long after there was any rational chance for such confederacies to succeed. Slave revolts on mainland North America faced similarly long odds, yet continued to terrify white Americans nonetheless. And instances where slaves and Indians seemed in cooperation could bring such horror to a boil.

If conspiracy theories made sense regarding Crown policies of taxation, or slaves' desires to seek freedom, it made even more sense to attribute Indians' motives and actions to secret plots. As Wood argued, the growing interconnectedness of eighteenth-century society dramatically increased the complexity of peoples' worlds. "Unprecedented demographic and economic developments in early modern Europe were massively altering the nature of society and politics. There were more people more distances from one another and from the apparent centers of political decision making."[14] The very nature of Indian attacks—lightning guerilla strikes that mystified and horrified their victims—destroyed not just lives and property, but peace of mind. As Peter Silver argued, "Indian warfare's close-up killings could change the way the world looked. Its special power to unnerve and stun disordered people's faith that they understood how things around them worked."[15] If uncertainty and doubt encouraged conspiracy theories, few realms were less known to Anglo-American officials than Indian Country. Few peoples remained more mysterious, more *suspicious*, than Indians.

Slavery engendered parallel fear and angst. Colonies or states with large enslaved populations lived in constant terror of a slave uprising, and one might argue that a deep feeling of guilt—a semiconscious recognition of the horrid injustice of slavery—remained even under the glossiest veneer of paternalism. These feelings continually challenged notions of white American righteousness when the other proved less than willing to accept their supposed fate. If white Americans were truly chosen by God, why were other peoples so unwilling to accept their own manifest destiny? As Alan Taylor notes, "Armed blacks and Indians haunted the overactive imaginations of [white] Americans, who dreaded darker-skinned peoples as ruthless savages."[16]

With Britain's victory over France in 1763, the Crown inherited a vast number of new diplomatic challenges with the nations of the American interior and also another challenge, a massive debt. While the Army and the Indian Department had a number of skilled operatives, the picture as a whole was enormously complicated. Aside from the dozens of Indian nations who had until recently been enemies, each tribal unit had a social and political structure that few white men understood. One village of Creeks (for example) might be mostly hostile to the English, while another could be largely allies. They might, as individuals or collectively, change their minds with astonishing speed as well. This made it extraordinarily difficult to determine just who one's friends were, let alone determine the origins or reliability of war rumors.

Further, Indian diplomacy baffled most Anglo-American officials, who tended to miss the subtle cues of Indian chiefs' speeches in council, and the nuances of native cordiality. When Indian leaders' speeches urged peace and warriors struck out anyway, it was far too easy to assume that the speeches had been deliberate lies. That Indian leaders generally lacked coercive authority was often overlooked. European (and later American) leaders also insisted upon creating a position of recognizable, coercive authority in Indian chiefs. At times this appears to have been for the convenience of land cessions, but perhaps as often was also a psychological defense mechanism—trying to artificially create a more comfortable, familiar mental environment for diplomacy. Outsiders simply felt better telling themselves that they were speaking with the man in charge, even if this was entirely fictitious.[17]

Enlightenment optimism in discoverable truth, mixed with uncertainty, led generals and politicians to believe in Indian conspiracies. Ordinary folk had equal motive, if not equal reason. Pious Anglo-Americans needed look no farther than Satan himself for the root cause of Indian wars. Mary Beth Norton has shown how easily New England colonists identified "hostile" Indians as minions of the Devil. While historians still contest just how literally eighteenth-century colonists took the concept of Satan, colonists saw Indian war parties as the manifestation of earthly evil. Other immigrants to America had their own colonial experiences with native insurgents to draw upon. The Scots-Irish, for example, had dealt with rumors, and a few actual seventeenth-century incidents, of Irish natives' plots to wipe out the newcomers who took their lands.[18]

Unlike the alleged New York slave plot of 1741, or the "Nasty Plot" of the King's ministers against American colonists, there were numerous efforts by Native Americans to form pan-tribal alliances. As deadly as regional tribal confederations had been—Metacom's New England Indians in 1675–1677, Pontiac's Great Lakes/Ohio Valley war from 1763–1765—even the dullest student of Indian affairs realized that a true coalition of tribes from both sides of the Ohio River could threaten the expansion, perhaps even existence, of Anglo-America. Evidence abounded that Indians had repeatedly tried to effect just this scenario.[19]

The land itself often seemed hostile to Anglo-Americans, even as they lusted after its potential for profit. The Trans-Appalachian West was poorly known to whites. Thousands of square miles of terrain and tens of thousands of native peoples seemed to confront them. Few roads suitable for wagons or coaches could be found, though trails blazed by animals like deer and bison proved convenient for Indian peoples. Dozens of rivers, which Indians seemed to navigate with frightful ease, cut across that land. While the rivers hindered the movements of armies and sometimes traders, Indians used them like highways. Settler communities, even as they felt they had a right to their claims, nevertheless knew they were but outposts in a dangerous place, surrounded by people they saw as alien and potentially malevolent.

Still, Anglo-Americans tended to discount Indians' capacity for truly great efforts: British officials in the 1760s feared that the French or Spanish were inciting Indian alliances against them. The Americans later assumed that British (or sometimes French or Spanish) perfidy lay at the root of all Indian efforts to resist them. Rarely did native peoples receive credit for a fairly obvious if difficult to achieve strategy to reestablish their autonomy. Indeed, while America's Revolutionary generation and their descendants reveled in their radical break with Britain and the perceived vices of Europe, their views and actions regarding Indians remained remarkably consistent. Americans increasingly came to see themselves as being defined in opposition to the other. As Indians (and their British allies) were demonized, so Americans were beatified, at least in their own minds. In defeating pan-Indian confederacies, real or imagined, Americans would come to feel they had legitimized their own empire. In an unfortunate twist, the American confederation did not feel it could coexist with Indian unity.[20]

The most immediate change to Indian affairs after 1783 seems to have been that British officials could suddenly appreciate the benefits of pan-Indianism, at least south of Canada. Indians for their part often feared Anglo-American conspiracies directed at them. Their understanding of the motivations of their neighbors to the east could be just as cloudy as their rivals'. British officers saw potential in advocating abolitionism, haltingly during the Revolution, and then with greater conviction during the War of 1812. Doing so allowed them to attack and punish Americans who cried out for liberty on a rhetorical and literal level.[21]

It is impossible to determine exactly how many efforts were made to form pan-Indian alliances. As British and American officials would find, sorting out the serious threats—and what exactly constituted a *serious threat?*—from wild rumors and ruses often proved quixotic. The general lack of hierarchy and centralization in native societies that often thwarted establishing broad confederations served equally to thwart confirming their existence. And, Native Americans might encourage the idea that pan-Indian coalitions were in the making—even when they were not—in the hopes of strengthening their own leverage to redress grievances.[22]

The question is this: How did the fear of pan-Indian alliances drive Indian policy in the years prior to 1815? While such fear was often genuine, it was also used as a political tool for unifying non-Indian populations. (Peter Silver has demonstrated just how true this was for Pennsylvania.) Fear of a general Indian war was one of the few unifying features of early American life.[23]

This book is divided into three parts, detailing three distinct, yet interrelated phases. Fear of pan-Indianism evolved over time, and that fear's evolution and consequences comprise the heart of this book. Part I chronicles the late colonial period, and describes the impact of what came to be known as Pontiac's War in the mid-1760s. For eighteenth-century Anglo-Americans, this war proved the most frightening instance of pan-Indian alliance. Many of the tribes, or portions thereof, in the Great Lakes and Ohio Valley rose to attack the insolence of British colonial practices west of the Appalachians. Nearly all of George III's posts there fell, and thousands of his subjects died. Late in 1763, the king issued his royal proclamation that indefinitely suspended English settlement west of the Appalachian Mountains—a move too late to prevent the current war, but that did help prevent costly Indian wars for the next decade. Pontiac's War showed the haughty British military just how vulnerable it was in Indian Country, and Crown officials took a number of steps, some quite drastic, to maintain a semblance of control. While they felt the increasingly demonstrative colonists needed a show of force and determination, Crown officials, including the king himself, advocated appeasing Indian allies.

Part II examines the impact the fear of pan-Indian alliances had on Americans in the Revolutionary era through the mid-1790s. As Colin Calloway has noted,[24] the Revolution proved devastating for Indians, sparking intense divisions and even civil war in Indian country. While all Indians would eventually end up losing in the war, whether they allied with the Americans, the British, or tried to be neutral, the war saw repeated attempts to forge an alliance between the Northern and Southern tribes. Had large Southern tribes, like the Creeks, firmly supported the British cause, it might well have changed the war's course in the Southern colonies. The war also exacerbated divisions between hawks and doves in many tribes. Warriors preaching an all-out war against settlers gained (and sometimes

INTRODUCTION   13

lost) clout in these struggles. It was the aftermath of the war, however, that gave pan-Indianism its greatest boost.

In 1783–1784, most Americans sighed in relief when told of the generous terms of the Peace of Paris, especially the massive grant of land. Many assumed that the land would be quickly and easily sold and settled, to the benefit of the U.S. Treasury and citizenry. Proud, well-armed Indians on both sides of the Ohio River disagreed. While a confederacy grew north of the Ohio to violently oppose American encroachment, both they and George Washington's government realized that the key issue was the disposition of the Southern Indians. The 1790s would prove the decade when pan-Indian efforts had their greatest chance for success. The enormous complexity of Indian affairs in this decade sprang from the fears, real and imagined, of foreign agents working with various nations to hobble America's territorial ambitions. While armies tilted north of the Ohio River, all sides kept a cautious eye toward the south, where Spanish officials seemed far more assertive to both Americans and Britons. Even after major treaties theoretically secured peace between Indians and the United States, the later 1790s were wracked with fears that Spanish- or French-backed natives would fall upon American or Canadian forces. A revolt by slaves on the French sugar island of St. Domingue further complicated the picture, as Americans and transplants from the colony wondered if rebel slaves would join with Indian warriors.

Part III examines the last great effort toward pan-Indianism east of the Mississippi River, as natives tried to block Thomas Jefferson's manifest policy of acquiring Indian lands. Both Jefferson's confidence in peaceful conquest and his Francophilia would be sorely challenged. The Shawnee chief Tecumseh's dream of pan-Indian resistance to the United States paradoxically helped fuel the rationalizations of Andrew Jackson and others to strip Indians of their lands. By the early nineteenth century, Americans had consumed a steady diet of tales of Indian "savagery," and Southerners especially felt the gnawing fear of slave rebellions, possibly with pan-Indian links. The War of 1812, the "Second War for Independence," saw Americans recycle the imagery of British-Indian-slave collusion. By the time war was declared, Indians still dreamed of pan-Indian alliance, and Americans retained the nightmare. Yet American preemption and poor timing in the British-Indian alliance made the long odds of stopping American expansion even longer. When Tecumseh's coalition fell apart, it made it all the easier for Andrew Jackson to effect his plans for American hegemony in the Southeast.

The epilogue discusses the last gasp of pan-Indian efforts in the eastern United States. Predictably for one of Tecumseh's former disciples, the Sauk leader Black Hawk hoped to rekindle a pan-Indian alliance with British aid to block American expansionism in the 1820s and early 1830s. The epilogue summarizes both the potential and the reality of such dreams. The potential gains of a successful pan-Indian alliance had always been tremendous. In 1832, Black Hawk would badly overestimate the odds of forming and maintaining such an alliance. Around the time of his birth, however, the opportunities had seemed limitless. The story concludes in Florida, where American fears of Indians, free blacks, and slaves most directly merged with the ambitions of empire.

Key peoples, towns, and battles, 1763–1815. © 2015, University of Oklahoma Press.

PART I

Tenuous Empire

In the wake of the Seven Years' War, Britons in America and elsewhere began learning the true cost of empire. Administering North America would prove far more difficult than conquering it from the French. Inheriting French land claims also meant inheriting French diplomacy with the Indians, and from the start it was clear that many British officials were in over their heads. At first they tried to reconcile the numerous Indian nations, while simultaneously insulting former enemy and ally alike with an imperious attitude and impolitic policies. But when a coalition of Indians from the Great Lakes/Ohio region attempted to drive British influence out of the West, and even sent embassies to the more populous Southern nations, Britain opted for the practicality of divide and conquer. From 1763 until the American Revolution, British policy became one of quietly encouraging intertribal rancor, to save money and to save Anglo-American lives.

Pontiac's multitribal coalition had wreaked such terrifying destruction and cost such blood and treasure that it cast a shadow over British–Indian affairs for decades. Officials in Whitehall knew that frontier colonists and officials who recklessly speculated in Indian lands would continue to prod and provoke the king's so-called red children. Yet budgetary limitations would preclude the manpower necessary to enforce order on Trans-Appalachia, and Crown officers would resort to fomenting dissent and expanding existing rifts among the Indian nations to ward off pan-Indian efforts. The covert campaign to keep Indians divided would end, paradoxically, with the increased unity of the thirteen colonies as they slid closer to open rebellion.

CHAPTER 1

Pontiac and Pan-Indianism

After nearly three years of relative calm in North America, British officials felt they could exhale and finally start enjoying their victory in what William Pitt had called the "Great War for Empire." Predictably, they did so with a sense of smug self-satisfaction. The relief and joy they felt with the Peace of Paris in 1763 soon vanished, however. And that would have been predictable for them, had they been paying closer attention to America's natives. While many Indians were now presumed to be conquered peoples, and others had recently been valuable allies, they all shared at least some common goals. Political sovereignty, financial independence, and territorial security had all been factors that swayed Indians in the Seven Years' War, regardless of whose side they had taken to reach those goals. Only imperial myopia could prevent British authorities from seeing it was so. Only their ethnocentric tone deafness could keep them from hearing the warning cries.

The story of what became known as Pontiac's War is well known. Starting in May 1763, most of Britain's forts in the Great Lakes region were suddenly captured, destroyed, or abandoned. The western settlements, especially north of the Ohio River, were thrown into a panic. The cost in Anglo-American lives and treasure, particularly coming in an era of astounding debt for the Crown, was shocking and disheartening.[1] Historians often forget what contemporaries could not; the conflagration could have been much worse. Pontiac's War was but another in a series of panics where not just a fight with Indians in one region, but the dreaded general Indian war, might have broken out. After Pontiac's War, both the British and their American successors remained ever mindful of the horrific threat of pan-Indian alliances against them, and would take whatever measures necessary to prevent such a doomsday scenario.

Indian coalitions and the intense fear they engendered in British America easily predated Pontiac. In 1622, upon learning of the Powhatan Confederacy's desperate surprise attack to wipe out the Jamestown colonists, the settlers at Plymouth, more than 600 miles distant, "responded by taking careful stock of the Indians around them." Three decades later, the United Colonies of New England seriously considered launching a preemptive strike against a rumored alliance of Indians and the Dutch of New Netherland, who were supposedly bent on wiping out the New English. (Cooler heads prevailed, and the alliance came to nothing.) Still, as Cynthia J. Van Zandt notes, it is striking that the Puritans "found it quite plausible" that "their fellow European Calvinists" could "make an alliance with Indians to exterminate the New England colonies."[2]

During King Philip's War (1675–1676) in New England, wherein a multi-tribal coalition led by the Wampanoags did battle with their Puritan neighbors, Englishmen again feared even broader Indian conflicts. Virginia's governor, Sir William Berkeley, worried that Philip's men might strike up an alliance with the Indians of Virginia and Maryland, who were coincidentally embroiled in their own war against colonists, the result of Bacon's Rebellion (1675–1677). "The infection of the Indianes in New-England," Berkeley maintained, "has dilated it self to the Merilanders and the Northern parts of Virginia."[3] If pan-Indian alliance was an "infection," then it was a virus for which Britain's American colonies had no inoculation.

During the conflicts collectively known as the French and Indian Wars (1689–1748), Anglo-America had been largely fortunate in Indian alliances. France and Spain continued to enjoy the bulk of native auxiliaries, but they rarely seem to have carried out concerted attacks against Anglo-America. Further, some, like the Iroquois League of northern New York, remained allies. But during the 1750s, the groundwork for broader Indian alliances, and even cracks in the Anglo–Iroquois alliance, began to show.

In the mid-1750s, Anglo-American arrogance and ignorance helped throw important allies into the anti-English (though not rabidly pro-French) camp. In 1753, South Carolina authorities foolishly intervened in a Shawnee raid against South Carolina Catawbas, holding the Shawnees prisoners for months. The Shawnees responded not only by abandoning the English, but seeking Huron help to fight their erstwhile allies. South Carolina had not only lost valuable allies, but largely initiated what would be forty-some years of Shawnee resistance to Anglo-American settlement.[4]

British officers had themselves engaged peripatetically in the business of pan-Indianism, sometimes encouraging, sometimes discouraging, but always trying to manipulate the situation to the Crown's advantage. In December 1755, for example, Governor Robert Morris of Pennsylvania wrote nervously to Governor William Shirley of Massachusetts regarding the Delawares and their hostility to the British cause. While the Southern tribes, in particular the Cherokees, were numerous and valuable allies, Morris noted, intelligence reports indicated that they had favorably received Delaware embassies seeking aid against the English. Yet by the summer of 1758 Sir William Johnson, the Mohawk land speculator and Indian superintendent, sought to promote greater coordination between the British-allied Iroquois League and the Southern tribes. Johnson argued that "a Union between our Indian allies to the Southward & Northward, is a desireable Event & worthy of our Endeavours to compass."[5] Johnson later came to curse the very thought.

In late 1758, Virginia backwoodsmen attacked a party of Cherokees moving through the western part of the colony, killing several. The Cherokees had been stalwart allies of Britain, and were returning home from offering their services to the Crown. The Virginians carried the fratricidal insult to the point of trying to disarm the chief Attakullakulla (Little Carpenter), and matters took a turn. "These differences I fear will not tend to our advantage," groaned Indian agent George Croghan. The only hope of precluding a general Indian war would be military victories in the northern quarter to dissuade their cousins to the south. "Nothing in my opinion could prevent a War with the Southern Indians but our Success at Ohio, and it yet depends much on our keeping possession of what we so luckily got."[6]

The situation continued to deteriorate into 1760, when official neglect and colonial impertinence had managed to infuriate the Cherokees into not only breaking their alliance, but actually attacking British forces and destroying Fort Loudoun in what is now eastern Tennessee. (The loss was doubly shocking, as Fort Loudoun had been built at the insistence of the Cherokees.)[7] This time it was the Cherokees and Choctaws who sought help from the Ohio Valley Indians. Britain averted disaster once more, and again largely through luck, when the Ohio tribes declined. Timing had favored the Crown: by 1760, the Ohio Valley tribes had largely come to an armistice, or even outright peace with Britain. Disaffected Creeks had long called for Cherokee aid in their war against the colonists in Georgia, but they too—after an intense effort by the British to keep them neutral— were now quiet and disinclined to join in a broader war. After a brief campaign of "chastisement," and of course another round of land cessions, South Carolina made peace with the Cherokees.[8]

Perhaps Britain's greatest allies were the old feuds that made unifying the Northern and Southern tribes so difficult. But they were never absolute. By the winter of 1762, reports circulated that the Shawnees, Delawares, and some Ohio Valley Senecas—the westernmost peoples of the Iroquois League—were preparing to fight off an anticipated attack from the English. Indeed, Seneca embassies, complete with red wampum belts, had been calling for such a league since at least 1761. Britain's refusal to supply arms and ammunition, necessary for both hunting and raiding their traditional Southern enemies, helped convince these tribes that the English would attempt their destruction. Further, as Gregory Dowd has demonstrated, Indians increasingly felt common cause through spiritual means.[9]

Ohio Valley tribes, especially the Lenni Lenapes, or Delawares, had spoken of pan-Indian movements for years. Delaware prophets—male and female—had preached of radical visions at least since the "Walking Purchase" of 1737, when Pennsylvania's authorities shamelessly defrauded the Delawares of some 1,200 square miles of land. They spoke of a separate creation of whites and Indians, with whites being malevolent beings from across the ocean. They spoke of sins committed by Indians that had angered the Great Spirit—alcohol abuse and greed for the material goods of the fur trade. In essence their preaching was quite similar to that which the Delaware Prophet Neolin would offer in the early 1760s. The message of the separate creation of Indians and whites carried implicit notes of pan-Indianism, and Delaware prophecy also became increasingly critical of domination from outsiders, especially the Iroquois League to the north.[10]

As the Delawares became increasingly influential in pan-Indian circles, their connections with the Southeastern Indians also grew. The phenomenon of the Black Drink, a powerful emetic consumed for physical and spiritual purging, had long been used by the peoples of the Southeast. It became common with the Ohio Indians of Neolin's era, perhaps introduced to the Delawares by their well-traveled Shawnee neighbors.[11] As harnessed by Delaware prophets, the Black Drink demonstrated that pan-Indian sentiment was winning converts both body and soul. The Delaware–Shawnee connection proved important for pan-Indianism as well, because of the Shawnee ties to the southeastern tribes. Especially with the Creeks, the Shawnees had a long history of kinship and diplomatic ties to a region with a large population and many warriors to recruit.[12]

At times it seemed that there were as many cultural forces hindering cooperation between Indians north and south as there were aiding them. While most peoples north of the Ohio had a well developed sense of "covering the dead," of ritual condolences and gift-giving that could heal rifts (even homicidal ones) between individuals or tribes, the main nations in the South generally adhered to the theory of "crying blood." For the Cherokees, Creeks, and others, if a member of one's clan were killed, whether by malice or accident, the universe was suddenly out of balance. The only way to restore that balance, in a rationale Hammurabi would certainly have appreciated, was the taking of another life from the group—clan or tribe—responsible for the death of the relative. Until they had done so, the spirit of the departed clansman would, essentially, haunt the living, unable to enter the afterlife. Similar to the "mourning war" practiced by other Iroquoians to the north, Cherokees in the seventeenth and eighteenth centuries were quite insistent in following this practice, even though it made warfare (at least on a small scale) a never-ending cycle.[13]

Furthermore, for the Southern tribes in particular, during this time period they viewed humanity as a fairly simple dichotomy: there were relatives, whose kin ties gave their lives meaning, and outsiders/strangers, who had no kin ties. Southern Indians saw such a person "as an enemy, and enemies had no rights, not even the right to live." Diplomacy certainly could involve a temporary assignment of kinship to outsiders, but outsiders emerged from "chaos," and they "were leery of anything that emerged from the chaos."[14]

Only two months before Pontiac began his siege of Detroit, intelligence again indicated that there were at least attempts at a grand North/South Indian alliance. A Shawnee chief reported that the Cherokees had sent a war belt—passed on by the French still in the Illinois Country—but that the belt "was not unanimously accepted of." Still, the same report boded ill, noting that "all the Indian nations were," as he said, "become very jealous of the English, who had erected so many Posts in their Country, but were not so generous as the French." According to some Miami chiefs in a speech in late March 1763, the Shawnees had also passed on a similar belt that originated with the Senecas, who were "very much enraged against the English" and wanted to "put the English to Death all about this place." The Miamis took pains to note that they themselves sought ammunition and war paint to attack the Cherokees, rather than the English.[15]

War belts calling for a broad multitribal alliance "had in fact never ceased to circulate among the western Indians after the conquest of Canada." Some of the belts were politically obsolete, having been sent out by the French during the war and never officially recalled. Newer ones sprang from the Geneseo Senecas, who had grown angry with the British at Fort Niagara, and sought allies to smite them. It is possible that spiteful French still living in the Ohio Valley circulated some of the belts. The primary evidence for this comes from outraged British officials, rather than any direct source, however. In late 1762, Colonel Henry Bouquet, safe in Philadelphia, passed on reports of what he called "a pretended new conspiracy" of Western Indians. General Jeffrey Amherst, the commander-in-chief for North America, proved equally dismissive of the notion.[16]

Adding to the confusion, in the spring and early summer of 1763 there were at least some signs that pan-Indian efforts would be held at bay. Newspapers reported warfare between tribes from both sides of the Ohio River, such as the Shawnees attacking the Catawbas of South Carolina. There were also accounts of the continuing violent feud between the Creeks (in present Alabama and Georgia) and their neighbors, the Chickasaws to the west and the Cherokees to the northeast. Nevertheless, General Amherst, on the eve of Pontiac's attack in the Northwest, was thinking of the Southeast. Amherst was troubled by the Crown's decision to demolish three key forts there. "I am persuaded the Indians will always be best Neighbours, when they See that We are in a State to Defend Ourselves, should they be inclined to Mischief." He also mentioned that the governors of the colonies south of Maryland, as well as John Stuart, the Southern District's Agent for Indian Affairs, were to call for a great council with the Southern Indians to allay their fears and explain "His Majesty's Just and Equitable Intentions towards all the Indian Nations."[17] At least Amherst was honest enough to note that the kind intentions toward Indians were the king's, and not his own.

In fairness to Amherst, his policy of reducing Indian access to arms was not as obviously foolish as it now seems. As David Dixon notes, Amherst saw the Cherokee War end favorably in large part because the Indians ran out of ammunition, and assumed that this would work universally. And, a year prior to Pontiac's War, Amherst could note that in dealing with Indian affairs, specifically some scalpings perpetrated by a party of Shawnees, Sir William Johnson knew best. "I would not have you take any steps against them until I have his advice," he wrote Colonel Bouquet.[18] Yet Amherst would soon ignore Johnson's advice regarding the sagacity of diplomatic gifts to Indians, infuriating both Johnson and his subordinate, George Croghan. Croghan tried to resign even before the war broke out, noting, "there is no ocation [occasion] for an Agent here on Sir Jeffrey Amhersts present Plan." Amherst did at least have the sense to oppose Croghan's resignation in the midst of the subsequent crisis, though that only deepened the agent's enmity for the general.[19]

Pontiac launched his attack on Detroit on May 7, 1763. Soon the idea had spread throughout much of the Great Lakes/Ohio Valley region, and with great fury. The war in the Northwest caught Amherst completely by surprise. Ironically his parsimony regarding the Indian trade, meant to lower administrative costs and raise his own stock with his superiors, would help bring on a nearly catastrophic frontier war. The cost in currency and casualties would lose Amherst the job he hoped to keep.[20] Soon after the initial reports of violence at Detroit and outside Fort Pitt, Amherst wrote to the governors in Montreal, Trois Riviers, and Quebec, directing them to take precautions lest Pontiac's allies "seduce as many of the Nations as they can, to Joyn them in their Wild & Treacherous Schemes." Defensively, Amherst quickly added that the hostile Indians were "a Giddy Tribe," and that "Should they Persevere [in their war], it must End in their Total Ruin, and Extirpation." Displaying the slow comprehension of Indian affairs that brought on Pontiac's War, Amherst waited three more days before writing to John Stuart, to similarly direct him to stop "any of the Nations to the Southward from Hearkening to any Messages that may be sent from those misguided Tribes."[21]

Once the full import of the war hit them, Army and Indian affairs officials belatedly paid considerably more attention to reports of attempted pan-Indianism, even when those reports seemed a bit far-fetched. While

Indian agent George Croghan was understandably worried in July 1763 that the successful attacks on British posts in the North might encourage the Southern Indians to "take this Opportunity of breaking out again,"[22] others nearly gave in to hysteria.

While Amherst continued to talk of the warring Indians as "misguided," and threatened them with "extirpation," much of his blustering was an attempt to conceal his increasing horror as the war spread. Previously contemptuous of Indians' military capabilities, by August 1763 he was applauding British forces in Nova Scotia—never seen as particularly vulnerable to Indian warriors—for being on their guard. Still, Amherst insisted that if the Canadian tribes did rise against the Crown, it would only be from "false Reports of the Success of the Western Tribes." In January 1764, General Thomas Gage, who had replaced Amherst as commander-in-chief for North America, gave further credence to reports that emissaries from Pontiac's Detroit-area Ottawas were trying to recruit Indians from Massachusetts and even Nova Scotia.[23]

The North American command also had plausible fears of the possible spread of the Indian war outside the Northwest, and the encouragement that would offer Indians elsewhere. Southern Indian Agent John Stuart could encourage Amherst by noting he had sent warning to the various tribes of the Southeast to steer clear of joining their cousins to the north. Still, Stuart raised another specter when he confided reports that the Creeks, the most numerous and potentially dangerous of the Southern tribes, were receiving "as much Rum as they can carry away" from nearby Spanish and French forces.[24]

Students of early U.S. Indian policy know that whenever tensions rose between natives and settlers on the frontier, America's citizenry and officials were quick, even reflexive, in blaming foreign influences. Usually they castigated the British for inciting Indians to violence. Americans rarely bothered to consider that their own practices had often led directly to Indian wrath. It is perhaps comforting that British officials had themselves tended to blame France or Spain for Indian troubles during their heyday. The king's army and civil servants were equally quick to assume the worst—that the Indian war would spread across a broad front.

Civil and military officials were certainly pleased, but also wary, that the Southern Indians had shown little inclination to join the war. They welcomed reports of Northern tribes, like the Shawnees, attacking the

PONTIAC AND PAN-INDIANISM

Cherokees or Catawbas, as signs of Indian division, but the very idea that they might put aside their quarrels and unite against the British proved deeply unnerving. One could never be too sure of Indians' intentions.[25] By the early summer of 1763, even the civilian press in the Northeast had heard of the outbreak of violence, and editors' and readers' fears were broadcast to a wide audience. A Rhode Island newspaper reprinted an extract from an Albany man, noting, "Before this reaches you, you must have heard the disagreeable News of the many Murders lately committed on the English, by different Tribes of Indians, and at different Places, which makes many fear the Rupture is or will become general, amongst the Southern Tribes."[26]

If British officials had been asleep regarding pan-Indian alliances, Pontiac shook them awake. In addition to recalling Amherst and replacing him with Gage, Whitehall also divided Indian affairs into Northern and Southern districts, with the Ohio River as the dividing line. Sir William Johnson proved the obvious choice for the Northern District, while John Stuart was promoted to the Southern district's superintendent. Both incoming and outgoing officers realized that bureaucratic maneuvers alone would not restore British control. They proved willing, in these dire circumstances, to contemplate any number of disquieting solutions. Considerable attention has been paid to the dastardly and desperate solutions conjured up by the military. Several British officers, including Amherst, had considered using biological warfare in the form of blankets exposed to smallpox, and one, Captain Simeon Ecuyer at Fort Pitt, actually made the attempt. Colonel Henry Bouquet had further opined that loosing massive war dogs on the Indians, as the Conquistadors had, would also do the trick.[27]

Considerably less attention has been given the more direct and infinitely more plausible solution British officials did widely utilize—encouraging the intertribal warfare they normally decried. As early as November 1763, Sir William Johnson recommended recruiting "a Number of the Cherokees, Catawbas, Chicasas [Chickasaws] &c to Join agst any of the Northern Inds." Doing so would be easy, Johnson reasoned, because of the long-standing grudges between the Northern and Southern Indians. (Indeed, Cherokee warriors, despite or perhaps because of their recent breach with Britain, ignored the calls for Indian unity and sent some parties against the Ohio Indians to strengthen their trade alliances with the British.) However, Southern Indians should only comprise perhaps a third of the forces engaged "until they are heartily entered in the Quarrel."[28] Even with the long-standing hatred between the Northern and Southern Indians, Johnson was wary that they might still band together against the Crown.

Johnson's fairly simple solution still faced complicating factors. John Stuart, his Southern Department counterpart, agreed in principle with the plan. He would send Johnson's recruiting message on to the Cherokees, as well as the Choctaws (who lived along the Mississippi), who had recently joined Britain's "Covenant of Friendship." The Chickasaws, neighbors of the Choctaws, were certainly game warriors and steady allies of the Crown. They also remained bitter enemies of the Northern tribes. But they had only 450 warriors available. With their numerous local enemies, they would not be able to send a sizable party north. Similarly, the Catawbas of South Carolina were "willing and brave," but disease had reduced them to only "60 or 70 Gunmen." Part of the ease in recruiting them was also the reason they would be largely ineffectual. They had suffered numerous casualties and captives from Northern Indian raids in the previous year.[29]

Obviously the British desired the aid of the Creeks. Stuart demurred on that front, though, arguing, "It would be a delicate Point to propose any thing of this Nature to the Creeks at this Juncture, when they are apt to construe every Proposal as containing some hidden Design; the Impressions left on their Minds by the French, and their Jealousy on account of the late Cession of Florida and Louisiana, not being as yet totally effaced." As Joshua Piker notes, the 1760s and early 1770s saw considerable tension in Creek–British relations. Indeed, some Creeks, like the chief Mortar, favored Pontiac's path. Diplomatic and economic interests—a desire to keep the English trade—as epitomized by the efforts of the aptly named chief Gun Merchant, won out. Clearly Stuart understood that Spain's cession of Florida to Britain had left the Creeks uneasy, and he feared that if pushed they might well join the war on Pontiac's side. The superintendent also followed basic divide-and-conquer logic by saying that he would try to get some parties of Northern Indians "within my Department to go and act jointly with His Majesty's Troops employed against the nations at War with us."³⁰ In this Stuart might have been behind the curve: he should have been asking just what those Northern parties were doing in the South in the first place.

Thomas Gage, for all his laudable Enlightenment humanism, was willing to go one step farther. In January 1764, he noted reports that the Creek Indians had suddenly proved quite amenable to peace with Britain and her colonies, and that the reason behind this was an anticipated war against the Creeks by the Cherokees, Choctaws, and Chickasaws. "And it's my Opinion as long as they Quarrell with one another we shall be well with them all. And when they are all at Peace, It's the Signal for us to have a good Look out," Gage concluded. Gage at this point discounted the idea that Indians were capable of sustained peace, and argued that if they insisted on fighting someone, it suited the Crown's interests to let them fight each other.³¹

Other serving officers also realized the danger of fighting a two-front Indian war. Major Arthur Loftus, writing from Pensacola about a skirmish between Redcoats and the Creeks, hoped it would not widen into a war. Or, if it did, that it could at least be delayed until the situation north of the Ohio had been resolved. "We are hardly Equal to Carry on Another War to the Southward till this shall be finished," he offered. "By that time, We may be able to Strengthen ourselves, & be in a better Condition to Oppose them." Loftus added that he felt wars with Indians in general were to be avoided, as they brought no benefit to British aims. From Mobile, Major Robert Farmar worriedly contradicted earlier reports of Creek pacifism, noting they appeared ready to "join the Northern Indians, and commence a War in these Southern parts" and were "expecting the War belt from the Northern Nations."³²

One of the great self-serving myths in Britain's command circles was that Pontiac's War had been both fomented and significantly aided by French agents. Gregory Dowd demolished that assertion, which was simultaneously dismissive of both native grievances and capabilities.³³ In the 1760s and 1770s, however, the idea enjoyed great longevity among His Majesty's military and Indian Department officers. As Peter Silver writes,

"A dread of Catholic–Indian conspiracy had long pervaded colonial society, and nearly two centuries of panics over Catholic plots against British governments had trained English-speakers to *chercher les catholiques* in times of trouble."[34]

The panicky insistence that foreign elements were fomenting pan-Indianism, with little or no proof, would be a recurring theme in the fear of Indian wars. For Britons, and later their Spanish and American rivals, outside intrigue was a consistently unquestioned assumption. As officials and citizens groped in the dark for an explanation of their pan-Indian nightmares, they tended to both increase the terror and exacerbate the actual danger.

British military and diplomatic efforts in the first months of the war must be seen in the context of their desperate scramble to contain the virus of pan-Indianism before it could spread to the Southern nations. Ideas both sound—recalling Jeffrey Amherst, sending Henry Bouquet to relieve Fort Pitt—and reckless—biological and canine warfare, arose from this pressing fear. The ever-present realization that their efforts at economy had backfired horribly only ramped up officials' concern.

CHAPTER 2

Dueling Diplomacies

In the summer of 1764, General Gage notified John Stuart that "The French at the Illinois have furnished the Delawares and Shawnese with Ammunition." Traders sending gifts or merchandise to Indians was not unusual among the *habitants*, despite having been banned by Amherst. Gage noted that the shipment might well be sent up the Ohio River. If so, he offered, Stuart might be able to entice the Cherokees to capture the "Persons & Goods of the Traders as they go up the Ohio."[1] Recruiting the Cherokees to squelch this transaction would have served the twin goals of denying enemies ammunition and continuing to stir up enmity between Northern and Southern Indians, forestalling their alliance. Squabbles in the South Carolina legislature frustrated the effort, as they could not decide what to offer the Cherokees for the proposed service.[2] For Gage and the British high command, it served as yet another example of a colonial assembly failing to act decisively for the defense of the Crown's territory.

In fact, French officers did take the initiative in holding councils with the Southern Indians. They did so not to bedevil the British, however, but to literally save their own skins. Having learned of the preliminary peace terms of 1763 that April, by early May French officers in New Orleans had grown concerned. Knowing that France ceded lands it did not really own, they rightly feared that their former Indian allies would become angry and slaughter the French settlers who chose to remain.[3] On November 14, 1763, Major Robert Farmar, commanding officer at Mobile, and Governor-General Jean Jacques D'Abbadie held a joint council with representatives of the Choctaws in an effort to smooth the transition from French to English imperialism in the Southeast. In most respects, holding the council with French help proved a prudent move for British interests. The Frenchman's insistence that neither power would trade with them if they attacked whites may well have dissuaded some Choctaws from attacking the British as well as the habitants. However, Farmar may have unwittingly raised Indian expectations higher than the increasingly parsimonious Crown was willing to go. At one point in their joint address, Farmar and D'Abbadie promised the Choctaws that "*vous avez reçu tous vos besoins du grand Empereur des Francois, vous les recurés egalment de celui des anglais.*" (My loose translation—"You have received all your necessities from the king of France, and you will in the future receive them equally from the English.")[4]

Indian diplomacy remained contradictory and complicated. At almost the same moment, John Stuart presided over another Indian conference in Augusta, Georgia. While the French in New Orleans, waiting for a transfer to Spain, were proving most cooperative to Major Farmar, Stuart's opening speech implored the assembled Indians—Chickasaws, Upper and Lower Creeks, Choctaws, Cherokees, and Catawbas—to ignore the "lies" the French had spread about the English. The council resulted in a treaty of friendship being signed on November 10, 1763, but not before the Chickasaw chief Pia Matta noted that though he had "great regard for the White People," the presence of so many white traders among his people nevertheless caused trouble.[5]

Through the direct diplomacy of such councils, and through new legal measures, like the Royal Proclamation of 1763, the Crown hoped to avoid future Indian wars on the frontier and to preserve the valuable fur trade. The Proclamation of 1763 banned the king's subjects from settling west of the Appalachian Mountains, and ordered any who were already west of the line to return. Though often assumed to have been a desperate response to Pontiac's War, the Crown had actually been contemplating such a move since at least 1761.[6] The Proclamation, despite its presumably temporary nature, was welcomed by most Indians. It did not, however, quell all pan-Indian, anti-Anglo sentiment, largely because of the pitiful efforts to enforce it. While the Proclamation effectively froze the assets of (furious) land speculators, settlers were a different story. Contemporaries estimated that about 30,000 whites violated the Proclamation from 1765–1768 alone.[7]

Pontiac's war did not end cleanly at a fixed date, but rather faded slowly, with occasional up-ticks in attempted pan-Indianism. At least one of the

Ottawa's confederates, the Shawnee "beloved man" Charlot Kaské, had traveled to the Creeks looking for allies in late 1764. Even years after Pontiac himself had made his peace with Britain, officials continued to receive intelligence of supposed plots. Frequently, these reports focused on the efforts of the Senecas, the westernmost nation of the Iroquois League, seeking alliances with Ohio and Southern Indians against the Crown. According to George Croghan, the Senecas had, in 1765, utilized Shawnee and Delaware go-betweens to "Seliseat [solicit] a General Union in order to putt a Stop to the English Coming into thire Cuntry to Setle any further, & ye Deputys of the Shannas & Dallaways when they Came to Fort Stanwix brought back ye answers of all the Westren Nations & Delivered them to the Sinicas." While this realization was frightening enough, Croghan also offered that as the Cherokees had now recently made peace with the Iroquois, "itt inlarged thire plan." The Shawnees and Delawares were now seeking to broker a peace between the Cherokees and the Wabash River area tribes. While Croghan allowed that this would be very difficult, if the reports it had taken place were true, "there is No Doubt butt a very Severe Blow will be Struck on ye Suthren provinces Soon."[8]

At least, Croghan continued, the easternmost Iroquois nations, the Oneidas and Mohawks, were most likely not involved, and would probably oppose the plan. This was a ray of sunshine for Croghan. He noted that his personal business interests (some of which were actually legal) would suffer greatly if such a war took place. He remained very pessimistic for the future, though, as "I Must Confess I am Much affrede [afraid] of when I Consider, that all Nations of Indians are a Restless people who Never forgett Nor forgive Injuerys & often think they are Injured when they are the agresors."[9]

Overzealous (or perhaps just Indian-hating) colonists could wreck the most carefully conceived plans to defeat Indian confederacies. The *Boston Gazette* reported in April 1764 that renegade Creeks had murdered fourteen South Carolinians, and had sought shelter with the Cherokees. The Cherokees, however, had offered to help South Carolina obtain justice in the matter. Coincidentally, at the request of Superintendent Stuart, Cherokee war parties were then headed north to attack the Shawnees and others. Such war parties served the twin goal of suppressing Pontiac's allies while rendering it difficult for them to recruit Southern nations. The Cherokees no doubt expected presents like powder and lead in return. They did not expect such gifts to be delivered by the gunfire of Virginian backwoodsmen, who may or may not have mistaken the Cherokees for hostiles, ambushing one of the parties on its journey home.[10]

A similar incident had sparked the Cherokee War of 1760. Yet when the Cherokees sent headman Attakullakulla to negotiate with Virginia officials, he "informed [Governor Francis] Fauquier that the British government could compensate the Cherokees for their losses by using its enormous political and economic influence to help them make peace with the Shawnees—the very people their war party had been planning to attack when it had itself been set upon by the Virginians." The Cherokees also wanted to bury the hatchet with the Delawares and the Iroquois League. Within three years, "with the sometimes-grudging assistance of British officials, the Cherokees achieved their goal of peace with the Shawnees, Delawares, and Six Nations."[11] It was a diplomatic (though temporary) masterstroke from the Cherokees, and it made the potential of a coalition of Northern and Southern nations all the more plausible.

Gauging the intent of the Southern tribes proved tricky as well. British officials back in Whitehall have often taken criticism for not understanding the American situation well. Certainly in many instances they displayed appalling ignorance of North America. Yet given how wildly contradictory the reports of even agents on the ground could be, it is little wonder that the king's ministers could be left guessing. In the spring of 1765, Superintendent Stuart wrote confidently that he had quashed efforts by the Northern tribes and some of the Creeks to forge a pan-Indian union. The Creeks, he continued, would become far more "modest and Tractable" once they realized that they were surrounded by British-allied tribes, and that the "Northern Rebellious Tribes" had been crushed. Little more than a year later, Stuart received word from Pensacola that a war with the Creeks was imminent—in fact it was not—and that the Creeks would likely heal their rift with the Choctaws. Those two numerous peoples would then fall jointly upon the English. "Charles Stuart [the superintendent's brother] is gone to Mobile to use every Means, consistent with Secrecy in order to prevent this," he offered.[12] While the king still preferred to see himself as a benevolent father to the Indians, officials in America, from General Gage on down the line, readily adopted divide-and-conquer when it suited them.

By that time Stuart appreciated the growing danger. In May 1766, he noted that the Creeks, unintentionally shielded from Northern Indian raids by the Cherokees and Chickasaws, were far too numerous. Further, the pan-Indian impulse had not died. "Whatever enmity or Misunderstanding may subsist amongst the Indian Nations, yet they all think themselves Concerned in every encroachment on, or injustice done any Tribe by us," he lamented. "The Complaints of the Cherokees on account of their Hunting Grounds and the Murder of their people in Virginia have been Echoed thro' all the Nations." The formidable Creek chief Mortar—a tireless advocate of anti-Anglo–Indian unity—had reportedly offered seven hundred men immediately to help the Cherokees take revenge against the Virginians for the 1764 incident described above. The Creeks were trying to spur not just the Cherokees, but the Choctaws, Britain's "new Allies," to join them, as well as the Chickasaws and the smaller nations along the Mississippi River. Between the Cherokees and Creeks alone, Stuart estimated that they could produce as many as 7,000 warriors. And, with French propaganda still fresh in Indian minds, "A Rupture with the Creeks and Cherokees would soon become general."[13]

Stuart had been so desperate to avoid a great native alliance against the Crown that, like Gage and Johnson, he had tried to foment or exacerbate fighting between the nations. Now he offered an even more diabolical plan to avoid disaster—fairness: "I am not without hope . . . that their bad intentions may be defeated by removing all Cause of just Complaint from, and Rendering Justice as far as is in our Power to the Latter."[14]

"Rendering justice" could take many forms. Gage, Johnson, Croghan, and Stuart all recognized that many Indians had significant grounds for complaint against the British colonies, and for a variety of reasons. Perhaps the most pressingly irksome issue was the lopsided system of justice in cross-cultural crimes, especially murders. Many of the Crown's appointees and officers eagerly sought to punish colonists who murdered Indians, but local juries rarely showed the same initiative. Yet colonists insisted that Indians who killed whites be handed over immediately for trial and execution. Predictably, it became an increasingly hard sell for diplomacy-minded chiefs to convince their people of the wisdom (or fairness) of such a system. Johnson, for example, feared that unpunished murders would keep Pontiac from officially ending his war with Britain. Even when that particular fear was allayed, the question of how to mollify Indians remained.[15]

Sir William, Gage, Stuart, and others realized that lacking a true universal peace with North America's natives, their best chance was to frustrate efforts at Indian confederacies by manipulating and even fostering jealousies among Indian peoples. Johnson in particular, though generally remembered as a friend to Indians, engaged in these Machiavellian tricks as a budgetary necessity. He eventually admitted: "We cannot expect to keep them in Temper but at an Expence too great (at least in the opinion of Government) for the Object, Consequently all that can be Expected from the present Establishment is to keep some of them [like Johnson's Iroquois neighbors] in our Interest, and endeavour to divide the rest, and I am hopefull that the Constant pains I take and Influence I have over many of them will at least have these Effects."[16] One sure way to foster enmity between the nations was to encourage squabbles over land.

Predictably, as the Empire grew, so did the disparity between the center of power and its periphery. George III's benevolence, condescending or not, carried poorly outside of London. Official policy became, from the Crown and Whitehall down, to secure natives' goodwill through more conscientious treatment. In so doing, Anglo-colonial policy would, in true eighteenth-century fashion, blend the public interest with private financial ones to the point where both goals were eventually undermined. Recognizing that boundary issues proved a great source of frontier friction, the king's cabinet decided that Indian boundary lines should be surveyed, with Indians observing and consenting, to prevent further misunderstandings. In theory it was perfectly sound, even rational. However, the ministers did not fully appreciate how self-serving, or even insubordinate, officers in the colonies could be.

In the summer of 1766, surveyors ran the boundary line between South Carolina and the Cherokee Nation. The Cherokees seemed happy enough with it that General Gage suggested fixing the North Carolina and Virginia boundaries as well. Of course, one reason that the Cherokees were on their best diplomatic behavior was that colonial officials had dangled the offer of helping to mediate between the Cherokees and the Iroquois and Ohio nations who still sent war parties after them. Cherokee desires for peace with the Iroquois, Gage reasoned, could be used to secure Cherokee war parties to send against the Creeks. If this could be accomplished, "we should endeavour to Negotiate for them with the Six Nations, Shawanese, &c., but not otherwise as their Conduct . . . Seems somewhat Suspicious." Gage further opined that, should the Cherokees, Chickasaws, Choctaws, and Catawbas be brought to bear, only a small body of provincial and regular troops would be needed to "bring the Creeks to Reason."[17]

Sir William had his own plan for strengthening the Crown's hold west of the Appalachians, and keeping potential pan-Indian alliances in check. It would also reap potentially huge sums in land sales for himself and his Iroquois neighbors. If to do so he had to largely ignore direct orders from London, so be it. In 1768, Johnson called for a great Indian Council at Fort Stanwix, near modern Rome, New York.

Lord Hillsborough, the Secretary for North America, sent instructions clearly stating that Johnson was to seek a boundary where the Kanawha and Ohio Rivers met, near present-day Gallipolis, Ohio. This had, up to that point, been the generally acknowledged western extent of Iroquois territory. Johnson instead sought a boundary extending nearly 400 miles deeper into the West, to modern Paducha, Kentucky. Rather than sticking with their already tenuous claims to the Ohio country, the Iroquois were now claiming to own, and therefore rightfully sell to the Crown, most of Kentucky and western Virginia. For this, they would receive £10,000 in trade goods—the most the Crown had ever paid Indians for land up to that point. The Ohio Indians, meanwhile, received a paltry £27 worth of trade goods.[18] The League proved perfectly happy to assist Johnson in their fictitious ownership of this territory, because it would increase their monetary reward and strengthen their alliance with Johnson and the British. Johnson obviously sought to improve the material and diplomatic situation of his Iroquois kinsmen, and aid the land speculations of both himself and his agent George Croghan.[19]

As Eric Hinderaker has noted, "The personal motives of Johnson and Croghan in these years are highly suspect." Both men were, by the 1760s, up to their eyeballs in western land speculation. Croghan, in particular, had been reckless in his speculations, and he desperately needed "a careful readjustment of the Indian boundary" to remain solvent. Johnson had negotiated at Stanwix not just for the Empire, or even the Iroquois, but for private individuals as well. He served as the silent partner of a broad speculation group that included a number of both future Revolutionaries and Loyalists: Benjamin Franklin and his son Gov. William Franklin of New Jersey, Joseph Galloway, Croghan, and the Philadelphia trading firm of Baynton, Wharton, and Morgan. All hoped to secure title to more than a million acres of land in the West. Calling themselves the Illinois Company, the group decided that Johnson's membership, given the astounding conflict of interest it represented, should remain secret.[20]

In addition to Johnson's financial motives, he also wanted to stymie any desire of the Cherokees and Iroquois to form a great alliance. This the Fort Stanwix Treaty would do, because the Cherokees had long asserted ownership of the prodigious hunting grounds of Kentucky. In fact, the Fort Stanwix council took place only a month after John Stuart had negotiated the Treaty of Hard Labor with the Cherokees—a treaty that had recognized their claims to Kentucky.[21] However, it was here that Johnson played an exceedingly dangerous game.

Prior to 1768, one of the few things that Ohio Valley Shawnees and the Cherokees could agree upon was the beauty of Kentucky, and the necessity that it be maintained largely free of human settlement, as this was the key to its abundance of game. The two tribes had often been at each other's throats as to just who did have the rights to it. But the Treaty of Fort Stanwix removed this major obstacle to Cherokee-Shawnee cooperation, and at the same time gave them both a clear enemy to unite against—Anglo-America. In 1668, Johnson's stratagem would have been brilliant. But by 1768 epidemic disease and the attrition of war had led Iroquois population (and military might) to decline steeply,[22] while the Shawnees were well on their way to earning their reputation as the fiercest opponents of Anglo-American expansion.

The Shawnees had perhaps the most at stake in Kentucky. All tribes needed access to hunting territory to remain in the European trade. But unlike most Indians living south of Canada, the Shawnees actually drew only about a quarter of their calories from horticulture. Game animals, especially deer, comprised the bulk of their meals.[23] Losing Kentucky would put the Shawnees on an involuntary diet. Croghan and Johnson knew the Shawnees would resist the sale of their hunting grounds, and therefore excluded them the deliberations regarding the cession. The Shawnees became so infuriated that their "leaders took the extraordinary step of circulating among the western leaders to suggest that they 'unite and attack the English as soon as the latter become formidable'" before the conference had even ended. They got some immediate support from Mingos and Delawares, and over the next two years their diplomacy culminated in several councils held on the Scioto River in Ohio. The "Scioto confederacy" would draw support from the Anishinabeg peoples (Ottawas, Chippewas, Potawatomis), the Wyandots, the Illinois, and the Miamis. Rumors circulated freely in the spring of 1768 that the Shawnees, Delawares, and Lakes Indians would strike the English and had already taken Detroit.[24]

The Cherokees, meanwhile, seemed perpetually on the verge of launching retaliatory raids against the most exposed portions of the colonial frontier. Johnson was not simply playing with fire; he was dancing brazenly through it. The Scioto Confederacy "agreed not only to cooperate with one another but also to seek peace with the Cherokees, the Creeks, and the other southern tribes in order to create a single, united front of Indian resistance to British power on the continent."[25] The Kentucky borderlands that had divided Cherokees and Shawnees now brought them together.

Sir William's recklessness in Indian diplomacy was matched only by his gall in disobeying orders. The instructions sent by Hillsborough had been in no way discretionary. The new purchase not only inverted previously understood boundaries between Indians, but also made a mockery of the Proclamation of 1763. Johnson simply barged ahead, reasoning that his reputation and the predictable approval of most colonial officials—particularly those who were also involved in land-jobbing—would pull him through. He proved correct.[26]

In fact, when Lord Hillsborough and others had the temerity to question the treaty, Johnson made his own pan-Indian bluff. He could not possibly deny the Iroquois their cession, he argued, because it would infuriate them, and the Six Nations would become "Worse Enemys than the Cherokees." They would attack British colonists, and induce all the other Indians of the continent to follow suit. The Board of Trade swallowed Sir William's tortured logic. His victory was pyrrhic, however. By pushing an absurdly fictitious interpretation of Iroquois power in the Ohio Valley, he effectively ended any real influence they might have held there. After Fort Stanwix, the Iroquois League might still be allowed to follow pan-Indian impulses, but in the minds of the Shawnees and others they had abdicated any right to lead.[27]

Johnson's treaty with the Iroquois also put John Stuart in a perilous position. Hanging on to the Cherokee alliance was paramount for him, if for no other reason than to provide a check on the volatile Creeks. Fort Stanwix threatened to wreck that, by robbing the Cherokees while simultaneously strengthening the hand of Virginia in western settlement. Aghast,

Stuart wrote to Lord Hillsborough to remind him that "by having suffered the Claims of the Six Nations . . . [Sir William] has, in a great measure, given rise to the Pretensions of Virginia." Indeed, the House of Burgesses had recently petitioned Parliament that they be granted Kentucky.[28] "Which inconveniency," Stuart continued, "the Right honble Board of Trade foresaw and were solicitous to avoid." Stuart was not in any way opposed to purchasing Indian lands but argued that taking Kentucky away from the Cherokees without offering them any compensation was "extremely improper."[29]

Stuart was not the only one who saw the impropriety (or poor policy) of such a purchase. In the fall of 1769 he again wrote Lord Hillsborough, reporting that the Cherokees had sent him a letter noting their extreme displeasure and "alarm" with Fort Stanwix. Hillsborough worried about the Burgesses' petition for Kentucky as well as Johnson's land grab, on two fronts. He noted Stuart's concerns that the issue of Kentucky might well "be productive of a general rupture with and coalition of all the tribes on the continent." And as a landlord in Ireland, Hillsborough also feared losing any more tenants to wild promises of available land in America.[30]

Previously, the Cherokees had refused to believe the Fort Stanwix cession was real, and Stuart was in no hurry to tell them otherwise.[31] He tried to calm them, but the situation remained quite tense. Reports indicated that the Spanish were flirting with the Creeks of Coweta, supposedly promising to drive the British out of Creek Country. Spanish mestizo traders were encouraging other Creeks to visit Havana to hear His Catholic Majesty's proposals and receive his gifts. Forty-five hundred Spanish troops, "and some Mulattoes and Negros," were said to have arrived at New Orleans, which Stuart felt was far more than needed simply for garrison duty there. (This was an early example of reports of armed blacks causing consternation among Anglo-speaking whites in the South.) The Choctaws, angry that they now received far fewer presents than when the French held sway, had taken to harassing the British settlers in West Florida. The only mildly encouraging news for Britain was that the Creeks were still warring with both the Cherokees and Choctaws. Still, Stuart was worried that anger over the Fort Stanwix cession could push the Cherokees to make peace with the Creeks, or worse. "I shall use my utmost endeavors to satisfy [the Cherokees] and preserve their Attachment at this time when the Western & Northern Tribes seem disposed to be troublesome."[32]

King George III and his cabinet provisionally approved the treaty, despite Lord Hillsborough's misgivings. They did so only after heavy lobbying from Superintendent Johnson and Lord Botetourt of Virginia—both of whom would profit handsomely from the Fort Stanwix cession. The Crown maintained that if Virginia agreed to pay for the cost of a new council to soothe the Cherokees, which Stuart estimated would cost about £2,000, the treaty would be upheld.[33]

The Cherokees stated that they could no longer even come to the aid of their Catawba neighbors when attacked from the north. They needed colonial, specifically Sir William's, aid and mediation to end the bloodshed. They nevertheless warned that war might spread to the colonists as well. Asking for the governor of Virginia to restrain his settlers from stealing land and deer, the chiefs complained, "the Virginia people will not Listen to anybody but do as they please." If Governor Botetourt could not restrain his frontiersmen, it would soon lead to "bad Consequences for our Young fellows are very angry to see their Hunting Grounds taken from them."[34]

Stuart continued to fight the cession into 1770. "The rapacity of the Land Jobbers in Virginia is insatiable," he exclaimed. He foresaw a host of potential calamities if it went through. The western settlements of Virginia would be beyond the reach of the government in Williamsburg. He argued that it "would immediately revive all the Jealousies and Apprehensions of the Indians on account of their Lands." Further, the land in question, mainly Kentucky, "altho' a very fine country, is absolutely necessary for the Cherokees & Chickasaws as Hunters." Britain's commerce would not be noticeably increased by this purchase, and it might actually give Spain easier access to the Indians generally and the Ohio Valley in particular. These points did nothing to improve Stuart's popularity among Virginians.[35]

Stuart persisted anyway. In a more direct letter to Governor Botetourt, he argued that in addition to immediately infuriating the Cherokees and Chickasaws, pushing the Indian boundary west would soon enrage the other Indians of America as well. He laid out the nightmare scenario:

> The Creeks consisting of Four Thousand Gunmen, have lately complained to me of Settlements being made by Emigrants from Virginia, on the unceded Lands on the Mississippi. . . . At this very Time there are in the Creek Nation, Deputies from the Shawnese, Delawares, &

other Northern Tribes accompanied by some Cherokees, endeavouring to form a General Confederacy on the Principle of Defending their Lands from our daily Encroachments.

The Cherokees, it was true, had yet to show great interest in a confederacy. But the agitation of Virginians on their frontiers could change Indian opinion quickly. Lest Botetourt underestimate Cherokee commitment to the idea, Stuart pointed out that their principal chief Occonostotah had, in July 1769, personally led a thirty-man Cherokee reconnaissance of Virginian settlements on the Holston River in what is now Tennessee.[36]

Lord Hillsborough praised Stuart for his efforts in dissuading the Creeks and Cherokees from joining a great confederacy. Their not doing so was "a very fortunate Event." The Cherokees' "friendly dispositions," the secretary added, encouraged him to see a favorable settling of the Cherokee–Virginia boundary. Later, Hillsborough cautioned Stuart that while the king wished him success in mediating the Creek–Choctaw war, His Majesty's name was not to be mentioned.[37]

In the end the Virginia land jobbers did not profit from either their petition or the Fort Stanwix cession. As Woody Holton observes, "the total yield of the Virginia land rush set off by the Fort Stanwix treaty was a pile of rejected land petitions and worthless surveys." But the cession's impact on the Ohio and Cherokee hunters who used Kentucky was far greater. While the Proclamation of 1763 and subsequent decisions in London had hamstrung the efforts of speculators, nothing had stopped the flood of hunters and squatters into Kentucky. In fact, the lack of legal title and process there actually made it easier for the poor and indebted to flee to the West.[38]

CHAPTER 3

Stuart Besieged

Among the more nerve-wracking facets of watching for an alliance of Northern and Southern Indians were the great distances and number of people involved. While Superintendent Stuart might temporarily feel optimism south of Virginia, officials to the north might be filled with dread. Throughout 1770, General Gage continued to forward to Whitehall reports of Shawnee embassies among the Cherokees, Creeks, and other Southern tribes, even while Cherokee war parties continued to attack tribes on the Wabash. Agent Croghan reported from Philadelphia that Indians were buying nothing from the traders but ammunition, even to the point of trading their horses for it. This detail he found "very uncommon, and I think discovers a design of an open rupture in the Spring." Further, a group of Senecas, Shawnees, and Delawares had met (privately) in the Huron Village near Detroit with Huron, Chippewa, Ottawa, and Potawatomi embassies. The Hurons and the Anishinabeg had "agreed to confirm a Peace with the Cherokees as soon as they returned from amongst the Six Nations which," he added ominously, "I think must be Detrimental to the Publick Interest."[1] As Woody Holton notes, "even as the anti-British league became more and more a phantom, imperial officials became increasingly frightened of it, and their determination to prevent British colonists from provoking an Indian war continued to grow." Despite the considerable difficulties inherent in building a pan-Indian alliance, Shawnee travelers continued to worry British officials. As Gage observed, "The Shawnese have been very Active for some time and are certainly hatching some great Piece of Mischief."[2]

When the Shawnees and other Ohio nations held a council at the Scioto River in Ohio in September 1770, Croghan was confident that his spies would relate that pan-Indian pretensions had once more been undone by old rivalries. But "he was stunned" to learn that the delegates there had all agreed to make peace with the Southern nations—paving the way for a great intertribal coalition against the British.[3] The threat of a pan-Indian coalition opposed to British interests brought extraordinary pressure to bear on the minds of Crown officials. That pressure continually exposed cracks in the carefully crafted veneer of Britain's paternal interest in Indians. Sir William Johnson, who more than any other British official cultivated an image as a man with great sympathies for Indians, echoed General Gage's cold calculations. Reiterating his concern about the new peace between Northern and Southern Indians, Johnson worried "because the Northern Indians [including his Iroquois neighbors] cant [sic] be idle." He then rationalized that, "Whereas a peace if Sincere would be naturally attended with an Union of Measures amongst the Indians, and under these Circumstances Humanity Should Yield to good Policy, as the preservation of our own People should be the first Object of consideration." Any such union, he concluded, "may be prejudicial to Us."[4]

By the early 1770s, Sir William was not long for the world. But to the end he would remain relentless in furthering the interests of himself, the British Empire, and his Iroquois neighbors, usually in that order. As Johnson biographer Fintan O'Toole asserts, "On behalf of a dying empire, a dying man orchestrated the tensions, jealousies and resentments among the different Indian nations, successfully preventing the formation of a hostile alliance by the Shawnees."[5]

Poor John Stuart. While Sir William schemed for land and influence in the North, Johnson's colleague to the south had to contend with the most numerous and potentially dangerous Indian nations in British America, as well as the repercussions of Sir William's machinations. In the latter half of the eighteenth century, Superintendent of Southern Indian Affairs may well have been one of the daunting administrative positions in the British Empire. Stuart's optimism in the summer of 1770 had evaporated less than a year later. He warned that the Fort Stanwix cession was encouraging the Western Indians—those of the Ohio Valley and Great Lakes—"to be active in forming confederacies & an Alliance with other Nations." It proved particularly unnerving to Stuart that these Western tribes were "indefatigable" in their quest for peace among themselves and with the various Southern tribes, sending innumerable messengers to do so.

Michael N. McConnell describes a Shawnee "diplomatic offensive in 1770 and 1771" to counter white expansion. Virginia's royal governor, Lord Dunmore, reported to Lord Dartmouth that native leaders were "meditating some important stroke," and that if they could "effect a General Confederacy the Country must suffer very great misery."[6] The manifest design was to bypass and even usurp the Iroquois League, which had threatened (rather hollowly) to use force to support the treaty.[7]

As if Stuart did not have enough to worry about with Indians trying to form broad alliances, by 1772 he had to contend with one of his own deputies doing the same, though ostensibly for different reasons. John Thomas, agent on the Mississippi River, had been encouraging Indians to move from west of the Mississippi to the east—the opposite of the Crown's desire. Further, working with the governor of Spanish Louisiana, Luis de Unzaga, Thomas was actually trying "to form confederacies, between said [Spanish allied] Indians, and the Cherokees Chickasaws and Shawnese." Thomas was most likely naïve, rather than traitorous. While Unzaga hoped to form a confederacy against the powerful Osages of Missouri, Thomas foolishly assumed he could mold an Indian alliance to fight the Kickapoos of the Illinois and Wisconsin lands, who had been hostile to British interests. Stuart considered such confederacies "impracticable," presumably because of the differing interests of Britain and Spain, and could not have been happy with Thomas encouraging any Indians, especially Shawnees, to form great alliances with the Southern tribes. Thomas was not only insubordinate, but Stuart and Hillsborough later agreed that he had probably gone mad. Stuart wanted to cashier him entirely. When the Earl of Dartmouth replaced Hillsborough as Secretary for North America however, Dartmouth intervened on Thomas' behalf. Stuart reluctantly kept him on in a reduced role, or, as he might have argued, a diminished capacity.[8]

Some Cherokee leaders tried to reassure the Southern Department that there were no secret confederacies in the works. The numerous delegations from north and west of the Ohio were merely in Cherokee country to "finish the Peace our Father & you Set on Foot between us," and not to join "in a War against ... the White People."[9] Old feuds and cultural quarrels made Shawnee diplomacy with Cherokees (and other Southern tribes) difficult. From Lord Dartmouth down to his field agents and settlers on the ground, however, the British remained skeptical, even fearful. Dartmouth worried over reports that the Spanish, "our Neighbours on the

Mississippi," could send speeches to the various Ohio Valley tribes for the purpose of "keeping up that jealousy, Discontent and Enmity towards us . . . which may hereafter when an opportunity offers prove fatal to the Security of the British Dominions in that part of America." As that enmity grew daily, Dartmouth continued, Britain's only "hope of preventing that dangerous Union of Interests that appears to be forming rests upon the friendship of the Six Nations & their acquiescence in that extension of Settlement which has apparently given so much offence to other Tribes who both claim & possess the Country." Though it was the Iroquois League's absurd pretension of owning Kentucky, at Sir William Johnson's urging, which had given common cause to so many Indians to oppose Britain, Lord Dartmouth's solution was to cling all the more desperately to the Iroquois. He does not seem to have seriously considered voiding the dubious purchase.

Stuart, not having Lord Dartmouth's luxury of distance from a potential Indian war, tended to be far more pessimistic. Fort Stanwix, and hunting ground encroachments in general, infuriated natives on both sides of the Ohio. By the first week of 1773, he again warned that Shawnee and Delaware embassies circulated among the Southern tribes. They had even adopted the strategy of trying to mediate between warring tribes, like the Creeks and Choctaws, to establish a general Indian peace that might then facilitate a general Indian alliance. As Stuart reported to Dartmouth:

> The great Emigrations from Virginia and the Northern Colonies, who pass through the Cherokee, Creek, & Chickasaw hunting Grounds on their way to the Mississippi, the great Number of white Hunters who destroy their Game, and the want of Regulation among the Traders, give great Umbrage to these three Nations; and I cannot doubt but a great many of them are inclined to favour the views of the Western Confederacy, if a Peace could be accomplished between the Chactaws & Creeks.[10]

The only encouraging news, Stuart continued, was that the Choctaws and Creeks at the moment seemed far from reconciliation. Stuart felt that the best he could do in this situation of growing unrest was to try to enforce the laws and treaties already in place, especially by prosecuting whites who squatted on Indian lands. Stuart recognized that these squatters were violating the King's Proclamation of 1763, but (perhaps in resignation) declined to note that Fort Stanwix had done much the same, and greatly encouraged violations of Indian boundaries. While the king and his ministers had reasonably good intentions regarding Indian land rights, by neglecting to enforce the king's word to Indians—which would have been expensive—all promises made after 1768 proved mere platitudes. "The Event of the Process will show how far the Law will afford a Remedy against the Evil," Stuart wearily continued. "Should this fail, I humbly submit it as my opinion that nothing will prove effectual but an act of Parliament." Surely Stuart realized that the most magnificent law imaginable was no match for colonial rapacity and indifferent enforcement. For his part, Lord Dartmouth felt that "the dangerous Spirit of unlicensed emigration" into the West would be impossible to stop, but agreed to "concur in any Measure" Stuart came up with to halt it.

If Stuart hoped that the June 1773 congress with the Southern Indians at Augusta would clarify the situation and ease his mind, the council soon dashed his hopes. Some of the talks he heard were certainly designed to comfort British officials. Emistisiguo, a prominent chief of the Upper Creeks, assured the superintendent that while wampum belts from the Cherokees were circulating among Northern tribes, most, especially the Western nations (on the Wabash) had rejected them. Indeed, the Wabash tribes continued to make war on the Cherokees. Further, Stuart noted, it was exceedingly difficult to get an accurate read as to what the belts actually said. Emistisiguo stated that he could detect nothing sinister in those he had seen.[11]

Stuart, however, could not shake the grinding fear that even those chiefs he trusted, like Emistisiguo, or the Cherokee chief Attkullakulla, were misleading him to cover the formation of a pan-Indian union. Occonastotah, the principal chief of the Cherokees, had begged off attending Stuart's council. Instead he met in the Cherokee town of Chotah with Mortar, the anti-British Upper Creek chief, and some "Deputies from the Shawnese, Six Nations, and Canada Confederacy, as well as from the Creeks, Chickasaws and Arkansas," according to Attakullakulla. Supposedly, they were meeting to discuss "chastising the Insolence" of some Wabash Indians— Weas, Piankeshaws (both members of the Miami Confederacy), and Kickapoos—who refused to make peace with their cousins to the south.[12] That was all well and good, assuming it to be true. But for a man in Stuart's precarious position, it proved far easier to assume a more menacing interpretation: The tribes sought peace with each other to more effectively make war on Britain's colonists.

Stuart hastened to add that he felt Attakullakulla had "very candidly and faithfully told me all that he Knew." But with tribes as far away as Arkansas and Canada conversing about a broad alliance, it seemed dangerously easy for them to alter their goals. Widespread cooperation among Indians did not, in any sense, further British imperial interests in North America. Indeed, it constituted the single greatest potential threat. With the Creeks being "already very insolent and troublesome," Stuart helped stifle their attempts to enlist the Cherokees and Chickasaws in their fight with the Choctaws. He had no qualms about this, because he felt that if the Creeks did win such a war, and secured a peace on their own terms, "their Superiority would render them . . . intolerable neighbours to the New Colonies."[13]

Despite his friendship with Attakullakulla, by August Stuart could write that, "Notwithstanding the pacifick professions and behavior of the Cherokees, I am not without some Suspicion of their sincerity." They had long (if often hostile) associations with the Shawnees and other Ohio Valley nations, and had been active in circulating, and helping to circulate, wampum belts whose meanings were kept from Anglo-Americans. Nor had they "relaxed in their Endeavours to form a Coalition of all the Tribes." Stuart clearly did not buy the idea of a pan-Indian confederacy for the purpose of punishing three Wabash valley tribes. In addition, the royal governor of Virginia, Lord Dunmore, accused them of taking part in the murder of a party of whites in the Virginia backcountry. Combining his senses of both fear and fairness, Stuart noted that the colonies' inability to capture and prosecute the white culprits in three recent, unprovoked Cherokee murders greatly increased the odds for hostility. On the question of murders, in fact, Stuart argued against getting immediately into specifics with the Cherokees, as they would have far greater right to complain. Cherokee neutrality, Stuart concluded, was of paramount importance, because of tension on the frontiers of Georgia and Virginia. He hoped to negotiate with the Creeks in the fall to help ease the situation of Georgia.[14] As it happened, Virginia's frontier proved the true flashpoint, inaugurating two decades of brutal warfare in the Ohio Valley.

CHAPTER 4

Dunmore's Fleeting Victory

From the fall of 1773 through the first half of 1774, the Trans-Appalachian frontier reverberated with stories, both true and false, of startling violence between whites and Indians. The most frightening intelligence insinuated a growing alliance between Northern and Southern Indians—former enemies coalescing against their common foe, the British-American encroachers. Affidavits from Fincastle County, Virginia, sworn before justices Arthur Campbell and William Russell, proved so alarming that they were forwarded all the way to Whitehall. A party of fifteen Delawares, two Shawnees, and two Cherokees had passed from the Cherokee towns to the Virginia frontier in September 1773. They murdered five white men and a slave belonging to one of the victims, a Captain Russell. The murders were provocative enough, but deponent Isaac Thomas added that though Great Warrior of the Cherokees disapproved of the mission, "that said Northward Indians came on an Embassy to excite the Cherokees to commence Hostilities against the English."[1] It was difficult enough to placate Indians when whites murdered their people and eluded justice. Keeping backcountry settlers from retaliating against Indians was next to impossible. Yet colonial officials would do most anything to avoid a general Indian war on their frontiers.

The situation proved so volatile that it provoked a response from Virginia's governor. Writing to Superintendent Stuart, John Murray, the fourth earl of Dunmore, relayed reports that Virginia backwoodsmen were attempting to buy a large tract of land, from Indians, "to the South West of our last Established Boundary Line." Such, Dunmore asserted, was improper, and he hoped that the Southern Department's agents would be able to dissuade

49

the Indians from "entering into any Bargain with our People in such an Irregular Manner."[2]

Dunmore was referring to what would become known as the Watauga Association, a group of backcountry settlers principally from North Carolina who sought to carve their own futures out of the Watauga River drainage in what would become eastern Tennessee. Led by James Robertson and John Sevier, both of whom would soon become famous among frontier folk, the association set up its own system of jurisprudence and land ownership far from the reach of colonial officials. Dunmore's condemnation of the Wataugans might have drawn a smirk from Lord Dartmouth. The Virginia governor had endorsed a similar private purchase (also from Attakullakulla's Cherokees) made by burgess John Donelson three years prior, and it was also "A clear violation of imperial policy," but one that Dunmore hoped would result in a massive land grant for himself.[3] The Wataugans' deal was not a perfectly clean purchase, as many Cherokees, especially the more militant ones, opposed it. Compared to many official land deals, however, Robertson's and Sevier's looked angelic.[4]

In a final irony, the Wataugans' relatively good relationship (for the first few years, anyway) with the Cherokees actually aided Dunmore in his schemes, by helping to squelch yet another attempt at a North–South Indian coalition. By sheer coincidence, in 1774 a Wataugan peace delegation was in the town of Chota (concerning the murder of a Cherokee man by whites from another settlement) at the same time that Cherokee emissaries were meeting with Shawnees north of the Ohio. The latter nation was again seeking a coalition with Southern allies, though this time for a specific conflict breaking out along the Ohio. The Cherokees did not feel they could honorably join the Shawnee effort while still negotiating with white settlers who might well be caught in a crossfire.[5]

Governor Dunmore had, since 1771, sought a large grant of land to the west from His Majesty. A few leaders in government still took the Proclamation line seriously, however, and denied the request. Dunmore instead had to rely on brutal misfortunes and naked opportunism. As in most cases, this proved far more successful. Summed up by Patrick Griffin, Dunmore "tried to take in the name of the Crown for Virginia what was denied by the Crown to Virginia."[6]

Even had colonial governors sought to avoid invasions of Indian lands west of the Proclamation line, they would have faced extraordinary difficulty in doing so. As hunters and settlers flooded west, tensions on the frontier predictably rose. A series of intercultural murders and retaliatory strikes took place in the Virginia backcountry in the spring and early summer of 1774, culminating in the murder and scalping of about ten relatives (including several women) of the Mingo war captain John Logan.[7] Previously known for his friendship toward Virginians, Logan announced his intentions for vengeance and swiftly struck back at settlers in the region. Still, it was a bloody but restrained revenge. Logan's Shawnee allies pressed him to limit the scope of his attacks to only Virginians, not Pennsylvanians, and Logan agreed.[8] Chroniclers often cite the murder of Logan's family as the spark of the ensuing war, but the powder keg had been filling rapidly since Fort Stanwix in 1768.[9]

The ensuing panic and clamor for action among Virginians, however—and Indian attacks always generated an outsized amount of hysteria[10]—allowed Dunmore to marshal Virginia forces for a major campaign against not just the Mingos, but especially their neighbors (and in some cases relatives), the Shawnees. The fact that the Shawnees had vigorously protested the Fort Stanwix Treaty, and any attempted sale of Kentucky, was doubtless also a factor.

Though much suspected by British officials for their efforts in building a pan-Indian alliance, in truth by 1774 the Shawnees themselves had been splintering for years. Some factions favored militant resistance, some accommodation, and some voluntary removal to the West. In part, their sense of division had led them to invite Mingos to live with them. The Shawnees did not seek a broader war at first, and sent peace overtures to Virginia.[11] Shawnee and Mingo leaders insisted upon, and received, assurances from Logan that his retaliation would be limited to Virginians, and only those west of the Monongahela River. His entire party consisted of only thirteen men, and having returned to his village in July with thirteen scalps, they announced they would listen to peace councils. Other tribes, especially the Delawares, sought to mediate the impending war, but unintentionally their efforts would simply leave the Shawnees exposed and without their nearest neighbors and allies.

Some Virginians argued that Logan's raid constituted a declaration of war on Virginia, and it is possible that the governor had been misled by the "inflammatory rhetoric" of some frontiersmen into believing the Shawnees were more culpable in the violence. Still, "Dunmore did nothing to bring the conflict to a speedy and equitable end." The governor insisted that he would have no peace until the Shawnees were "severely chastised." The Virginians' insistence upon a war with the Shawnees was not only opportunistic, but calculated as well. Governor Dunmore handled the Cherokees—also claimants to Kentucky, but far more numerous than the Shawnees—quite differently. When a Virginian named Crabtree murdered an Indian known as Cherokee Billy in the spring of 1774, Dunmore sought to mollify the Cherokees by offering a reward for his capture. In all likelihood no frontier jury would have convicted Crabtree, who withdrew deeper into Kentucky nevertheless. But Dunmore clearly wanted to avoid conflict with the Cherokee Nation, population 8,500, while he went out of his way to fight the Shawnees, whose population in 1774 was but one-third that number.[12]

Understandably, other officials watched the outbreak of "Lord Dunmore's War" with some apprehension. North Carolina's governor Josiah Martin noted in July that he had received word from Dunmore "that he has some Reason to believe they will be joined by the Cherokees, Creeks & many other Tribes." Martin remained confident, though, that the continuing war between the Choctaws and Creeks would keep the latter from joining the Cherokees. Martin added his compliments to Superintendent Stuart for having aided the Choctaws—and blocking a potential Southern alliance—in anticipation of just such an event.[13]

Almost with his last breath, Sir William Johnson pressured the Northern tribes to avoid mixing in the coming fight. Johnson knew that his Fort Stanwix "purchase" remained a constant irritant for the Shawnees. Conciliation would have been extremely difficult, even if he had the slightest inclination toward it. Instead, he spent 1774 gathering intelligence and fomenting discord that would leave the Shawnees isolated should a war break out. He held a conference at Johnson Hall in January 1774 with the Ohio Valley Senecas. Johnson wanted to avoid any possible splintering of the Iroquois League (as had happened during Pontiac's War). The Ohio Seneca chief Kayagshota, likely with Johnson's prodding, did his best to distance his people from the Shawnees. In March, Johnson sent him on a mission to the Miamis, hoping to dissuade them from joining their Ohio neighbors against the Crown.[14]

April brought an alarming report from Indian agent Alexander McKee. McKee, whose mother was of the Shawnees' Kispoko (warrior) sect, relayed a conversation from a Shawnee informant living in the Creek country. He spoke of an imminent meeting on the Scioto River of the Western and Southern nations. Though a number of chiefs had spoken of their desire for peace with the English, "the Warriors [were] of difft sentiments" and they allowed the speeches of the more pacific chiefs "as a Cover to this General Design." Further, while there had already been considerable violence on the frontier, only a general desire to avoid putting the English on their guard had prevented more bloodshed up to this point. The universal grievances of land encroachment, slaughtering of Indian game, and "the ill treatment recd from the frontier people" made a massive war inevitable, the Shawnee opined. The "Chenussio" (Geneseo) Senecas, despite their denials, were also taking an active part in the plot. The plan for a broad, trans-Ohio alliance to drive back the English, he continued, "is no new one, but has been in Being since our first Acquaintance almost with the English, & particularly since the French left their belts to the Northwd." Recalling those belts and banishing their intent would be nearly impossible, he felt, as the Ohio Indians were already committing to attack any settlers moving down the Ohio River. Finally, the Shawnee offered his most distressing intelligence: "I must likewise inform you that I am well acquainted with the Policy of all the Southern Indians and I can assure you That their Designs are exactly the same against the English." He again warned McKee not to take seriously any protestations of amiable intent, for "it is from their Lips only, and not from their Hearts."[15] Johnson had to know he was dying by this point, and McKee's report, if taken at face value, doubtless did little to ease his mind. Yet contradictory missives from the southward may have cheered him.

John Stuart, it seemed, was largely successful in diverting the Southern tribes' potential interest in joining the coalition, in large part by stoking the fires of mutual resentment among them. As General Frederick Haldimand informed Sir William, though there were troubling signs of a possible alliance between the Shawnees and the Upper Creeks, the Creeks as a whole seemed of divided opinion on the issue. Further, he noted, "a happy circumstance in our favor is the war now Subsisting between them [the Creeks] & the Chactaws." For the moment the Choctaws seemed solidly in the English camp, and Haldimand felt that if the Cherokees could be kept from aiding the Creeks against them, the whole affair would likely turn to Britain's favor. And if there were any way, he added, to solicit some Northern Indians to pitch in against the Creeks as well, so much the better.[16]

On May 2nd, 1774, Sir William wrote one of the longest letters of his career, reporting on a broad range of issues to the Secretary for North America, Lord Dartmouth. Even Johnson had become at least somewhat suspicious of the repeated claims that the French government, including King Louis himself, sought to stir up Indian alliances against the English. Yet he concluded, "The Religion Government & Genius of the French conspire to render them dangerous to us." Furthermore, he added, "their enterprizing Disposition with the plausible manner they use to lull us into security until they compass their Views has often been felt, & may as often be Experienced hereafter." Thus Sir William, as a true child of the eighteenth-century, felt confident in the assertion that a lack of real evidence against the French merely proved how cunning and deceptive they could be. (Other Anglo-American officials would make similar conclusions about Indians as well.) He did offer that French Canadians were probably even more dangerous to British America: "as they have less liberality of Sentiment, Stronger prejudice founded on greater ignorance, so that they are never without Inclination to hurt us, or hopes of success. . . . In short their [particularly their former leaders'] disposition & Attachment to old Interests is still so Strong that I have known Some of them when Speak[in]g to the Ind[ian]s who even in my presence could scarcely be restrained from Reflections on the English & Encomiums on the French."[17]

Six weeks later Johnson again wrote Lord Dartmouth. He lamented the murders committed by "Cresap," [the primary culprit, especially against Logan's family, was actually a Daniel Greathouse].[18] Johnson correctly acknowledged that settlers' wanton slayings of Indians helped make peace-keeping nearly impossible on the frontier. He then completely (and deliberately) mischaracterized the role that the Fort Stanwix cessions played in fostering mistrust and violence in the West. The treaty had been, he hastened to assert, "secured by the plainest & best natural Boundaries." Further, "the Indians freely agreed to make it the more ample that our people should have no pretext of narrow Limits."[19]

For someone with Johnson's detailed knowledge of North America's natives, such a convenient generalization as "the Indians" could not have been accidental. Of course *some* Indians, Johnson's Iroquois allies, had readily agreed to make the cession larger, for it cost them nothing and brought them profit. George III might have ceded Normandy to Catherine the Great with as much glee and legitimacy as the League had sold Kentucky. Johnson's self-serving narrative argued that only the lawless frontiersmen who pushed across the Ohio were to blame for the bloodshed, as if the purchase had somehow been designed to discourage western migration. Little could be done, he offered, until "better order is restored" and Indians' just complaints could be addressed, and until then war remained a constant threat. "Under such circumstances, my Lord, I fear the most that can be done, is to prevent the evil from becoming general, to encourage the fidelity of those Nations on whom I can rely, with those that will Joyn them, & secure as much of the Frontiers as possible from Incursion."

"My Lord I have daily to combat with thousands who by their avarice, cruelty or indiscretion are constantly counteracting all judicious measures with the Indians," he continued. One might debate Johnson's own cruelty, but his policies had absolutely displayed avarice and indiscretion. One also detects hubris, and a misplaced sense of martyrdom. "But I shall still persevere, the occasion requires it, and I shall never be without hopes, 'till I find myself without that Influence which has never yet forsaken me, on the most trying occasions."[20] For Johnson's purpose—an *apologia*—it was a terribly well constructed letter. He sought to insulate himself from any hint of wrongdoing for past events, and by blaming lower-class colonists and reminding Dartmouth of his "Influence which has never yet forsaken me," Sir William basically argued that if he could not prevent a general Indian war, no one could.

To the last, Johnson missed the point. He minimized, even ignored, his own role in provoking the rage that made pan-Indianism a threat, and simultaneously underestimated Indians' capabilities to think for themselves. Perhaps, in the end, Johnson was not unlike the great nineteenth-century historian Francis Parkman, whose magisterial prose placed Johnson's Iroquois friends on a pedestal. Parkman did so, aside from literary style, as a means to denigrate Indians in general.[21] As a loyal servant of the Crown, Johnson did so as well, though he still seemed to favor the Mohawks. He died on July 13, 1774, and the Iroquois League mourned him sorrowfully and sincerely.

Lord Dunmore's War was, until its final battle, really just a number of desultory skirmishes between a small segment of the Ohio Indians and backcountry Virginia. But the hype and terror it engendered roared on after Sir William's death, and threatened to denude the backcountry of white settlers. It would be left to his nephew, Guy Johnson, as well as John Stuart and General Thomas Gage, to sort out British strategy to prevent the dreaded general Indian war. Gage and Guy Johnson both seemed to agree that great efforts were needed to keep the lawless frontiersmen from starting a pan-Indian war—perhaps even including the Iroquois League— against His Majesty's colonies. Neither mentioned the impact of Sir William's treaties upon the current crisis. John Stuart, who had repeatedly complained about the questionable legality and dubious utility of the Fort Stanwix cession, also managed to keep his pen in check on that score. He could not resist, however, blending his tactful condolences for Johnson— "[who] would have been a great loss but is particularly so at this juncture which with respect to the Indians is very Critical"—with a tactless request that he be given the late man's job.[22]

British diplomacy, working through the Delawares and others, helped keep the Shawnees isolated. The Cherokees seemed rather quiet during this time, perhaps correctly seeing they had little stake in a conflict between Logan and some frontiersmen, but failing to see that the rapacious Virginians would opportunistically try to claim their hunting grounds. The Creeks also declined sending parties north, despite their inclinations to do so, because they feared stretching themselves while engaged in a war with the Choctaws. Gage referred to the Creek–Choctaw war as "a lucky Circumstance," neglecting to mention the efforts of Superintendent Stuart and others to foster it.[23] So the Crown's officials did put some effort into the conflict, but committed neither men nor great sums of money to it.

The British Army was in the process of abdicating its role in the West. Indeed, they had abandoned Fort De Chartres on the Mississippi, and had ceased shoring up Fort Pitt at the forks of the Ohio, despite its seemingly crucial location. They had no interest in joining this fight. As Paul W. Mapp notes, in the wake of the Seven Years' War Britain's imperial interests were increasingly focusing on the Atlantic World (and India) rather than interior North America.[24] For most of the British establishment, the military included, by the early 1770s the unrest of colonists on the eastern seaboard over taxation and soldiers in their midst seemed more troubling. Indeed, General Haldimand opined to General Gage that "all the settlers on the frontier were not worth what a campaign would cost." Further,

British officials were actually hoping that the threat of Indian war or slave rebellion would keep the unruly colonists from rebelling. If a true pan-Indian alliance had risen, Virginia would have been in serious trouble. General Gage heartily disapproved of the colony's rash saber-rattling, and noted that if they did bring on a war, "which as they rush into without Necessity, they must get out of as they can." Yet despite his fairly reckless insistence upon broadening the war, Dunmore would be rewarded. As Richard White notes, "In the unequal test of strength between the Shawnees and Virginia, the Virginians prevailed."[25]

The only sizable battle of the war took place at Point Pleasant, in what is now West Virginia. The Shawnees, in the hope of preempting an invasion of their Ohio villages, attacked the Virginian army while it was still gathering. In a hard fought and bloody day, the outnumbered attackers nearly succeeded. But the Virginians held,[26] and in the aftermath forced the Shawnees to sign the Treaty of Camp Charlotte, in which they ceded their claims to Kentucky. (Dunmore did receive a reprimand, but no more, from the home government.)[27] Most Shawnees, even those who marked the treaty, were furious, and had little intention of honoring it. They burned with the knowledge that with even a few supporters from the other Ohio villages—Miamis, Kickapoos, or perhaps Cherokees from the southward— "if there had been only a part of the league the Shawnees envisioned, the outcome would have been far different."[28] (Of course, a broader league of Indians probably would have brought a broader league of Britons against them. The Yamasee War on the Southern frontier in 1715 had proved one of the few forces capable of forging an alliance between South Carolina and its rival Virginia.) Still, the Shawnees forgot neither their grievances nor the need for alliances to redress them.

The mood of Indian superintendents, like the tone of Indian affairs, could change with astonishing speed and annoying frequency. By mid-November 1774, John Stuart could report happily that the Shawnees were accepting the loss of Kentucky, and that the Cherokees had agreed to turn over some of their men involved in the murder of several whites, including the aforementioned Captain Russell of Virginia. General Gage could write that while the home government frowned somewhat on Lord Dunmore's actions, the Shawnees had been thwarted in their efforts to enlist the Northern tribes, including the Iroquois. Yet by the end of the month

Gage, not knowing the outcome of Point Pleasant, fretted over the battle: "which Event may spread the War throughout the Nations, the Six Nations were with Difficulty restrained before from joining them, and declared they would do it if the Virginians persisted in Marching forwards with Design to extirpate the Shawnese. The Indians your way especially the Cherokees may take the same Resolution, and as they know no Difference between one Province and another may as well fall on Carolina as Virginia."[29]

CHAPTER 5

Revolution and Realignment

As 1774 gave way to 1775, both Stuart and Gage became increasingly alarmed not just with the state of Indian affairs, but also with the growing anti-government sentiment of American colonists. Gage reported that "Ill affected People" had been circulating among the Iroquois "with Design to persuade them that the King had deserted their Interest." These miscreants, Gage continued, had even hinted that the king hoped to destroy the Shawnees, which was perhaps a revealing bit of psychological projection on the part of the king's opponents. Gage warned Stuart to be on his guard in the Southern district for similar shenanigans, "for you have People full as ill inclined to Government as any to the Northward of you." An Indian war, particularly a "general" one, was the last thing His Majesty needed in the increasingly rebellious colonies, and Gage knew it.[1]

January 1775 presented at least some good news for Anglo-Americans. Reports indicated that the Upper Creek war captain Mortar had been killed in a skirmish with the Choctaws. Gage would be doubly glad to hear of this, as Mortar had opposed encroachments on Creek lands, while his death at the hands of Choctaws would help ensure that those two nations continued to fight each other, rather than Britons. Further, Shawnee and Delaware embassies to the Chickasaws had failed to sway the latter into joining their confederacy. Compounding their failure, the delegation killed two Choctaws very near the Chickasaw Town, which offended the Chickasaws and Choctaws gravely. Still, Stuart concluded, Indians would never coexist peacefully with colonists as long as the colonials maintained their "insatiable" hunger for Indian lands.[2]

In April the landscape of British policy for North America shook. A clash between Colonial militia and British soldiers in Massachusetts suddenly ratcheted up the stakes for His Majesty's relationships with his Indian children. It was obvious that Indian allies could potentially play a vital (or catastrophic) role in any ensuing fight, yet the growing spirit of rebellion made it that much harder for British officials to project their power. Superintendent Stuart assured his superiors that both the Creeks and Cherokees remained "attached to His Majesty's Interest," though both nations complained about the dearth of arms and ammunition available to them. Yet at this crucial juncture Stuart felt compelled to flee Charles Town (soon to be Charleston, South Carolina) because of the "total subversion of Government" there. He further noted that some Cherokees were now very dissatisfied with their sale of land on the Holston River (now eastern Tennessee) to Richard Henderson's private land company. Shawnees had waylaid Henderson's party before they could actually survey their purchase, killing four. More potentially ominous was the intelligence that Creek headmen were once more sailing to Havana to talk with the Spaniards, while Shawnee and Delaware emissaries were expected among the Cherokees that summer.[3]

Stuart did flee Charles Town—so precipitously in fact that he left his wife and daughter behind. He removed to Georgia, but found the rebels there so worrisome that he left again for the safety of St. Augustine. Part of the reason Stuart fled South Carolina was the charge, made by the provincial (Patriot) legislature there that he had sought to have the Cherokees and Catawbas "fall upon the provinces of North & So. Carolina & Georgia." In all likelihood, Stuart was simply trying to hold on to the Crown's allies. The superintendent happily reported that his deputies all found "the Indians as perfectly pacifick & well disposed." But in the fervor and paranoia of those days it would have taken little to convince the legislators (or a jury) of Stuart's guilt. Even more damning, and equally unsubstantiated, was the charge that Stuart would try to free the colony's slaves to help suppress the rebellion. "As nothing can be more alarming to the Carolinians than the Idea of an attack from Indians and Negroes," Stuart noted, he was probably fortunate to escape with his life. Indeed, in the fall of 1775 Charlestonians would execute a free black man named Jemmy, "who was found guilty of having endeavoured to cause an insurrection." Governor Dunmore of Virginia, who as late as March of 1775 had received the public thanks of a Patriot convention for his "noble, wise, and spirited conduct" against the Shawnees in the late war, would soon arm the Shawnee hostages he kept from that conflict for his own protection. In November 1775 he issued a proclamation offering freedom to the slaves of rebellious planters.[4] Both moves were designed to shore up his control and intimidate rebels into submission. Dunmore soon found they had the opposite effect. Fear could spur men to be dangerous.

While "Patriot propaganda depicted Dunmore as promoting a bloody and indiscriminate massacre of white people by slave rebels"—an inaccurate but easily sold version of events—the home government had specifically ordered him to do no such thing. At the same time, planters resorted to draconian measures to discourage slaves from running off to join Dunmore. Slaves were flogged publicly, their ears severed, were hanged, and (not unlike the Wampanoag pan-Indianist King Philip) were beheaded, and the heads placed "atop posts placed at crossroads as a warning to passing slaves."[5] While Indian affairs at this point required some diplomacy, slave owners saw no need for subtlety with their human property, and would likely have viewed such as a sign of terminal weakness.

Typically historians of Indians in this era paint both the Americans and British as reluctant to employ Indian allies in the beginning of the Revolution. Assuming this to be true, it is nevertheless clear that the reluctance gave way within a few months of the clashes at Lexington and Concord. At the very least, both sides greatly feared the other would successfully recruit Indians first. By July 1775 Stuart, knowing the key role of trade goods for Indian alliances, was concerned that the war would hinder Britain's Indian trade. This in turn would provide opportunity for the Americans. "The great supply of Ammunition and other presents which [Patriot] Agents will be enabled to carry," Stuart feared, "will possibly have a great Effect on the Indians." Fortunately for Great Britain, the reverse proved true—in most cases the Americans failed in Indian diplomacy, because their underdeveloped industries could not match Britain's capacity for providing Indian trade goods. It looked very dark for Stuart in those first months however, epitomized by an incident where the Patriots seized a supply ship stocked with Indian trade goods, including eight tons of gunpowder. This was an especially tough loss for the Creeks, who desperately needed ammunition to continue their war with the Choctaws. As it happened, by the fall of 1775, Stuart would have to negotiate an end to this intertribal war that he had helped foster.[6]

Patriots, both at the local and national level, initially viewed Indian neutrality as the best-case scenario. When the Shawnees Young Cornstalk and Wolf paid a call to Albemarle County, Virginia, in September 1775, they received a talk from Dr. George Gilmer. Gilmer asked that the Shawnees "not harken to the wicked talks that be against us." King George had "by wicked Councils & by the advice of bad men" attacked the Virginians' "houses, our wives & children." Gilmer spoke euphemistically of the king's taxation without representation, but was then quite concrete about his desire for something even grander than a pan-Indian confederation—a truly pan-American union. He hoped that Virginians and Shawnees would "bury our Tomahawks in the Center of the earth," and then "Let every nation & every people on this side of the big water enter into a mutual League, unite our thoughts & councils by our strong chain, banish all contention, & shew our deluded brothers that we have courage confidence & strength enough in each other never to be forced to submit . . . to the yoke of evil men." Gilmer's pleas to Wolf and Young Cornstalk for peace were not remarkable, nor were his admonitions against trusting the soon-to-be exiled royal governor, Lord Dunmore—"He is deceitful." Certainly Americans would seek to counter British attempts to secure Indian allies against them. But Gilmer's call for a unified white-Indian league opposed to Britain demonstrates either a strikingly naive or brilliantly progressive vision.[7] While a tantalizing window into contingency, Gilmer's talk succumbed to frightful odds. Americans' lust for Indian lands and Indian dependence on British trade goods would prove too much for a pan-American alliance.

Officials in Whitehall, given the lag for carrying reports across the Atlantic, wasted little time in calling for help in suppressing the rebellion. Citing reports that "the Rebels having excited the Indians to take a part," Lord Dartmouth wrote Colonel Guy Johnson, Sir William's nephew, to "induce [the Iroquois League] to take up the Hatchet against His Majesty's Rebellious Subjects in America." Besieged in Boston, General Gage agreed, noting that the local rebels "have brought down all the Savages they could against us here." Gage wrote to Agent Alexander McKee at Fort Pitt the same day, ordering him to secure as many Indians as possible for an expedition against the Virginia frontier to take place the following spring.[8] Fear of facing a broad coalition of Indians allied with the enemy pushed men in both Britain and America to seek native allies, resulting in a physical and rhetorical "arms race" for native warriors.

British and American officials were not the only ones fearing a withering assault by a broad Indian confederacy. The Oneidas, founding members of the Iroquois League, became unnerved in early 1776 when a Cayuga sachem hinted at talks with the Western Indians. They had not been privy to such talks. Fearing that they could not depend on their League membership to protect them from outside attacks, or even other League members, they "sought security against their closest traditional allies." So great was the fear of pan-Indian warfare that the Oneidas formed a secret defense pact with the Tuscaroras (junior members of the League), the Kahnawakes (Catholic Iroquois from Canada), and Oquagas.[9]

While Lord Dunmore had hoped his war with the Shawnees had clarified ownership of Kentucky, North Carolina's Judge Richard Henderson continued to muddy the waters. Henderson saw opportunity in the chaotic frontier, and hoped to buy up much of the Cherokees' claims to both Kentucky and Tennessee with a speculator's group known as the Transylvania Company. He had been inspired to do so in large part through the encouragement of a "longhunter" who had repeatedly made the dangerous but profitable journey deep into Kentucky—Daniel Boone. Henderson, like the Wataugans Sevier and Robertson before him, had been audacious enough to try to buy Indian lands from Indians who actually had some claim to them. In so doing, he trod over the claims of Virginians—including Lord Dunmore and George Washington, and numerous North Carolina authorities as well. Henderson's purchase incensed them.[10]

While greed certainly helped fuel their fury with Henderson, Colonial officials had legitimate reasons to rage against his purchase. Josiah Martin, the royal governor of North Carolina, proclaimed that the purchase violated the Proclamation of 1763, which it certainly did. He also railed that Henderson's colony would become a refuge for brigands from the other colonies—a charge that had often been made against northern Carolina in the previous century—and that it would hinder future settlement. Probably the most troubling aspect was Henderson's form of payment, which had been distinctly to the Cherokees' liking. Henderson had provided "a considerable quantity of Gunpowder, whereby they will be furnished with the means of annoying his Majesty's subjects in this and the neighboring Colonies." In theory a royal governor should not have opposed a transfer of much needed gunpowder to the king's allies, but in the uncertainty of the times Martin felt justified in being overly cautious. He declared the purchase "illegal, null, and void." Dunmore made a similar decree in March.[11]

As different white factions squabbled over the disposition of what would become Kentucky and Tennessee, the Cherokees themselves were increasingly divided. One flaw in all Indian land cession treaties, whether conducted by Europeans or Americans, was the tendency to treat with Indians as if they constituted monolithic blocks of opinion. Indian nations were far too de-centralized and fond of individualism for European-style treaties to ever truly represent "Indian opinion." Land cession treaties were especially tricky because the European concept of fee-simple land titles for individuals simply did not translate for Native Americans. Strictly speaking, it would be difficult to imagine a scenario where any land cession treaty between Indians and outsiders would have been considered legitimate from the native view. Anglo-American negotiators could be quite ruthless in exploiting this fact to get a treaty signed. However, that rarely ended conflicts, and frequently exacerbated them. Among the Cherokees, the issue of selling western lands actually followed the arc of Greek tragedy.

When Henderson made his purchase, his principal ally among the Cherokees was the venerable chief Attakullakulla (Little Carpenter). The chief and many of his followers hated to sell the land, but felt that their debilitating war with the Choctaws made the land less necessary than the gunpowder Henderson offered. Many Cherokee elders supported Attakullakulla in the endeavor, though his right to actually make the sale was questionable. His most vocal detractor at the council was his son, Tsi'yugûnsi'ni, or "Dragging Canoe." (In Cherokee matrilineal fashion, Dragging Canoe was reared by his mother's clan, though he still would have had a relationship with his father.) Dragging Canoe bitterly opposed the idea of selling any Cherokee lands, and had no intention of honoring any such treaty. Toward the end of the council, he told Henderson ominously, "You have bought a fair land, but you will find its settlement dark and bloody." Dragging Canoe led a faction of militant Cherokees, soon known as the Chickamaugas, who spent the next decade doing their best to make their chief's words a reality. In May 1776, Dragging Canoe attended a conference at Chota with Shawnee, Mohawk, and Ottawa militants. A headman from Chillhowee took up the militant belt, and as he began singing "the war song . . . all the Northern Indians joined in the chorus." As Gregory Dowd notes, "the British had earlier provided Dragging Canoe with three thousand pounds of gunpowder; here were northern militants suggesting how to use it."[12]

Pan-Indian efforts had failed during Dunmore's War, though not by much, and by 1776 Dragging Canoe's Chickamaugas embraced Shawnee allies in the common cause of driving settlers from the backcountry. Given how often Cherokees and Shawnees had traded war parties along the Warrior's Path in the past century, this was quite remarkable. Perhaps a delayed reaction to Dunmore's aggression and Henderson's purchase, Shawnee military cooperation with any faction of Cherokees would probably have astounded warriors from a previous generation. As Stephen Aron asserts, "A confederation of Shawnees and Cherokees had once seemed as unlikely as a union of American colonists," and even more radical. Of course, radicals are rarely in the majority. Though there were joint Shawnee–Cherokee parties raiding the backcountry—including those who briefly kidnapped Daniel Boone's daughter Jemima—"The symbolism of age-old enemies fighting side by side as yet outweighed the military significance of this and other raids."[13]

By the spring of 1776, America's more zealous rebels were beginning to gain the upper hand on moderates and conservatives, and proved perfectly willing to utilize rhetorical mash-ups to further their cause. Effortlessly marrying the language of bondage with cries that "our Negroe slaves have been incited to rebel against us," and conflating "Indian savages" with German mercenary "savages," American propagandists had mastered what Peter Silver calls "violent self-pity" long before the Declaration of Independence.[14] With such deplorable, villainous, frightening enemies, how could the American Patriots ever lose the moral high ground?

The Declaration itself famously listed among the king's crimes "inciting domestic insurrection among us"—a reference to Dunmore's emancipation proclamation—and attempting to bring war from "merciless Indian Savages" upon the frontier. During the Revolution, and again in the War of 1812, "American writers demonized the British as race traitors who allied with savage Indians on the frontier and fomented bloody slave uprisings in the South.... [in so doing] the British betrayed the white Americans, who claimed a unique capacity to enjoy freedom and sustain a republic."[15]

In the months after the Declaration of Independence, the Southern frontier braced for a full-on war with the Cherokees, who retained their alliance with Great Britain. The fact that American settlers poured into, and even past, the Transylvania and Watauga purchases only heightened tensions. One of the few things American and British officials agreed upon was that such settlers greatly tried Indians' patience and invited attacks. Though some felt that the Cherokees were "drawing on their destruction" by attacking American settlements, reports took on a far more sinister air when it appeared they had secured alliances with the neighboring nations. When "certain Intelligence" indicated a Cherokee party of 600 men was but part of a 2,400-man force of Cherokees, "Creeks . . . & 15 Northern Tribes," it merited a letter from the provisional president of Virginia to the North Carolina Council of Safety. Virginians no doubt exhaled a bit when, two days later, the *Virginia Gazette* reported a successful skirmish between the militia and the large war party.[16]

In fact, by mid-August 1776, the *Gazette* would happily report that "the Cherokees have been so completely checked in their career," and the Northern tribes seemed primarily defensive in their posture, "we may hope that there is not much to be dreaded from the terrible combination of Indians we have been threatened with by our enemies." Summer punitive campaigns against Cherokee towns appeared to deliver results similar to those in the early 1760s, which ended the Cherokee War, and it looked as though the Creeks and other nations had little inclination to join them. By the fall, the Cherokees were suing for peace. A closer look, however, reveals that while the campaigns against the Cherokee towns did burn cornfields and impoverish many, few warriors were actually killed, or even seen.[17] They would lie low for the moment, weighing their options.

As 1776 demonstrated that the war would become more general, British officials made increasing preparations to both keep and utilize Indian allies. Major General Sir Guy Carleton, commander of the Canadian posts, wrote from Quebec in late 1776. He notified the Lords of the Treasury that while he could not be exact as to department's budget, it would cost at least £50 to 60,000. In addition to repairing fortifications, a considerable amount would be needed for "Presents to the Indians, whom it was so necessary to attach to the King's Interests." Carleton also complained that "The Indian Presents sent out this year, I know not by whom, have been so improperly chosen, that they were of little use." Carleton had therefore been obliged to give extra gifts to his department's Indians, "As it is of so material a consequence to gain these People."[18] To the south, the far more precariously situated John Stuart agreed.

Stuart wrote his new superior, Lord George Germaine, who had replaced Lord Dartmouth and would be Great Britain's last Secretary for North

America. He acknowledged that some of the Cherokees "who have been severely chastised" for remaining loyal to the king, had made peace as a temporary measure. The vast majority, however, "hold out and wait for nothing more than being joined by the Creeks and some white Leaders to act vigorously." While some of the Lower Creeks had been misled by American promises of plentiful trade goods, "A Chief from the Chehaw Town" led a party against some Georgia (Patriot) Rangers, killing four of them near Fort Barrington on the Altamaha River. This successful party returned just as a number of English traders arrived in Chehaw with a great supply of goods. According to Stuart, the battlefield success and the plentiful trade goods "so discredited [the Americans' promises] that the whole Nation immediately declared for [the king's] Government."[19]

Stuart happily reported that several hundred Creeks had gone to aid the Cherokees, while others led by local Tories were scouting the Georgia frontier. He also noted that his younger brother, Indian agent Charles Stuart, "is out upon a tour through the Chickasaw & Chactaw Nations." John Stuart had called a conference with their principal chiefs at Mobile in April. "I make no doubt," he added confidently, "of being able to attach them firmly to his Majesty's cause, and to join firmly in a Confederacy with the Creeks & Cherokees." In little more than a year, Stuart and the British Empire had made an abrupt about face. After twenty-some years of actively trying to scuttle (by any means necessary) a grand alliance of Southern Indian nations, Stuart hoped now to effect one. Of course, proposing and succeeding were two different things.

Predictably, the Creeks in particular found it very difficult to trust His Majesty's word. In all likelihood they suspected British agents' role in prolonging their war with the Choctaws. Stuart said perhaps more than he realized when he noted, "the great bulk of the [Creek] Nation continue at Home or are hunting near their Town ready to oppose any Invasion of their Country, or to assist this Province in case of its being attacked."[20] For decades, Creek diplomacy would be defined by keeping the nation's options open, preferring the threat of war (at least against non-Indians) to its large-scale application.

In trying to encourage pan-Indian forces against the rebellious colonists, Stuart could not have been pleased by the peace between another great Southern nation, the Cherokees, and Patriots in Georgia and the Carolinas. In the Treaty of Dewett's Corner, completed in May 1777, the Cherokees acknowledged that American forces had "repeatedly defeated" them in the summer of 1776, and they would cede to South Carolina lands they had taken during the campaign, particularly the lands east of Unacaye Mountain. South Carolina promised an immediate shipment of trade goods to the Cherokees, and pledged to promote a regular and regulated trade among them. The Cherokees further promised to arrest any Tories who had aided or encouraged their fight with the Americans, and to hand them over to South Carolina's Fort Rutledge.

In an attempt to reduce the friction created by the lawless on a frontier, the Cherokees promised to hand over for execution Indians who murdered whites. Any whites "or other Person"—slaves—from South Carolina or Georgia who murdered Cherokees would, after being "duly convicted thereof," be executed as well, with the Cherokees permitted to witness the event. (The fact that white juries almost never convicted the killers of Indians was not mentioned.) All Indian and white prisoners from the late war were to be freed, while stolen horses and "all negroes taken during the late War"—at least those stolen from Virginia, the Carolinas, or Georgia—should be taken to Fort Rutledge. South Carolina also promised the Cherokees 100 lbs. (weight) of leather for every escaped slave they returned to proper authorities. Finally, the treaty declared, "an universal Peace and Friendship re-established between South Carolina and Georgia and the Cherokees." Notably, the treaty also stated that the Catawba Indians—who remained allies of South Carolina—were part of the peace settlement.[21]

Cherokee militants had a multitude of good reasons to oppose ceding more land to the colonists, most especially the region of the Holston River in what is now eastern Tennessee. In addition to its value to hunters, the Long Island of the Holston River, which settlers coveted, sat astride the Warrior's Path, which ran roughly north–south, as well as serving as an intersection to major rivers and trails leading to the West. The Warrior's Path in particular was "perhaps the most significant and ancient route of Cherokee geopolitics." Through the efforts of Dragging Canoe and others, the Treaty of Long Island (1777) did not actually cede the eponymous piece of land.[22] Losing Long Island to white settlement would severely hinder pan-Indian ambitions by closing off the major route from the Cherokee country to the north.

Cherokee delegations also visited Virginia that spring to solidify the peace. One group of about "forty gentlemen and ladies of the Cherokee nation," the *Virginia Gazette* noted with pleasure, journeyed to Williamsburg. The delegates, including chief Occonostota, "favoured the public with a dance on the green in front of the palace, where a considerable number of spectators, both male and female, were agreeably entertained."[23] Doubtless the news would not have made the ailing John Stuart dance. His own pan-Indian dreams—which had until recently been nightmares—were crumbling before his eyes. And things would only get worse.

PART II

Pan-Indianism and Policy

With the American Revolution, British policy toward Indians would shift again. Agents initially sought to keep natives quiet as the colonists became more rebellious. Soon however, both American and British officials realized Indian warriors would not remain neutral, and both sides sought them as allies. While the Crown and the Patriots might both use the rhetoric of unity, Britain would have an early interest in now suddenly promoting pan-Indian unity against the American colonists, who had long been a source of friction with Indians on the frontier. Yet misfortune and mismanagement would plague the British–Indian alliance, which never reached its potential during the war. Americans also witnessed British attempts to use African Americans against them. Particularly for Americans in the South, the image was as indelible as it was terrifying. After abandoning their Indian allies in 1783, Britons were effectively intimidated into appeasing pan-Indian designs in the early 1790s, as nativists seemed poised to repeat the destruction of Pontiac's War if Britain continued to ignore them. From fear as much as policy, the British agents would embrace pan-Indian rhetoric, only to abandon their allies once more when war with the United States became likely. For the new American nation, an obvious imperative was preventing a comparable union of Indian nations that could oppose its western ambitions. Adding to U.S. concerns was the return of Spanish influence among the natives of the Southeast. If Southern Indians and runaway slaves with Spanish guns acted in concert with Northern Indians bearing British ones, the cost of putting down such a war might well break the Treasury.

The early 1790s proved the era with the greatest potential for pan-Indian resistance. The old obstacles to Indian unity briefly seemed to fade, and both Britain and Spain seemed willing to support Indian coalitions whose battlefield successes could stall American expansionism. But battlefield reverses north of the Ohio and the deaths of prominent leaders to the south, combined with shifting European priorities resulting from the French Revolution, killed hopes for a broad Indian front to oppose the United States. The Americans, first as a confederacy, and later a Federal Union, meanwhile, forged their own national identity in part through their ability to stifle and defeat Indians' attempts to unite. In many respects the Union's foundation was built on the ruins of attempted pan-Indian confederacies. American patriotism became entwined with anti-Indian rhetoric and expansion.

CHAPTER **6**

Britain's Pan-Indian Gamble

Maintaining Britain's Indian alliances often impressed British officials as a chore, though a necessary one. Maintaining a broad, pan-Indian coalition of course brought extra difficulties. In the Northern theater, General Haldimand could note the sorry condition of the Indians who had joined General John Burgoyne's campaign in New York. Writing only four weeks before the disastrous end of Burgoyne's efforts, Haldimand noted that because they had not been able to hunt the previous year—denying them not only meat but also the increasingly crucial currency of pelts—the warriors and in particular their families would be in great need. While doing so would not be cheap, the Crown had little choice but to keep them alive with food and stores. The general offered, "I conceive the assistance of the Indians is most essential to our success, and their attachment to His Majesty is at all times to be secured." Stuart faced a similar situation in the Southern theater. He apologized to the Treasury for his unusually high expenses for the winter of 1777–1778, noting that the Cherokees had been much "Distressed." Further, the Rebels were actively competing for Indian allies. Because of this, as well as an acknowledgment of those who "ventured their lives in fighting His Majesty's enemies," Stuart had little choice but to "expend an extraordinary quantity of presents."[1]

Despite Stuart's efforts, he could never keep any nation entirely in the British camp. By 1778 the Cherokees could note that while their treaty with the Americans had been costly and even humiliating, the Americans were nevertheless arming them with powder and shot to keep them neutral, if not allied. The Upper and Lower Creeks had also, according to Stuart, "been alienated from His Majesty's interest," which would necessitate more councils and of course more expense.[2]

The struggle for Indian alliances remained fluid, however, and eventually the weight of British maritime resources would make it exceedingly difficult for the United States to keep its Indian friends. As one Patriot official in Georgia correctly predicted, "Should the Trade from this Country with the Indians be once open and interrupted, the Enemy will find not the least difficulty, whenever they have a mind in bringing the Savages upon the Frontiers of Carolina." Paradoxically, it was Britain's sway with Indians, and perhaps especially its willingness to abet pan-Indianism, that helped convince many settlers in the Southern backcountry to side with the revolutionaries.[3]

In many respects the entire British war effort during the Revolution seemed half-hearted. Certainly the British public had misgivings about making war upon their American cousins. Early in the war the British military proved strikingly passive and unwilling to exploit its advantages. Many Indians and some British nationals realized that the native arm of His Majesty's forces, though so critical for any success, was poorly utilized. The British commander at Detroit, Lieutenant Colonel Henry Hamilton, sought to "concert a general invasion of the Frontiers." Hamilton, taking his lead from the vast array of tribal spokesmen gathered at Fort Vincennes, sought to gather warriors from the Cherokees, Chickasaws, Shawnees, Delawares, Senecas, Miamis, Wyandots, Pottawatomis, Chippewas, and others. The confederacy would also include warriors from Iroquoia and the Great Lakes to the Gulf Coast, acting in a relatively coordinated series of assaults on the Rebels' frontiers. Hamilton rightly had great hopes for this venture, which would surely put tremendous pressure on the already strained American war effort.[4]

Yet this truly pan-Indian attack—which some of the Southern nations were already planning independent of Hamilton—proved ill-fated. Modern schoolchildren in Illinois and Indiana learn that the intrepid Virginian George Rogers Clark "conquered" Illinois and Indiana in 1778 and 1779. He of course did no such thing, but merely staked a claim for Virginia to some villages in the Illinois Country.[5] But Colonel Clark's audacious assault on Fort Vincennes in February 1779—after Hamilton had re-taken it from the Americans in December 1778—had enormous ramifications. Clark's capture of Vincennes disrupted the timing and leadership of the British–Indian alliance, as Hamilton was led away in chains to Virginia. Hamilton, as will be discussed in chapter 9, never forgave the Americans this indignity, nor lost his interest in utilizing Indian proxies to vex them.

Clark also intercepted the invaluable trade goods and weapons Hamilton had intended to distribute to his Indian allies for the grand campaign of 1779. Indeed, "one of Clark's chief objectives in his daring Vincennes campaigns was to prevent the planned Indian council from being held at the mouth of the Tennessee River." While remembered primarily for the harrowing conditions his men faced crossing the flooded and nearly freezing Illinois prairie to take Vincennes by surprise, his assault accomplished far more. "Deprived of their supplies and temporarily divided by Clark's successes at Vincennes and elsewhere on the Wabash, the Indians could not plan their assault."[6]

After 1778, in fact, the North ministry's enthusiasm for utilizing Indian allies to the hilt faded rapidly, long before they had given up hope of winning the war. The relatively lackadaisical effort to support a pan-Indian union that would have crushed American efforts in the backcountry fell apart because of the British public's reaction to the murder of one American woman: Jane McCrea.

In July 1777, McCrea, the fiancée of a New York loyalist, was killed (likely by mistake) by Indians allied to Britain. A small component of John Burgoyne's disastrous campaign that culminated in the American victory at Saratoga, McCrea's death became a huge propaganda victory for the Patriots. Actual information about the killing remains elusive, but the lack of evidence proved advantageous for the American press. "Literary anti-Indianism," Peter Silver notes, had been tailor-made by the Revolutionary era to generate a sense of sympathy and martyrdom for Anglo-Americans. Their "sense of indignant vulnerability" or "violent self-pity" became a deadly cudgel in the hands of American propagandists. A narrative emerged that McCrea had been deliberately murdered, and (it was strongly implied) raped by the *savage* allies of Britain. The lurid stories only furthered the American conflation of Indians and Britons in the American mind, and their alliance was portrayed as a force of pure evil.[7]

Aside from ignoring the basic facts (or lack thereof) surrounding McCrea's death, Americans also ignored the unmitigated horror with which the British public greeted the news. Britons generally had long been ambivalent at best concerning the use of Indian allies, even against the hated

French. In the Revolution, native warriors would obviously be falling almost exclusively upon Anglo-Americans, which did not sit well with many in Great Britain. As Troy Bickham notes, "Indians were again called upon to be enforcers of Britain's political will, but they were a more politicized variable than they had been two decades before." While the North ministry was not initially troubled by the idea of Indian allies potentially killing civilians, it "nevertheless appears to have been somewhat sensitive to public sentiment on the matter." The press and the loyal opposition made great use of the McCrea tragedy, just as George Washington and Horatio Gates had on the other side of the Atlantic. None other than Edmund Burke castigated the ministry's use of Indian allies (and McCrea's resulting murder) in a February 6, 1778, speech, which was widely reported and reproduced in the British press. Lord Germain, the Secretary for North America, who had earlier been a strong advocate of using Indian warriors to bring the colonists to heel, was criticized so heatedly during debates in the House of Commons in the spring of 1778 that he "reportedly challenged Henry Luttrell, a leading opposition spokesman, to a duel." Burke moved to stop using Indian allies altogether, but the motion was defeated by more than eighty votes. Nevertheless, the horrified British press and public put so much pressure on the government over the issue, Bickham concludes, that by late 1778, "the ministry had all but washed its hands of Indian affairs."[8]

Understandably, then, 1779 turned out to be an awful year for the British–Indian alliance. The Iroquois League—or four of its six nations, more precisely—had been steadfast allies to the Crown. Yet the Iroquois and those who knew them could complain loudly and justly that they received very little protection from their Father the King. After a large American force invaded and devastated the Iroquois heartland in 1779—retaliation for Iroquois–Tory raids the previous year—the League sought more British aid. They also sent out war belts to the Western and Southern tribes. In so doing, they hoped in the words of a Cayuga speaker, "to reestablish us once more in our former Situation."[9]

While Royal efforts to establish a broad, coordinated Indian assault on the Rebels proved stillborn, native efforts persisted, and the fear of such a calamity raged unabated.

"Through a fascinating pattern of cooperation, the Shawnees and Chickamauga Cherokees kept alive their militant networks, networks that drew together peoples as distant from one another as the Creeks near the Gulf of Mexico and the Chippewas of the Great Lakes." By March 1780, British-hosted councils at Niagara were already seeking to repair the damage by sending war belts from the Shawnees, Delawares, and Six Nations to the Western and Southern nations. Arent DePeyster, the British commissary at Detroit, thanked his counterpart among the Upper Cherokees for the intelligence that the Southern tribes strongly supported Britain. He gleefully noted that the same could be said of Indians from as far away as Michilimackinac, Canada, and the Sioux country (in modern Minnesota). The Shawnees, Delawares, Mingos, Wyandots, and Hurons continued to fight well, and the Hurons would soon circulate war belts to the Southern tribes, with the Cherokees (presumably the Chickamaugas) acting as envoys to the Chickasaws, Creeks, and Choctaws.[10]

Seven hundred Ohio Valley and Great Lakes warriors—Mingoes, Delawares, Shawnees, Potawatomis, Chippewas, Hurons, and Ottawas—accompanied by Captain Henry Bird and 150 British soldiers, left Detroit for Kentucky in late May, 1780. While Bird wanted to attack Fort Nelson, held by George Rogers Clark, Bird's Indian allies preferred to go directly after the civilian "stations," and he reluctantly agreed. The size of the force, and the fact that they had two small fieldpieces, gave the expedition an extraordinary opportunity to drive the settlers from Kentucky, as none of the wooden palisades there could withstand artillery. By late June, they had captured both Ruddell's Station and Martin's Station, taking numerous prisoners. Bird, however, was incensed that his allies—against his fervent demands—had not only killed a number of prisoners, but also the livestock that Bird hoped would feed his force. He decided to withdraw, and it proved the last time that Indians had the crucial allied artillery at their disposal for an invasion of Kentucky.[11]

In the last years of the war, British strategy focused on retaining the more financially rewarding Southern colonies. Old practices, like fostering animosity between slaves and Indians, certainly proved a hindrance. As Jim Piecuch notes, trying to unify white Loyalists, Indians, and the slaves of rebels, "would certainly have been . . . difficult, but not impossible." (Indeed, this would prove a strong formula in the War of 1812.) But by not really trying, they negated their great potential advantage.[12]

For winning in this region that was relatively under-populated by settlers, Indian alliances would be all the more crucial. While John Stuart's death in March 1779 deprived His Majesty of an experienced and loyal superintendent, Britain was fortunate to retain his successor, Alexander Cameron. Cameron knew Indian cultures and understood fully that, accountants be damned, "it will be an insurmountable difficulty . . . to preserve an influence over Indians and secure their attachment to His Majesty, without having presents, Provisions and Ammunition in my own power." Worse, the Spaniards, who had officially joined the war against Britain (though not in alliance with the United States) in 1779, sought to woo the Southern Indians away from King George III. Such would only increase the costs of alliance in the Southeast. "It may be attended with bad consequences to deal Sparingly with [the Indians]," Cameron further noted, "least the Spaniards, who are indefatigable in their attempts to bring the whole Chactaw Nation over to their Interest, should succeed in Exciting them to take up the Hatchet against us." Though British agents, like Cameron's deputy Ferguson Bethune, could tell themselves that Indians would fare better as their allies than those of another power, they also understood that such arguments could easily fall flat with Indians. "Reason & Rhetoric will fall to the Ground unless supported by strouds and Duffles," Bethune offered. "Liberality is alone with Indians true Eloquence without which Demosthenes & Cicero, or the more modern orators Burk & Barre might harangue in vain."[13]

Spanish agents, eager to regain their influence in West Florida, used the volatile situation to their advantage. They sought to detach the Chickasaws from the British alliance through Arkansas intermediaries. Losing the Chickasaws meant losing a fierce people living on the crucial Mississippi River. It also boded poorly for retaining the more numerous Choctaws, who were now closely associated with the Chickasaws. Cameron tried to counter by repeatedly calling for a troop of mounted soldiers to personally escort him to the Choctaw Nation—a request that was just as repeatedly denied. That same month, the American general Benjamin Lincoln received encouraging reports that Spanish efforts were succeeding in neutralizing the Indian threat on the Mississippi. "On the whole," said one Andrew Williams, "I believe we have little to fear from that Quarter."[14]

Yet by late 1780, despite official disinterest from the ministry, British officers and agents were once more gaining ground in the contest for Indian allies in the South. They had prevailed upon a number of moderate Cherokees to aid the Chickamaugas in their assault on the Wataugan settlers.

(Sending a quantity of arms, ammunition, and clothing to the Cherokees no doubt helped carry the point.) The Upper Creeks—about five hundred of them—had agreed to help the Cherokees in this endeavor. Thomas Brown, a hard-fighting Georgia Tory, had managed to help Augusta, Georgia, become an "Indian town" once more by 1780–1781. "Augusta became the center of a vast frontier communications network," with Indian couriers bearing letters to and from Pensacola, Detroit, and Quebec. Even the Abenakis, a New England people who had been dwindling since the Seven Years' War, had a village among the Cherokees and agreed to scout and block the Mississippi River's passage for the Crown.[15]

By the spring of 1781, the war in the South had taken a strong turn in favor of the United States, especially in South Carolina. The victory at Kings Mountain by backwoods militia in October 1780 basically ended the active campaigning of Tory militia in the South. Daniel Morgan's stunning defeat of Banastre Tarleton at Cowpens in January 1781 had also significantly weakened Lord Cornwallis' army. Cornwallis's naked contempt for his Indian allies, and their potentially deleterious effects on the rebels, did not help. Tory leader Thomas Brown's proposed attack on the Wataugua settlements with Indian warriors, for example, might well have prevented the backwoodsmen from slaughtering the Tories at Kings Mountain. Yet Indian raids (both real and threatened) still took a serious toll on the American war effort. Col. Arthur Campbell of Washington County, Virginia, lamented to Governor Thomas Jefferson that more of his neighbors would join the Continental Army, "were it not for the daily apprehensions of attacks from the Northward and Southern Indians." It would be misleading, however, to state that these men were out of the fight. Many launched raids into the Cherokee lands, devastating towns and helping to bring about new peace talks with the nation.[16]

By late February 1781, General Nathanael Greene, the American commander in the Southern theater, commissioned eight frontiersmen/militia leaders to treat with the Cherokees and the Chickasaws. Among them were Arthur Campbell of Virginia and John Sevier of North Carolina. Though the American government would be glad to end the hostilities with those nations, the old problem of Anglo-American land hunger, and a tendency to minimize its negative impact on Indian–white relations, persisted. Robert Lanier of Surry County, North Carolina, wrote General Greene in April to update him about the negotiations.

"You may be assured that nothing are more sallaciaous [*sic*] than the report of the late rupture with the Cherokees was Occasioned by the incroachments on their Lands—It was a measure of the British Generals to facilitate their inhuman Projects of ruin and subjugation a number of Documents now in Possession of the Executive of Virginia can prove this to the world."

In his own bid to break pan-Indian designs, as well as to punish the Cherokees, the next month Lanier offered to call on tribes from the Illinois country to attack them. He also stated that, if allowed, he "could raise a force and make them [the Cherokees] cede lands."[17] Lanier's frank letter exemplifies perhaps the greatest source of frontier warfare from the mid-eighteenth century through the War of 1812 and beyond. For many white frontier folk, making war on Indians had at least as much to do with securing valuable land (or plunder) as it did with fear, personal revenge, or imperial designs.

In October 1781, a Franco-American army led by George Washington and the French General Comte de Rochambeau, aided by a French fleet, managed to trap and force the surrender of Lord Cornwallis's army at Yorktown, Virginia. The loss of 7,000 British fighting men, on top of the similar humiliation under General Burgoyne in 1777, proved too much for the average Briton—especially taxpayers. After learning of the defeat at Yorktown, British officials would begin seeking to extricate themselves from the American war with at least a scintilla of dignity. The great paradox is that while the British war effort east of the Appalachians fizzled out, the king's Indian allies were holding their own, perhaps even gaining the upper hand, in the Western country. Only days after Cornwallis' surrender, an oblivious General Haldimand could giddily write Lord Germaine concerning Mohawk war captain Joseph Brant's victory over George Rogers Clark. As the Virginian assembled a large force to punish the Ohio Indians' villages—and possibly even Detroit—Brant with only one hundred warriors managed to disrupt Clark's whole invasion, killing dozens and taking sixty-four prisoners. Such successes only gave heart to other British-allied war parties throughout the backcountry. "It would be endless and difficult to enumerate to your Lordship the Parties that are continually employed upon the Back Settlements," the general reported. These attacks struck terror into rebel frontier settlers, many of whom fled, he noted, and "from the Illinois Country to the Frontiers of New York, there is a continual succession." As Indian allies could re-establish themselves in their old haunts, Haldimand noted, they would prove less of a financial burden to the Crown as well.[18]

American frontiersmen had no intention of surrendering their lust for western lands, however. As Virginian Colonel John Floyd wrote to Colonel John May, they burned to go on the offensive against pan-Indian designs. Floyd offered that the best place to attack would be the area surrounding the Falls of the Ohio River (near modern Louisville, Kentucky). "Its situation is exactly centrical [sic] to the Northern, Southern, & Western Tribes. The distance to Holston, Clinch, New River, Green Brier, &c very trifling— Their supplies already here provided, & the communication to the British Posts in Canada very safe and easy." Floyd argued that the area "must be laid waste," lest the exposed American frontiers "once more experience the disadvantages of a Savage War." He feared that neglecting to do so would bring "ten times" the number of Indian war parties previously seen.[19]

Other Virginians also sensed Indian war parties—and broad tribal alliances—reforming, and hoped to check their power. Arthur Campbell nervously reported that while South Carolina militia had invaded the Chickamauga country, "but for want of the energy of Government," Virginia was not able to help them complete their invasion. "The Northward Indians has form'd an intercourse with the unfriendly Cherokees and continues their depredations," he lamented. While they had already "distress[ed]" some western counties in Virginia proper, he worried that in Kentucky "the scene is likely to be more bloody." Moreover, George Rogers Clark had opined to Campbell that "if measures are not taken early this spring to divert or crush their confederacys," at least 1,000 more warriors would join the enemy's force. Campbell offered a final note of bitterness, which became increasingly common for Western settlers over the next decade. "Pardon this intrusion!," he added sarcastically. "I am sensibly led into discussions with men living in security, which may let affecting scenes pass with indifference. I have a predilection for my native Country. It hurts me sorely to hear her Government despised, and her citizens destroyed by the Enemy."[20] Indian attacks, especially pan-Indian ones, could unite Anglo-Americans in their resistance. They could also, as would be repeatedly seen, widen political and geographical schisms when they inspired different sentiments.

In Georgia, British and Tory raids to free Patriots' slaves—at first primarily as a punitive measure toward the rebels—of course elicited alarm.

In the spring of 1782, Georgia governor John Martin complained that Tories (from Florida)—in what proved a preview of British strategy in the War of 1812—had "collected a large property belonging to this State, consisting of Horses, Cattle, & negroes." Martin suggested, however, that if the army could recover Georgians' walking property, it would considerably help the lackluster recruiting for the Continental Army there. Rebecca Read of Lancaster, Georgia, wrote the Army for assistance in apprehending a young Tory man–"I much fear this Lad is one of the East Florida Scouts"— who had "forced away" three of her slaves and trying to "entice" the others away. She despaired of actually catching the lad, who might well "make his escape to St. Augustine." American officers would write passes for citizens (which the British tended to ignore) allowing them to pass through the lines "for the purpose of Identifying negroes belonging to themselves & friends." As had so often been the case in earlier eras, foreign control of Florida was seen as a terrifying security risk to Southeastern slave owners. In March of 1783, nearly a year after it was known that the United States and Britain were trying to negotiate a peace, General Nathanael Greene issued orders for the protection of the state of Georgia. In particular, the troops were to note that "Incursions may be expected from the enemy principally from St. Augustine and for the purpose of Plundering provisions and negroes."[21]

The Southeast was especially ripe for a multiracial, anti-U.S. alliance. General Anthony Wayne, now fighting in Georgia (and seriously considering becoming a plantation owner there after the war), exclaimed "We have to contend with one of the most Heterogeneous Armies ever produced, composed of British, Hessians, new levies, out layers, tories, Crackers, Ethiopeans & Indian *allies* to the number of thirteen tribes!" Still, he did feel that proper diplomacy on his part had won over the latter, to the point where he might have even taken "an Alliance with the Charming Princess of the lower Creek Nations," had he so chosen.[22] In all likelihood, that was not the only instance of Wayne overestimating his powers of persuasion over the Creeks. A year later the Tallassee King and others complained that in complying with the American insistence that they return horses and slaves taken during the war, they made themselves footsore and poor.[23]

The British–Indian alliance in the South suffered setbacks, most notably the death of the principal Creek warrior, Emistisiguo—"our great Enemy," one American officer noted—killed in brutal close combat with some of

General Wayne's men. Wayne not only confirmed Emistisiguo's death, but noted that many of the more pro-American Creeks heralded the warrior's demise as a good sign for future peace between the United States and the Creek Nation.[24] Wayne would become, in the 1790s, the U.S. Army's most successful "Indian fighter" of the eighteenth century. In particular, he would be known for defeating a broad coalition of Indian peoples. Between 1782 and 1792, though, natives tended to have the upper hand on the battlefield, if not at the treaty council.

As the last full year of the Revolution wore on, frontier Americans grew increasingly troubled. While the armies in the East were largely quiet, Britain's Indian allies in the West and South seemed to gain enthusiasm for the war, while American interest flagged. The Indian alliance was far too great to defeat at once. It needed to be whittled down. If the Chickasaws and Creeks made peace with the United States, "it would Effectually put a stop to the Cherokees and Chickamogga Indians committing depredations on any of our frontears," noted one Virginian. It would also "Greatly Discurrage the Shawnees, and other Western Tribes." But if Indian raids continued, it would be extremely difficult for settlers to realize their dreams of peaceful (and vast) land ownership in Kentucky and Tennessee. Colonel Joseph Martin stated the obvious when he noted that as the path from Kentucky to Tennessee was subject to attacks from both Northern and Southern warriors, it would "make it a place of very disagreeable residence." For their part, Chickasaw headmen, including Piomingo, admitted that their young men had attacked Americans, but insisted they had been urged on by Cherokee, Creek, and Delaware militants, as well as American encroachment on their hunting grounds.[25]

Martin wrote in the aftermath of the August 1782 battle of Blue Licks, wherein Kentucky militia had been defeated in an embarrassingly one-sided ambush by a force of Ohio Valley and Great Lakes tribes and a few British rangers. Among the seventy-two Kentuckians killed was Daniel Boone's son, Israel. As the war in the East faded, keen observers saw the fight for the Western country growing, sometimes with remarkable prescience. Arthur Campbell wrote to a fellow militia officer that "they [the British] are uniting the Savage Tribes, and endeavoring to sow the seeds of deep laid animosity, which will lengthen the Indian war to a longer period than most imagine." Like most frontier leaders, Campbell felt that only "a decided blow" against the Indians in their homelands would provide the setting for an advantageous peace for the United States. He saw that frontier troops needed more training with "The Bayonet and Scymeter [scimitar, or sword]," and with maneuvering both infantry and horsemen in the woods. He added that capturing Canada would not hurt either.[26]

Into the late winter of 1783, American officers feared the apparently growing sense of Indian unity. Joseph Martin despairingly wrote to Virginia governor Benjamin Harrison of his recent visit to the Cherokee Nation. He warned of "Warriors sent from four different Tribes of Indians from the neighborhood of Detroit" who would soon meet with the Cherokees, Chickasaws, Choctaws, and Creeks, and then "proceed to San Augustine" (presumably for British arms and munitions, and perhaps advice). Over 1,000 Cherokees and Choctaws, it was said, had already joined this group. The Cherokee headman Old Tassel had informed Martin that these like-minded warriors would gather as many fighting men from the Southern tribes as possible for the campaign of 1783. While an assault on the Southern frontier would presumably be launched with these warriors from St. Augustine, "all ye other nations are this Spring, to Imbody in the neighborhood of Detroit & march from there with a party of British forces against Fort Pitt." After reducing Pitt, they would head for the Falls of the Ohio, and finally move on to Illinois to destroy the Kaskaskia Indians. On the same day, Continental Army General Nathanael Greene wrote of his own frustration that "some general plan is not adopted for settling a general peace with all the Southern Indians." Greene hoped that Congress would intervene for the public good, as he felt that the individual states could not be trusted with the matter.[27]

Despite the rather tepid support from Whitehall, the Crown's native allies were holding their ground, perhaps even gaining some, against Americans in the West. Yet as Richard White states: "And then in 1782, with more warriors engaged in the British cause than ever before and with those warriors inflicting costly defeats on the Americans, the British made peace." Or, as the Cherokee chief Raven of Chota put it, "The Peacemakers and our Enemies have talked away our land at a Rum drinking."[28]

CHAPTER 7

A New Nation with Old Fears

Excepting the sizable number of Loyalists, the majority of Americans practically shook with joy at the official recognition of their independence from Britain. They reveled in what they saw as the culmination of a great crusade against tyranny. Further, on its face the Treaty of Paris, concluded in 1783, seemed to prove just how spectacular a victory, and an empire, had been won. It was time to celebrate. In Philadelphia in late January 1784, the state of Pennsylvania put on an "exhibition" in honor of the American victory. The Philadelphia exhibition would prove an unwitting metaphor for the next decade of U.S. history. Having won a long, tumultuous revolution, the leading citizens of Pennsylvania wanted a proper, tidy, orderly celebration of the supposed end to chaos.

Central exhibits included fireworks, a Roman-style triumphal arch, fifty feet high, as well as a number of Charles Willson Peale's striking oil portraits of Revolutionary heroes, at the north end of Market Street. The arch also featured an image of Cincinnatus that reportedly was "a striking resemblance of General *Washington*." The Pennsylvania Assembly took pains to publish just how the unruly public would view these tributes to revolution. Very specific instructions laid out how those approaching the exhibit from the north or south, on foot or on horseback, were to proceed. By following these one-way instructions, spectators would then be free to "pass and return as often as they chuse [sic]."[1]

The Assembly had every reason to be particular for such an important event. They had appropriated up to £600 for the display. Because it was state money, they insisted that "no person or persons whatever will presume, in defiance of the authority of the Commonwealth, to require or to make any other demonstrations of joy upon the occasion, than those directed and authorized as aforesaid." The ink of Paris had barely dried, yet the Commonwealth was declaring a monopoly on patriotic celebration. Furthermore, lest the august celebrations be marred, the Assembly noted that "Any Boys or others, who disturb the Citizens by throwing Squibs or [fire] Crackers, or otherwise, will be immediately apprehended and sent to the Work House."[2]

To ensure that the exhibit was visible in the evening hours, the Assembly decided that "there should be no other illumination in the city," while "twelve hundred lamps" would bathe the arch and paintings. In tragicomic fashion, the exhibit came to a terrifying conclusion two days later. The paintings caught fire "by a rocket being put too near the paintings," and Peale's labors were consumed in ten minutes. One of the celebratory missiles hit "a sergeant Stewart" of the artillery in the head, killing him, and several others were wounded. Peale himself had been atop the arch when the rockets fired, and was hit with several which burned his head, hand, and clothes until he fell and suffered bruising that kept him in bed for several weeks.[3]

While perhaps anecdotal, the story of Philadelphia's fire serves as an important metaphor for the position of the United States in the 1780s and early 1790s, especially vis-à-vis Indian affairs—enthusiasm and hubris followed by shock and sorrow. As with their British predecessors, Americans would learn that it was far easier to claim North America (and its natives) than to rule it.

The terms of the Peace of Paris, known to most Americans at the time as "The Definitive Treaty of Peace," ceded British claims to all the lands east of the Mississippi River (not including New Orleans), north of Florida and south of Canada. Florida was (separately) ceded to Spain, though its specific northern boundary would remain disputed for years. Americans universally took it to mean that the formerly "British" land, excepting Canada and Florida, belonged to the United States. The tens of thousands of Indians who actually lived there—having been neither defeated nor included in the negotiations—thought differently. For the next ten years they (with aid from Britain and Spain) provided their own fireworks as a rebuttal. The resulting flames consumed the lives of settlers and soldiers on the frontier, as well as the reputations of some heroes of the Revolution, as surely as those celebratory flames had consumed Peale's heroic canvasses in Philadelphia.

Ministers in Whitehall and some members of Parliament were initially intoxicated with the relief of peace with America, and disposed to accommodate their former colonists.[4] This soon wore off, however, especially as the United States showed little interest in honoring their weak promises to compensate the Loyalists who had suffered so grievously in the war. As Timothy Willig notes, immediate British interests would have been far better served by holding onto the western lands and Great Lakes region, protecting Indian allies and British forts and trading posts. The Shelburne ministry soon "collapsed under a storm of protest."[5] Within months the British brought the full weight of the Navigation Acts to bear on their outclassed American competitors. Meanwhile, British Indian agents on the ground sought to repair the damage wrought to their alliances by years of neglect and an insulting peace treaty that had abandoned Indian lands to the Americans. Still, postwar poverty hamstrung both British and American officials' efforts in Indian affairs.

By the end of 1782 all major combat operations had ceased, at Britain's behest, as a new ministry sought to extract itself from the American war. Native leaders and warriors largely, if grudgingly, complied. General Haldimand in Quebec had the unenviable task of soothing his angry allies while simultaneously cutting costs. Public Indian councils should, he noted, "be conducted with the greatest Decorum and Formality," because it was "very pleasing to the Indians."[6] What would have pleased them most would have been more Redcoats and arms to safeguard their lands from the Americans.

Even in the latter stages of the war, Indian affairs had remained expensive. The January 1782 Estimate of Indian Presents for the service of the Western Indians in the Michilimackinac division of the Detroit District, prepared by Sir John Johnson, included "45 Gross Scalping Knives, and 500 Tomahawks, 800 Fuzils [muskets], 120 Rifles, small bore, 40 Pair[s of] Pistols, 10,000 lb. Gunpowder, 25,000 lbs. [of lead] Ball, 10,000 lb. shot," and "An Assortment of Files for Armourer and Blacksmith." Indian agent Alexander McKee estimated 12,000 plus Indian allies living in the Detroit area in the same year, and many of them would need and expect rations and blankets as well. McKee also made a separate notation for "140 Cherokees and Creeks [living] in the Shawanese Country since the Winter of 1782."[7] He therefore dealt with a broad, diverse group of Indians, bound primarily by their fear of the United States and their increasingly gloomy material prospects.

Military and Indian Department officials tried to keep a lid on the terms of the provisional treaty with the United States "in the vain hope that the final peace would bring better news." American officials, of course, as well as their Indian allies (who rationally if incorrectly assumed their lands would be untouched) gleefully spread the news that Britain would cede the lands east of the Mississippi and north of Florida to the United States. Moreover, the Indians were to cease viewing George III as their father, and instead look to the Americans.[8]

Understandably, this turn of events brought considerable anger and frustration to the King's old native allies, and from the summer of 1783, British policy toward the Indians shifted once more. Britain held on to its forts, even in some of the lands that would be ceded to the United States, touted the Fort Stanwix line of 1768—which was now being used to *protect* the Ohio Indians' land claims—and even endorsed a pan-Indian confederacy. Americans would interpret all of these moves in the coming years as an effort by Britain, especially in the case of the pan-Indian alliance, to reclaim the lands recently lost in the war. What they failed to realize was that the British were primarily trying to prevent a repeat of Pontiac's War, rather than aggressively counter the United States. The British felt that if they did not endorse pan-Indian efforts to defend their lands, they themselves would be attacked by the confederacy. In the first years after the war, the king's men acted not out of spleen, or ambition, but fear. Many British officers in America had personal memories of what Indian coalitions could do to soldiers on the frontier, while younger officers and enlisted men had doubtless heard the bloodcurdling stories. Other concerns faded into the background when frontier soldiers and agents considered the threat of pan-Indianism.[9]

In September 1783, Alexander McKee addressed a council of Hurons, Shawnees, Delawares, Mingoes, and once more, Cherokees and Creeks. He admonished them that he could not "harbour an Idea that the United States will act so unjustly or Impolitically as to endeavor to deprive you of any part of your Country under the pretence of having conquered it." The king still valued his native allies, McKee insisted, and they should accept their "losses with manly forgiving and forgetting what is past looking forward in full hopes and expectations that on the return of the blessings of Peace and cool and just reflection all animosity and enmity will cease." It is most doubtful that either McKee or Simon Girty, who acted as a translator at the council, truly believed those words, but for the time being they followed orders.[10]

Sir William's ghost continued to haunt the Crown's Indian policy in 1782 and 1783. Britain's vision of the Western Indians had not changed significantly since the Fort Stanwix cession of 1768. Governor-General Haldimand, without authorization, declined to evacuate the posts (including Detroit), now in U.S. territory. He hoped to avoid an Indian war against the Americans, while still hindering American settlement of the West.[11] The Secretary of State's office asserted that Indian affairs would be conducted as if there were two distinct groups—others, and the Iroquois Confederacy, who remained close allies to His Majesty thanks largely to "the indefatigable pains the late Sir William Johnson took with them since the last Peace." In reality, the Iroquois were anything but united, and those who had fought alongside His Majesty's troops were seeing common cause with the Ohio Indians. They vented their increasingly typical frustrations.[12]

In the first week of October 1783, the Six Nations held a council with a deputation of Shawnees and Delawares, as well as some Cherokees— perhaps those mentioned above—at Niagara. As reports of the Peace of Paris, especially the land cession, had become rather notorious in Indian Country by now, tensions ran high. Tagaia, a Cayuga chief, lamented, "you have repeatedly told us you wou'd remain with and share the same fate with ourselves, but on our serious consideration, we have reason to fear that we shall be left alone to defend our Women & Children, and a country that has so long supported them, against a people who seem determined to overrun it." He further complained that his warriors had only stopped fighting the Americans at Britain's request, strongly implying that the Crown had significantly hindered Indians' defense of themselves and their territory. With little tact and less honesty, Brigadier General MacLean and Colonel John Butler responded that Britain had ceded only the Fort Stanwix lands fixed by "your late Worthy Friend & Brother Sir William Johnson." They therefore denied that any land south of Kentucky had been given away, because the king had never claimed it—an assertion the Royal charters of the Carolinas and Georgia refuted. They somewhat desperately added that the Americans could not "with propriety ask [for] it."[13]

Maclean and Butler were toeing the government line for late 1783. In his own way, Joseph Brant did the same, though a close reading of his speech to American General Philip Schuyler in October 1783 hints at his mindset.

Brant assured Schuyler that the Six Nations, as well as "a deputation from our younger Brethren the Southern and Western Nations" had "unanimously agreed to live in Peace and Friendship with Congress." The sticking point, however, for the "Six Nations & [their] Confederates," was that Congress would leave their "possessions undisturbed." In an equally logical attempt at wishful thinking, Brant added that the Indians could not "think ourselves in the least blameable for . . . giving a helping hand to our good and antient allies."[14]

The vast majority of Americans, of course, held exactly the opposite opinion. The United States, they insisted, had conquered their British and Indian foes, and this "victory" over Britain's allies fully entitled Americans to the lands east of the Mississippi. It was a game for the highest of stakes. As François Furstenberg notes, "in many respects, the ultimate success of the settler rebellion—long-term national sovereignty—would hinge on the outcome of the indigenous one; one had to fail for the other to succeed."[15]

During the war, and for decades after, American propaganda conflated British soldiers and their Indian allies, branding both as "savages." Doing so had presented the dual benefits of painting America's enemies as less than truly human, and also justifying any potentially questionable acts Americans undertook to combat these foes. This subhuman vision of Indians "became a means for white Americans to identify themselves in opposition to what they deemed to be the savage, ferocious, uncivilized nature of the Natives. The image of the Indians was thus a vision of the Other that delineated in refraction the image of the new, national self." Americans could thus heap any negative imagery of North American life—and the acquisition of their growing empire—onto Indians, while keeping the wholesome and noble characteristics for themselves. Furthermore, as the stereotype of Indians became more uniform, it mattered little to Americans in the immediate postwar years just whom Indians had sided with during the war; their lands would now be taken.[16] This postwar enthusiasm, at once myopic and grandiose, would influence American negotiations with Indians in the Ohio Country for years. Even when the United States began to see the true situation more clearly, the clumsy steps toward empire in the early 1780s would continue to color the Ohio lands with blood.

Andrew Pickens, one of South Carolina's Revolutionary heroes, would note that one of the primary causes of friction with the Indians was that "many disorderly persons goes up amongst the Indians [in this case the

Cherokees] and Creates uneasiness amongst them." As British officials had before him, Pickens hoped the government would appoint a good superintendent who could regulate trade the Indian trade, which would "graitly [sic] add to the security and safety of the Fronteers of this State." The next month he reiterated the problem of white encroachment, now noting that it "much Dissatisfied" the Creeks, Chickasaws, and Cherokees, who were frequently joined by emissaries from the Choctaws and the "Norward Indians," offering "their assistance to Defend their just Rights." Pickens concluded that only by Congress' setting rigid boundaries and halting such unlawful incursions on Indian land, could they hope to "prevent Mischief."[17] Congress did appoint an agent, but had little power to do anything else, and the situation only worsened.

A rebellious frontier offshoot state, calling itself Franklin (comprising the twelve northeastern counties of modern Tennessee),[18] caused serious friction not only with North Carolina and the Congress, but with the Cherokees. North Carolina's governor noted the severity of the situation in a letter to Evan Shelby in Franklin, offering that Franklin and North Carolina needed to avoid a civil war, "as we have great reason to apprehend a general Indian war—in which case there is no doubt but they will meet with support from the subjects of Foreign powers—at least, they will be furnished with arms and ammunition, and if the Northern and Southern Tribes should unite with your neighbors (the Cherokees), you will stand in need."[19]

Joseph Martin, the U.S. agent to the Cherokee Indians, noted in September of 1785 that it had been his worst summer ever professionally. The Cherokees' blood boiled partly because of the "raised encroachment" of the Franklinites, but also because of martial talks from "the Spanish and Western Indians." Four Wyandot chiefs (from the upper Ohio Country) were acting as emissaries to the Chickamaugas, who needed little encouragement to resist invading settlers. Old Tassel, a venerable Cherokee leader from Chota, diplomatically asked the governors of North Carolina and Virginia for help as the rapidly encroaching Franklinites insisted they had purchased the land near the French Broad and Nolichucky Rivers (modern Knoxville). "We hope our Elder Brother will not agree to it," Old Tassel pleaded, though presumably both he and the state authorities realized that younger warriors would be almost impossible to restrain in such circumstances.[20]

Europeans and Euro-Americans (by design) had a tremendous impact on Native American diplomacy, particularly where gender was concerned. Though most native peoples had traditionally utilized, at the very least, vigorous input into decision-making from influential clan matrons, European and Anglo-American patriarchy waged its own campaign against women taking a role in the public sphere. This was especially true among the Cherokees, whose women had long held a great influence over going to war. The European-style rejection of war based on clan or blood vengeance in favor of military and diplomatic goals "denied most women a role in the escalating warfare with which the Cherokee political system was increasingly concerned. . . . As the significance of kin ties in military decisions waned, so too did the connection of women and war." Further, by engaging in large-scale military endeavors more frequently, calling for the nation, rather than one clan, to commit to war, it pushed Cherokee warriors and male peace chiefs into greater prominence, while leaving women behind. When the influential Cherokee *beloved woman* Nancy Ward (Nan-ye-hi) warned American soldiers and settlers of pending Chickamauga attacks in 1777 and 1780, she was no doubt trying to keep peace and avoid greater destruction for her people.[21] She might also have been trying to reassert Cherokee women's rights to endorse or condemn war.

Pan-Indianism remained the connecting thread to fears of a renewed (or really, an expanded) Indian war throughout the 1780s. These fears circulated not just in army posts and bureaucratic offices, but in letters from the frontier to family back east as well. And they frequently made it into the popular press for the public to absorb. Newspaper editors realized that talk of Indian wars could help boost their subscription lists, but most no doubt also published accounts of rumored impending attacks as a public service as well. A 1785 letter from an officer at Fort Harmar in the Ohio Country pronounced, presciently: "A war with the Indians will Inevitably commence next Spring." Adding considerably to the gloom in his prediction, he further stated that a "Grand Council" at the headwaters of the Miami River had featured a great "numerous number of the Chiefs from different Nations, the Western Indians determined for war, and were sending Belts to those nations not present to make it a common interest."[22]

The obvious collusion of warriors from both sides of the Ohio drew worried attention. Kentucky militia officer Samuel McDowell reported to Virginia's governor Patrick Henry, "We are not only troubled with the

Wabash Indians but the Chickamagies, a part of whom have lately settled over the Ohio on a Creek called Paint Creek." That Ohio Indians, like the Shawnees, had not only cooperated with the Chickamaugas, but even suffered them to live north of the Ohio, spelled potential disaster for Kentucky's settlements. Only aid and support from Canada could make the scenario more frightening. Joseph Saunders' "Report Respecting the Behaviour of the Western Indians," though written for a "Captain Finney," made its way into the newspapers as well. Saunders stated that the Cherokees (presumably, though not necessarily, Chickamaugas) were a constant presence in the Shawnee towns, so much so that he considered them "in the same light." "If the British give them the least encouragement," he concluded, "they will be at war with us." Reports from the Southern backcountry echoed the theme of a dangerous combination of Britons and Indians.[23]

In such a tense climate, newspaper editors also sought to quickly pass on any encouraging news from the frontier, sometimes without verifying its accuracy. Middletown Connecticut's *Middlesex Gazette* happily published a missive from Pittsburgh, reporting that Joseph Brant had died, and while on his way to meet with the Southern Indians no less. Brant's death would, the *Gazette* offered, "greatly damp that spirit for war which has lately prevailed throughout the Indian country." With a heavy heart, the next month newspapers had to correct the earlier report, affirming that Brant had not actually been killed in an engagement with George Rogers Clark on the Ohio. They did, however, soften the blow by asserting that the skirmish had prevented Brant from making "his intended visit with the Southern Indians."[24]

Plenty of Northern and Western Indians did complete their diplomatic sojourns to the South. Alexander McGillivray, the painfully shrewd and calculating métis Creek leader, wrote American officials to inform them that on the tenth of June 1787, "we had a general council of the Creek nation to receive a deputation from the Northern Indians." The deputation consisted of "the Head Warriors of the Mohawk, Iroquois, Hurons, Oneidas and Shawanese." As the Oneidas had largely either aided the Americans or remained neutral during the Revolution, their inclusion no doubt raised eyebrows. Further, McGillivray noted, a Mohawk chief called for a renewal of "the friendship and confederacy formed with you and other red people, our brothers, formed at the beginning of the last war." As McGillivray certainly hoped, the letter was widely reprinted in numerous papers throughout the country, and served as an unnecessary reminder (especially to the troublesome Georgians) that a major campaign against any Indian nation—such as the Creeks—might well result in a massive, general war. Indeed, later that year Virginian Arthur Campbell wrote to his delegate in New York, noting sorrowfully that "There is now a probability that the peace will be broken, from the injudicious and ill-concerted war begun against the Creek Indians, which I fear will spread to Holstein [Holston River], Kentucky, and Cumberland; and eventually make enemies of the three other Southern Tribes.—And all this mischief impending for want of proper men, to adopt proper measures in due time." It should be noted that Campbell was seeking a job as Superintendent of the Southern (Indian) Department. Still, he was not alone in his dire assumptions about Indian affairs.[25]

While the army and militia on the frontiers knew how serious the threat of Indian wars, especially the dreaded "general" Indian war, could be, the legislation being passed by the Congress in the mid-1780s seemed breezily unaware of the struggles ahead. The Ordinance of 1785, better known as the Land Ordinance, detailed how the land north of the Ohio River would be surveyed (on a rectangular grid in one-mile square sections) and sold (at public auction for a minimum of $1 per acre, with a 640-acre minimum). Even more confidently, the Ordinance of 1787—the Northwest Ordinance—described how the lands north of the Ohio River would be settled and eventually become co-equal states of the Union. Though Article III did mention the Indians living there, stating that they should be treated fairly and with benevolence, it also reserved the right for Congress to declare "just wars" against them if necessary.[26] On paper mechanisms for the dispossession of the Ohio Indians were now neatly in place, but the reality on the ground was far more chaotic and fluid.

The ratification of a new constitution from 1787–1789 laid the foundation for a powerful new federal order, which could raise taxes and therefore great armies to enforce the government's will. Still, wielding that power would remain a tricky proposition for some time. The majority of Americans opposed taxation and a standing army. Henry Knox, continuing as Secretary of War,[27] now answered directly to his old commander, George Washington. Both Washington and Knox felt the weight of the new government's poverty. Both also felt the burden of something more—the conflict between the high morality espoused by the new nation, and the realism its weakness imposed.

As with their British predecessors, American officials continued to struggle with the brutal violence of the frontier, and in particular Americans' knack for murdering the voices of peace and moderation among the Indians. While the Chickamauga Cherokees rightly hold their reputation for militant resistance to white encroachment, especially in the 1780s, Cherokees from "peace" towns were spurred to lash out. The 1788 murder of some Overhill Cherokee headmen, in particular Old Tassel, who had only recently warned Americans about Chickamauga raids and calls for them to be "cut off," seemed especially egregious. Allegedly in retaliation for the murder of the family of John Kirk, Jr., Old Tassel's murder led to a wave of raids by up to 1,200 Cherokee warriors. As Tyler Boulware notes, "Fighting in the winter of 1788–1789, in fact, proved to be the bloodiest and most unified engagements for the Cherokees of the entire war."[28] The Chickamaugas were more than an ample threat to frontier security, and when joined by other Cherokee towns, they only amplified the possibility of a true multitribal coalition in the West.

Knox certainly knew that a massive pan-Indian alliance was a possibility, as he had been receiving reports of its attempt since at least 1789. Colonel Arthur Campbell, of the Washington County (Virginia) militia, noted intelligence indicating that Alexander McGillivray had "sent a deputation of Creek Headmen to the Wabash to encourage their hostilities against our Western settlements." Campbell further worried the ammunition the United States was providing to the Chickasaws would be intercepted by hostile Indians, or that the Chickasaws themselves might suddenly break their alliance, and use the powder and ball against the Americans. Knox took Campbell and his pan-Indian warnings seriously. He found one such Campbell letter so direly important that he personally handed it to Washington, who noted it in his diary.[29]

In mid-June 1789, Knox wrote a report on Indian affairs for the president. Typical of his correspondence, Knox's report was cogent, detailed, and strikingly logical. He began by noting a number of murders in the Ohio Valley, both north and south of the river. He pointedly added, "The injuries & murders have been so reciprocal, that it would be a point of critical investigation to know on which side they have been the greatest." Knox knew full well that frontier settlers missed few opportunities to make trouble, and Revolutionary propaganda aside, Indians were not always to blame. To drive the point home, Knox acknowledged that "Indian-hating"

Kentuckians had killed a number of "peaceable Piankeshaws who prided themselves in their attachment to the United States."[30]

Knox discussed the cause as well as the symptoms of these frontier ills. The United States had yet to form any treaties with the western Indians, especially those on the Wabash River, and those tribes and the Kentuckians had warred continually since the Revolution. Suffering that situation to continue, he feared, would allow the fighting to spread even to tribes with whom the United States had already officially made peace. "It is well known how strong the passion for War exists in the mind of a young Savage & how easily it may be inflamed so as to disregard every precept of the older & wiser part of the tribes who may have a more just opinion of the force of a treaty." (Perhaps he considered adding a line about their lawless white counterparts but thought better of it.) Without "some decisive measures" to end the fighting, the war would "become general among all the Indians northwest of the Ohio."[31]

The United States had essentially two choices to deal with the problem, Knox offered. It might raise a great army for "extirpating the refractory tribes entirely," or it could seek peace treaties that would specifically delineate the tribes' rights and territorial boundaries. The treaties would need to be enforced "with the most rigid justice," and the United States would have to "punish . . . the whites who should violate the same." Knox quickly and emphatically rejected the first option: even as ardent and proud a Patriot veteran as Knox openly questioned whether the United States had "a clear right, consistently with the principles of justice & the laws of nature" to simply destroy or drive off the Wabash Indians. It would not be possible for "a nation Solicitous of establishing its character on the broad basis of justice." Further, "the bloody injustice which would stain the character of the Nation, would be beyond all pecuniary calculation." Exemplifying a classic eighteenth-century grasp of two seemingly unrelated thoughts, he also cautioned that in any case the army necessary to do so would not be "easily attainable."[32]

While Knox still allowed (as had the Ordinance of 1787) a loophole for a conquest "in case of a just War," it was nevertheless impracticable to drive the Wabash Indians out. "The finances of the United States would not at present admit of the operation." Here Knox came to the crux of the issue: to defeat the 1,500 to 2,000 warriors thought to live on the Wabash, he estimated (perhaps optimistically) that it would require 2,500 regular troops, which would mean raising almost two thousand more men than he currently had on the frontier. In all, a six-month campaign would cost $200,000—"a sum far exceeding the ability of the United States to advance consistently with a due regard to other indispensable objects." Knox's projected campaign costs assumed a fight only against the Wabash tribes—he estimated there were another 3,000 more warriors in the Great Lakes or Upper Ohio Country, and they would not likely remain neutral. Knox expanded on the idea of such a campaign being manifestly unjust, and then once again came back to the conclusion that it was also financially unfeasible.[33]

The Wabash peoples could be pacified, asserted Arthur St. Clair, a former Continental Army officer who was the appointed governor of the newly created Territory Northwest of the River Ohio. In St. Clair's estimation, about $16,000 in treaties and gifts would do the trick, and Knox concluded that it would be "highly expedient" to adopt such a "liberal system of justice" with Indians. In time, such a "Conciliatory system," Knox felt, could attach all the Indians living east of the Mississippi to the United States for about $15,000 a year—a condition he foresaw as lasting for fifty years. The secretary, in effect, continued what Article III of the Ordinance of 1787 had begun; arguing that Indians did in fact have the rights to lands they occupied, yet feeling that they could eventually be removed or absorbed peacefully if Americans were patient.

Still, Knox opted not to connect all the dots for the president. Having estimated that a campaign against the 2,000 warriors in the Wabash region would cost $200,000, he then stated that there must be nearly 14,000 warriors living south of the Ohio and east of the Mississippi. Obviously if a campaign were needed to reduce those warriors, it would be astronomically more expensive. The elephant sitting quietly but ominously in the room remained: even assuming it were possible, what would it cost to fight a pan-Indian force of warriors from the Great Lakes to the southeast, with an estimated manpower of almost 20,000? What would happen to the nascent nation if Britain or Spain (or both) chose to actively support those warriors? Indeed, even without a true pan-Indian conflict, in waging war north of the Ohio from 1790–1796 Congress would spend "$5 million, almost five-sixths of all federal expenditures for that period."[34]

The Chickamauga Cherokees, led by Dragging Canoe, had been seeking arms from both powers, and allies from all points, for years. Their emissaries had asked for arms from the British at Detroit in the spring of

1783, and the Spanish at Pensacola that summer. They initially found the Spaniards more accommodating. Hoping to secure native allies against a possible American incursion into Florida, Governor Esteban Miró gave Dragging Canoe's men a great cache of arms in 1784. The Chickamaugas enthusiastically used them (as well as encouragement from the Shawnees to form alliances) to raid the frontiers. The Americans failed (or refused) to recognize, however, that for the next several years Miró declined to further aid the Chickamaugas, "since he had come to the conclusion that the Chickamauga villages lay outside the jurisdiction of either Spanish Florida or Louisiana." Their continuing war against the Americans, and the pursuit of broad tribal alliances—Dragging Canoe's parties included Shawnees and Upper Creeks as well as his own dissident Cherokees—was a native, not European, idea.[35]

CHAPTER 8

The Talented Mr. McGillivray

By 1790, as the ugliness deepened across the Ohio Valley, the Chickamaugas raided the Tennessee settlements, and the Creeks continued to battle Georgia's expansionists. The Washington administration saw making peace with at least some of the Southern nations as imperative to avoiding a disastrously general Indian war. The Creeks, with their wily but pragmatic *beloved man* McGillivray, seemed a logical, even crucial, choice for negotiations. Knox estimated that the Creek Nation, composed of the Upper Creeks in sixty towns along the Alabama River, and forty towns of Lower Creeks along the Apalachicola River, combined, could field about six thousand "gun-men." Even as the war accelerated north of the Ohio, taking the Creeks out of the pan-Indian equation would be a priority. That priority had its own difficulties. While each town had its respective chief, he noted that "the Creeks appear, at present, to[o] much under the influence and direction of Alexander McGillivray."[1]

Knox inferred that McGillivray, the son of a "principle woman of the Upper Creeks" and a Georgia Loyalist whose entire estate had been confiscated by Patriots, held "resentments . . . probably unbounded against the State of Georgia." "He had an English education [and] his abilities and ambition appear to be great," Knox continued. Showing just how good American spies could be, he added that McGillivray was "said to be a partner of a trading house which has the monopoly of the trade of the Creeks." Indeed, Panton & Leslie, the Scottish firm with Spanish imprimatur, kept him on as a silent partner, to considerable mutual benefit.[2]

With remarkable restraint, Knox then described a series of treaties Georgia had concluded with Creeks, noting that one in particular featured representatives from only two of the one hundred Creek towns. Tacitly admitting that Georgia had behaved badly, Knox saw an opportunity for the federal government to intervene for the greater good, in this case defined as keeping both costs and a general Indian war down. Specifically, he asked, "Whether, in the present state of public affairs, any proper expedients, could be devised for effectually quieting the existing hostilities between the State of Georgia and the Creek nation, other than by raising an army?"[3]

After the failure of the Rock Landing conference in the fall of 1789, Knox and company wisely decided that holding a conference with the Creeks anywhere near Georgia (or Georgians) would be disastrous. Anthony Wayne, the transplanted Pennsylvania general-turned-Georgia planter, insisted, "we never shall have a permanent peace with the Creek Nation until they experience our Superiority." Further, he would "with avidity" take the opportunity to take a strong army "to produce a Glorious speedy & happy Issue . . . with those Savages & after defeating them in the field," conducting a treaty that would be honorable for the country and "Satisfactory" to the Creeks. He further added that being made the commander of the Southern District and Superintendent of Indian Affairs would help him in this task.[4] Though part of Wayne's suggestions would be successfully adopted to the north, with the Southern Indians the Washington administration preferred a more diplomatic approach. When asked his opinion, Senator Benjamin Hawkins of North Carolina, probably the foremost expert on the Southern Indians in government, suggested having a private conference with the Creeks in New York.[5] By inviting McGillivray and the Creeks to New York City, the administration could not only control the setting and tone of the conference, but hopefully awe the Creeks with the majesty (such as it was) of the nation's capital. The ensuing treaty illuminates some realities of the Federal government and Indian policy in the early years.

Washington did not leap blindly into his meeting with the Creeks. Upon Knox's suggestion, he had sent three companies of soldiers from the Ohio, where they were sorely needed, "to the Oconee River, where they would prepare for an offensive." Knox also began seriously considering recruiting native allies, especially the Chickasaws. Piomingo's warriors had practically begged for some type of military alliance with the United States since the early 1780s, and the resumption of the Creek war against the fierce but heavily outnumbered Chickasaws in 1789 only deepened that need.[6]

Still, the Treaty of New York, finalized in August 1790, was largely about Alexander McGillivray and his vision for Creek geo-politics. He spent considerable time as the guest of Henry Knox, and was almost always escorted by American officers in an attempt to keep foreign agents from being able to negotiate with him. Spanish and British officers did manage to steal some time with McGillivray, but rather than secure concessions for their kings, it seemed that their courtship only made the Americans more generous with the Creeks.[7] Additionally, the beloved man no doubt hoped that his work in negotiating this treaty would further elevate him above his main rival for Creek leadership, the Loyalist adventurer William Augustus Bowles (discussed in chapter 11).

McGillivray and the Creeks did agree to cede lands that the Georgians already occupied—for an annuity, of course—but maintained sovereignty over any lands that were not already part of the United States. In effect, this put considerable weight upon the disputed boundary between Spain and the United States—the greater the Spanish possessions, the better for the Creeks. Georgia, however, felt itself a loser, as it wanted the lands at least as far west as the Altamaha River, which the Creeks maintained as hunting grounds. American efforts to break Panton & Leslie's monopoly on the Creek trade failed, with the provision that in case of emergency— if a war with Britain prevented Spain's bringing goods across the Atlantic— Americans could pick up the slack. That provision in particular—made a secret clause of the treaty—must have been particularly satisfactory for the firm's silent partner. Also kept secret was McGillivray's commission as a brigadier general in the U.S. Army. One might ask what benefit derives from being a "secret general"—who would know to follow your orders? The answer is that the commission carried a $1,200 yearly salary.[8]

Consciously or not—and he certainly would have hated the comparison— Washington was in a sense borrowing from Lord Dunmore's playbook. That is, he flattered and bargained with a larger, powerful Southern nation, while treating smaller Ohio Valley nations with contempt. Recall that when Lord Dunmore sought to acquire Kentucky, he chose to fight the less numerous Shawnees while appeasing the more formidable Cherokee Nation. While McGillivray and the Creeks did part with some of their valuable lands, they would receive financial compensation, and the Beloved Man himself received some lovely gifts. A year previously, American commissioners had met with representatives of the Wyandots and six other Ohio Valley/Great

Lakes tribes at Fort Harmar to reconfirm the land cessions of the Fort McIntosh treaty (1785), including that the tribes would receive no compensation for their lands. (Arguably, the Fort Harmar treaty violated both the spirit and letter of the Ordinance of 1787, which espoused a belief in fair treatment for Indians.)

Though Washington was probably playing a very shrewd game in avoiding pan-Indian war through his treatment of McGillivray, the Georgians were predictably furious with the public version of the treaty, and probably would have had a collective stroke had they learned of the secret provisions. Representative James Jackson thundered in the Congress that the Federal government had "given away [Georgia's] land, invited a savage of the Creek nation to the seat of Government, caressed him in a most extraordinary manner, and sent him home loaded with favors." Four U.S. senators voted against the treaty, including James Gunn of Georgia and Pierce Butler of South Carolina. Butler lauded Senator Gunn's protesting of the treaty, and himself remained convinced that it was deeply flawed. He particularly chafed at what he felt was the weakness of the provision to recover slaves captured (or sheltered by) the Creeks.[9]

Georgians and South Carolinians were of course reflexively touchy on the issues of slavery and Indians. Georgia had been founded largely to protect South Carolina from Indian raids, staged from Spanish Florida, that targeted plantations. South Carolina had blamed the 1739 Stono slave revolt, and almost every subsequent whisper of one, on Spanish offers of freedom to runaways. (Georgians, it should be noted, also raided into Florida to steal slaves.)[10] The fear of Indian–slave collusion encouraged from St. Augustine would continue for nearly a century. When Anthony Wayne ran for a U.S. Senate seat from Georgia in 1788, he would remind Georgians of his defending them against "a Cruel and Savage Enemy" during the Revolution, and that during "this Crisis, when Actually engaged in an Indian War who are aided by the tories of Providence Florida &c & Countenanced by the Spaniards," he would offer his services.[11]

A month after the Treaty of New York's conclusion, Butler was still unhappy, but given the military threat the Creeks posed to the frontier, he concluded, "I would have consented rather than have no Treaty." The Georgia legislature had little choice in the matter, though they bitterly noted that the Creeks refused to return slaves or other property they had taken from the citizenry, and even stole the horses or fired on those who bore passports from the governor to enter Creek country. Though many Southerners were furious with the terms, as Celia Barnes notes, "Federal treaties in reality represented only the *intentions* of Congress, as they could not be implemented."[12]

Unbeknownst to Butler and Gunn, Spain was equally upset, fearing that McGillivray had sworn allegiance to the United States—which he had—and that he had granted the Americans both a commercial treaty and sovereignty over the Creek Nation—which he had not. After recovering from their initial shock over McGillivray's signing of the Treaty of New York, Spanish authorities engaged in a sort of double game with the Beloved Man. They raised his Spanish salary from $600 to $2,000 per year, while instigating a "whispering campaign" against both McGillivray and the treaty itself.

The chill in the Spanish–Creek relationship remained until July 1792, when the new Louisiana governor, the Baron de Carondelet, negotiated a new treaty with McGillivray in New Orleans. The treaty promised that Spain would recognize, and guarantee, the same boundaries of the Creek Nation that Britain had. Further, the governor promised "sufficient supplys of Arms & Ammunition" to the Creeks to defend that territory—far larger than recognized in the Treaty of New York—against American interlopers. (Reports from Knoxville confirmed that West Florida governor Arturo O'Neill had issued "arms and ammunition in abundance" to the Cherokees and Creeks, "stimulating them to go to war against the frontier inhabitants of the United States. Even worse, O'Neill had stated that "now or never was the time while the United States were engaged with the northern tribes.") McGillivray's biographer concludes that these terms, which he had sought since the 1780s, might have had a major influence in containing American territorial expansion in 1787. By 1792–1793, however, the strengthened American government under the Constitution, the enlarged settler populations in Kentucky and Tennessee, and perhaps even Spain's being pulled into war with Revolutionary France, had all served to change the geo-political and demographic dynamics of the American Southeast.[13]

Regardless of his efforts to improve relations with McGillivray, Carondelet felt that the Treaty of New York had stripped away an important barrier between the Spanish possessions and "the ambitious projects of the Americans." Americans were trying to muscle their way into the Muscle Shoals area, and until Spain could completely prevent it, Carondelet argued that it would be "convenient . . . to persuade those [Indian] nations, that their existence depends absolutely on a defensive Confederation." He directed Governor O'Neill in Pensacola to call Indian chiefs, especially the Creeks, for a great conference, and to impress upon them the stubborn American desire to separate Indians from Spanish aid and then to destroy them. He was further to remind them that only Spain would oppose American expansion onto Creek lands. Erroneously estimating U.S. troop strength in the Ohio Valley to be about 16,000—a comically high number—Carondelet added that O'Neill should avoid giving the United States "any just complaint" against Spain, but that as long as the United States tried to usurp the territory of Spain's allies, the king intended to aid those allies.[14] In so doing, Carondelet set up the sort of impossible diplomatic task that Britain's Indian agents had been struggling with since 1783—how to firm up a defensive military alliance without seeming provocative.

In the end, the Treaty of New York demonstrated just how desperate the federal government was to remove the Creeks from a possible pan-Indian alliance. It showed that for the moment, the Washington administration was far more concerned with keeping the Creek Nation, rather than Georgia, content. Pointedly, when Georgians continued to protest the treaty and call for a military campaign to destroy the Creeks, the Secretary of War restated (with some annoyance) how economically disastrous such a war would be for the United States, and reminded Georgians that the Treaty of New York—in his estimation—had largely been for the benefit of Georgia. They had to stop antagonizing the Creeks with land grabs and murders. Otherwise Georgia might well find her Spanish neighbor gaining "an ascendancy over the Southern tribes," and then letting them "loose with all the horrors of their warfare" upon the state,[15] which could have been construed (though was certainly not intended) as a warning to behave or fight a confederation of Indians alone.

Knox and the War Department proved quite willing to use nonmilitary means, like bribing a Creek headman, when it seemed the more cost-effective method for conflict resolution.[16] (They dealt with the Barbary Pirates in a similar fashion.) Using payoffs as a means of pragmatic diplomacy placed them far closer to standard European practices than many would likely have wanted to admit.

Not surprisingly, the 1780s witnessed a series of attempts by Indians, Americans, Britons and Spaniards to form broad coalitions. In the uncertainty following the end of the Revolutionary War in 1783, the numerous nations jockeyed for position in North America, and frequently misread each other's intentions in doing so. British officials sought a graceful exit from affairs south of the Great Lakes, but their interest in the fur trade, and more importantly their fear of a horrific sequel to Pontiac's War directed at their outposts, led them to grant numerous concessions to their Indian allies and neighbors. U.S. officials, as would be their wont, consistently misinterpreted the efforts of British agents as instigating, rather than reacting to, pan-Indian impulses against American expansion. Spain's Indian policy in the 1780s proved fitful, at times encouraging Indians across tribal boundaries to resist American expansionism in their quarter, and then seeming to withdraw that support arbitrarily. Americans in the West, especially in Kentucky and Tennessee, seemed willing at times to flirt with both British and Spanish officials in the 1780s and 1790s, in an effort to make the Congress (and later the federal government) more conscientious of their needs. George Washington certainly "took the threat very seriously," even mentioning the necessity of avoiding Western secession in his Farewell Address.[17]

The most consistent players were Indians themselves, as the call for pan-Indian resistance to the American invasion of their territory came repeatedly from many places, though especially from the Ohio Valley, and most particularly the Shawnees. Southern nations, like the Cherokees, never "openly threatened a Spanish alliance or a united Indian war, but they surely found it useful to raise the possibility in the Americans' minds."[18] Still, native opinion never really approached the unanimity that outsiders would assert it did.[19]

As the summer of 1790 drew to a close, both Knox and Washington could feel some much needed relief and satisfaction in the realm of Indian affairs. The treaty with the Creeks had, they assumed, taken the most dangerous of all the Southern Nations out of a possible pan-Indian confederation. An almost giddy Washington wrote his old comrade the Marquis de Lafayette, noting, "This event will leave us in peace from one end of our borders to the other." The president did allow that there might be brief interruptions to this peace, but only from "a small refugee banditti of Cherokees [probably the Ohio Cherokees who had settled on the Scioto] and Shawanese, who can be easily chastised or even extirpated if it shall become necessary." With that last line Washington surprised himself, and he quickly added that *extirpation* would only be carried out "In an inevitable [he meant *unavoidable*] extremity." He further intoned to his old comrade—who had been noted for his sincere friendship with Indian allies—that as long as he had any connection with the federal government, "the *basis* of our proceedings with the Indian Nations has been, and shall be *justice*."[20]

Having (they thought) purchased a measure of peace on the Southern frontier, Knox and Washington hoped that General Josiah Harmar's punitive expedition into the Miami heartland would do the same in the Northwest. Yet by the late fall of 1790, when accurate reports of Harmar's campaign began to filter back, their optimism dimmed. They could not realize that it was only the beginning of the most gut-wrenching and horrifying fourteen months of their war for the American West.

CHAPTER 9

Ohio Confederates Triumphant

Between October 1790 and November 1791, the United States waged two major offensives against the Indian confederacy north of the Ohio River. The first, led by General Josiah Harmar, resulted in 183 Americans killed and Harmar's eventual acquittal in a court martial. *It was by far the more successful of the two campaigns.* General Arthur St. Clair's army was nearly annihilated at the headwaters of the Wabash River (modern Fort Recovery, Ohio) on November 4, 1791, with 630 American soldiers and militia killed. The Indian confederation had been led by the principal Shawnee war chief, Blue Jacket, and the Miami Little Turtle, who had embarrassed Harmar the year before.[1] Though none could know so at the time, it would prove the worst disaster the United States ever faced at the hands of Indians, easily dwarfing the loss of George Custer's detachment at Little Big Horn eighty-five years later. This crushing defeat loosed a wave of panic upon the citizenry and the government. St. Clair became the target of the first-ever Congressional investigation in U.S. history.

As was customary in Europe, the commanding officer's incompetence was attributed to poor performance by his men, and St. Clair was officially cleared of wrongdoing. Washington's cabinet, excepting only the president himself, argued for a cessation of hostilities, even the bribing of the confederation with both cash and the retrocession of some parcels of land ceded in 1789. Americans generally, except for those already living in the West, showed little interest in renewing the war, and recruiting for the U.S. Army became, if it were possible, even more difficult.[2]

Newspapers reported on the possibility of a pan-Indian alliance even before the American disasters in the West made it more likely. The *Vermont Gazette* published a letter from a "General Chapen" [Israel Chapin] in

Western New York to his son, noting that the Southern Indians had demanded the Iroquois join them, though with relief added that the Six Nations had refused. The *Pennsylvania Mercury* (Philadelphia) offered a letter from a gentleman in Mercer, Kentucky, stating, "Although we are in a fair way to scourge our Northern neighbors, yet we are greatly harassed by the Southern Indians."[3]

By December 1791, major American newspapers were reporting the carnage on the Wabash. While there were some tiny rays of light—editors were quick to report the courage shown by the contingent of Chickasaw warriors who had aided the Americans, and that Mountain Leader (Piomingo) was not among the slain, the public and private accounts were overwhelmingly gruesome and chilling. Famed Philadelphia physician Dr. Benjamin Rush committed the observations of a fellow doctor to his commonplace book. Dr. Charles Brown, who had been with St. Clair's army and survived, boldly revisited the site a few weeks later. He noted that the corpses at the immediate battle site had their eyes and genitals (and one woman, her breasts) chewed away. Yet the remains on the path of retreat were largely skeletal, and broken at that. "He supposed that the Buzzards had chased the wolves from the *field*, & that the wolves had eaten those bodies only which fell in the retreat."[4]

Five weeks after the battle, George Hammond, the British minister in Philadelphia, had heard unofficial reports of "the total defeat of the army under General St. Clair, by the Indians . . . at the distance of about ten miles from the place where Brigadier Harmar was defeated last year." A month later Hammond noted a rumor circulating that the Senecas, previously "well-affected to the United States," were preparing to join the war against it. That the Senecas could make such a dramatic policy swing after St. Clair's debacle, he reported, doubtless implied "a sort of concert and correspondence subsisting among the different Indian nations, and . . . furnishes a reasonable ground of concluding that a general confederacy and junction of a majority of the tribes, bordering on the frontiers of the United States, is ultimately an event not wholly improbable." Indeed, Philadelphians were so terrified of the Senecas joining the confederacy against them, a New Hampshire paper reported, that when forty-seven Senecas visited Philadelphia to offer their services against the Southern tribes, the locals greeted them with abandon. "The bells were kept ringing. This is the first time we have heard of joy bells being rung at the approach of savages."[5]

The question of whether or not to continue the Indian war, and if so, how to conduct it, divided the country. Antifederalists, like Senator Pierce Butler from South Carolina, felt that Indians were the lesser of two evils. "The standing Army will be the result I fear," he noted to a friend in Charleston. "My negative shall stand on record against it." Months later, Butler was convinced that peace with Indians both north and south of the Ohio was at hand, and that his Federalist colleagues had simply exaggerated the Indian threat. "The Indian War has been made a handle of to encrease [sic] the military establishments—A pretext for borrowing of the New Bank—And, with the specious appearance of the laying the General Government under obligations to the Stockholders, made the means of increasing their profits."[6] In reality, the Indian War threatened to engulf the entire West, bring direct British and/or Spanish intervention, and cripple the republic in its infancy.

Students of the Early Republic have long noted the dramatic effect that American military reverses in the Ohio Country had on U.S. policy in the early 1790s. Less well known is the wave of euphoria, even ecstasy, that shot through not only the Indian confederation, but Britons interested in North America. For them, "Harmar's Defeat" and "St. Clair's Defeat" offered an unprecedented opportunity to safeguard Indian homelands and British Canada. For the exceedingly ambitious, they might even offer a chance to reverse the American Revolution itself.

As news spread of the Amerindian victory over Harmar, British officials from the West Indies to Whitehall saw a great opportunity to exploit. The governor of Bermuda, for example, felt compelled to offer his thoughts on the subject to Lord Melville (Henry Dundas, an MP soon to become Home Secretary). If it seemed unusual that the governor of a small Atlantic island would bother to weigh in on events in the Great Lakes region, in this case it made perfect sense. The governor was none other than Henry Hamilton, the former British commander of Detroit. No doubt recalling his humiliating defeat and captivity at the hands of George Rogers Clark during the American Revolution, Hamilton retained a keen interest in Indian affairs in the Ohio Country. He noted that while U.S. policies had given Indians "an implacable hatred" for the Americans—which he of course shared—conversely British aid had "given the Indians considerable confidence in the good faith of the English Nation."[7]

When Hamilton learned of the Confederacy's victory over St. Clair, he could not restrain himself from treading upon the chain of command. "I hope you will pardon my stepping aside from the direct road of correspondence," he wrote Lord Melville, "and troubling you with my ideas on the Subject—it appears to me to be of infinite consequence to the American States." In a postscript he wrote a quick line about the possible "connexion [sic] with the business of a commercial treaty with America" having spurred him to write the letter, before adding, "I have heard that the Indians have sent Belts to all their confederacy from the Six Nations to the Cherokees."[8]

Hamilton's missive to Melville was accompanied by an extract of his letter to George Hammond, the British minister to the United States, which contained the kind of wild-eyed optimism for intrigue that diplomats typically prefer not be recorded. In the wake of the "entire defeat of General Sinclair's [sic] force," the "extended frontier" of the United States had now become a liability, Hamilton insisted. "After the heavy loss of officers and men, the difficulties attending the raising of new levies will be (I should think) next to insurmountable." Not only had American fighting morale been crippled, he noted, but "Taxes will now be felt with all the disadvantages of inexperience, and whatever measures are adopted will no doubt be censured with all the bitterness of invective." (Tariffs were in fact raised in 1792 to fund the army, though they did not prove as disastrous as Hamilton predicted.) Hamilton felt that the United States would be so weakened by the Amerindian victory that they would be forced to accept British mediation to secure peace. Britain could then secure a great Indian buffer state in the Ohio country, stalling American expansionism and safeguarding the Great Lakes region fur trade for Britain simultaneously.[9]

"My idea on the subject will probably meet with few abettors," Hamilton offered, but he was "most intimately persuaded it is the only one applicable in the present emergency." He proposed that "to make a serious compact" between the United States and the Indians, British mediators would sanction "taking the British Governors on the Continent as Guaranties, to give the Savages respectable hostages for the performance." The governor of Bermuda was suggesting that to solidify a peaceful boundary between the United States and the Indians—which would provide a great "Indian territory" in the Ohio country, British governors "on the Continent" (presumably excluding himself)—would be given to the Indians as hostages. [!] Further, Loyalists who had already been granted Indian lands would have them restored, and agents from the United States and Britain would be posted in Indian country to insure that the articles of the peace were not broken. At a future date, "When peace and Mutual confidence shall be restored," Indian land sales could resume, though a "Complete register of all Indian deeds" would be kept in a joint Anglo-American office where they might be inspected by "all persons interested in contracts of Whites with Savages." Hamilton had to know that these proposals would be unpalatable to the United States. Yet he insisted that his experience told him that this elaborate "Scheme" was the only way to preserve the fur trade and prevent "a bloody contest" for the Americans and would "sap their Treasury and Cost the dearest lives of the community."[10]

British officials in Canada and London echoed Hamilton's enthusiasm, if not his proposals. John Graves Simcoe, lieutenant governor of Canada, offered, "The recent defeat of Mr. St. Clair may be productive of beneficial consequences to the Government of Upper Canada [Ontario]." Lord Melville, now the Home Secretary, agreed, further spelling out that "the great object to be attended to is to secure such a Barrier against the American[s] . . . by the intervention of the Indians" in the event of war with the United States. Blue Jacket's victory over St. Clair had, it seemed, opened up a world of opportunities for British trade and Canadian defense. Minister Hammond would now be directed to negotiate with those directives in mind.[11]

Despite what Americans of the early republic reflexively thought, however, British support for the Indian confederacy's war against the United States was neither chronic nor universal. Neither Haldimand nor his successor Lord Dorchester (Sir Guy Carleton's new title) wanted to "increase the British presence among the tribes" within American territory prior to November 1791. Dorchester had expressly forbidden Indian agents from acting in the Indian trade, for example, though agents like the Girtys routinely ignored the order.[12] In the months leading up to the battle on the Wabash, leaders in Whitehall—and the king himself—hoped for a speedy termination of the frontier war. While officials in Canada, especially Lt. Governor Simcoe, seemed to Americans to be actively encouraging the Indian Confederacy, Lord Grenville wrote Minister Hammond to mediate for peace. "The British Government feel . . . that they have a strong commercial and political interest in the restoration of Peace." Home Secretary Dundas wrote agent Robert Prescott that while the Indian Nations had given "such decided proofs" of their loyalty to the king, Prescott was to try "effecting, if possible, a speedy termination of the War." Even the normally bellicose Simcoe would write in the summer of 1791 that "The Indian War is so detrimental to Commerce and uncertain in its Events, that I am anxious to be permitted, (if it were possible), to mediate for its Termination."[13]

Aside from the detrimental effects on trade, officers in Canada continued, prior to November 4, to fear that their Indian allies would be turned against them. Col. John Butler, who had led Indian auxiliaries during the Revolution, warned his superior that from the American efforts to draw the Iroquois into a council, that "they are Determined the Indians [i.e., the Iroquois] shall not remain neuter." (Indeed, Knox and company were making significant efforts to revive and recruit the Iroquois League to help them defeat the Northwest Confederacy.) Simcoe, as he typically would, stated the matter more bluntly: if the Confederacy obtained a satisfactory peace with the United States without Britain having played a role, "on whom will their young Warriors wish to exercise their prowess or whom will the Congress point out as a proper Enemy?"[14]

Within months of the battle, and within several weeks of the giddy sense of opportunity and excitement it engendered, Simcoe began to doubt once more. By April 1792, the lieutenant governor felt that the moment had passed and momentum had been squandered. That the war continued, with the Confederacy having failed to destroy any American forts after the battle, gave him "a considerable degree of uneasiness." He therefore renewed his request for "a central force [of regular troops] in Upper Canada"—not to fight off an American invasion, but to forestall an Indian uprising. Simcoe grimly concluded that the requested force would serve only as a deterrent, and would not actually "be adequate to support a War with the Indians" if that deterrent failed. Some even feared that the Americans would attack British frontier posts in retaliation in the spring of 1792. Indeed, "It seemed all courses of action carried a risk, and this uncertainty led to a virtual paralysis of British Indian policy in 1791."[15]

Perhaps what Simcoe needed to snap him out of his fears of an Indian war gone awry was a borderline absurd, pie-in-the-sky assessment of the situation, which he received from his good friend Charles Stevenson. Captain Stevenson was one of the many secret agents Simcoe had ordered to infiltrate the United States to seek out Loyalists who might bedevil the republic. Stevenson, posing as a Montreal trader in New York City, reported back to Simcoe. Assuming that the costs (human and financial) of the Indian war were now too much for the United States, and that the Bank of the United States would fail under a panic of its depositors, Stevenson assured Simcoe that the state of New York, in its distress, would likely bolt to the king. And of course if New York seceded to Canada, "Vermont must . . . belong to us." West Point, New York, "where all the cannon and stores of Gen. Burgoyne's and Lord Cornwallis' Armies are deposited," could then easily be taken, and Forts Montgomery and Stony Point "might be occupied in one night." He then concluded that Alexander Hamilton might be made "a secret friend" of Britain,[16] which was probably a bit more plausible than British armies re-occupying the Hudson Valley.

Simcoe yearned for the opportunity to strike militarily at the United States, but he was constrained by the official (and perpetually months out of date) policy of his superiors at Whitehall. For example, in 1792 he had to admonish agent Alexander McKee that "in no case are the Indians to expect our Interference by any other means than mediation." Simcoe knew this was asking a lot, especially given the tightrope that agents were expected to walk with Indian policy, not to mention McKee's own strong ties to the militant Shawnees. Nevertheless, he continued, "it will be a part of your difficult Duty, . . . to counteract any assertions of self-interested & venal Traders, that G Britain will sooner or later engage in a War with the States in defence of the Western Indians."[17]

Simcoe did not mention, of course, that while some in both the Indian country and the United States speculated that Britain might come to the defense of its native allies, the Northwestern Confederacy was hardly taking its cues from Britain at this point—it was the other way around. In 1792 and 1793, the Confederacy grew increasingly bold in threatening not only the Americans, but also any potential allies who balked at pan-Indianism. In the summer of 1791, Mohawk Joseph Brant had already called for the British to build a new fort at the Miami Rapids, near modern Toledo, Ohio. Building a new post deep within the recognized American boundary line—and while continuing to occupy Detroit—would be an explosively provocative move by the king's troops. Perhaps with feigned casualness, Brant also mentioned that the Confederacy (of which he clearly considered himself a part) would have about 2,000 warriors in the area—more than enough to cause serious trouble for under-manned Upper Canada. (Despite the Home Secretary's rebukes, British troops completed the post, dubbed

Fort Miami, in 1794.) Warriors of the Confederacy also killed two American peace emissaries and their entourages in 1792.[18]

American officials and civilians were so desperate to thwart the growing pan-Indian menace that they managed to convince themselves for a time that staunch opponents like Brant had their best interests at heart. Around the time Brant had insisted upon the construction of Fort Miami a leading newspaper happily communicated that while Brant was heading south with a retinue of warriors, it was not "with design to join the Indians in that quarter . . . but by the desire and at the request of the officers at Niagara, to gain intelligence, and endeavor to bring about a reconciliation between those Indians and the United States." Knox himself sought to recruit the Mohawk, writing him that Brant's "general character for intelligence and attachment to the Indian interest" would prove useful to tell the Indians that Washington had their best interests at heart. The United States showed somewhat better sense in recruiting Hendick Aupaumut, a Mohican who had actually fought *for* the United States during the Revolution. Aupaumut's embassy to the West was not especially successful either, as Brant repeatedly informed him that the peace messages would work best if they went through his British friends.[19]

As Washington guessed, negotiating while the Confederacy was flush with victory had little hope for success. At the 1793 conference at the Miami town Auglaize, the Indian Confederacy boasted terrific, even fearsome, potential. As one unidentified native speaker noted, "Father, as the Creeks and all the Southern Indians will attend the proposed Council we have requested you to be strong & Encourage the other Nations to meet us there, & we shall then be able to speak our minds without fear." Nativist leaders would be so confident in their chances for successful resistance that they suggested (with a glint of smugness) that the United States would be money ahead to simply give cash to the Ohio Country's prospective settlers, rather than pay for a great army which would simply lose anyway. At the council in February, the assembly admonished the Iroquois that they should include the Confederacy's demands in their talks to the Americans. "It is incumbent upon you our Brethren, to make them fully acquainted with every particular which concerns the establishment of so important a work, as the peace of this Country."

The speakers' wish was that the Americans "be prepared to perfect a peace *which we have offered* [emphasis added] on just and equitable terms."

While stating that they desired "the advice and assistance of our Elder Brethren in the great Work which we are about," the talk reads more like a demand than a request. "The Western Indians are all prepared and in daily expectation of the arrival of Our Brethren the Creeks, Cherokees and the other Southern Nations Who are on their legs to join us agreeable to their promise. And we desire You will put the Seven Nations of Canada in mind of their promise last fall to be early on their legs to join us and that you will bring them in your hand."[20] Students of Washington give him credit, and justly so, for continuing to prepare for war while he attempted to secure peace. Equal esteem is due his native rivals.

Throughout 1792 and 1793, Simcoe and the British continued the dangerous game of trying to hold on to their Indian allies and, with thinly veiled threats of force, encourage the United States to allow British mediation—without seeming to have actually promoted open war. For example, Home Secretary Dundas officially approved the idea of seeking a "permanent" Indian buffer state in the Ohio country in May 1792, *provided* the deal was approved by the Americans. Getting that American approval was of course a different matter. Even in the wake of the debacle on the Wabash, secretaries Knox and Jefferson—war and state, respectively—were quite clear to Minister Hammond that a permanent Indian territory within the bounds of the United States was a nonstarter.[21]

Furthermore, considerable confusion reigned between administrators (even in Canada) and the Indian agents themselves. That the governor-general's secretary could write, without irony or sarcasm, that officials in Quebec did not know whether "any presents were issued in the Miamis country about the time of Mr. Harmar's expedition," spoke volumes. That he could add "but if it was the case, certainly none were given with a hostile intent. No Officer of the Indian Department would presume to act so opposite to his instructions," displayed a remarkably naive view of how the Indian Department actually operated.[22]

The threat of a true pan-Indian confederacy remained crucial to forcing the United States to accept British interference, and Indian agents like Alexander McKee were certainly willing to prime the pump. In seeking the input of Joseph Brant and the Iroquois, McKee reminded him that "the General Indian Confederacy" was "a business so Essentially necessary to the Interest, Welfare & Happiness of the Indians in General." McKee also noted to his superiors that, to nurse the growing confederacy, "It will also be requisite on this occasion . . . to be a little more liberal in the distribution of the Provisions & and other Necessaries usual[ly] delivered to them at this Season of the year."[23] This proved to be the heart of the conflict between the United States and Britain. To avoid having an angry Indian confederacy attack British posts in Upper Canada, as well as to have allies enough to safeguard them from an American invasion, British agents aided and abetted the pan-Indian movement. By giving arms and encouragement (that Indians themselves demanded), British agents gave the Americans greater reason to fear their influence with the Indians, and to seek to remove that influence by attacking British posts.

Simcoe and others were not above conjuring strange rhetorical bedfellows to support their Indian allies, and to convince them that they needed the king's protection. Sir William Johnson's Fort Stanwix treaty of 1768, which had defrauded both the Shawnees and Cherokees of their claims to Kentucky, was once again touted as a savior of Indian lands.[24]

While Simcoe, against his instincts, tried to avoid the appearance of directly instigating the king's allies against the United States, Lord Dorchester's reply to the Indian council on the Maumee sounded far more inflammatory. Dorchester assured them that war was imminent, and that they should prepare to fight the Americans. American officials and newspaper editors were understandably outraged when they heard of this, though in Dorchester's defense, he had assumed that the United States would honor its military alliance with France and attack British Canada. (The Washington administration felt differently.) In a talk to the Seven Nations of Canada, he addressed their request for passports to visit New York. "You shall have a passport that whether Peace or War You shall be well received by the Kings Warriors." He added that he felt the Americans had "broke the Peace" of 1783, and that while "on our Part we have acted in the Most Peaceable Manner . . . I believe our Patience is almost exhausted."[25]

The Washington administration, despite the obstacles to taking the Ohio Valley, nevertheless felt they had to press on. The Treasury desperately needed the cash Ohio land sales would bring. Most importantly, however, was the fact that the Southern nations were far too large to tangle with. U.S. policy dictated that they would pursue whatever treaties or concessions were necessary to keep them out of a pan-Indian alliance until the Northern Indians were subdued.

CHAPTER **10**

Henry Knox's Nightmare

By the fall of 1793, after multiple failed attempts to secure a peaceful cession of land from the undefeated Northwestern Indians, Americans were prone to bleak assessments of the situation. South Carolina's Pierce Butler had abandoned some of his distrust of the federal government, and replaced it with terror of an Indian war across the frontier. He noted that the latest round of negotiations with the Ohio Indians had featured "a deputation from the Creeks accompanied by a British officer . . . [and] they cordially approved of War. There can no longer be any doubt of a general Indian War or combination under the auspices of the British, and I imagine the Spanish also." As much as he feared the standing army, the specter of a combined pan-Indian coalition with European military aid was too much for Butler. He agreed with James Gunn of Georgia that "most men are of your opinion; that the Indians generally must feel the arm of America," and that "A general Indian War may be looked upon as certain." A month later he reiterated his opinion of a general Indian war to a friend in Savannah, Georgia, and included the advice that would become especially relevant for Southerners when Indian wars threatened: "Place Your Negroes therefore in security."¹

Slaves had long been considered a grave security risk, most obviously so in the South. Their value as property (or as potential, well-motivated allies) had made them sought-after targets for Indian antagonists as well. While treaties with Indians generally featured a call for the exchange of prisoners, Southerners logically insisted on the return of their human property as well. At the 1789 Treaty of French Broad, North Carolinian John Steele and his Cherokee counterparts agreed upon the return of prisoners, "papers, horses, negroes & other property . . . without delay." Americans seemed to have more trouble with the Creeks. Transplanted Georgian (and future Major General) Anthony Wayne, griped to a friend that "we are all in confusion here on account of the Indians and Spaniards—the first carrying off our Negroes and other property—the latter Countenancing and protecting them! Thus circumstanced, I believe there will be an other attempt to Convince the House—and should it meet, it's more than probable decisive measures will be taken against the Creek Nation." Andrew Pickens and Henry Osbourne had to write a personal appeal to McGillivray in 1789, pleading that the sons of a widow whose eight slaves had been taken by a Creek party be allowed to enter the nation to look for them, lest she be left destitute. A few weeks later, reports surfaced of the Creeks taking still more slaves from Georgia settlers.[2]

The 1790s proved a decade to frighten slave owners to no end. An unforeseen ramification of the late-eighteenth century's revolutionary ideals came in the form of the Haitian Revolution. From its outbreak on the island of St. Domingue in 1791, the most successful slave revolt in history, led by Toussaint Louverture, sparked mixed emotions in Europe and America. True republicans in France and the United States reveled in the idea of human liberty, yet many French would belatedly lament the loss of such a valuable sugar colony. Presidents Washington, Adams, and Jefferson could applaud a weakening of France's grip in the Americas, and (at least in the abstract) the blow to slavery. Adams' administration even secretly provided Toussaint with supplies and critical troop transportation. Yet they feared that the insurrectionist fever could spread to the United States, and would not be confined to slaves.[3]

As Paul Lachance notes, the Haitian Revolution had an almost immediate impact on Louisiana from its outbreak in 1791. Nearly 40,000 refugees—slave and free—descended upon the colony when fighting broke out. Toussaint's war further influenced nominally Spanish Louisiana by encouraging a switch from producing tobacco to sugar—a far more labor-intensive crop that the disruption of St. Domingue's sugar production made even more wildly profitable. The abolition of slavery in the French colonies in 1793–1794 threatened slavery, and it encouraged slave revolts in Louisiana, which were in turn crushed "quickly and ruthlessly" by Louisiana's ruling elites. A failed 1795 revolt in Point Coupée, Louisiana, saw fifteen slaves executed. As with previous pan-Indianists and rebel slaves, the condemned were beheaded, and their heads placed on posts to serve as a grisly warning to future rebels.[4]

Louisiana was not the only mainland region terrified of the revolt's example. In 1793, Charleston, South Carolina, the destination for many of the early expatriates from St. Domingue, witnessed a particularly bad scare. Rumors swirled that French revolutionaries would spread a rebellion through the Southern states,[5] with abolition presumably being one of their goals. The American press carried reports from French newspapers which noted not only the apparent formation of a great league of Southern Indians at Spanish behest, but that emigrants from St. Domingue might join them as well. The St. Domingans moving into the Southern states, they noted ominously, would "carry with them their slaves, their follies, and their vices." One correspondent from Charleston eschewed the innuendo for full-blown panic. He noted that a fear of slave insurrections—spurred by the seditious speech of the slaves of the island refugees—had led the city to keep the militia and light horse patrolling the streets all night, every night. "We are in a dreadful alarm, . . . and much to be apprehended from the Indians, domestics and disaffected people now among us," he concluded.[6]

Whether the "disaffected"—be they slaves or displaced planters—were actually trying to forge a multiethnic revolt of white and mulatto refugees, slaves, and Southern Indians, is impossible to know. French agents were certainly involved in machinations involving Spanish Florida, though perhaps not ones as immediately disastrous for the United States as Federalists might have feared. France's consul to the Carolinas and Georgia, Michel Mangourit, hoped to cause an invasion of Spanish Florida that would establish it as an independent republic allied to France. To effect this, Mangourit and his allies did seek to form an alliance with the Creeks, Choctaws, and Cherokees, or at the very least break Spain's ties with them. (These negotiations would have given harrowing plausibility to charges of an attempted Indian confederation.) Mangourit's plans certainly threatened Spain and troubled the U.S. government, the latter hoping to eventually take Florida for its own from a weakened Spain. Still, Mangourit's efforts did not pose the immediate existential threat to American citizens that Federalists claimed. Indeed, both Mangourit and Thomas Jefferson doubted that there was any real conspiracy among Charleston's slaves, and Mangourit suspected the plot rumors were spread by Federalists trying to weaken his ties to South Carolina's governor, William Moultrie.[7]

Though the fears of slave revolts and Indian confederacies was so common as to seem almost organic, historian Robert Alderson argues that in the case of the Charleston panic of 1793, the rumors might have been deliberately spread. They were perhaps fostered, as Mangourit thought, by Federalists (trying to discredit their Francophile Republican rivals), or St. Domingue's expatriates (seeking to discredit the French government that had failed them). Or, it could have been an actual plot that was discovered in its infancy. It is worth noting, as Simon P. Newman does, that the fear of "black revolutionaries bringing race war into the communities of the United States" was not confined to the South in 1793. After slave arsonists set fire to part of Albany, New York, "rumors of similar fires spread through such communities as Philadelphia, Schenectady, Waterford, Boston, Hartford, New London, and Elizabethtown."[8]

Thus Americans in the early 1790s may well have been suffering from a form of anxiety overload, as a staggeringly deep and broad array of threats from within and without confronted them. The Northwestern Confederacy's smashing victory over St. Clair still combined with the continuing and rather obvious pan-Indian overtures to complicate American officials' tasks in dealing with Indians. Even those who were quite blatant in advocating the acquisition of native lands had to consider the risks of antagonizing native peoples at this crucial moment. As the Southwestern Territory's Governor William Blount noted, he now felt he had to be especially diplomatic in dealing with the Cherokees and Creeks, as "The Unfortunate affair with General St. Clair [has] in my opinion made attentions to the Indians more indispensably necessary than before."[9]

Among the victorious confederacy at the "unfortunate affair" was a contingent of sixty Chickamauga warriors sent by Dragging Canoe. They appear to have had a marvelous time, and when they brought tales of their exploits back home, their chief was inspired to pursue pan-Indianism with even more vigor. He had already "forged ties with William Augustus Bowles, a former Loyalist adventurer and self-appointed "Director-General of the Creek Nation," employing Bowles' associate George Welbank at Running Water to keep up a correspondence with Alexander McKee, the British Indian Agent at Detroit." Now he sought closer ties to Alexander McGillivray and the Creeks—a potentially sticky situation, as McGillivray teetered between tolerating Bowles and trying to have him assassinated. But McGillivray appreciated not only the Chickamaugas' ferocity as allies, but also their ability to work as go-betweens. He hoped they might bring the Chickasaws—continually, if not continuously, at war with the Creeks—into a pan-Indian union. During the winter of 1791–1792, they would labor, unsuccessfully, to have the Chickasaws join the growing Shawnee–Creek–Chickamauga coalition.[10]

Blount grew increasingly alarmed as Creek and Chickamauga war parties moved through Tennessee and into Kentucky in the spring of 1792. Those warriors proved frightening enough on their own, but absolutely horrifying when he warned his militia officers that "I am sure you have to fear the depredations of marauding parties of both nations as well as the Northern tribes." Even if the pan-Indianists were not working in close coordination, Tennesseans could easily be caught in a cycle of deadly assaults from north and south—effectively pincers. As if this were not enough, Blount soon became convinced that Spanish agents would excite the Chickasaws and Choctaws—who, it should be noted, often fought the Creeks—to attack Americans as well.[11]

Understandably, Governor Blount wanted help from the federal government, specifically in the form of a large punitive expedition against the Chickamaugas. Henry Knox did not acquiesce. In a missive that ran for eleven pages, he answered seven letters the governor had sent him in the previous two months. He replied to Blount that President Washington did not feel empowered to unilaterally levy war against the Chickamaugas, as only Congress "are vested . . . with the powers of War." While regrettable, Knox continued, the Chickamauga assaults were probably the result of their being antagonized by white settlers' continued encroachment. More to the point, neither Knox nor Washington, or the general citizenry for that matter, would be so foolish as to start a major war south of the Ohio while a vicious one already raged north of it. "I can however with great truth assure that the extension of the Northern Indian War to the Southern Tribes would be a measure which the Country would enter with extreme reluctance. They view an Indian War in any event of it as unproductive either of profit or honor, and therefore to be avoided if possible," he noted. Washington, Knox insisted, wanted to keep things as quiet as possible in "the Southern quarter," for "he is exceedingly apprehensive that the flame of War once kindled in that region upon the smallest scales will extend itself and become general."[12]

The administration was so alarmed that in February 1792 Knox wrote a letter to Alexander McGillivray which, read between the lines, practically begged him to restrain his warriors from joining the Northwestern Confederacy. Knox also explicitly asked for three hundred Creek warriors to fight against them. Though now technically an American brigadier, less than three years earlier McGillivray had been one of the most prominent advocates of pan-Indian union and resistance. That he was once again calling for such a confederacy, even asking Dragging Canoe to bring Piomingo's Chickasaws into the fold, could not have been encouraging for the Washington administration.[13]

Knox would spend much of 1792 veering wildly from optimism for peace to pan-Indian doomsday scenarios. In April he wrote to South Carolina's Andrew Pickens, a fierce veteran of the Revolution, Indian fighter,[14] and future treaty commissioner. Knox described the deteriorating situation in the Ohio Country, how the American settlers and Indians fought for the valley's rich lands, and how the U.S. Army would have to intervene forcibly. Then he got down to business, noting, "there can be no doubt that the hostile Indians are endeavouring to excite the Southern Indians to join them—This event would be attended with the most pernicious effects—and it must if possible be avoided." Pickens, for his part, would reply that the United States should "*carry a vigorous campaign into the Creek country*," [emphasis in original] to awe the other Southern nations and "prevent the junction of more tribes against [us] than is now expected."[15] Less than three weeks later he would write the governor of Virginia, avowing that "it would appear that the United States have much to hope, and but little to apprehend from the disposition of the Southern nations of Indians." Knox felt that if the war in the Ohio country continued, he could get "five or six hundred Southern Indians to Join our Army." True, he noted, some Chickamaugas and other Cherokees had "held considerable intercourse with the Shawnese for some years past." But with the death of Dragging Canoe (in March 1792, apparently from natural causes),[16] Knox was thrilled at what he perceived to be an opportunity for peace with the Chickamaugas, and even to "settle the remnants of the war on the Southern frontiers."[17]

Unfortunately for Knox, the Chickamaugas, now led by the métis John Watts and joined by Creek and Shawnee warriors, fought on for another two years. As Tyler Boulware asserts, when Watts, who lived in the Upper

Cherokee Towns, accepted leadership of the Chickamaugas, he demonstrated how frustrated the "non-militant" Cherokees had become with settlers' depredations. Watts' political connections to both the Upper and Lower Cherokee towns helped broaden the Cherokee war effort. Parties seeking scalps and horses often originated from so-called "peace towns." They proved so effective that "congressional delegates considered a motion to grant the president (as opposed to Congress) the right to call out the army to defend the frontier against them." For some, growing pan-Indian resistance proved more alarming than the growth of the executive branch. Only when a punitive militia expedition finally destroyed two of their principal towns—Running Water and Nickajack—would the Chickamaugas sue for peace.[18]

Blount and the Tennesseans were not the least bit surprised that the Chickamaugas fought on after Dragging Canoe's death. Blount reported that while some Cherokees had destroyed a "War pipe" the Chickamaugas had brought from Detroit, Dragging Canoe's brother had commissioned a replica from a local pipe maker so that "he might have it to show to the Northwards, whom he daily expected at the lower towns." Equally disturbing, Arturo O'Neill, the governor in Spanish Pensacola, had been liberally supplying arms to the four principal Southern nations. According to Blount's source, O'Neill had even exhorted the Southern nations to "to join quickly in war against the United States while they were engaged in a war with the Northern tribes; if they did not, that as Soon as they (the United States) conquer the Northern tribes, they would be upon them and cut them off."[19]

Blount's informer was spot on. That summer the Baron de Carondelet in New Orleans had specifically told O'Neill to encourage the Creeks to defend their lands from the Americans. Then he essentially confirmed the worst possible scenario for the United States. "This diversion will prevent the Northern Indians, who are aided by the English, from being annihilated during this campaign, and with this the Americans will be stuck between two fires and it will compel them to return what they have taken, or they will be exposed to a general devastation of their Settlements on this side of the Appalachians." American newspapers carried the essence of that report, with some myopic criticism of Indian "hypocrisy," by the fall of 1792.[20]

Within days of learning about St. Clair's disaster on the Wabash, Knox reported to the president that in "contemplating the probable consequences of the late defeat," the Southern tribes deserved greater scrutiny. True, he noted, the United States had treaties with all the Southern nations, and all seemed "tranquil" for the moment, "except the Creeks." Nevertheless, Knox was forced to admit, "The hostile Indians can easily, and will, probably, repeat their invitation to the Southern tribes during the present winter." While the U.S. Army had just been badly beaten by the Northwest Confederacy, which Knox now estimated as having about 2,200 warriors, he guessed that the Southern nations could field "about fifteen thousand."[21]

As scholars have noted, for a time after the Battle of the Wabash, George Washington was the only figure in the executive branch still advocating the pursuit of military victory north of the Ohio. Yet he managed to seek peace sincerely even as his gut told him to prepare for war. That he was able to grasp both the olive branch and the arrows simultaneously does him much credit, though Indians both allied and opposed to him disagreed.[22] In 1792 and 1793, Washington continued to offer a peace settlement to the Northwestern Confederacy (though the terms were, to them, laughable), with an eye toward forestalling a pan-Indian alliance. It proved a nerve-rattling game. He noted to the Congress in 1792 that "It must add to your concern to be informed, that, besides the continuation of hostile appearances among the tribes north of the Ohio, some threatening symptoms have of late been revived among some of those south of it." A year later the president vented his irritation that attempts to end the war in Ohio "having been frustrated, the troops have marched to act offensively." Meanwhile, his "anxiety . . . for peace with the Creeks and the Cherokees" had necessitated giving "corn and clothing" to the Cherokees, and he had also banned "offensive measures against them [meaning, primarily, the Chickamaugas]" while Congress was in recess. For Knox and Washington, the risk of killing friendly or neutral Indians with a campaign in the South, which would then bring on a "general confederacy," was simply too great. Still, as Cynthia Cumfer notes, Washington had shown far greater interest in using massive force against the Whiskey Rebels than the Indian killers on the frontier. The closest the settlers came to punishment was the secretary of war refusing to pay them militia wages, though once Tennessee joined the Union, fittingly, "congressman Andrew Jackson succeeded in reversing even this rebuke."[23]

Still, Washington felt that the army would play a major role, certainly north, and perhaps south, of the Ohio. He settled upon Anthony Wayne to be its new commanding general. Though not his first choice, Wayne would prove to be an excellent one. He had experience fighting Indians—the Creeks in Georgia—as well as British regulars during the Revolution. He had been advocating a military campaign against the Creeks—"I am decidedly of Opinion that we never shall have a permanent *peace* with the *Creek Nation* until they experience our Superiority in the field"—since the late 1780s, and was also in agreement with Washington and Knox about the need for greater federal control of the frontier areas. The Georgia resident, admiring the government of the Northwest Territory, said more than he knew when he added, "I would be much gratified by an Appointment Similar to that given to General St. Clair."[24]

"Mad" Anthony Wayne was thoroughly professional, and professionally thorough, when it came to both training and deploying the new Legion of the United States. British officials remembered Wayne from the late war. Minister Hammond offered, "General Wayne is unquestionably the most active, Vigilant and enterprizing officer in the American Service," and would "be tempted to use Every Exertion to justify the Expectations of his countrymen & to efface the Stain, which the late defeat has cast upon the American Arms." One of his own soldiers would write that Wayne was "as usual, warm for fighting. Every body knows he loves it." The confidence Wayne bred in his men made "*another thirty mile flight*," like that of St. Clair's army, highly unlikely.[25] Part of Washington's genius was his realization that the Legion needed to awe and impress not just pan-Indian militants or foreign agents, but American citizens themselves, especially in the West.

For Westerners like Arthur Campbell, the Indian wars were intensely personal. They were unified in the idea that a peace with the Indians could only be obtained through strong military efforts, and nearly as unified in the belief that Easterners might sell them out at any moment. Secretary for Foreign Affairs John Jay's 1786 agreement to give up the Mississippi River to Spain in return for "commercial benefits favoring the eastern states," though overruled by Congress, only added to that concern. As Andrew Cayton reminds us, "The right to unrestricted access of the Mississippi was the *sine qua non* of western loyalty." Kentuckians had flirted with detaching the district to both British and Spanish agents in the 1780s. They were hoping to secure access to the river, though most likely the direct goal was to force the Congress (and later the federal government) to take that need more seriously. Nevertheless, the prospect of rebellion and even secession in the West would remain a potential nightmare until the implosion of Aaron Burr's schemes in 1806.[26]

When it seemed that many in the Congress wanted to abandon military measures for more diplomatic means toward peace, Westerners viewed their talk as tantamount to surrender, perhaps even treason. Especially in the years after the Revolution, tales of Indian savagery, of homicidal attacks on white settler families, and captivity narratives, grew in popularity and influence. These stories were rife with gendered and racialized imagery—often they involved the patriarch's absence or being killed early in the attack, leaving the wife to "overcome . . . the savages not because of her technical superiority . . . but because of her moral superiority and cleverness." Almanacs and other publications focused "not [on] talk of conquest, but defense." The basic narrative structure in the media did not allow for a complex narrative, or discuss the dispossession of Indians. Tales of Indian attacks followed a simplified story line, where *innocent settlers* were attacked by *murderous savages*. The gory specifics of Indian attacks made it easy enough for whites to gloss over the broader context of frontier warfare, and also to excuse any horrible deeds committed against *savages*.[27]

Furthermore, because whites on the frontier saw themselves as civilians and farmers first—acting as the Bible had decreed—Indian attacks could be seen as especially unjust and heinous. This was never truer than when marauding warriors killed women or children. There was brutal pragmatism in the murder of white women, who would of course bear the next generation of potential militiamen. Further, knowing how ghastly such attacks appeared to nonnatives may have been a blunt "rejection of European codes of behavior." For the Cherokees in particular, the murders of women may have been deliberately symbolic—the matrilineal Cherokees felt that a lineage lived and died with its women. The murders of women, especially pregnant women, may well have been their signal that it was a fight to the finish. Still, when traditional gender mores were upended in this way, "both white and Indian women suffered."[28]

In fairness one must note that even with the race-baiting propaganda used against Indians, and the disproportionate casualties inflicted upon them, there were some truly ghastly incidents for frontier people to cite. In late 1792 Governor William Blount of the Southwestern Territory forwarded an account of settlers killed or wounded by Indians in the previous ten months. The list ran to 119 names, over a quarter of them women or children. Depositions forwarded to the War Department included that of Michael Cupps and Nancy Smith, who witnessed: "about thirty Indians firing upon and massacreing Richard Thresher, two children, and a negro wench; at the same time the wife of the deceased, with an infant, ran and leapt into the river, the Indians firing upon her as she fled. The woman was found alive, scalped, wounded in both her thighs, and her right breast with balls, and stabbed her in her left breast with a knife, her left arm nearly cut off, as is supposed with a tomahawk, of which wounds she died in about twenty-four hours. The infant was found drowned, without any marks of violence upon it."[29]

Thus while Anglo-American terror of Indian wars had almost always been somewhat exaggerated, there were nevertheless sufficient horrific incidents to keep that fear alive. It was rarely so plausible as in the 1790s. Arthur Campbell was no doubt sincere when he wrote his friend John Steele in Richmond, in the spring of 1792, noting, "I read with no small degree of indignation, some of the Speeches in a certain hon. Assembly on the Indian War. I wish they and their Wives and little ones were placed One year near the frontiers of Kentucky. They would know and feel some of the hardships and ills we have long struggled with." More troubling still, he relayed reports from the Cherokee nation that at least sixty Cherokees (Dragging Canoe's Chickamaugas, in fact) had joined in "the battle on 4th Nov. last"—that is, the Confederacy's victory over St. Clair. Finally, he fretted that "the British Emissary Bowles,"—the aforementioned adventurer William Augustus Bowles, who styled himself a leader of the Creeks— "will outwit our Superintendent [James Seagrove], the ensuing Summer." Decisive action was needed, Campbell insisted, or the U.S. would lose all hope of allies among the Southern nations. With more despair than hope, he concluded, "This ought to arouse the patriotism and valour, of the sons of freedom, and friends of humanity within the United States."[30]

While nearly at his wits' end, Agent Seagrove was not witless. In early 1793 he sought to have his subordinate, Timothy Barnard, "to overset the plan of the Northward Indians" among the Creeks. There could be no better tactic than that practiced by John Stuart, and he admonished Barnard, "As to the Shawnese that are in that nation, you must, by every means possible, stir up the Creeks against them." Still, indiscriminate assaults by American frontiersmen, as Stuart had often lamented, could bind that which American diplomacy had set asunder. Barnard responded to Seagrove, asserting that if Americans responded to the depredations of Cowetas and other Lower Creeks by attacking the nation as a whole, "it will bring on a general war, in which they will receive every assistance by supplies from the Spaniards, and it is probable the Choctaws, Chickasaws, and Cherokees, will join them." That several Cherokee chiefs were known to be receiving the most solicitous treatment in Pensacola only deepened this fear. Seagrove was already well aware of Spanish efforts among the Southern nations. The "barefaced" efforts of Spanish agents, and the U.S.'s paltry efforts to halt them, he warned Knox, were being interpreted by Indians and whites alike as a sign of American weakness. Seagrove hoped the government would take steps "that the bloody-minded agents should fall into the pit which they have dug for the servants and friends of the Union."[31]

Arthur Campbell continued to keep a wary eye for any signs of pan-Indian alliance. In the spring of 1793 he warned the governor of Virginia about a massive party of seven hundred Chickamauga Cherokees, supposedly headed for either Tennessee or Kentucky. Campbell's great fear was that the Cherokees proper had joined in a "conspiracy," as they would not "attempt to brave the whole power of the United States" by themselves. He added, "it is known that a formal embassy came from the Northward Indians to the Cherokees in the winter, and that some of the Heads of that Tribe accompanied them on their return." Fellow Virginian Andrew Lewis proposed taking a party of forty men to the head of the Kentucky River, to lay an ambush "where the Southern Indians pass going to and from the relief of the Northern Tribes." Lewis hoped that surprise would allow his men a victory and strike a blow for frontier security. Governor Lee apparently passed on the proposal.[32]

Sir William Johnson. The highly skilled superintendent for Northern Indian Affairs sought to forestall pan-Indianism and promote his land speculations with the Fort Stanwix Treaty of 1768. *Sir William Johnson* (1715–1774) by Edward L. Mooney, 1838, after a lost portrait by Thomas McIlworth; oil on canvas, 30 x 25 inches; negative #6871. Courtesy of the collection of The New-York Historical Society.

William Augustus Bowles. Equal parts pan-Indianist and con-artist, Bowles sought to create a great Indian union centered in Muscogee and headed by himself. He infuriated both Spanish and American authorities, especially slave owners, until his death in 1805. *William Augustus Bowles,* mezzotint print engraved by J. Grozer after Thomas Hardy, 1791, London, England. Ink on paper; HOA: 14-5/8 inches; WOA: 11-1/4 inches. Courtesy of the collection of the Museum of Early Southern Decorative Arts (MESDA), Acc. 3765, Given in memory of Allene Dalton.

Henry Knox. The first Federal Secretary of War, Knox struggled to maintain both the nation's territorial integrity and its honor in an era dominated by financial constraints and suspicion of standing armies. Given the degree of difficulty involved, he was remarkably successful. Portrait by Gilbert Stuart. Courtesy of the Library of Congress.

Tecumseh. The most famous advocate of pan-Indianism, Tecumseh's ambition, skill, and insistence on humane treatment of war prisoners captivated Americans. His 1813 death crippled the movement, and led to his quasi-lionization in the pantheon of American heroes. Courtesy of the Indiana Historical Society.

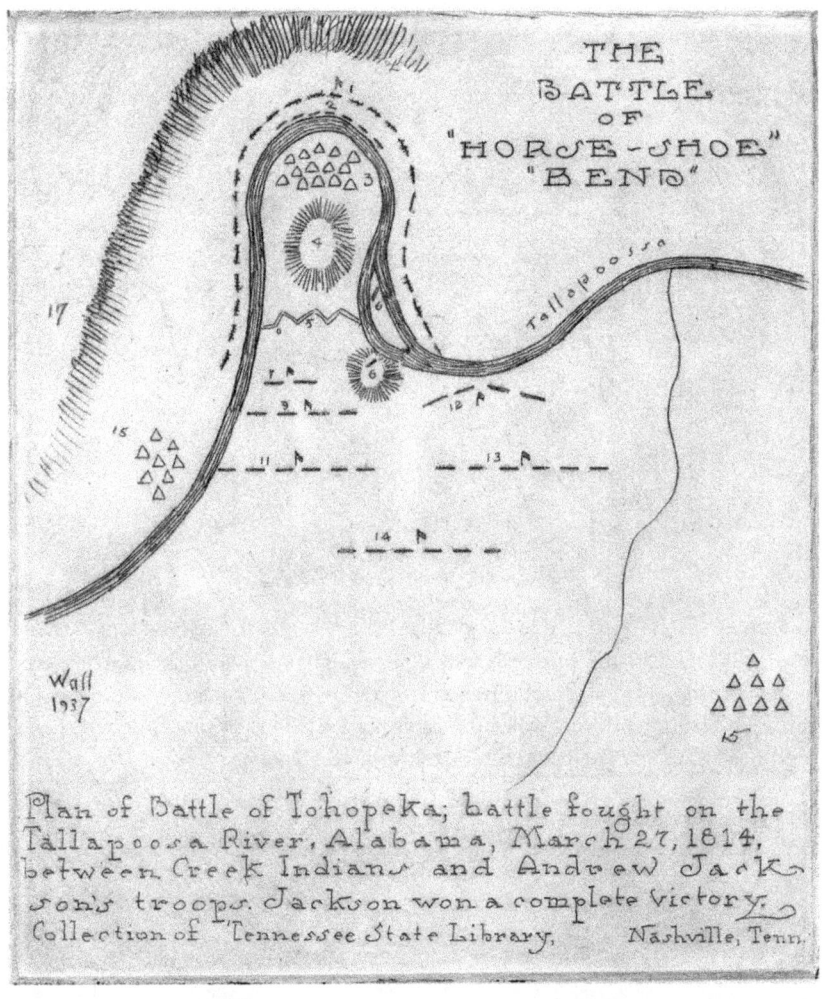

Horseshoe Bend. The Red Sticks made this bend in the Tallapoosa River a formidable fortress, but the courage and ingenuity of Andrew Jackson's Creek and Cherokee allies turned it into a deathtrap. Courtesy of Tennessee State Library and Archives.

William Weatherford Surrendering to Andrew Jackson. The métis Red Stick surrendered to Jackson shortly after the disaster at Horseshoe Bend. Both men would spend considerable time hunting down the surviving Red Sticks in years to come. Courtesy of the Alabama Department of Archives and History.

Black Hawk. The Sauk war captain and comrade of Tecumseh outlived both the Shawnee and the feasibility of pan-Indian resistance. Americans could not resist putting Black Hawk's 1832 struggle into the narrative framework of Tecumseh and the Prophet, which had ended to their liking. Courtesy of the Indiana Historical Society.

Osceola. The Seminole leader was also compared to Tecumseh, though his people's alliances with maroons and slaves in Florida made him briefly seem an even greater threat to white hegemony in the Southeast. Courtesy of the Alabama Department of Archives and History.

CHAPTER 11

Bowles, Part One

In 1792–1793, despair proved a perfectly rational response for Westerners worried about pan-Indian alliances and their foreign abettors. North of the Ohio River the undefeated confederacy swelled with confidence, and British officials began to seriously consider that their allies might win. And the Spanish, who typically followed a defensive, even moribund, Indian policy, had become suddenly aggressive. The years 1792 and 1793 would see Spain's most serious efforts to not only foster pan-Indianism but to work with their British rivals at the expense of the Americans.

In a letter marked "confidential," Luis de las Casas, the governor of Havana, could write back to Spain that he strongly supported: "The Plan of forming a general alliance of all the Indian nations in between the King's possessions and those of the United States, attracting them and preserving them with our Party, inspiring them to be opposed to cede lands to the Americans in order to contain their borders farther away from ours, and forestall them extending their continued disguised usurpations." Encouraging pan-Indian resistance to the Americans was "the most advantageous to the interests of the state in that Continent," and he would continue the policy as long as it did not give the United States a just complaint.[1] Therein of course lay the rub. Any measure by a foreign power that would make it more difficult for land-crazy Americans to acquire Indian lands—like, say, giving those Indians arms and ammunition—would automatically be seen as a hostile gesture. Indeed, as Las Casas confidentially admitted, stifling the growth of the American states was a primary goal.

Nevertheless, the Spaniards were far too steeped in European legal and diplomatic culture not to try. Enclosed with the above letter was one from Carondelet to Las Casas, in which the governor in New Orleans stated that the king would not consent to (re)building forts at the Muscle Shoals or on the Tombigbee River unless the Choctaws, Creeks, Chickasaws, and Shawnees all "unanimously" consented to form a "defensive federation," and that "all should confess"—presumably to any Americans who might ask—that they had asked the Spaniards to build those posts "solely for their protection and utility."[2] One doubts that William Blount, or Andrew Jackson, would have been swayed.

The spring of 1793 found Spanish officials lamenting the difficulty in negotiating a cease-fire between the Creeks and the Chickasaws, and they suspected that Governor Blount might well be clandestinely stoking the fires of "rancor" between them. (They were correct.) More serious still was the renewal of Creek raids on Georgians across the St. Marys River. Aside from bringing American retaliation against the Creeks, it also led the Americans to believe that the raids were "instigated by the Commander of Pensacola," which was not an unreasonable assumption. (Indeed, Washington remained deeply distrustful of Spain's influence in the South.)[3] Spanish officials now lamented what they saw as the greater efficacy that the British had enjoyed in "handling" their Indian allies—like the Americans, they did not fully understand just how reactive, rather than proactive, British policy was. Governor Gayoso de Lemos in Natchez even opined that if Britain threw a decent force of regular troops into Detroit, they could detach the western American provinces and make a far better claim to the Mississippi River than the Americans could. Far from feeling threatened, de Lemos offered that Spain might ally itself with Britain if George III declared war on the United States.[4]

The fluid near-anarchy of European power politics greatly influenced the chess game for Indian allies in North America. Initially, Revolutionary France's declaration of war against Great Britain in 1793 made England and Spain allies for the first time in modern history. Indeed, Carondelet's greater emphasis on Indian alliances sprung in part from a fear that Spain's under-manned American possessions would be attacked by French-backed American adventurers, like George Rogers Clark. Thus, it was not necessarily bad news when Alexander McKee reported in the spring of 1794 that "speeches brought lately into that Country from the Mississippi in the Name of the Spaniards, Southern & Western Indians which seems to have given the Indians in this Quarter great Spirits and made the Nations in General more unanimous than ever in supporting one another and their common Interest."[5] On the contrary, if it frightened the Americans into approving a favorable boundary for the Indian Confederacy, it would be a net gain for Britain. But once Spain made peace with France in 1795, and became a formal military ally against Great Britain in the 1796 [2nd] Treaty of San Ildefonso, the fear of a Spanish-led confederacy would come to deeply influence British–Indian politics.[6]

Centuries of rivalry in the Americas and elsewhere, not to mention Spain's alliance with France during the American Revolution, made some level of tension between George III and Carlos IV unavoidable. In the first few months after the Harmar campaign, Lord Dorchester forwarded reports that "the Spaniards have been tampering with the Indians on the Mississippi," especially the Potawatomis, and that they had also sent war belts "to all the Nations hereabouts, declaring their intentions of going to war with Great Britain."[7] Spanish intrigue among Indian alliances certainly threatened British and American interests in North America, but could never hope to match the panache of a renegade British soldier who claimed to lead the Creek nation.

Though the actors could not have known so at the time, pan-Indianism's greatest chance for success would come in the early 1790s. The diplomatic and military conditions in North America were complex and chaotic. Chaos tends to bring opportunity along with its dangers. Few could provide a better example of this than William Augustus Bowles. While rarely discussed in works about pan-Indian alliances, in many ways Bowles would come to epitomize Americans' fears about race, rebellion, and resistance.

Born in Maryland in 1763, Bowles remained loyal to the Crown and became a teenaged Redcoat ensign during the Revolution. (Pointedly, after 1783 the American press exclusively referred to Bowles as a "British" adventurer, choosing to forget that he spoke with a Frederick, not a London, accent.) Stationed in Pensacola, he resigned his commission in a huff at age sixteen, apparently after having had a falling out with his commanding officer. Casting his uniform coat into the Gulf of Mexico, the suddenly isolated teenager took up with a band of Lower Creeks, with whom he lived off and on for some time. He would marry a Cherokee (probably Chickamauga) woman, and later take a Creek wife as well.[8]

Spain's entrance into the Revolutionary War as France's (though not America's) ally, and her attacks on British Florida, suddenly made New Orleans a tempting target for British troops and Indian warriors. Bowles rejoined the fight as Creek, Chickasaw, and Choctaw war parties sought to be part of the action. Bowles had fought in such Lower Creek parties against Spain, and would at this point have been nominally an ally of Alexander McGillivray. Fighting the Spanish led to his regaining his commission in the British Army and his first (though not last) capture by Spanish forces when they took Fort George in Pensacola. He was paroled from Havana to New York in time for the Patriot victory. There, according to his not especially objective memoir, Bowles was accused of "ungentlemanly conduct" by "jealous" fellow soldiers, primarily because he had been seen bringing in scalps during the war. Though he was officially cleared, the young Marylander had been soiled in the eyes of many. With few other options, he returned to his Creek relatives, who would subsequently make him a chief.[9]

After 1783, Britain relinquished its Florida claims to Spain, which brought a new problem of supply and demand. Spain could not hope to provide all the desired trade goods for its Indian allies in the Southeast, as the Creeks alone may have numbered eighteen thousand. American merchants were eager for the trade, but American land hunger made them incompatible with both Spanish and Indian interests. Reluctantly, Spain would allow the Scots firm of Panton, Leslie & Co. a monopoly on the Indian trade in the Southeast. This made Alexander McGillivray, who had tied himself to William Panton's company partly from necessity, even more influential as he tried to assert his leadership over the Creeks.[10]

Trade monopolies are rarely beneficial to consumers, but the arrangement became truly obnoxious for the Creeks and their neighbors when, in 1788, Spanish policy shifted to a curtailment of arms to their Indian allies in an attempt to win the favor of American frontiersmen, who would (Spain hoped) secede from the United States and become part of, or client states to, the Spanish Empire. In so doing, Spain placed its trust with Westerners like James Wilkinson of Kentucky (already on the Spanish payroll as a "confidential" agent), over Indian leaders like McGillivray. That this was intensely foolish became apparent only in hindsight. That it would be potentially catastrophic for the Southern Indians was readily apparent to the natives themselves, and to Bowles, and it spurred him to seek a solution.[11]

Bowles's decision to outflank Panton and supply the Indians with goods from the Bahamas, while certainly beneficial to them, was not altruistic. It might also make him rich. He enlisted not only traders, but a powerful friend in John Murray, the 4th Earl of Dunmore, who had been appointed the Bahamian governor at Nassau some years after the Revolution drove Bowles from his post as governor of Virginia. The American press proved skeptical, even hostile, toward Bowles, even before they had his name.

A Philadelphia paper printed an extract from a Georgia gentleman's letter, which noted: "A banditti of rascals, consisting of 70 or 80 men from the Bahama Islands, have lately arrived in the southern parts of our state, professedly to join the Indians and plunder the state. They have an armed vessel in an Indian river, south of Augustine, to receive the plunder, consisting of negroes, cattle, &c. It is said with confidence, that Lord Dunmore, Governor of the Bahamas, gives countenance to their proceedings, and that the officers of this abandoned corps frequently dine at his table. By this you may see what you have to expect, should it be your unhappy lot to be attacked under the present poor, weak and unenergetic government of the United States."[12]

It is noteworthy that the correspondent immediately assumed that the "banditti" would be stealing slaves as well as other property. One of Bowles' close associates was the Afro-Creek chief Philatuche, "who had fought for the British in the last war." The headman of Chiaha, Philatuche "probably contributed to its attraction of a sizable black population in the 1790s." This came at a time when the number of both slaves and fugitive former slaves was growing in the Creek and Seminole nations.[13] It is certainly possible that Bowles' interaction with blacks was as troubling to American and Spanish settlers as his close ties to pan-Indianists. Surely Governor Dunmore would have been the last man to object to the idea of arming former slaves to strike at rebellious American colonists.

Ruffling Spanish (or American) feathers, especially for profit, did not bother Dunmore at all—he had taken the job in Nassau largely to rake in profits from illegally trading with Spanish colonies. Further, Dunmore (much like Henry Hamilton) had never relinquished his interest in the Trans-Appalachian West, nor his desire to take revenge upon the Americans. In the Earl's case, he even held out the hope of someday cashing in on old land warrants that had been dashed by the Revolution. But the first priority would be to ingratiate their project to Creek leadership. Dunmore et al. sent Bowles, laden with gifts, to make a deal with McGillivray.[14]

The two men initially got on well—both were Loyalists who "had the dream of uniting the southern Indians with those in the north to form a general confederation to stop the relentless American advance," and both recognized that a steady supply of arms was a necessity. Biographers note the differences between the two—Bowles was a respected warrior, McGillivray an admitted coward. McGillivray had support from the Upper Creeks, while some of the Lower Creeks favored Bowles, and so on. But the key source of their eventual conflict was the inescapable rivalry: both men wanted to be the sole leader of the Creek Nation. McGillivray, related through his mother to the powerful Wind Clan, had a distinct edge in that quest.[15]

Before this deal, which required McGillivray to betray his business partners, could be fully consummated, the Beloved Man was drawn back to the Spanish fold. Madrid had reconsidered the wisdom of trusting the American backwoodsmen, and they reversed their goods embargo. From this point on, the Bowles-McGillivray rivalry would intensify.[16]

By the spring of 1789, Bowles had begun calling himself "Director General of the Creek Nation," a position the Creeks had not previously recognized. In this capacity he and the Lower Creeks at Coweta received "an important Cherokee delegation," led by Dragging Canoe of the Chickamaugas, as well as Hanging Maw and Little Turkey. Bowles promised British protection against the Americans, in the form of reasonably priced wares from his trading partners through Dunmore, as well as a positive answer to the Cherokees' request that George III "take them by the hand" as he had the Northern Indians. Not realizing that Bowles' British authority was unofficial at best,[17] shading toward nonexistent, they further authorized him to take a small diplomatic party with him to make their case in a personal audience with the king. That he was able to con his way to first Quebec, then London, with British officials picking up the tab, spoke volumes for his personal charms and sharp wits.[18]

Part of the difficulty in analyzing diplomacy with Indians in this period comes with the realization that the early West was but one component in a massive global chess game between the United States and the European powers. Bowles' schemes gained credibility and feasibility in British circles because of the ongoing Nootka Sound Crisis. Briefly, Anglo-Spanish rivalry in the Pacific Northwest—Nootka Sound is part of modern Vancouver Island, B.C.—threatened war in early 1790, after Spanish authorities had arrested several British traders and confiscated their ships. Officials as high-ranking as William Grenville, the Home Secretary, held enthusiasm for Bowles' proposals.[19]

Bowles offered to take 20,000 Creek and Cherokee warriors (a considerable exaggeration of their true numbers), and another 20,000 Choctaw and Chickasaw warriors (exaggerated again, and not taking into account the historical antipathy both those nations held for the Creeks), with which he could easily capture Florida, Louisiana, and perhaps Mexico. In a perfect mood for just such ridiculous assertions, Grenville happily scheduled Bowles and his delegation for an audience with the king. But the meeting never took place, thanks to the sudden news that an Anglo-Spanish war, for the moment, had been averted. Having signed the first (of eventually three) "Nootka Conventions" with Spain in October 1790, George III could not risk publicly receiving an envoy who openly advocated an attack upon His Catholic Majesty's holdings in America. Further, as even Lord Dorchester had realized when Bowles visited Canada, American officials were not pleased to hear of Bowles' efforts at pan-Indianism, and in 1790 Britain was eager, even desperate, to avoid open warfare on the American frontier.[20]

Bowles nevertheless boasted of his importance and potential contributions. He claimed that in 1788 the Americans had asked him to lead an attack on the Northern Indians and British outposts in the Great Lakes. He insisted that it was his loyalty to the Crown, and not the nonexistence of the offer, that made him decline. Instead, he could (with British support) forge an alliance between the Creeks, Cherokees, and the Northern Indians. He further claimed that the American settlers of Cumberland, 6,000 of them, would join him in an attack on the Spanish. Out of the absurdity of his claims, or from British diplomatic goals, Bowles' efforts came to naught.[21]

His voyage to Britain threatened to become merely a long holiday—an American paper included an account that in February 1791 Bowles had been "initiated into the mysteries of free masonry." (Given the social-climbing opportunities the Masons provided—George III himself was a member—it might eventually prove useful.) He did manage to prevail upon one Benjamin Baynton to publish what he called the *Authentic Memoirs of William Augustus Bowles, Esquire, Ambassador for the United nations of Creeks and Cherokees, to the Court of London.* The less than subtle exercise in self-fashioning noted that the arms he brought to the Creeks and Cherokees might "one day, perhaps, shake the power of the Spanish empire in South America, and give freedom to the long oppressed and enslaved natives of Montezuma's realm." The memoir tactfully omitted Bowles' challenge to

American settlement, but did note that the Spaniards had placed a price of six thousand dollars and fifteen hundred kegs of rum on his head.[22]

Understandably crushed by the Crown's sudden lack of interest, "Bowles [was] forced to lower his sights." Specifically, he sought to break Panton's monopoly, not only by negotiating with the Spanish—who must have been more amused than interested—and by a more novel approach. The official British position was that, legally, the Creek, or Muskogee, Nation, could dock ships in Nassau for the purposes of trade. Of course, ships required flags to denote their nationality.

Upon his return to Nassau, Bowles had a flag of the Muskogee Nation fabricated: "He specified that a blue cross be superimposed on a red background; the blue background of the upper left hand corner had a sun with human features resembling both an American Indian and Bowles himself." In 1791, the "Director General" sailed for the Indian River in Florida with a cargo of goods for Indian presents and trade, including some three-pounder bronze cannon, pondering both profits and pan-Indianism. By early September, American newspapers had learned of the flag and Muskogee assertions for free trade. Bowles further opined that "in a few years . . . [Muskogee would] vie with, if not exceed, the progress and rapid strides of the states of America."[23]

At the Coweta council in the fall of 1791, Bowles made his case for leadership of the Creeks, blending truth with rumors and wild exaggerations, primarily at the expense of McGillivray. He contended that the latter had committed treason against the Indians at the Treaty of New York. He alerted the assembled that American land speculators, including the Yazoo Company, had made McGillivray a partner. That charge was false, though they had approached McGillivray, and Bowles conveniently neglected to mention that he too had been lobbied by the speculators. The Indians, he argued, "beset by land-grabbing Americans, defrauded by Panton and Spain, and deceived by McGillivray's forked tongue, [and] had no recourse . . . but to follow his lead." Only he could save them, he asserted, ludicrously promising that he could produce "six thousand Bahamian Loyalists" to join the fight against the Americans. As one of his biographers notes, not only did Bowles not have the fleet necessary to carry that many men, but to produce that number "he would have removed almost every man, woman, and child, black or white, from the Islands, and even then he probably would have had to scour the Out-Islands or rob a few graves."[24]

The Director General showed far greater logic and factual consistency when he insisted that a cooperative alliance be formed with the Northwestern Confederacy, and that British arms could flow to the Southern tribes from the Bahamas just as they came to the Confederacy from Canada. Predictably the Upper Creeks disliked his denunciations of McGillivray, and mostly left, but the Lower Creeks and their Seminole relatives were more receptive. McGillivray was of course furious, but ill health made it difficult for him to do more than flee to Pensacola and plot revenge. Bowles, meanwhile, would argue to the Spanish that keeping the Americans at bay served both their interests. Furthermore, if McGillivray seemed determined to let the Americans take Spanish lands through the Treaty of New York and its boundary survey, Bowles on the other hand—with Creek warriors and British guns—could prevent it.[25]

Bowles also tried to negotiate with the Americans, to little positive effect. As later Indian leaders, including those north of the Ohio, would soon find, the United States had little interest in a peace built upon Indian wishes. Further, "The 1790 Creek treaty was a cornerstone of American Indian policy, and Bowles was the chief instrument in preventing surveying the boundary line." Bowles' efforts looked baldly hostile to U.S. designs. Reports filtered in about his trip to London with Indian emissaries, and the uncertain degree of support and authority he had from the British government. He was also (falsely) described as the man who had scuttled the Rock Landing Treaty with the Creeks in 1789—he had already embarked for England before the conference.[26] Articles like "Authentic Intelligence of fresh Disturbances from the Creek Country," coming just as reports of St. Clair's disaster at the Wabash were filtering back from the West, no doubt added to the sense of alarm. The American press noted Bowles' attempts to scuttle the Treaty of New York, and generally held up Alexander McGillivray as a model of faithfulness and decorum in comparison.

Anthony Wayne, only months shy of his appointment to lead the new Legion of the United States, would write of troubling reports that the Creeks would not abide by the Treaty of New York. Part of the problem, it seemed, was "that Mr. Bowles (alias) Genl. William A. Bowls [sic] has rivaled General McGilvery [sic] in the confidence of that Nation." Furthermore, Federal troops in the Georgia theater would be increased to between four hundred and five hundred effectives in case "the Indians become troublesome." Other accounts noted that Bowles was supplying British arms to the Southern

Indians, drawing the ire of Spanish officials, and also fomenting Indian resistance—in the king's name—to American encroachments. More troubling still, he was openly stating that Alexander McGillivray "has deceived the Indians in their treaty made at New York: but that he is willing to form a treaty with the United States in behalf of the Creek nation, and declares that the former treaty shall not be executed."[27]

When reports began circulating (almost a year prematurely) that McGillivray had died, one paper noted, "The probable consequence of this great man's death . . . will be peculiarly unfavourable to the *interests* of the United States; especially when it is confided that Bowles will use every stratagem he is master of to effect the object of his wishes." His *wishes*, of course, included a free Muskogee nation, secure in its lands and sovereignty, which was essentially what McGillivray also wanted. The intractable rivalry remained, however, and the American press had noted with little sorrow that "Indeed, his [McGillivray's] importance, and life, probably depend on Bowles being driven out of the nation."[28] That Americans readily sided with Alexander McGillivray, himself a slave owner, in this contest clearly demonstrates how much they feared Bowles' potential to sow the seeds of pan-Indian resistance, made all the more frightening by his plausible British backing and links to black Creeks like Philatuche.

Westerners obviously followed the Bowles story with heightened interest. Virginian Arthur Campbell deemed him "an infernal Tory," who was "likely to stir up discord to the Southwardly, of which Georgia may be the First victim." McGillivray he dismissed as "by no means a man of firmness." Samuel Newall offered that Bowles was "amongst the Upper Creeks endeavouring to engage them in a war against the United States," and that the stroke would come soon.[29]

Upper Creek chiefs sought advice from the Federal government on how to deal with Bowles, and upon what authority he made his "disturbances." Even the British minister to the United States, Henry Hammond, could not vouch for Bowles' authority, and had to write back to England for guidance. The *Federal Gazette* reported, "There is . . . no room to doubt but that Bowles is assisted in his present operations, and expects to be supported in them, by the government of Great Britain." Yet as with the Shawnees and other pan-Indianists in the North, encouragement of Bowles was strictly unofficial, no matter how many of the king's muskets he handed out. Henry Knox informed McGillivray that Hammond had disavowed

Bowles, and stated the perfectly obvious when he advised that the "bold adventurer" be driven from the Creek Nation. With redundancy as well as urgency, Knox offered, "The United States will support you in any proper measures which you may think proper to pursue" against Bowles—a tacit endorsement of assassination. Knox made a similar note to James Seagrove, the U.S. agent to the Creeks, with the caveat that to avoid exciting McGillivray's "Jealousy," any "strong attempts" against Bowles should first be coordinated with the Beloved Man.[30]

With Spanish naval vessels hindering the efforts to open trading ports in Florida, Muscogee flags be damned, in 1792 Bowles hit upon an idea that would cost him dearly: Why not just attack the thinly defended Panton and Leslie warehouse at St. Marks? Panton had already put a bounty on Bowles' head, after the last time he plundered Panton's stores back in 1788. So what, the Director General figured, did he have to lose? In fact, his bloodless surprise assault on the warehouse, though initially successful, convinced Spanish authorities that to protect Panton, and (through McGillivray) their influence among the Southern Indians, Bowles had to go. Lured onto a Spanish vessel under the pretense of negotiations to be had in New Orleans, Bowles was eventually sent to rot in a Spanish dungeon, with only feeble British diplomatic efforts to secure his release. A correspondent in Havana offered, "it is thought the depredations he has committed on the Spanish settlements will cost him his life," adding (incorrectly) that Bowles had fought against St. Clair's army. With considerable reason, his friends and his enemies assumed Bowles' career among the Creeks, even his existence, had ended. McGillivray, meanwhile, sent word that he would now be attending the running of the boundary line from the Treaty of New York.[31]

Though Bowles' capture was cheered by Knox and other Americans—he noted to the governor of Virginia that it would (along with Agent Seagrove's efforts) "probably restore entire tranquility" among the Creeks. Nevertheless, considerable angst remained that his followers, or even his example, would lead to a broader war. Seagrove was instructed to show the greatest and most polite concern to his Spanish neighbors. If any "desperado similar to Bowles" threatened their citizenry or claims, Seagrove was to alert the closest Spanish officer immediately. Not surprisingly, McGillivray asserted, "Bowles' partisans are some violent fellows . . . who eagerly listen to any vagabonds that will call themselves Englishmen, and will set them on to mischief against the Americans." Agent Seagrove came to fear Bowles had not really been imprisoned by the Spaniards, but was in fact being converted to a double agent, citing (erroneous) reports that Bowles was not actually confined in Spain. Perhaps feeling the strain of his job, Seagrove wrote a second letter the same day, to the same recipient, arguing that Bowles and McGillivray were really in cahoots to "injure Spain" and "re-establish the English with the Creeks."[32]

By August 1792, as some Creek warriors continued to attack settlers along the Tennessee River, Knox noted to McGillivray, "it is painful to reflect, that, after the capture of Bowles, any of his pernicious influence should remain," and blamed this "banditti" upon the "ignorance" of the Creeks who had followed Bowles. A Savannah correspondent wrote to Supreme Court Justice James Iredell that "Great Confusion still prevails among [the Indians] in consequence of the influence of Bowles and his party." Further, given the Indian–white tension on the frontier, he "would not be surprized, if they provoke each other to commit hostilities." Seagrove admonished the Creeks that Bowles' adherents were "rascals" who deserved "severe punishment" for having "kept your land in flame for years." Even worse, Seagrove later wrote President Washington, stating that McGillivray continued to be untrustworthy, and all available data indicated that "the Spaniards will if possible . . . involve the United States in a War with the four Southern Nations of Indians. Every exertion is making by the Spaniards and undue measures taken with the Savages to stir them up against us."[33]

CHAPTER 12

Pan-Indianism Crests

Though Alexander McGillivray was a man of great ambition, he had never been of strong constitution. In February 1793, he died. While he had been one of the primary proponents of pan-Indian resistance in the 1780s, the human tectonics of the frontier and geopolitics had shifted so in the intervening years that some Americans mourned his death, while others concluded that while something of a weasel, he was the weasel they were accustomed to dealing with. One Georgia gentleman, who had an astonishingly short memory, opined that the general Indian war that loomed would not have come were the Beloved Man still alive, "as he was always the friend of peace."[1] McGillivray's death came at a crucial time in the politics of pan-Indianism.

Even while Spain and Britain were ostensibly allies in the European war, they might still be played off against each other for Indian favor, something Indians themselves were quick to utilize. In the spring of 1793, Creek headmen could complain to Alexander McKee in Detroit about the Spaniards' intercepting a ship of trade goods sent them by Governor Dunmore of the Bahamas. They also lamented the Spanish insistence that they trade only with Panton, Leslie, & Co., and that Spanish authorities had arrested William Bowles. The Creek headmen used the pan-Indian alliance as a lever here, noting: "Our whole Nation has taken the Talks of our Brethren the Northern Indians and have commenced War, we have therefore to desire you to give us all the Assistance in your Power, as we are informed by our Brethren the Shawnees you promise us."[2] (Several months later British officials were complaining that the Shawnees had made just such a promise without authorization.)[3] The micos then pointedly noted that "the want of arms & ammunition will be the only thing that will prevent our prosecuting the War, [and] as we have none but what we get from the Spaniards, & which is very little, we are on that account obliged to hold in with them."[4]

Meanwhile, American papers continued to carry accounts of the Creeks being "joined by some tribes of northern Indians, which must prove a stimulus to more open and outrageous operations," as well as stealing (liberating) slaves. In early May, men as expert as South Carolina's General Andrew Pickens felt that "a general Indian war, on the western frontiers at the southern states seems inevitable," though the renewal of Chickasaw–Creek hostilities did give Americans some hope. Creek chiefs, including Cussitah King and Mad Dog, offered Agent Seagrove some perspective, noting that only certain Creek towns, "Cowetas, Broken Arrow, Uchees, Ufuchees, and Talassee," were hostile to the United States. They pleaded that the other towns, "or any friendly Indians that might be out hunting," be spared American vengeance. A piece from the Knoxville *Gazette*, reprinted in Philadelphia, eschewed such nuance. After listing Creek depredations across the Cumberland River, including murder, horse theft, and the scalping of a child, it pronounced that "The Creek nation must be destroyed, or the south western Frontiers, from the mouth of St. Marys to the western extremities of Kentucky and Virginia, will be incessantly harassed by them; and now is the time. Delenda est Carthage," the author concluded in unmistakable, if not especially good, Latin.[5]

While fearing and loathing the Creeks, Americans on the southwestern frontier kept a wary but hopeful eye to the north. General James Robertson in Nashville wrote to Kentucky's governor Isaac Shelby asking for news of Anthony Wayne's progress against the Ohio Indians. "I think much depends on the success of that army," he offered, as Indians would not make and keep a peace until conquered. Further, while Robertson felt the loyalty of the Chickasaws was "past a doubt," the Spanish would nevertheless try to prevent an American peace with the Southern nations generally, and the Chickasaws might have to "accept a Creek vision," and join the war against the United States.

Isaac Shelby, governor of Kentucky, was more cynical. He noted that Chickasaw missives to Robertson, promising to fight the Creeks and the Northern Indians, might prove encouraging news, "if an Indian was to be relied on." Shelby was reluctant to rely on Indians, however. "I am clear that they are too good a Judges of their own interest on both sides to carry this dispute to any considerable length," he concluded. Two months later, his counterpart to the south William Blount believed that peace would be achieved with the Ohio tribes, as Wayne would be aided "by the Militia of the Southern Territory." Once the Ohio victory was achieved, he enthused, then the army could "chastise our perfidious Yellow Brethren to the South."[6]

In the summer of 1793, Lt. Governor Simcoe could note, "the Spanish Governor's pushing on the Choctaws to join the Confederacy, and . . . that the Chickasaws will soon be added to the Confederacy, and that it will be universal through the whole extent of the nations on this side of the Mississippi." Reports indicated the Shawnees held the same view "to the very moment of their returning to the Miamis, [and] that they concealed the treaty now pending, and that Colonel McKee was angry with their proceedings." Simcoe offered, "In this State of Affairs . . . all attempts at pacification will prove abortive." He nevertheless directed McKee, as Indian agent, to try to effect it. Perhaps having learned of France's declaration of war against England, Simcoe felt that any move that might provoke a war with the Americans would draw fire from his superiors—and openly aiding the Southern Indians would certainly do that. For his part, Anthony Wayne noted that a large force of Cherokees and Creeks was making for the Miami country, and that "a Strong confederacy is actually forming against us." Though Simcoe was actually trying to get his Indian allies to stand down, Wayne felt he was only delaying until he was in a position to "dictate boundary lines" or "to let slip the dogs of war."[7] Compounding the already complex situation, British Indian agents on the ground, as well as the confederacy's warriors, openly hoped that Britain would actively intervene, at least in opening up the arms trade to the Southern tribes.

Loyalist trader John McDonald wrote from the Cherokee country that the Southern nations had "throwd [sic] themselves under the protection of his Catholic Majesty" at a treaty conference in Natchez with Governor Gayoso de Lemos in the fall of 1793. The result had been the Treaty of Nogales, which in theory placed the Chickasaws, Cherokees, Creeks, and Choctaws in a mutual defense pact, but because the tribes were so de-centralized, in reality it did nothing.[8] They had done so as a last resort "to enable them to keep possession of the remainder of their country." While McDonald thought that this move would "be attended with happy consequence to the Indians," it would only suffice if they could receive ample arms and goods to continue to resist the Americans. Spain, many concluded, simply could not supply the quality, quantity, or price of goods for this to work. "I cannot help looking in the General way, of the Southern Indians[,] in wishing the return of the British once more to the Floridas," McDonald concluded.[9]

Finances and demography made Henry Knox and other officials wary of any move that might expand the sporadic Indian raids on the Southern frontier into a general war. When confronted with how to counterbalance potential enemies short of outright war, the Americans did what the British had done before them: they sought to strengthen alliances with at least some of the Southern nations, and where possible to quietly encourage wars between others. Like Thomas Gage before him, Knox sought to cultivate the Chickasaws.

The Chickasaws were the least numerous of the four principal tribes in the South, though they also had perhaps the fiercest reputation as warriors. Their territory lay along the Mississippi in western Tennessee and what would become Mississippi, which made them of immediate strategic use. They were also allies and neighbors of the far more numerous Choctaws, who could help balance out the terribly populous Creeks. Further, unlike those of the Cherokees and Creeks, the lands of the Choctaws and Chickasaws were not currently the focus of land hungry settlers—though they obviously would be eventually. So for reasons geographical, military, political, and Machiavellian—Niccolo had advised allying with the weaker of two rivals against the stronger—aiding the Chickasaws in their war against the Creeks made sense.

For the Chickasaws, allying with the United States seemed a practical move as well. While they had been rock-solid allies to the British until 1783—largely because of their enmity toward the French—by the mid-1780s Chickasaw pragmatism dictated an alliance with the former rebels. Further, with the massive Creek advantage in manpower and their strong ties to the Spanish for arms, the Chickasaws desperately needed friends.[10]

While American officers, including George Rogers Clark, had made overtures to the Chickasaws since the early 1780s, by the end of the decade there were serious efforts made by both sides of the courtship. In 1789 Arthur Campbell had suggested that Knox send "An intelligent Officer of the American Troops on the Ohio" to the Chickasaws, to impress the chiefs with America's might—though one could ask, "With what?"—and possibly to bring them in as allies against the Ohio Indians. In a separate letter to Washington, Campbell suggested, "It is a desirable event to confirm the Chickasaws in their ancient goodwill to the Anglo-Americans."[11]

Tennessee settlers understood the dangers and potential benefits of dealing with the Chickasaws and the Choctaws as well. As governor of the Southwestern Territory, William Blount lamented, "the Spaniards are determined to excite the Chickasaws and Chactaws to War." While the territory reeled under the assaults of the Chickamaugas and Creeks, staying in the good graces of the other tribes was imperative. Blount knew that when the Chickasaws asked for corn to stave off starvation, giving them some was prudent and necessary. While he penuriously added, "but it must be done as sparingly as possible as to give them satisfaction," he concluded that maintaining the Chickasaws and Choctaws as allies was "of the utmost importance." He further decreed that "in case you should discover that any part of them are about to Join the Creeks and Cherokees," he should be immediately notified.[12]

Understandably, Blount craved any intelligence possible concerning Indian dalliances with foreign powers. He scolded the Cherokee chief Bloody Fellow, not (he argued) for meeting with the Spanish, "but I have expected that you from your friendship for the United States would have made me acquainted with what was done there." He was quite happy to learn, in early 1793, that the Chickasaw–Creek war would flare up once more, and hoped only for some guidance from the federal level as to what role he should play.[13]

While territorial and federal officials agreed that some aid to the Chickasaws would be prudent, considerable confusion reigned as to how much and what type to send. The Chickasaws had asked repeatedly for arms, ammunition, and other supplies, which would be relatively uncontroversial. But their calls for small artillery pieces caused some to balk. Yet William Tatham, a trader who worked with the Chickasaws, assured the governor of Virginia that they should receive whatever they asked for. The Chickasaws were far too honest, he intoned, to plunder Americans. He advocated giving them not only their own artillery, but also "a strong garrison" at the Muscle Shoals to help protect them and secure a key American post on the Mississippi River. "It is Nature's master-piece for an immense and powerful city. It intercepts the main communication between the Hostile Tribes of North and South. It secures the Chickasaw and Choctaw Nations as effective Light Infantry in our service." And, having strong allies on the Mississippi could only help the Americans in their dealings with Spanish authorities. When unidentified settlers murdered a Chickasaw chief on a friendly visit to Knoxville, Arthur Campbell groaned that the "unlucky accident" might well "give serious offense to the only nation of Indians that are disposed to be a faithful ally."[14]

General James Robertson of Tennessee's Mero district (named after the Spanish governor Miró in the days when American settlers—Robertson included—had flirted with Spanish protection) thought giving the arms, even the fieldpieces, to the Chickasaws a capital idea. Chickasaw headmen had sent him a talk directly, in which they bluntly stated that the Creeks and Northern Indians had tried unsuccessfully to bully them into joining the war against the United States, and that now they made war on the Chickasaws, who were desperately short of food, whisky, and arms. They specifically asked for ten swivel guns—small cannon for mounting on walls—as well as small arms. The complete lack of any secrecy on the frontier brought this information to the Spanish governor of New Orleans, the Baron de Carondelet, who strongly disapproved. Even a small cannon, he intoned, "is an Arm too dangerous in the hands of the Indians." Though there had been some European artillery supplied to Indians in the seventeenth century, cannon were strongly associated with national power and sovereignty in the eighteenth century. Louis XIV's artillery pieces carried the Latin motto *Ultima Ratio Regum*—the Last Argument of Kings.[15] Most European and American leaders sought to exclude native peoples from such debates. Carondelet further asserted that both Spain and the United States should keep the "knowledge and practice" of firing cannon "carefully concealed." He had done as much in his dealing with the Cherokees when they had asked him for such weapons, and prevented attacks by them on the Cumberland region, he claimed, which might easily have been interpreted as a threat of retaliation if the Chickasaws received cannon. The governor further insisted that he had avoided giving such arms to the Creeks, and had even "distracted [them] from being hostile to the Georgians." He also refused to supply arms to Creeks or Chickasaws while their war continued, tactfully omitting that pan-Indianism held far greater benefits for Spanish policy.[16]

While noting that official U.S. policy was to discourage Indians from fighting each other, Knox's War Department nevertheless authorized a sizable shipment of arms to the Chickasaws in 1793. General Anthony Wayne, who at the moment had his hands full training an army north of the Ohio River, was to send the Chickasaws "500 stands of arms [typically a stand of arms meant a serviceable musket, cartridge box, and bayonet] 2000 lbs. Powder[,] 4000 flints[,] 4000 lb. lead[,] 1500 Bushels of corn[,] 50 lbs. Vermillion [paint], [and] 100 gallons whiskey." For such an important task, Wayne took no chances. He sent one of his ablest lieutenants, William Clark—a decade prior to his fame—to deliver the goods, and insisted that the young officer show the greatest tact and prudence when he passed Spanish posts on the Mississippi. Should anyone inquire about the huge shipment of arms, Clark was to say only that they were "compensation to the *Chickasaws* for past Services." It is worth noting that the Chickasaw population was roughly three thousand in the mid-1790s, with approximately nine hundred to one thousand men. The American shipment therefore was arming half the Chickasaws' available warriors— a rather high percentage.[17]

Wayne was also to seek out an armorer from Fort Washington (Cincinnati) to live among them to service broken weapons, and to pay him from the government account. Spanish authorities found the delivery, of which they had strikingly accurate reports, irksome in the extreme. Baron de Carondelet complained bitterly that while he had labored to bring peace between the Creeks and Chickasaws, the arms and supplies went to "Piamingo . . . who has always fomented . . . a party adverse to the interests of the King, and desiring the continuation of the war."[18]

Frontiersmen were always ready, unfortunately, to deliver bullets to Indian allies in a more direct fashion. As David A. Nichols notes, since the late 1780s "gunfire had become the dominant form of communication in the region."[19] In the midst of this perilous era in American relations with the Creeks and Chickamaugas, militia captain John Beard led an unauthorized raid on the village of Hanging Maw, killing nine followers of one of the few Cherokee chiefs who opposed fighting the Americans.[20] It was now "generally believed it will cause them to join with the Creeks and make a general war against this country, from which Cumberland cannot be exempt," noted the worried acting governor of the Southwestern Territory, Dan Smith. While he hoped that the Cherokees could wait patiently until the federal government offered them satisfaction, "I believe at this hour war will be unavoidable by fall at any case, I mean a general one."[21]

For Americans, 1794 began with a strong feeling that an expanded, even general, Indian war would engulf the West. Governor Isaac Shelby of Kentucky predicted "that we shall be attacked by the Creek and Chickamaggy Indians as soon as the winter breaks." Colonel Andrew Lewis in Fort Lee, Virginia, worried that the settlements were particularly vulnerable while the Northern Indians flirted with peace. He reasoned, "those that are unfriendly disposed . . . [may now] fall on our frontiers, with an expectation that the Southern Indians will be blamed for it."[22] It should be noted that scuttling the peace process with what seemed like irrational murders was not a solely white activity. To the north, with chagrin and annoyance Anthony Wayne would report to Secretary Knox that, for all his courting of Joseph Brant, the Mohawk was "tampering with the Hostile Chiefs, & will undoubtedly prevent them from concluding a treaty of peace with the United States if possible."[23]

Francis Preston, a Kentucky congressman in Philadelphia, wrote to his brother back home. When it came to the prospect of peace with the Northwest Confederacy, local opinion, he offered, was "somewhat similar to the Kentuckians," that is, pessimistic. Yet he was sure that most people would welcome a peace "to avoid a further effusion of blood and the amazing expense these wars have occasioned." He glumly added that having run into Governor Blount, he learned that "there is no prospect of a permanent peace with the Southern Indians."[24]

The national government, having no feasible alternative to peace with the Southern Indians, continued to try anyway. The Congress' Committee on Indian Affairs released a report outlining Indian policy, and paid particular attention to provocations in the Southern quarter. Perhaps chastened by the attack on Hanging Maw's village, and the colossal threat it posed for a Creek–Cherokee war on the United States, the committee wanted to give President Washington a firmer hand. In delineating the structure of how militia would be organized in the Southwestern Territory, they noted that Indians should be held to strict compliance with federal treaties. They also laid out the dire consequences for any yahoo (like Captain Beard) who launched an unauthorized assault on the Indians.

> That every officer, noncommissioned officer or private of the militia of the United States, who shall go armed over the mutual boundary line; and commit murder or other depredations upon the Indians,

without being legally authorized thereto, under the President, every such person so offending shall be considered as having voluntarily put himself under military power, and shall be tried by a Court martial, and if convicted of the murder of any Indian, shall suffer death; and if convicted of any offence, short of murder, shall suffer such fines and penalties as shall be adjudged by the said Court martial, not extending to the taking of life.[25]

The committee's findings would heavily influence Secretary Knox's report to the president of December 29, 1794, entitled "Preservation of Peace with the Indians," which was quite blunt in blaming the incursions of "frontier white people" for bringing on much of the violence. Lest anyone miss the dire necessity of preserving peace, Knox wrote that while

> It is certainly an evil to be involved in hostilities with tribes of savages amounting to two or three thousand, as is the case Northwest of the Ohio. But this evil would be greatly increased, were a general Indian war to prevail south of the Ohio; the Indian Warriors of the Four Nations in that quarter not being much short of fourteen thousand, not to advert to the combinations which a general Indian war might produce with the European Powers, with whom the tribes both North and South of the Ohio are connected.

For Knox, that general Indian war south of the Ohio, and the repercussions it would have with the U.S.'s foreign rivals, meant Armageddon. Following Knox's lead, in early 1795 the Senate would pass a bill with wording quite similar to the committee's report, to "Prevent depredations on the Indians South of the river Ohio." It failed in the House by seven votes.[26]

If the American depredations on the Southern nations were unstoppable, then encouraging the Southern tribes to war against each other—stifling pan-Indian sentiment in the process—would have to suffice. Even better, Piomingo and a contingent of pro-American Chickasaws were already helping Anthony Wayne's army in the Ohio country, as were some Choctaws. Piomingo was a man of his word. He accompanied Wayne's army after scolding General Robertson that treating with the "Northward tribes" was foolish, as they were "all ways at war with you, and will be till you whip them." In August 1794, Governor Blount reported that a war between Hanging

Maw's Cherokees and the Creeks was likely. As the Creeks "will have no peace with us," he further asked James Robertson to help him with his "secret Wish." Robertson was to "encourage . . . both the Chickasaws and Choctaws to fall on the Creeks."[27]

The year 1794 proved the high water mark for pan-Indianism's potential. Despite the deaths of Dragging Canoe (1792) and Alexander McGillivray (1793), and the involuntary departure of William Bowles (1792), had the Northwest Confederacy defeated another American army, it might have convinced fence-sitting warriors south of the Ohio to join in the resistance. Instead, Anthony Wayne's army, though it did not crush the confederacy on the battlefield at Fallen Timbers (August 20, 1794), did drive them from it. The true American victory came from diplomacy. Wayne marched to the very gates of Fort Miami, and to the shock and horror of the Confederacy's warriors, the British refused to start an Anglo-American war by helping their Indian allies. More damningly, rumors would slowly filter into Indian country of John Jay's treaty (1794) with Britain, in which the king agreed to pull his troops not only from Fort Miami, but also from Detroit and the other posts in American territory. Wayne would call the Confederacy to a treaty council at Fort Greenville (Ohio) for the summer of 1795.[28]

From Upper Canada, John Graves Simcoe had sensed the impending collapse of pan-Indianism, and the Indian buffer state he so desperately wanted, since at least March 1794. He warned, five months before Wayne's victory at Fallen Timbers, that reports indicated that the Iroquois would "be as submissive as the Western Indians to such terms as General Wayne shall dictate." He concluded that if the Northwestern Confederacy made peace, the Southern nations' resistance would prove futile, and repeated his request for more regular troops to forestall a possible American or Indian assault on the Canadian posts.[29] Americans, especially in the West, could rejoice that peace might finally be established north of the Ohio (for the first time since the mid-1770s). With (understandably) far more enthusiasm than Simcoe, Arthur Campbell confidently wrote the governor of Virginia in early 1795 that "The intended treaty North-west of the Ohio will have an influence with the Southern Indians," who would certainly have spies at the council.[30]

One might assume that in the aftermath of Fallen Timbers, and particularly after the Greenville Treaty, Wayne could relax and savor the victory. Quite the opposite was true. Rumors and threats of pan-Indian alliances, with foreign intervention, continued to plague the general. Francis Vigo, the Vincennes trader and Patriot, notified Wayne (incorrectly, it turned out) that the French had taken Fort Mobile, and that the commandant of New Orleans had declared war on the U.S. Creek and Cherokee war parties continued to strike at the Cumberland settlements, and would "Seldom leave that place without borrowing a few Scalps and Some Horses." While Timothy Pickering, the new Secretary of War, could write enthusiastically that the "hostile Indians" were sincere in their calls for peace, Wayne received intelligence that wampum belts from the south circulated north of the Ohio, inviting "all Red peoples not to make peace with the United States, but to continue the war."[31]

Wayne wrote Col. James O'Hara in February 1795, "Had I the means I wou'd prefer separate treaties in order to avoid the idea of *a General Confederacy*, but the disposition of those people must be consulted." Shortly before the negotiations at Greenville were to begin, Wayne felt beset on all sides, and the desperately needed peace treaty seemed in jeopardy. "The British agents have descended to mischief of the basest & meanest Artifices to prevent an amicable treaty from taking place," he groaned. Worse still, "they have been but too much assisted by such men as [William] *Whitesides* [a frontiersman] belonging to the State of Kentucky [who had murdered a sugar-making party of Miamis, including women and children] upon a very recent Occasion!" Wayne continually referred to the situation north of the Ohio as "the Crisis." Not being one to shrink from a challenge, however, Wayne simply re-doubled his efforts. He noted to Secretary Pickering that he would make a great show of strength at the treaty council, "should the Indians be stimulated to imitate the conduct of the famous Pondiac in his attempt on Detroit."[32]

As the specter of Pontiac continued to haunt the minds of Anglo-Americans, more concrete threats on the ground also drew Wayne's attention. First, American settlers themselves were often to blame. Three days after blasting British agents for stirring up opposition to the Greenville treaty, Wayne bitterly concluded that "It wou'd appear that certain evil disposed people in the State of Kentucky are determined to prevent an amicable treaty taking place between the United States & the Indian tribes North west of the Ohio & to whose aggressions may justly be attributed all the recent depredations committed by the Savages." In addition to the "gang of marauders" under Whitesides who had murdered the Indian sugar-makers in Illinois, other Kentuckians, including a Parson Findley, had attacked Indian camps on the Ohio, bent on plunder and murder. Knowing that such outrageous acts could extend the war and bring retaliation upon other settlers, an exasperated Wayne offered that the parson could "not be a disciple of the meek Jesus, otherwise he wou'd not thus wantonly bring war & desolation upon the innocent, by the simple aggressions of his Guilty horde of plunderers." The only bright spot was that timely notification of a similarly homicidal expedition was thwarted when the local Army officer was able to warn the intended Indian victims.[33]

Wayne was able to negotiate a successful treaty at Greenville in the summer of 1795. In addition to a great cession of land, the treaty also ushered in a general peace to a region that had been continually at war for two decades. Still, the American situation west of the Appalachians, and with a potential pan-Indian confederation, remained in "crisis." The Greenville Treaty had barely concluded when Wayne received reports that the Spanish were building a strong post at the Chickasaw Bluffs on the east side of the Mississippi River (present Memphis, Tennessee). In so doing, the Spanish had obviously secured at least a small cession of Chickasaw territory on what the United States clearly considered its own land. While American officials might have presumed that the large shipment of arms sent the Chickasaws in 1793 had purchased some loyalty, neglecting to build the fort Piomingo's people had also requested left Spain some diplomatic daylight. In a time-honored technique, the Chickasaws sought multiple means of support during their ongoing war with the Creeks.

Wayne was, of course, furious. He was too smart to start a war, however. In September 1795 he sent a "flag"—once again the very capable William Clark, to politely inquire of the Spanish just what the hell they were doing building a new fort on American soil. Wayne also sent private instructions to Clark. Not only was he to take notice of Spanish troop strength and any advantageous geographical features, but also to bring any packages from the Spaniards addressed to anyone in the Army directly to headquarters unopened, which was likely a veiled reference to General James Wilkinson's Spanish shenanigans.[34]

Wayne had immediately recognized the inherent dangers of simply allowing the Spanish such direct intercourse with a Southern Indian nation. He noted that the precedent could easily escalate, and allow the United States to seek land cessions from the Creeks, Choctaws, or other nations living in the Floridas. Wayne held his tongue, to the Spanish at least, and waited for further instructions. Eventually, diplomacy won out. With the treaties of San Lorenzo (Pinckney's Treaty) and the second treaty of San Ildefonso, Spain decided that peace with the United States and France, respectively, was more important than maintaining broad Indian alliances in the American Southeast. This proved a bitter pill for the Baron De Carondelet, as the situation "snatched defeat from the jaws of victory," and negated the laborious efforts to secure alliances with the Southern nations. Spain evacuated and burned the post in 1797. It proved yet another damaging blow to pan-Indianists seeking to stem American expansionism.[35]

Several factors both within and without the United States had combined to kill off pan-Indianism in the mid-1790s. Wayne's victory at Fallen Timbers had broken the Northwestern Confederacy's momentum. Britain's refusal to join them in an outright war, demonstrated both after the battle and with Jay's Treaty (which Wayne read to them for the first time at the council), broke their hearts.[36] At the Treaty of Greenville, they would mark a document ceding almost three-fourths of what would become Ohio to the United States, and inaugurate a peace north of the Ohio River for the first time in two decades. Indian militants in the South fell victim to forces beyond their control. Spain misinterpreted Jay's Treaty, which had prevented war between Britain and the United States, as a strong alliance. Not wanting to be left out in the North American cold, they signed the Treaty of San Lorenzo (ratified 1796). The treaty considerably thawed Spanish–American relations, as Spain guaranteed American navigation of the Mississippi River and agreed to abandon its posts north of Florida, including at the Chickasaw Bluffs. In addition, Spain's capitulation to Revolutionary France (1795), and declaration of war on England (1796), ended any hopes of a joint Anglo-Spanish war against the Americans, and decidedly shifted Spanish priorities back to their defensive doldrums.[37] A brief return to the plight of the Chickasaws illustrates just how the game had changed.

In early 1795, months before Wayne's Treaty of Greenville, James Robertson and William Blount had responded with borderline glee to the news that some Chickasaws had fallen upon a party of Creeks, scalping all five. This Creek party had apparently been making for the Nashville area with malice aforethought, "evidenced by a war Club and other tokens of the kind, as much as Halters bridles and Spurs [for horse-stealing], and Pack

Saddles which they were making." Blount in particular was thrilled with the news, though he did allow that President Washington would probably not approve of the renewed violence. Blount's solution: continue to encourage the Chickasaws to kill Creeks until they got official word from Washington to stop.[38]

The Baron de Carondelet was still calling for a pan-Indian alliance in the South, but by the spring of 1795 he had chosen a new target. While exhorting the Creeks to continue to fight the encroachments of the Georgians, who had sold the lands of the Creeks, Choctaws, Chickasaws, and Cherokees "against the right of all nations," he also warned of the "French[,] enemies to your nation[,] to the Spaniards and the English." The French, he argued, would take Creek lands in East Florida. French agents had indeed remained on Amelia Island (northeast Florida) in 1794 and 1795, hoping to aid an invasion of Spanish Florida, though their desire to take Creek lands was most likely a fib on the baron's part.[39]

"Instead of uniting your nations all together in one body in your own behalf," he continued, "and for your common defense, you go to war against the Chickasaws. Thus while you mutually and actually destroy each other, you will be expelled from your lands, and then what will be your fate & the fate of all your nations?" He admonished the Creeks to end their war with the Chickasaws, and to unite with them and the Choctaws. "Do not be so foolish as to kill one another," he intoned, adding, "and should you be attacked, the Spaniards your faithful friends and allies, will support you and give you as many arms and as much ammunition as you may want."[40]

Less than two months later, as Wayne's peace council with the Northwestern Indians loomed, Blount and the War Department sought to cap the Creek–Chickasaw war that they had encouraged for years. Blount warned General Robertson that Nashville's citizenry—who had decided to go to the Chickasaws to help them fend off an expected attack from the Creeks— should desist, as the president would surely not approve.[41] And any supplies they had for the Chickasaws should be on a "carry-out" basis only. It would be unseemly for Americans to be seen taking supplies directly to the Chickasaws. Timothy Pickering, who succeeded Knox as Secretary of War in January 1795, soon added that as a peace with Northwestern Indians was imminent, federal gifts to the other nations could be expected to drop off drastically. Furthermore, "of course no more Chickasaws or Choctaws [would be] required to join our troops." Blount also endorsed Robertson's idea to ask the Choctaws to serve as mediators in the Creek–Chickasaw war, and wanted the Chickasaws informed that if they continued the war "they are not to expect supplies of any kind from the United States."[42] If the Creeks were willing to keep the peace with the United States, and pan-Indianism seemed slain, then Chickasaw motivations were considered inconsequential.

The Chickasaws did eke out one small victory in the process. For years they had begged to have cannon sent to them for their defense. Americans and Europeans alike had balked at the idea of giving fieldpieces to Indians—recall Carondelet's protests. Secretary Pickering and Governor Blount therefore directed General Robertson not to forward them "the six Howitzers, with powder and ball" that had been sent from Cincinnati for their use. Both were more than peeved to learn that Robertson had already sent them on—perhaps the only instance of the United States providing cannon to Native Americans. Robertson was in hot water for a time—Blount began referring to him as "James Robertson, Esq." rather than "General Robertson,"[43] and he would be forced to resign his commission. Doubtless, however, the delivery made Robertson's job far easier when he was later named U.S. Agent to the Chickasaw Nation.

Carondelet was not the only one who thought France posed a threat in North America. French officials had high hopes in that regard. As François Furstenberg asserts, "From the perspective of Paris, it was unclear that France had been permanently chased from North America in 1763." Frenchmen had remained, as traders, military officers (in "Spanish" Louisiana) and settlers, all with strong ties to the Indians. French policy retained its goal of driving a wedge between any Anglo-American rapprochement, and hopefully to keep the United States as a small "French client state."[44]

French agents, especially the infamous Edmund Genet, did their best to violate U.S. neutrality in the Anglo-French War (which, to be fair, had abrogated America's 1778 "permanent" alliance with France.) In addition to recruiting privateers from American ports, Genet (through a French agent) hired George Rogers Clark, the down and out former hero of the Revolution, to take New Orleans from Spain. "Identifying himself in a published proposal for volunteers as 'Major General in the Armies of France, and Commander in Chief of the French Revolutionary Legions on the Mississippi River.' . . . Clark claimed that his soldiers had abandoned their allegiance to the United States in favor of France, a power they believed would look with greater solicitude on their commercial interests."

Despite what Clark might argue, the Washington administration was not amused. Though they would have welcomed a Spanish expulsion from New Orleans, they had no intention of risking a war with Spain (and possibly Britain) to do so. (In the *Centinel of the North-Western Territory*, for example, Clark's call for volunteers was printed on January 24, 1794, adjacent to a proclamation from the governor of the territory declaring that any man joining such an expedition would be arrested.)[45] As long as there was the faintest chance of foreign intervention in the American West, which would of course prominently feature pan-Indian auxiliaries, the young republic would remain uneasy and prone to nightmares.

CHAPTER **13**

The Fear Remains the Same

With the Treaty of Greenville in the Ohio country and subsequent pacts with the Southern nations, pan-Indianism slumbered for the remainder of the 1790s. By keeping the Indian nations from forming a true trans-Ohio confederation, the American government allowed the survival of its own union. Despicable murders on the frontier marred, but did not seriously threaten, the peace, and Indians and frontier Americans stood down, exhausted from two decades of ferocious combat. Though the chance of a general Indian war with foreign support was slight by the late 1790s, the fear itself continued to haunt the frontier. In March 1797, a Brooke County Virginian[1] wrote his governor about his recent visit to the Delaware Indians. They were, he gratefully acknowledged, friendly and peacefully disposed. However, they had also been "solicited to the contrary by the Spaniards (or their agents) from whom they informed me the nations had received a belt and speech purporting that the United States had deceived them" at the Treaty of Greenville.[2]

Later that summer, John Sevier, now governor of the new state of Tennessee, reported his concerns to his U.S. senator, William Cocke. Cherokees were "daily moving into the Spanish Dominions, and I am sorry to add, numbers of whites also." Sevier blamed the ineffectual nature of the federal government, which some settlers felt paid more attention to Indians' concerns than those of whites. If many more Americans migrated to Louisiana, and a war were to break out, he pondered, it might pose a major threat to Tennessee's security. More ominously, he added, "I have received information which I think can be relied on that a delegation from the southern tribes, and many of the northern, are holding a council with the Spaniards some where in the vicinity of New Madrid."[3]

165

Such rumors could not stay out of the newspapers for long. The *Kentucky Gazette* printed a letter from a Pittsburgh man who informed the editor that the fears of a rebellion among the people of Natchez were unfounded. Unfortunately, "It is at Kaskaskias and in the neighbourhood of that place, that the French settlers have been instigated by Spanish and French emissaries to throw off their allegiance to the United States and erect the standard of the French republic." Worse still, these "wicked French emissaries" were trying to recruit Indian allies against the United States, and "a party of savages . . . actually attempted to get possession of Fort Recovery." Even more troubling, French agents were reported to be speaking to the Senecas under the pro-American chief Cornplanter, stating that the Indians "would never be happy until their old friends the French were in possession of the country again . . . and there is reason to fear the vile incendiaries who are now among the western tribes will be too successful in their endeavours to kindle the flames of another bloody war on our frontier." One month later, however, the *Gazette* reported that the Indians to the west were friendly to Americans.[4]

Congress was not idle in the wake of the peace established in 1795–1796. To maintain, or enhance, control of Indian affairs within American borders, it was decided to block foreign traders from dealing with, and influencing, Indians within American borders. The Act for establishing Trading Houses with the Indian Tribes was passed in 1796. As one Congressman noted, "This bill has for its object the Promotion of Trade and Intercourse with the Indian Tribes, so as to conciliate their affections to the Citizens of the United States, and thereby defeat the influence of the Schemes and Intrigues of the British Traders which have had so much agency in creating and in protracting the disturbances between our frontier Inhabitants and the Indian Tribes." The trading houses were not meant to run at a profit, but to merely to establish a monopoly for both American goods and influence.[5] Establishing a monopoly on frontier imaginations, however, would be far more difficult.

The summer of 1798 saw still more rumors of French (and Spanish) agents among the Southern Indians, especially in Natchez. The Choctaws, in particular, seemed to favor the French, even to the point of bearing arms against the United States. The picture was further blurred by Zachariah Cox, the noted land speculator, who had formed a small army to help him trade along the Mississippi River.⁶ None could say for sure what his motives were, though "all seem to agree that his intentions are inimical to our government."⁷

Tennessee's Congressman William C. C. Claiborne, the future governor of the Mississippi Territory, was of course sensitive to Indian affairs and the possibility of foreign intervention in the Southwest. He recorded his frustration at the failure of recent councils to buy land from the Indians. Somewhat myopically, he observed that "The *Obstinacy* and *perverseness* of *the Indian*, cannot well be accounted for," in their reluctance to sell their most valuable resource. "It is attributed by some to French and Spanish Intrigue, but in my opinion, it arises *principally* from the improper management of Indian affairs, on the part of the U. States." The problem was not Americans' impatience and greed for land. Instead, Claiborne insisted, the Adams administration had made "too many sacrifices . . . to their friendship, and they are impressed with an opinion, that the General Government are more attached to their *welfare & happiness*, than to that of the Frontier Citizens." Claiborne, a Republican, was anticipating the Jeffersonian land policy that would dominate the early nineteenth century.⁸

By 1800, American officials still saw a plot to stir Indian resistance coming from Spanish authorities. Franchimastabé, a Choctaw headman, told American agents "that a great part of the Indians had gone to Orleans to receive their presents from the Spaniards, we passed on to the Six Towns all the Indians were gone from them, they said by invitation of the Spanish officers." Why the Spaniards would call a conference in the winter puzzled them. "Yesterday a chief by the Name of Tastehoma who we sent to Orleans as a spy returned, he says that the Indians received very good presents, and some of the old Spanish Chiefs received extraordinary presents, and invited them to return in the Spring and they should receive liberal presents." The Indians had been further informed that the Spaniards "were not in their hearts friendly to the United States, but by treaty they must act so." At the spring conference, it was feared, Spain's true colors would show, and "the results will be unfriendly to government." At least, the agent concluded that regarding the Chickasaws, there was "no danger of their joining any power against the United States."⁹

Nothing came of the alleged Franco-Spanish conspiracy, but a similar panic gripped Upper Canada. The pan-Indian rumors came at a particularly vulnerable time for Peter Russell, the acting Lieutenant Governor. Russell, a former soldier and problematic gambler, had been filling in for John Graves Simcoe, who—broken by illness and the failure of his plans for attacking the United States—had taken a leave of absence in late 1795. By this time, Russell surmised that Simcoe would not return, and hoped to be appointed in his stead.[10] His desire for the post—and a steady salary—probably made him more anxious than usual about his temporary position, and the anxiety only increased when he learned of the death of the venerable Indian agent Alexander McKee.

McKee had picked an awful time to die, Russell must have thought, when in February 1799 he began receiving disturbing reports. A runner sent by Joseph Brant informed him that "a Belt of white Wampum has been sent thro' the Caughnawaugas in Lower Canada by 4000 Southern Indians (Friends to the Spaniards) who are said to be assembled at the mouth of the Mississippi to the Ottawas & other Western Indians." The belt was said to be an invitation to join an "attack on the frontiers of the United States, or this Province and threatening Destruction to those Tribes, who shall refuse, or obstruct their designs."[A true war belt would have been colored black or red.] Russell had some doubts as to the veracity of the reports, in particular the notion that so large a body of Indians could have gathered without the Americans getting wind of it. But there was no such thing as excessive caution when dealing with pan-Indian alliances.

"I judge it my duty not to slight it," Russell continued, and detailed how he had sent orders to hold 2,000 militia in readiness, and had already directed the purchasing agent to contract for a year's worth of rations for 1,500 men. He felt that, with these resources, even without additional support from Lower Canada (Quebec), he could defend against the Indian force, as long as they were "unsupported by French or Spanish Troops." To secure the advance warning necessary for defense, Russell sent "Trusty persons" to scan the Mississippi River and its tributaries (which lay in U.S. territory) "to watch the Movements and designs of the Indians in those quarters." He even hinted at an alliance between Canada and the United States if "French Emissaries have actually persuaded the southern & Western Indians to join in an attempt against this Country." The suggestion of alliance between the United States and Britain, despite the hostility of much of the previous decade, was more than plausible. In the wake of the XYZ Affair and the Quasi-War with France, the Adams administration and Whitehall had become far closer, and the Federalists had even "offered to send troops to help defend Canada in the event of a French invasion." Presumably the offer would have stood for a French-backed attack by Indians as well.[11]

Russell was not alone in his fears of this massive Franco-Indian army moving up the Mississippi. Apparently the dying Colonel McKee had considered the threat viable, and had reflexively gone to the standard procedure for thwarting pan-Indianism—seeking native allies. He had suggested recruiting the Sioux and Menominees to join some British officers to meet the invaders. The Sioux, he offered, were "a Nation Unquestionably composing the best Indians Warriors in America, are all mounted and muster about 6000 men," while the Menominees were "our old friends & fellow soldiers." The situation remained tense for Russell and the citizens of Upper Canada until April, when he could finally report that the whole threat had been a false alarm. Two months later he learned that Peter Hunter had been appointed the new Lieutenant Governor.[12]

Pan-Indianism missed its chance in the early 1790s, undone perhaps by unfortunate timing as much as the extraordinary diplomatic difficulties involved. The years 1795–1805 saw a considerable relaxation of Indian–white tensions in the West, if only because exhausted warriors on both sides seemed uninterested in a full-scale military conflict. With growing hubris, American settlers and government officials began to take the notion of Indians' dispossession as inevitable. But the dreamy embers of a broad, multitribal alliance to defend Indian lands had not been completely extinguished. Events and policies during the presidency of Thomas Jefferson would fan them back into flames.

Despite having won the presidential election of 1800 by the slimmest of margins, and that by just barely edging his own running mate, Thomas Jefferson brimmed with confidence and self-righteousness. Nowhere was this clearer than in his direction of Indian affairs. With his penchant for simultaneously embracing opposing concepts—spendthrift champion of economy, antislavery slave owner, etc.—Jefferson sought a rapid acquisition of Indian lands on the cheap. He was correct in noting that purchasing Indian land title quickly and for pennies on the acre would please white yeomen. Just how he could alienate Indian land title without alienating (and infuriating) Indians went unanswered.[13]

One of Jefferson's contradictions—Francophilia mixed with Francophobia—was a common one. Especially since the "Quasi-War" during John Adams' presidency, many Americans had come to fear Revolutionary France, even as they still cheered the downfall of a monarchy. Concerns about France's influence—militarily and sociopolitically—came at Americans from a dizzying variety of angles, and many of them were perfectly rational.

For one thing, French traders, though not acting in any official capacity, had continued to work with Indians in North America since 1763. While never as dangerous as British officials had charged in the mid-1760s, the idea that Frenchmen held an almost magical sway over Indian sentiments remained a potent theme in Anglo-American minds. In the conspiratorial mindset of the eighteenth and early nineteenth centuries, few seemed ready to accept that the rants of an odd French canoeman or two did not necessarily constitute official policy. Rumors swirled from time to time about "painted Indians" being "exhorted by a Frenchman to 'accomplish the object for which they started'"—in this case to stop further surveying of Indian lands.[14]

Of course nothing made rumors of French perfidy and intrigue more frightening than the actual plans of French officials, and eventually Napoleon himself. Since at least the mid-1790s, "French policymakers came to realize that they could no longer depend on their fickle ally," the United States, for help in maintaining the Caribbean wing of their empire. Sugar and slaves generated enormous profits for France, just as they had for other nations with island plantation colonies in the region. For France, the cash machine of St. Domingue would be fueled by Louisiana. It took little effort for American imaginations to picture a massive "transracial" army of blacks, mulattos, and Indians bearing French muskets and wreaking havoc. Indeed, during the Quasi-War, French officials had "seriously considered" landing an army of black soldiers in the American South and in British Jamaica, with the explicit intent of sparking slave revolts. The idea of such a force attacking Southern plantations continued to haunt George Washington, even in retirement.[15]

When Napoleon took the Revolution's reins in 1799–1800, Louisiana remained a key part of his plans for St. Domingue, at least initially, which was why he duped Spain into a retrocession of the territory in 1800. In his "revived imperial system," Louisiana would serve as a combination food pantry/lumberyard for the Caribbean colonies, "thereby avoiding dependence on the United States for supplies." It was not to be, however. Efforts to retake (and re-enslave) the black revolutionaries, though leading to the treacherous capture and pitiful death of Toussaint Louverture, would eventually cost Napoleon at least 50,000 troops lost, thanks to fierce resistance and yellow fever. It was an unmitigated military disaster—even by French historical standards. Once St. Domingue was obviously lost for good, "Napoleon had neither the means nor the incentive to take control of Louisiana." Selling the vast territory to the United States accomplished two aims in particular: it brought much needed cash for new French armies, and like the cession to Spain in 1763, "it kept the territory out of British hands."[16]

For their part, American officials had lusted after Louisiana—and especially the all-important city of New Orleans—since at least 1783. Once rumors of the retrocession to France made it to Thomas Jefferson's ears, that lust mixed with terror to create a feeling of existential crisis. Jefferson feared not only Bonaparte's aggressiveness, but also the way that Indians welcomed news of a French return. As he wrote in early 1803 to the Indiana Territory's governor, William Henry Harrison, "The occupation of New Orleans, hourly expected, by the French, is already felt like a light breeze by the Indians. You know the sentiments they entertain of that nation; under the hope of their protection they will immediately stiffen against land cessions to us." Jefferson directed Harrison to grab what lands he could quickly. The governor did not disappoint.[17]

Jefferson was not alone in fearing French influence from Louisiana. Newspaper accounts from early 1803 on warned that Spanish officials had been telling Indians the French "would take their red brethren by the hand, and assist them to drive the Americans from the lands of which they dispossessed them." French agents had supposedly "already invited the head men and warriors of the Creeks, Chickasaws, Choctaws and Shawanese," to meet with the French at Mobile. "Those who recollect or have read of the French, and the ascendancy they gained over the children of the forest in times of old, can readily conjecture what kind of neighbors the French in Louisiana are likely to prove."[18]

Though Jeffersonians made a point of insisting that they operated from principles diametrically opposed to those of the Federalists, in truth they were at least as imperialist as the Hamiltonians, if not more so.[19] For Jefferson acquiring new lands and "civilizing" the people already living on them was both good politics and sound policy. Acquiring Louisiana, or at the very least New Orleans, became Jefferson's top priority, as it would become his presidency's greatest triumph. The president himself had noted to

Secretary of State James Madison that "St. Domingo" was impeding France's progress taking possession of Louisiana—though he did not know to what degree—and urged his fellow Virginian to make haste to France for the purchase. Once there, American negotiators skillfully used their military weakness as a diplomatic strength, noting that the British navy might move against New Orleans and the Mississippi if they remained in French hands. Napoleon agreed, and the deal was made. While Britain was perfectly happy to let the United States acquire Louisiana, denying it to Bonaparte, "Britain's Native American allies, alas, were not consulted, and would not have agreed."[20]

PART III

Paternalism vs. Pan-Indianism

Though pan-Indian efforts had their best chance of success in the early 1790s, the most famous attempt would come with the Shawnee war chief Tecumseh and his brother Tenskwatawa immediately before and during the War of 1812. Tecumseh's recruiting efforts among the Southern Indians, while far from original, became legendary. To Americans, the Shawnee brothers' connections to the British were the stuff of infamy. Having perfected their anti-Indian rhetoric and their conflation of British and Indian perfidy since the Revolution, Americans were as well equipped to fight Britons and Indians symbolically in the War of 1812 as they were unprepared to fight it militarily. The war against British forces was often humiliating, but the efforts to crush Indian resistance on both sides of the Ohio proved far too effective. Combining "Indian-hating" rhetoric with anti-British and anti-Spanish saber-rattling, Andrew Jackson and other Americans in the Southeast would attack pan-Indianism directly by crushing the "Red Stick" Creeks who had heard Tecumseh's calls to resist the Americans and assimilation. Jackson would also punish his Indian allies at subsequent peace treaties, driving home the point that opportunism as well as military security fueled his campaigns. Revealingly, having fought two major wars against Britain and its Indian allies, thwarting pan-Indian designs in the process, Americans would prove slow to relinquish those themes.

While the plausibility of pan-Indianism declined, the rising slave population in the South added credibility to the fear of slave rebellions, especially in conjunction with Indian warriors. Americans marshaled race-baiting and patriotism to rally against pan-Indian leaders, maroons, and their (tardy) British allies. The specter of slave rebellions with possible links to Indian militants was even more effective than it had been in the 1790s.

Though many in the United States bitterly opposed the Republicans' efforts to bring on the War of 1812, once it began in earnest enough citizens (especially in the West) rallied to the cause. While the effort against British military and naval forces was often lackluster, pan-Indian threats brought out the best (and worst) in fighting men on both sides of the Ohio. When white Americans' racial hegemony and the lust for Indian lands combined, pan-Indianists and former slaves stood little hope without significant foreign aid. Despite the protests of Andrew Jackson, William Henry Harrison, and others, that foreign aid was generally slight and, in the Southeast, terminally late. From 1814 on, when most pan-Indian bones were in the ground or bleaching in the fields, the American state slowly rolled over Indian friend and foe alike in the quest to possess more and more territory.

CHAPTER **14**

Bowles, Part Two

As if the disposition of the Indians, and the Southern Indians especially, had not seemed convoluted enough in the late 1790s, in May 1799 the American press began running reports from England that only deepened the confusion. Bowles was loose. Though the Spanish had clearly hoped to keep William Augustus Bowles quietly out of the way, he had other plans. Shortly after his capture in 1792, he was taken to Cadiz for confinement. Bowles "expressed himself much surprised that he was not treated as a state prisoner, and carried to the castle." A great throng of onlookers delayed his movement to his prison. "He threatened the Spaniards with the revenge of his nation on their American settlements for the treatment he received. It is expected he will shortly take his trial for the depredations committed, which will probably cost him his life." The next spring, some of his Creek followers expressed their dismay to Alexander McKee, noting that the Spanish had taken their "very good friend" Bowles, "for whom [they] grieve[d] much."[1]

But now, in a tale that could have been written by Homer, he had escaped. As a celebratory notice in a London paper noted, Bowles had been illegally detained by the Spanish for six years. (The paper tactfully omitted that the British government, despite the entreaties of Lord Dunmore, had done next to nothing to secure his release.)[2] After their "various interrogatories" failed, the Spanish "resorted to the singular measure of embarking him on board a galleon, for the Spanish colonies." He was taken to Peru, and from thence to Manila, then back to Europe, and finally to the coast of Africa, where Bowles eventually made his escape to England.

"His health had been extremely injured by the length of his confinement, and change of climate," the article noted in scolding tone, "but during a residence of five months in this country, it has been completely re-established." Now he would return to the Creeks. The article concluded, "he is now going to resume his station among a People, whose welfare and prosperity depend so much upon the exertion, good sense and activity of this extraordinary man."[3] While Americans increasingly self-fashioned their identity as the civilized opponents of Indian savagery, Britons came to see themselves as noble for aiding (pan) Indian resistance.

Predictably American newspapermen were far less pleased with the Director General's escape. "It is to be hoped that our government will not fail to order the seizure of this British emissary, who is coming into the heart of our Indian country," noted one Philadelphia paper. The timing of Bowles' release, as much as anything else, seemed to reveal a great conspiracy. Though flatly stating that the "numerous and warlike" Creeks could not seriously threaten the United States, the article also observed that if they attacked it would be "monstrous indeed." At this point the editor seemed incapable of stopping himself. Noting that John Graves Simcoe was leaving Upper Canada for, supposedly, the Gulf of Mexico, he offered that "Simcoe, is well acquainted with the leaders of the American Indian tribes, having studied that object in Upper Canada. It was given out that he was going to the government of St. Domingo [*sic*], though it is either French or is independent. This is a cover for Louisiana, perhaps. If, however, Bowles is sent from the British into our Indian country, it will be a violation of our territorial rights." He went on to postulate that a British fleet in the Gulf was probably heading for either Louisiana or Cuba, and that the 15,000 troops Britain was reportedly sending to Portugal (to fight in the Peninsular Campaign) would be an insignificant number there, ergo they must really be heading for Louisiana. The exhausting leaps of logic necessary to follow the argument concluded with, "We hope both *French* and *British* troops will keep of[f] this continent. If we can preserve our peace, thro' this extreme year, we shall probably be in little future danger."[4]

While it would be both humorous and easy to dismiss such musings as an early version of a tinfoil-hat conspiracy theorist, in truth the uncertainty and potential peril of the international picture, and Bowles' exact role it in, made such rants more commonplace than comical. Furthermore, officials in Whitehall in this era were willing to listen to some plots regarding Louisiana that sounded (in hindsight) rather farfetched. The ministry of Pitt the Younger had at least considered the possibility of sending some Royal Navy vessels to the mouth of the Mississippi to aid Aaron Burr's plot against Mexico.[5]

Some basic facts, unavailable to most Americans, might have calmed them down. First, Simcoe by this point was essentially a physically broken man, probably because of his unsuccessful attempts to do what Americans feared most—bring about a pan-Indian alliance that would reverse the American Revolution. He was heading back to England to try to recover his health, and would never return to North America.[6] Second, William Bowles had never received, nor did he now possess, the official sanction of the British government. In many respects this was, however, to the Crown's advantage. If Bowles achieved his goals of thwarting American expansion by unifying Indian resistance, it would work to Britain's advantage. If he failed, it had cost the Treasury next to nothing, and there was enough plausible deniability to perhaps avoid provoking an American war. Still, there was some risk involved: if the American public continued to believe that Bowles' mission was a sanctioned one, it could bring trouble.

An American in Kingston, Jamaica, reported home of Bowles' presence there later that summer. Bowles, he insisted, was "supported by the British government," and would soon embark on a British warship "with a long retinue of military men" for the Florida coast. "There can be no doubt that their views in this are political," the gentleman continued, and that Bowles intended to disrupt the peace that had existed between the Cherokees and other Southern tribes and the United States for the previous few years. As it became clear that Bowles intended to thwart the running of the boundary line between the Cherokees and the United States from the 1798 treaty on the Holston River, the alarm grew. Even more, he would most likely seek to attack Spanish officials, possibly violating American neutrality in the ongoing European war and drawing the United States into it. Worse still, "Bowles created havoc by encouraging Indians to steal slaves, livestock, and goods in Florida, which he would then "purchase" from them."[7] Bowles was now the ultimate nightmare for white Americans. He was a renegade Tory, who had "gone native," consorted with the British, promoted pan-Indianism, and stole, liberated, and recruited slaves to attack their former masters.

A Georgia paper, following these arguments, further added that Bowles' "patron," Great Britain, was "that common disturber of the peace of mankind in every quarter of the Globe . . . [and] the active mover in deluging three fourths of the world in blood, & [could not] suffer this quarter to have remained in peace." Now, the editorialist continued, "our unhappy frontier settlers will have the cruel savage let loose on them, while Britain's fleet is robbing and insulting us on the ocean, whilst perhaps a deeper and more serious plan is maturing to destroy our independence."[8]

Bowles' style, whether élan or delusion, had not dimmed during his confinement. In November 1799 he proclaimed that the Muskogee Nation would purge itself of dangerous foreign—read American—influences. He hoped that this would be accomplished without violence, he noted, but if they did not remove immediately they would "forfit [sic] the protection due to all men by the Law of Nations," and "Ought to suffer death by being hanged as conspirators against the peace and sovereignty of Muscogee." The threat of execution was directed especially against "Mr. Hawkins," who was "a dangerous man" who must "gow [sic] immediately."[9]

Benjamin Hawkins, the former senator from North Carolina and now U.S. agent to the Creeks, understandably followed Bowles' activities and threats with keen interest. He wrote to James Jackson, the governor of Georgia—who also had an obvious stake in Bowles's whereabouts—to note that Spanish vessels had sunk a small boat in which Bowles was traveling on Apalachee Creek, nearly capturing the Director General. The Spaniards, he continued, had put a considerable bounty of trade goods on his head, and were committed to "putting out of the world that common enemy of peace (Bowles)."[10]

Bowles had maintained his clout with the Seminoles, "despite their knowledge that he lied prodigiously and bore the public moniker 'Oquelúsa Micco' (King of Liars)." Yet at one point in the spring of 1800 estimates gave him only a handful of white and black followers. Then Bowles engaged in his biggest gamble yet—he laid siege to Fort San Marcos de Apalache (modern St. Marks, Florida). The fort capitulated on May 18th, 1800. Spanish retribution would not be swift, but it would be ruthless.[11]

Spanish officers threatened to destroy Seminole towns and crops, to kidnap their women and children, and to confiscate their cattle and slaves, if they harbored or aided Bowles. Peace would only come, they insisted, when the "Director General" was in chains, and all prisoners, deserters, and slaves were returned to Spanish hands.[12]

The summer of 1802 witnessed still more accounts of Bowles' war with the Spanish in Florida, and American newsmen found themselves in the odd position of rooting for Spain. The Creeks, reports ran, had been "deluded by Bowles," into resisting the Spanish, from whom they "had received all aid and assistance . . . and by whom they never were interrupted." While Bowles' reported piracy and other attacks on Spain were bad enough, given the potential to disrupt American neutrality, as a Massachusetts paper warned, "there are great apprehensions of disturbances among all the neighboring settlements, from the wanton cruelty of savages. Some reports are given that there were expectations of some internal broils in force of the western tribes, but no cause is assigned." The only positive—if inconsistent, given their view of Bowles—news they could offer was, "We learn nothing of the interference of any European nation."[13]

Bowles continued to steal/liberate slaves from Spanish subjects—one man lost thirty-eight slaves, and was said to be financially ruined by the loss. "Many of these liberated Africans savored their freedom and willingly joined Bowles." He brazenly camped outside Fort San Marcos with several hundred warriors, and more than fifty slaves liberated from Florida plantations. (Indeed, the Jefferson administration was particularly on edge after the recent squelching of Gabriel's slave revolt in Virginia, as well as the continued presence of free, armed blacks in Haiti.) But it became increasingly difficult for Bowles' Indian friends to stay with him. Spanish officials again threatened to regard those who stole and refused to return slaves as enemies of the state.[14]

The Spanish noose continued to tighten on the Director General throughout 1802, as His Catholic Majesty's agents managed to whittle down Bowles' native support network. The August 20, 1802, treaty at Apalache, accompanied with numerous presents, basically ended the war between the Seminole chiefs who signed, promising to return their prisoners, slaves, and plunder. Further, they had to agree to stop aiding the Director General. By a spring 1803 conference at the Hickory Ground (modern Montgomery, Alabama), delegates from the Creeks, Chickasaws, Choctaws, and Cherokees could proclaim near unanimity for putting an end to Bowles' career. Unable to supply the trade goods that his enemies wielded so effectively, in May of 1803 Bowles was arrested by a party of métis Upper Creeks— some of them friends of his late nemesis Alexander McGillivray. One of the principal captors was William Weatherford, whose later career in Creek leadership would not always please American officials. After one brief escape Bowles was taken to the Spanish at Mobile. There would be no further miracles for him.[15]

Bowles' capture was so momentous that the Spanish Crown issued "a royal order of October 2 that year," expressing the king's "appreciation to the persons involved in extinguishing the menace Bowles represented." Despite his crimes—including declaring war on Spain, killing Spanish subjects and recruiting Indians to fight the empire, Bowles was not denied any legal niceties of the era. But he refused to cooperate in his trial, declining to testify, and so he was simply held. Finally, he refused even to eat. He died a miserable death in a Spanish dungeon in Havana, two days shy of Christmas, 1805.[16] Pan-Indianism had lost a quirky advocate, and Americans had lost a charismatic boogey man.

CHAPTER **15**

Indians and the Jeffersonian Mind

With Louisiana purchased and Bowles dead—Americans learned of the latter by January 1806—fears of massive Indian wars on the frontier should have eased somewhat. Yet they actually grew worse after 1805. The Jeffersonian policy of rapidly purchasing Indian lands, in theory extraneous after the Louisiana Purchase, continued unabated. American settlers in the upper Mississippi Valley had proven so irksome to the Sioux and others that they formed a confederation and solicited British aid in 1805. (Canada turned a deaf ear until the war scare of 1807.) Westerners of all stripes continued to hear and pass on rumors that Napoleon would try to occupy Louisiana. Finally, for about a decade after the Louisiana Purchase, Spanish officials maintained that the sale had been illegitimate, noting reasonably that Napoleon had not fulfilled his part of the bargain, and lacked proper title. As chronically under-manned and under funded as ever, Spanish officials on the ground tried to offset their frontier defenses with Indian alliances, which brought scrutiny and anxiety from Americans.[1]

As Peter Russell had learned, being an acting administrator, naturally lacking ultimate authority, was especially nerve wracking when the possibility of Indian conspiracies arose. Cowles Mead, who served as acting governor of the Mississippi Territory during Governor Claiborne's absence, would have agreed. When he wrote the interpreter for the Choctaws, John Pytchlin, it was regarding reports "from a very respectable authority" that the Spanish were trying to draw the Choctaws "into hostile measures." Pytchlin was to pay close attention to the upcoming talk, and to "loose [*sic*] no time in acquainting us with the real situation of the Nation."[2] Nothing actually came of these rumors, though the Choctaws, and European interest in them as allies, continued to rankle Americans.

When a party of Choctaws rode into Natchez in the summer of 1808, they burned down a trader's house and fired several guns (perhaps warning shots) at him. A local posse pursued, and the resulting firefight left as many as five Indians dead and one of the posse wounded. A Kentucky paper asserted, "Whether this is a lawless act of revenge or an offering of protection, by our magnanimous ally Napoleon the Great," it added sarcastically, "we cannot undertake to say." The piece concluded with the hope that "the offenders may be brought to justice without involving us in savage warfare."[3]

By 1805 American policy toward the Indians of the Ohio Valley had helped create a new prophetic movement under a Shawnee named Tenskwatawa. The Shawnee Prophet, as Tenskwatawa was known, initially preached a return to "traditional" native values as the cure for Indian woes. Alcohol consumption, cultural degeneration, and land sales to the Americans, Tenskwatawa insisted, were all causing Indian misery, and abstaining from all would be the only cure. Until a witch-hunt among the Delaware Indians in 1806—the witches had ties to the Americans, and were gruesomely executed—he seemed relatively harmless. As his movement grew and became more obviously interested in pan-Indian unity, American agents feared him proportionately.[4]

It was thus disquieting when Indiana Territory's Governor Harrison wrote to Henry Dearborn, Jefferson's secretary of war, in May 1807. Harrison noted that he was "utterly at a loss to know what to do with the Banditti of Creeks which have so long infested this country." These refugee Creeks had been living along the Ohio, and had been "in the daily habit of committing every species of aggression excepting murder, &c." If these Creeks began murdering the settlers, he added, he would have little choice but to hunt them down "like wild beasts." Two months later, Harrison wrote of his fear that the Shawnee Prophet was "an engine set to work by the British for some bad purpose." Harrison was concerned about the Prophet's attempts to have chiefs who collaborated with the United States put to death, and especially troubled by the pan-Indian implications of his religious revival movement. Tenskwatawa's village in Ohio had seen "a considerable collection of Indians for many weeks," he offered. More ominously, he added, irrefutable intelligence stated, "that war belts have been passing through all the Tribes from the Gulf of Florida to the Lakes." Gratuitously, he added, "The Shawnees are the bearers of these belts and they have never been our friends."[5]

By later that summer, in the wake of the *Chesapeake–Leopard* Affair (June 22, 1807), the Prophet drew considerable negative attention from Harrison, Jefferson, and any Americans concerned with frontier security. When the deserter-hunting British warship *Leopard* fired upon the U.S.S. *Chesapeake* (in U.S. territorial waters) and then forcibly boarded, it created an international incident. While exacerbating years of tension regarding maritime (and now naval) issues between the two nations,[6] the incident did far more for Americans in the frontier territories. Governor Harrison blasted the Royal Navy and Britain's insult to American honor in a fiery address to his territorial legislature in August, 1807. Yet he breathlessly transitioned into reminding the assembled—and the citizenry as well, for he knew the address would be published—that "the tomahawk and scalping knife" had always been "employed as the instruments of British vengeance."[7]

Anglo-American fears of Indian warfare had begun, and begun evolving, from the dawn of colonization in the late sixteenth century. During the American Revolution it had crystallized into a default narrative, deliberately (and later reflexively) conflating Britain and her Indian allies as demonic agents. By the time of Jefferson's presidency, the vast majority of Americans had developed what we might characterize as a borderline Pavlovian response to any perceived threats coming from Indian country. As Peter Silver has argued, by the American Revolution:

> literary anti-Indianism was an electrifying set of images, purpose-built for the interpretation of suffering in terms of injury by outside attackers.... It was ready to be applied to the British and their allies. The sense of indignant vulnerability that many Americans felt—what could literally be called their violent self-pity—would be one of the new nation's most characteristic and long-lasting cultural products.[8]

While contemporary Americans can be heard complaining of our "media echo chamber," where stories are simply repeated and take on disproportional significance in the popular mind, there have in fact been many eras in American history where this proved to be the case. (Or has it ever not been that way?) While there were fewer forms of media available in the

Early Republic, they nevertheless achieved a striking amount of saturation, if not accuracy or objectivity. As Elise Marienstras reminds us, popular culture took on a huge significance in the years after the Revolution, both because of the growing literacy rate of perhaps 75 percent, and the conscious efforts of elites—like newspaper editors—to create a truly *national* culture. Though the disparate peoples of the United States had come together during the Revolution, creating a permanent, unifying identity was another matter. Defining Anglo-Americans as the opposite of Native Americans helped create a sense of a "distinctive *character*, a community of thought, morals, and values enabling them to adhere to the entity that had just come into being." This process would continue until well after the War of 1812.[9]

A host of print media including popular captivity narratives, newspaper editorials, stage plays, early American gothic novels like Charles Brockden-Brown's *Edgar Huntly* (1799), even graphic touring portraits like John Vanderlyn's "The Murder of Jane McCrea," combined with folktales and actual remembrances to give the Indian hating narrative a robust core. Certain key phrases and patterns of response are found over and over again. The phrase "tomahawk and scalping knife" was especially popular, perhaps because it not only hinted very strongly at direct and gory violence that Indians would inflict, but also because by definition those were two trade items that Indians secured from foreign, usually British, sources. During the War of 1812, when anti-war clergy criticized the Madison administration as essentially advocating homicide, the imagery of Crown-supplied Indians murdering women and children was an especially effective counterweight. Focusing on British–Indian perfidy allowed Americans to further the narrative of American exceptionalism. The United States seemed to gain virtue in direct proportion to its enemies' perceived wickedness. Especially for Republicans, Indian-hating became, in a real sense, an expression of patriotism.[10]

It would be easy to attribute such attitudes to cynical political opportunism, and indeed this frequent charge of Federalist newspapers was sometimes spot-on.[11] But in the western territories especially, there seemed to be little diversity in opinion on the topic of Indians, particularly when a war scare arose. Frontier Americans differed on a great many issues; slavery, the extension of the political franchise, the French Revolution. But there appears to have been little serious debate on whether or not to acquire Indian lands quickly and cheaply, or whether to prepare a vigorous military response in case of a war breaking out with Indians. For both those issues, the answer was a resounding and emphatic yes. The threat of pan-Indian alliances only increased the level of anxiety, and thwarting pan-Indianism became central to the American identity. As had become increasingly clear in the 1780s, the American confederation could expand and thrive only if it suppressed native confederations.

Without a doubt, Republicans realized that ginning up fever for an Indian war on the frontier held the promise of political and economic gains, particularly the lands of defeated Indians, as a number of historians have rightly pointed out. But the argument that Westerners raised such concerns fearlessly and recklessly for their benefit is an oversimplification. Since the Revolution, the war between Indians of all stripes and white settlers had become almost absurdly lopsided, most particularly in terms of relative population and casualties inflicted. The odds of an Indian being killed by whites were far greater than the reverse. Yet the pervasive fear of Indian attacks, and the disproportionate response it evoked, remained. Politicians in the late eighteenth and early nineteenth century certainly had little difficulty conflating public and private good. But the fear mongering directed at Indians, even at its most cynical, came from a sincere place—the deep-rooted frontier dread of an Indian war.[12]

In September 1807, Ohio governor Edward Tiffin called out the state's militia, the *Western Spy* noted, because "large bodies of Indians" had assembled near the Prophet's village at Greenville, Ohio. While native informants insisted they were only there to hear the Prophet's peaceful teachings, the paper's editor remained unconvinced. "We are led to believe they are prompted by a more powerful motive than curiosity—British Gold."[13]

Uncertainty and contradictory reports only exacerbated war fears. Indiana's Governor Harrison had written Secretary of War Henry Dearborn—less than a week prior to his saber-rattling address to his legislature—that he could vouch for the vast majority of his close Indian neighbors, who had rejected "overtures" from British and Spanish agents "with indignation." Yet an officer stationed at the post of Michilimackinac wrote his brother, "We are now much on the alert, expecting an attack from the United tribes of Indians north of the Ohio and east of the Mississippi." He reported, "A great prophet," probably Tenskwatawa, "pretends he is revived from the dead by the breath of Manitou (great spirit) to reform and unite his red children."

While purportedly seeking to reclaim Indian virtue, this prophet—an "impostor," he offered—was really seeking *"energetic war on our frontiers."* The garrison had discovered this plot from "an Indian woman who is attached to a trader in our interest." If the letter sounded strikingly similar to the beginning of Pontiac's War, it was in part because the author himself was quite familiar with it. Proof of an impending attack came from a trader having seen "a red war club and black wampum belt (never failing forerunners of war) carefully wrapped in a French flag." The author concluded that they were "precisely similar to those circulated immediately previous to the attacks of the celebrated Pontiac (See *Carver's Travels*)."[14]

Even before *Chesapeake-Leopard*, British Indian Department employees continued to seek any news of pan-Indian efforts that might either help or hinder the king's wishes. In May 1807, Thomas McKee, the agent at Amherstburg—just across the Detroit River from the United States—received intelligence from Létourneau, a principal Chief of the Chippewa Nation. The chief had spent several days at the Prophet's village at Greenville, Ohio. Létourneau offered that two Shawnees from the band living on the Mississippi had come to Greenville with word from Spanish New Orleans that Spain and the United States would soon be at war. The Spanish, said the Shawnees, had told them to remain neutral in the coming battle, "but strongly to hold the hand of their English Father who took such great care of them." An Anglo-Spanish alliance was in the offing, they were told, and the Americans would be defeated. Létourneau concluded his report by noting that "a large Party of Sackies, Foxes and Kickapoos are on their way to pay a friendly Visit to the Shawanoes at Greenville."[15]

After word of the *Chesapeake* incident reached Upper Canada—and London—a frontier war, for which Canadian defenses were completely unprepared,[16] looked increasingly possible. Britons and Americans eyed each other warily across the border, and both looked with considerable anxiety to Indians as potential friends or foes. For all the American insistence that British puppeteers manipulated the Shawnee Prophet, he and his brother, a reputable—though not yet famous—warrior named Tecumseh, declined a British offer to ally their growing Indian confederacy with the king's forces. Tecumseh, a veteran of Fallen Timbers, had not forgotten the unreliability of British promises, and was hoping that his brother's movement would be enough to halt rapacious American purchases of Indian lands. As his most recent biographer tells us, by 1810—in the wake of a new round of land purchases by William Henry Harrison—it would be the British who would have to restrain Tecumseh from launching a frontier war. Officers in Canada, for the time being, would have to console themselves as Francis Gore did. The Lieutenant-Governor of Upper Canada wrote to his friend, Under-Secretary of State for War Edward Cooke. Gore tried to reassure Cooke, and perhaps himself, that "the Influence which the American Government professes in their newspapers to possess over the Indian Nations, has no foundation in truth."[17] Undoubtedly, many nervous Americans would have agreed.

Almost a year after his negotiations at Fort Wayne had purchased nearly three million more acres of Indian land, which his under-populated territory neither needed nor asked for, Governor Harrison began to sense the potential perils involved. He wrote the new Secretary of War—President James Madison had brought William Eustis aboard—of recent intelligence and events from two years past. An Iowa Indian informed him that in 1808 a British agent had come to the Shawnee Prophet's Town, which had moved to the Tippecanoe River (near modern Lafayette, Indiana) The agent urged the Prophet to "unite as many Tribes as he could, against the United States, but not commence hostilities, until they gave the signal." That of course had been the basic British policy since the mid-1780s. For Harrison, who could not have known that Tecumseh had specifically rebuffed a more direct offer of alliance from the British in 1808, this was the smoking gun. "From this man and others of his nation," he continued, "I learn that the Prophet has been constantly soliciting their own and other Tribes of the Mississippi to join them against the United States." Winamac, a pro-American Potawatomi whom the Shawnee brothers despised, reported that they had tried to assassinate him—which was perfectly plausible. The Potawatomi warned that Tenskwatawa would surely "endeavour to raise the southern Indians, the Choctaws and Creeks particularly."[18]

Harrison had long since become quite adept at spinning his reports to the War Department to his advantage. "I was, Sir," he continued, "for a long time unwilling to persuade myself that there was any probability of a war between the United States and the Indian Tribes on this frontier." He had reasoned that past battle losses against the United States, combined with material dependence and a simple lack of manpower would have convinced the Territory's natives that armed resistance was futile. Yet, he was now "perfectly convinced" that war would have commenced, had not the Delaware Nation vetoed the project. He could not resist adding, "(I have as little doubt that the scheme originated with the British and that the Prophet is inspired by the superintendent of Indian affairs for upper Canada, rather than the Great Spirit, from whom he pretends to derive his authority.)" As Gregory Dowd asserts, Americans never understood Tenskwatawa, and his religion seemed so foreign to them that they tended to dismiss it as a false one. Harrison concluded by offering that he did not believe the British had actually wanted to start a war, but "it is probable that having given the impulse, they have found it difficult to regulate the after movements of their tawny allies." Thus Harrison dismissed the Prophet as both a charlatan and a puppet.[19]

The view from Canada, though seeing a different instigator, made a general Indian war seem inevitable as well. Indian agent Matthew Elliott, Alexander McKee's successor at Amherstburg, reported in October 1810, on the great Indian council at Brownstown (outside of Detroit) that August and September. McKee noted that the efforts of the Seneca chief Red Jacket—who advocated peace with the Americans and blamed British agents for trying to form a pan-Indian alliance—had failed completely. He further saw the war fervor among the Indian Nations as high, which would be of great help in the case of an American war. Still, there was the old problem of keeping them as ready allies, but not allowing them to actually precipitate the combat. Elliott was terribly concerned that his Indian friends would start a war, because "our Government will be (indeed always is) blamed for encouraging them, as may be seen in their public prints, particularly in some documents published at Vincennes by Governor Harrison." The next month, Elliott gave an excellent example of the hybrid bureaucratic/diplomatic challenge he faced.[20]

Enclosing a copy of "a Speech of the Shawanee Prophet's Brother"—Tecumseh—Elliott was now convinced that an Indian war was imminent, and that "the confederacy [was] almost general." Elliott promised to lose no time in forwarding their request for military aid to the king, but he begged his superiors for "ample and explicit instructions" for dealing with Tenskwatawa and his confederates. "I am well aware that I cannot and aught not during present circumstances of affairs do anything overtly, but whether or not it would be proper to keep up among them the present spirit of resistance, I wish much to be informed." The task was of course complicated further by the cost—Elliott had already supplied 6,000 Indian visitors with presents and over 70,000 rations, with almost two full months left in the year.[21]

In a postscript to the above letter, dated Nov. 18, Elliott added that he had held a private meeting with Tecumseh, who offered that the confederacy had wanted to keep their plans secret even from the British, until the pan-Indian alliance was completed. However, it was pressure from Harrison—presumably at the August 1810 council, which had nearly ended in a bloody melee—that drove them to tell Elliott of their plans. Tecumseh's speech, translated by James Girty (of the family infamous to Americans), stated that the Shawnee would head south—"to the mid day," and felt that by the autumn of 1811 "the business will be done." As long as Redcoats remained in a death grapple with Napoleon, though, British enthusiasm for a war between their Indian allies and the Americans fell off precipitously as one moved up the chain of command. Accordingly, Francis Gore assured the Earl of Liverpool that he had given unequivocal word "to restrain the Indians from Committing any Act of Hostility on the Subjects of the United States of America." The fact that Gore was largely successful until November 1811 would be lost on Americans for two centuries.[22]

Though Harrison did not respect Tenskwatawa, he did fear him. Toward Tecumseh, who after 1810 became increasingly prominent in the governor's correspondence, he seems to have felt both fear and respect, and even admiration. To Harrison, "Tecumseh has taken for his model the celebrated Pontiac and I am persuaded that he will bear a favorable comparison in every respect with that far-famed warrior."[23] After his second conference with the chief Harrison reported that Tecumseh admitted to bringing the Northern tribes together "under his direction." However, Tecumseh disingenuously insisted, "they really meant nothing but peace." Showing the native rhetorical eloquence that frustrated Harrison, he added that the Indians were merely following the American example of forming a confederation. Then Tecumseh, in what may have been his worst tactical move ever, also admitted to Harrison that he would now leave Vincennes for the South, to visit the Creeks and Choctaws in peaceful diplomacy and "get them to unite with those of the North." On his return he would cross the Mississippi and see the powerful Osages as well.[24]

Harrison was not even remotely fooled, writing the next day, "There can be no doubt but his object is to excite the Southern Indians to war against us." He further noted that informants said a British agent had been to the Prophet's town, insisting that the time for war had come, and offering arms for the endeavor. For his part, Harrison saw Tecumseh's absence as "a most favorable opportunity for breaking up the Confederacy." It was also in this missive that Harrison included an oft-quoted and strikingly laudatory assessment of Tecumseh, an "uncommon genius" who might found "an Empire that would rival in glory that of Mexico or Peru," were the United States not so close.[25] Though Harrison seems to have been sincere in his praise, it is equally clear that he was emphasizing the threat the Shawnee and his pan-Indian dreams posed, and setting up whoever might stop him for considerable patriotic glory.

CHAPTER **16**

Fear's Resurgence

Americans throughout the West, on both sides of the Ohio, spent the year 1811 increasingly convinced that a fight was coming. Intelligence indicated that a party of Indians from west of the Mississippi was trying to recruit tribes to the east, including the Shawnees, Delawares, and Southern nations, to join them in a war. While they were supposedly seeking to attack the Osage Indians, Secretary of War William Eustis was not entirely sure. He directed Indian Agent John Johnston at Fort Wayne, Indiana, to ascertain their true motives, and to discourage them from war. The War Department also worried that the embargo on British goods, resulting from Macon's Bill no. 2, would be interpreted by Indians as a hostile gesture toward them, or that British agents would encourage them in that interpretation. A circular letter was sent to U.S. Indian agents to help them counteract the "hostile dispositions" against the United States that might result. It authorized them not only to note that Britain could reverse the boycott at any time by honoring American maritime rights, but also to issue extra presents if necessary.[1]

A Federalist paper in New Orleans commemorated August 20, 1811, as being exactly "17 years since Maj. Gen. Wayne defeated the Indians on the Miami of the Lakes." Since that time, the article added, "the tomahawk and scalping knife (thanks to the immortal WAYNE) have not been stained with blood. . . . Wisdom & firmness then marked our councils—we then had to boast of a *Washington*, a *Hamilton*, and a *Knox*, in the cabinet, and *Wayne* in the field."[2] The Federalist charge that the Republicans were blundering and blustering the nation into an unnecessary war, a charge that unfortunately had considerable merit, would continue.

Still, in fairness to Governor Harrison and his Republican superiors, considerable evidence suggests that a great many Americans in the West agreed with him that striking a preemptive blow at pan-Indianism, especially at Prophetstown, was the judicious and expedient course. Harrison's colleague and old comrade, Governor William Clark in the Missouri Territory, as well as any number of common members of the frontier militias, wanted to strike before a massive war against all Western Indians became inevitable. One soldier in Harrison's army, in a September missive printed in the newspapers, opined that that when the Prophet's adherents spoke of peace, they were merely stalling to build their confederation. "It was evident . . . that all their objects were to get a little time, so that they might draw the Southern Indians to their assistance."

The same column carried an article from St. Louis, noting that Tecumseh had passed to the Chickasaws, and while he was unsuccessful in recruiting them, he had fared better with the Choctaws. "We may learn from the errors of Braddock and St. Clair," the author continued, "that an Indian enemy is never to be despised." While Indians probably could not wipe out all American settlement in the West, they could "inflict upon us, serious injury" and "deal death and destruction in [their] inroads on our frontier." Lest anyone minimize the threat, he concluded, one need only recall that "at the bottom" of the pan-Indian threat, was "a powerful nation [i.e., Britain]; that the instrument it uses, consists of an artful imposter [the Prophet,] who holds an unlimited power over the superstitious mind of the Indians, and the bravest, and most active Indian warriors that ever appeared on this continent." All that was needed, however, to forestall this calamity, was "One vigorous movement . . . and the present is the period when it should be made."[3]

William Henry Harrison mounted his campaign to disperse the Prophet's followers at his village on the Tippecanoe. The resulting battle of Tippecanoe, on November 7, 1811, nearly proved personally and professionally disastrous for Harrison. Though his men were kept dressed in readiness for battle, General Wayne's protegé failed to fortify his camp near Prophetstown, and although his men outnumbered Tenskwatawa's by about two to one, they were badly mauled—well over ten percent of Harrison's men were killed or wounded. Harrison himself appears to have escaped assassination only because in the predawn confusion he failed to find his distinctive white horse. His aide de camp, riding a light gray mount, was shot down in his place. But when the Prophet's warriors ran out of ammunition they withdrew, abandoning their town and supplies. Harrison burned the town, and soon set about explaining his "victory."[4]

A month after the battle, the Federalist *Columbian Centinel* (Boston), ran a blurb describing Harrison as "an officer of experience and merit—having served under Wayne." This was immediately followed by an editorial entitled "Serious Truth," which argued strenuously that the British could not be the sole instigators of "the Indian war." If President Madison had specific proof of British instigation, he should have told Congress, lest he be guilty of "treachery" to his country. Adding that the *Centinel* had made "diligent inquiry of honorable and impartial men from the interior and from Canada on the subject," they concluded that Britain had absolutely no role in the Indian war. "These reports are doubtless circulated by the advocates of a British War, for no other purpose, than to play on the passions of the public, and commit them into a justification of so ruinous a measure—situated as the U. States now are."[5] The editor had correctly seen that Republican "War Hawks," Kentuckian Henry Clay chief among them, were pushing mightily for a war, and that British Canada was desperately hoping to avoid combat. But in fairness to Harrison, even though his provocative campaign had inaugurated the war in the West, by now that war would have come anyway. The die had already been cast with the Fort Wayne cessions in 1809. Tecumseh and his followers had had enough.

To the south, American soldiers worried about giving Indian militants any more reason to join confederations (or European armies) against the United States. Captain John McKee at Ft. Stoddert (Alabama) had written to the Secretary of State (James Monroe) in September. In a treaty with the Creeks from 1805, the United States had claimed to "have a right to a horse path, through the Creek country, from the Ocmulgee [River] to the Mobile." It would pass from Athens, Georgia, to Fort Stoddert just north of Mobile. While a horse path might have sounded innocuous, McKee realized that it was a touchy subject for the Creeks, despite the treaty, and came at a time of rising tensions. (Indeed, since the invention of the cotton gin in 1793, the Creeks had seen even greater pressure to give up their valuable, arable country.)[6]

He warned that opening the road "without the consent and against the wishes of the Indians . . . is calculated to add them to our list of enemies." Further, he deduced that "should foreign and hostile troops be landed in Florida," an Indian alliance with European soldiers would "thereby greatly increase the difficulties of carrying on a war (if war must be) in this projected weak point." Apologetically, McKee added that he might have overstepped his bounds by writing so directly to Monroe, "but so fully am I persuaded of the embarrassment that Indian hostilities would add to a European War in this quarter, that I could not satisfy myself with saying less, and I hope it will be ascribed to its proper motive: a wish to promote the interests of my Country."[7] McKee need not have worried about seeming insubordinate. His superiors would have had to pay attention to his warnings to notice.

The opening of the roads through the heart of Creek Country proceeded. Governor Harrison's hometown newspaper carried a report from Tennessee, stating that a party of Cherokee Indians—they were in fact Creeks—had attacked a party of American soldiers building one of the roads.

"We should not be surprised to find, that this act has proceeded not only from the opposition to the opening of the road through their territory; but also *from a determination to co-operate with the northern Indians in their warlike expedition against the whites* [italics added]. —There is no doubt but that Tecumseh has made every effort in his late visit among the southern Indians, to sour their minds against us, and it is possible that his exertions may have succeeded to a very considerable extent."[8]

With the threat of pan-Indianism once more rising, it was perhaps with some relief that the *National Intelligencer*—a month after Tippecanoe—noted that reports from the Choctaws, Cherokees, and Creeks indicated their continued neutrality. "The Prophet's [and Tecumseh's] attempts to instigate them against the United States" had thus far failed. A trace of dread accompanied the next clause, though, because "some few Creeks . . . have gone to join his party."[9]

In truth, Tecumseh's 1811 recruiting tour of the Southern nations had been largely ineffectual. Most of the Southern nations' established chiefs did not care for a Shawnee usurper filling their younger warriors' heads with what they deemed dangerously implausible dreams of defeating the Americans in a war. Further, as Gregory Dowd notes, the pan-Indian militants faced competition from tribal nationalists, who sought to assert their own identity. "This was especially true in 1811, and especially true among the Creeks." Indeed, the one nation where he had attracted more than a smattering of followers was the Creeks, who had been creeping toward internal dissension for some years. Though the emerging Creek civil war defies easy categorization, in general those who opposed American physical and cultural encroachment, who became known as "Red Sticks" (for their painted war clubs) backed Tecumseh. Red Sticks and the followers of the Creek National Council—many of whom were mestizos—would soon fight viciously among themselves.[10]

Tecumseh may not have been a household name just yet, but his efforts to forge his coalition were already receiving considerable coverage in the newspapers. While Harrison had hoped that the Tippecanoe campaign would break up the Prophet's following, it had only dispersed them temporarily. The War Department seemed rather behind the curve for several months. As late as January 1812, they hoped that reconciliation in the Northwest was still possible. The Secretary of War wrote Governor Harrison, noting that he wished to have some of the disaffected Indian chiefs brought to Washington to smooth over their differences, including Tecumseh and the Shawnee Prophet. (Given the situation on the ground in Indiana, it may well have provided Harrison with a much-needed laugh.) Harrison was also authorized to note the President's displeasure, and to threaten the Indians with a large army to be raised in the spring. In March 1812 Indian agent William Wells, a former Miami captive, told Harrison that Tecumseh was furiously trying to "raise all the Indians he can" to "attack our frontiers." He had called for warriors from the Illinois and Mississippi Rivers, Wells asserted, and had personally gone to the Cherokees and Creeks "to hurry on the aid he was promised."[11] The confederationists were coming for their Southern brothers, and American officers in the region braced for impact.

Benjamin Hawkins, as agent to the Creeks, had the thankless task of trying to assimilate them to a more Anglo-American style economy. The North Carolinian was widely regarded in American circles for his knowledge of Indian affairs. He had served Congress in dealing with the Creek Indians in the 1780s, including at the Hopewell Treaty negotiations. As early as 1785, he noted his frustration and fatigue with these tasks. "If I have health in future, I mean to depend on my own exertions—and bid adieu to the cursed Indian business."[12]

Protestations aside, Hawkins would serve as a principle figure in American Indian affairs until his death. George Washington found him so capable that he appointed him both Agent to the Creeks and Superintendent for all the Southern Indians. James Robertson had certainly been impressed, noting in the summer of 1797 that he had been told that Hawkins was more influential with the Creeks than any previous agent. The Creeks seemed disposed to peace, and what was more, they actually seemed to like Hawkins, despite their antipathy toward Indian agents generally. Hawkins was more modest in his self-appraisal, noting that he had "heard of many personal threats" against him, and "been seriously advised to be on my guard." Yet he was not particularly moved by such intelligence. If anyone really wanted him dead, they would have innumerable opportunities.[13]

Following a paternalistic policy that both Federalists and Republicans applauded, Hawkins sought to have Creek women abandon their fields for spinning and domestic manufactures. Creek men, Hawkins insisted, had to give up the hunting bow and the war club for the plow. In so doing, the agent breezed over the complete disruption of traditional Creek gender roles this necessitated. Many Creeks did not. Hawkins's "civilization program" led to further dissension and division among the Creeks, far more complicated than a simple traditionalist vs. modernist struggle. The gender implications in particular, and Creek women's efforts to re-assert themselves in Creek society, infuriated warriors of the Red Stick faction. As Kathryn Braund notes, "Hawkins seemed oblivious to the intense strains that his efforts to transform Creek society and economy had placed on the Creek psyche," in addition to the pressures for land, etc. Red Sticks would engage in terrifying acts of brutality toward women, both Creek and American, in their quest to assert their dominant status.[14]

Hawkins, known to Indians and whites alike for his general humanity, nevertheless dodged repeated assassination attempts from within and without the Creek Nation. By 1812, the Red Sticks, inspired by millenarian, anti-American prophets, and by Tecumseh's calls for Indian unity, sought to rid the Creek Nation of outside, especially American, influence.[15]

The fear of Indian war in the South had other complicating factors. One was linked not directly to pan-Indianism, but to another classic American theme—desire for the Floridas. Since at least 1809, American civilians and military officers, with the tacit consent of Madison administration, had plotted to take over East Florida (and hopefully West Florida too) from the Spanish—legality be damned. Spanish authorities, like the British to the north, were compelled to supplement their manpower by calling for aid from Indian allies, in this case the Choctaws and Creeks.[16]

Whites in the South had also long had their fears of pan-Indian wars compounded by the dread of slave revolts, either independent or in league with Indians. In the 1790s, Caribbean slave revolutions had rocked the psyche of whites North and South, and there was great apprehension that the spirit of insurrection would spread like a virus when slaves from Saint Domingue came to American shores. (Indeed, the fear of such revolts does seem to have been spread in part by white expatriates from Saint Domingue.) In early 1811, events in Louisiana once more fueled white terror.

The American government had been concerned with slave rebellions in Louisiana at least since they purchased the territory. In the fall of 1803, governor of Orleans Territory W. C. C. Claiborne requested thousands of muskets and considerable ammunition with which to arm the white citizenry, noting that "The negroes in the Island of Orleans are very numerous, and the number of free mulattoes is also considerable." They might well become "riotous" with the transfer of the territory to the United States, he warned, and an armed white populace would be the best deterrent to such a catastrophe.[17] General James Wilkinson requested five hundred more [white] soldiers be sent to New Orleans, explaining, "The formidable aspect of the armed Blacks & Malattoes [*sic*], officered & organized, is painful & perplexing, and the [white] People have no Idea but of Iron domination at this moment."[18] Over the next two years, various reports of impending slave insurrection terrorized the white population of New Orleans. The rumors took on increasingly ominous tones with additional details. In 1805 a white man named LeGrand was "taken up . . . for endeavouring to bring about an Insurrection among the Negroes." That plot was apparently foiled, but the next year lurid stories involving "all the free Creoles of Colour, including one who wore a "Spanish Cockade," offering to free all blacks who joined them, swirled around the city.[19]

For Louisiana planters especially, these scares had nearly proven nightmares come true. In addition to the Pointe Coupée revolt in 1795, Louisianans had recent nearby slave rebellions in West Florida, Mexico, and Central America to bedevil their dreams. The Haitian rebellion was "burned indelibly on the consciousness of slave owners everywhere, all the more so in Louisiana because the white refugees from the holocaust were available in numbers to remind [them] of their potential powder-keg." The rapid pace of slave importation was "hardly calculated to allay to fears." After the failure of Gabriel's slave revolt in Virginia in 1800, several of those convicted in the plot were transported to Louisiana, "then a foreign colony." On top of that, authorities had thwarted an 1805 plot in New Orleans—the LeGrand plot—"which appeared to have involved substantial numbers of slaves . . . who planned to kill the city officials and take over the city." Repeated threats of this nature made whites in New Orleans "doubly susceptible to terror by virtue of the previous threats which seemed by then to be unrelenting."[20] Yet nothing came of these scares until after the American annexation of West Florida in October of 1810.

On January 8, 1811—only three months after the United States had annexed West Florida—a revolt began thirty-some miles north of New Orleans, on the east bank of the Mississippi. Charles Deslondes, "a mulatto from Saint-Domingue and a slave driver on the plantation of Col. Manuel Andry," led a force of fellow slaves and nearby maroons, attacking Col. Andry and killing his son. Deslondes's men were well organized, gathering some weapons that Andry had stored since the Burr Conspiracy scare, and "pillaged gunpowder from a nearby mill." Deslondes formed "his followers into companies, appointed officers, flagmen, and drummers, and armed them with guns and swords, and his 'troops' with farm implements." Deslondes killed or tortured those who would not join his force, variously estimated at between one hundred and five hundred. They marched south, chanting "on to Orleans," with the manifest goal of taking the city and liberating its slaves.[21]

To Deslondes's misfortune, a detachment of U.S. Army troops under General Wade Hampton, as well as some militia, were near enough to respond quickly. On January 9 Hampton's men attacked the rebels sixteen miles north of New Orleans. In what has been described as more "massacre" than battle, the engagement left sixty-six dead rebels and a number of captives, including Deslondes. A tribunal of five plantation owners eventually condemned twenty-one to death, including Deslondes. They were to be taken to their home plantations, shot, and, as was the fashion for rebels, their heads "cut off and mounted on poles as an example to the remaining slaves of what rebellion would mean."[22]

Like the other North American slave rebellions, the Deslondes Revolt was quickly put down, and resulted in a lopsided casualty count in favor of the slave owners. But the psychological impact was equally lopsided, this time against slave owners and whites in general. While reports of the revolt spread relatively quickly, some newspapers, like the St. Louis *Gazette*, refused to publish the story "until local authorities could take steps to tighten control of local slaves." As with Indian alliances bent on stemming territorial losses, whites assumed that slave rebellions were largely the result of foreign intervention, rather than a reaction to the inherent cruelty of the institution. General Hampton blamed the influence of Spain, and argued that disgruntled Spaniards had encouraged the revolt, an argument that had even less logic than evidence to back it. Some felt that French agents, including pirate Jean Lafitte—who did business with maroons—had been behind it. Governor "Claiborne and others in New Orleans, indeed probably most native whites, blamed slaves from the West Indies for instigating the revolt."[23]

The shockwave ran through most Southern states. St. Louis and the states of Kentucky, Virginia, and Georgia, all passed harsher slave codes in the aftermath. Tennessee, like the Orleans Territory, passed a law barring "blacks, Mulattoes, and Indians" from the militia. Whites were justly terrified when they considered that the Deslondes rebels had come perilously close to predominately black New Orleans, which "could have been catastrophic." With the specter of this seemingly ever-present threat to their lives and livelihoods, it was little wonder that, as they did with Indian militants, slave owners referred to the rebel slaves as "brigands" and "banditti." As the likelihood of war with Great Britain loomed—and Southern and Western "War Hawks" in Congress did little to dampen that feeling—"Fear of what slaves might do if a war with Britain drained off local militia forces greatly heightened concern for increased militia strength throughout the South."[24] Such fears would only multiply if an Indian war threatened.

The threat posed by Indians and slaves joining forces had weighed on white minds, especially in the South, nearly since the beginning of colonization. It had become especially acute during the Revolution, with Dunmore's proclamation and British efforts to emancipate the slaves of rebels. Those fears never really receded after the war, and the raids of William Bowles and his ties to pan-Indian efforts had maintained a level of anxiety, punctuated by actual and thwarted slave revolts, throughout the 1790s and into the 1800s. While slave owners might eventually exhale in the aftermath of the Deslondes Revolt, Americans in the South and West only grew more anxious for their security as the months passed. Any news that signaled an increase in Anglo-American, or Indian–white tension, brought greater likelihood of war and the total breakdown of security. Americans north of the Ohio River continued to fear being attacked by a multitribal coalition bent on their destruction. Whites in the South feared the same, with the added terror of being murdered in their beds by rebelling slaves, or possibly both at once.

Throughout 1812, the pace of reported murders and Indian attacks grew. In May the *Vincennes Western Sun* first noted Indians killing whites in Ohio, and then in June carried stories from the *Nashville Enquirer* that the Creeks and Cherokees (apparently false in the case of the latter) had risen to attack American settlers. The American Congress had declared war on Britain June 18, 1812. By the time the *Sun* carried the story of Martha Crawley's abduction by militant Creeks on the Duck River in Tennessee, war had broken out across the Western frontier.[25]

CHAPTER 17

Death by the River's Side

In May 1812, a small Red Stick war party had attacked a remote settlement on the Duck River in Humphreys County, Tennessee. They killed seven settlers and took Mrs. Martha Crawley captive. In the wake of Tippecanoe, and a series of isolated but increasingly frequent Indian attacks north of the Ohio, the "Massacre on Duck River," as Americans dubbed it, came at a key moment. The American temperature was rapidly rising to war fever, especially regarding Indians or Britons. Historian Tom Kanon asserts, "The Crawley kidnapping struck a collective nerve, not only in Tennessee, but across the nation—a nation eager to use the incident as a springboard to further anti-British sentiments, and to promote the expansion of territorial claims into Indian lands."[1]

The warriors did have tangential links to Britain. They were in fact a contingent of Creeks who had joined Tecumseh when he returned north from Creek Country after the battle of Tippecanoe—a battle in which other Creeks had fought and died. The assault on the Duck River cabins probably had more to do with Creek clan-dictated blood vengeance than with the broader war brewing, however. The warriors might have been retaliating for their brothers' deaths at the hands of Governor Harrison's army, but would appear to have been seeking vengeance for the alleged murder of the aunt of one of the warriors by a Tennessean. In fact, the Creek woman had not been murdered, but would later be killed by National Council Creeks when she sheltered her nephew. Despite the contention of American newspapers, all the warriors who took part in the raid met a similar fate.[2]

James Robertson, once more the agent to the Chickasaws,[3] offered a rather nuanced, if not entirely prophetic, interpretation of these events in a letter to John Sevier a few months after the War of 1812 was declared.

The Chickasaws and Choctaws were firmly in the American camp, he noted with some pleasure. The Creeks were "among the most faithless nations on Earth," yet they now could "see their situation." He did not anticipate trouble with them, though the Seminoles living near the Gulf Coast might be a problem "If the British were to land there." Robertson went on to explain that, through the exertions of Agent Hawkins, the Creeks had already put the Duck River murderers to death so promptly that "the crime cannot be considered a national offense." He concluded that despite his attention to such matters, Hawkins was terribly unpopular with Georgians and Tennesseans, and that Sevier might do well to seek his post.[4]

Many Americans would prove capable of ignoring the large number of Creeks who either openly supported the United States, or remained neutral in the war with Britain, and did so from a complex set of motives. It would appear that safeguarding their slave property was a factor for many pro-American Creeks.[5] No better example of these militants can be found than Andrew Jackson. At this point in his life, he was a successful lawyer and planter in Tennessee, as well as general of the state's militia. He had served briefly in Congress, and had a political following. He was not yet, however, famous. Jackson was certainly steeped in frontier "Indian hating," and also had legitimate reasons to fear an Indian war on the frontier. That is, while as a Jeffersonian he had perfectly good political reasons to rail about a British–Indian alliance menacing the Western country, it is too cynical by half to think he did not also believe his own rhetoric.

At the same time, Jackson was undoubtedly thinking of the rich lands that could be wrested from the Creeks in the aftermath of a successful Indian war. For at least a decade, Tennesseans in particular had openly lusted after Creek lands, not just for their arability, but also for the wonderful system of navigable rivers they contained. But he also shared a very typical frontiersman's attitude—in vogue at least since the 1780s—that Indian enemies needed to be struck quickly, ruthlessly, and if possible preemptively, to save American lives. Xenophobia, nationalism, commerce, ethnic hatred, and careerism all prompted Jackson to push for a war with the Creeks.[6]

Jackson had been in Georgia on business when the Crawley kidnapping occurred, but upon his return immediately asked Tennessee's governor Willie Blount for permission to launch a punitive expedition against the Creeks. He mentioned pan-Indianism, noting that the quicker the attack, "the fewer will be the nations or tribes we will have to war with." Given that the Duck River murderers had been with Tecumseh shortly before, and that Tecumseh's greatest success in recruiting warriors for his movement had been among the Red Sticks, it was not an unreasonable assumption that they acted in the pan-Indian cause. Jackson and other leaders in Tennessee certainly did predict, even desire, a war against the Creeks and their allies in 1812. That war failed to materialize, in part because the Creeks were busy fighting among themselves. The Muskogees' civil war itself was rarely mentioned, if at all, in the American press. Far more interesting and ominous stories circulated.[7]

When a bitterly divided Congress[8] declared war on Britain in June 1812, the probability of a nasty frontier fight leapt into near inevitability. The Vincennes *Western Sun* carried a story that the Spanish had demanded the surrender of Baton Rouge, and the Creek Nation had declared war against the United States—both reports proved false. Elihu Stout's paper also printed an extract of a letter from an officer in West Tennessee to General James Winchester in Ohio. The correspondent (who sounded a lot like Jackson)[9] noted his belief that "the Creeks are making formidable preparations to take the field against the U. States," and "the British have thrown into Pensacola." The Royal Navy had indeed just visited Pensacola and Mobile, and done so with a vessel Americans in the Southeast would have found appropriately named, the HMS *Brazen*. The ship's captain would note to his superiors that the Gulf Coast was ripe for the picking, and his visit proved more than enough to fill the air with rumors of joint Anglo-Spanish invasion of the American Southeast.[10]

The officer from Tennessee continued with (false) reports that "250 well disciplined black troops, commanded by British officers" had moved into Pensacola and handed out large quantities of arms to the Creek Indians—the Southern Republican's nightmare trifecta. Professing great "astonishment" at the Secretary of War's delay in authorizing a quick strike on Pensacola and St. Augustine, the author pledged to effect his invasion, whether it led to "laurels" or damnation. Aside from seeking to cut off the main source of Creek arms, he also felt the horror of black troops working with the British on the Southern frontier, and the resulting slave rebellion. Planters from Louisiana to the Atlantic coast, with the memory of the Deslondes Revolt and countless others fresh in mind, no doubt shared his concerns. "The southern states have an enemy within their bosoms worse than the Creeks," he added ominously. The *National Intelligencer* reported (inaccurately) that British forces were expected in Pensacola, while 280 black troops from Havana were leaving Pensacola for Mobile in U.S. territory.[11] Even those who most strenuously advocated a war with the Creeks knew the fabulously high rewards of victory were matched by catastrophic losses in defeat. As Adam Rothman asserts, the "War of 1812 represented [both] an opportunity and a crisis for the budding slave country of the Deep South."[12]

As tenuous as the American hold on the South might have been, the war in the North went exceedingly, humiliatingly wrong from the start. While raw numbers favored the Americans, raw talent favored the British–Indian alliance. Easily the most gifted British soldier in the theater was Major General Isaac Brock. He was under no illusions as to the severe manpower shortage he faced in battling an aggressive American neighbor bent on invading Upper Canada. He knew that Indian allies would be the province's most necessary bulwark, and that significant steps needed to be taken to regain their trust and support. A month after Tippecanoe he offered to Sir George Prevost that before Indian allies would take the field in significant numbers, "the reduction of Detroit and Michilimackinac must convince that people (who conceive themselves to have been sacrificed in 1794 to our policy) that we are earnestly engaged in the war."[13]

He was not particularly impressed with Tenskwatawa at this point, writing, "a few Tribes at the instigation of a Shawanese, of no particular note, have already (tho' explicitly told not to look for assistance from us) commenced the contest." Still, Brock was pleased at how they were holding their own against the American forces on the Wabash River—"about two thousand including Militia and Regulars"—and concluded that a "grand combination of Indians" would compel the Americans to tie down a vast number of troops for defense of the Ohio region.[14]

Brock's first opponent—it would be too generous to say *rival*—was General William Hull, the governor of Michigan Territory. Hull hoped to forestall Britain's use of Indian allies by issuing a frightfully naive proclamation on July 12, 1812. It read in part:

> If the barbarous and savage policy of Great Britain be pursued, and the savages be let loose to murder our Citizens and butcher our Women and Children, this War will be a War of extermination. The

DEATH BY THE RIVER'S SIDE 205

first stroke of the Tomahawk, the first attempt with the Scalping Knife, will be the Signal of one indiscriminate scene of desolation.— No white man found fighting by the side of an Indian will be taken prisoner: instant death will be his lot.[15]

Brock countered with his own proclamation on July 22. He took an interesting approach, blending fact with fiction. Hull's dictum, he asserted, would deny Indians the right to defend their own lands and property. He stated that they had been given lands in Canada to compensate them for the territory lost to the United States during the Revolution—neglecting to mention that the king had ceded their lands without consultation, and that many of his Indian allies, like Tecumseh, did not call Canada home. If Indian tactics, "being different from that of the white people[,] is more terrific to the enemy," he added, "let him retrace his steps." A final jab aimed at the frontier (especially Kentucky) militia who had adopted scalping and other tactics of the Middle Ground. Did Indian men not have a right to defend themselves, "when they find in the enemies camp a ferocious and mortal foe using the same warfare which the American Commander affects to reprobate?"[16]

The image of Indians attacking the frontiers, and the rhetorical use of the *tomahawk and scalping knife* had not really abated since the 1790s, or the Revolution, or Pontiac's War for that matter. That imagery at times facilitated the British–Indian alliance, as the terror of Indian warfare served as what the modern military would call a "force multiplier." Even a few Indian war parties could easily lead to a significant depopulation of enemy territory from fright alone. That Americans had been reared on tales of Indian savagery only made this more effective. As Alan Taylor asserts, the downside would prove to be the vicious revenge that the fearful settlers would exact when they had an advantage over Indians.[17]

The easy British conquest of Michilimackinac, which surrendered under the threat of extermination by Britain's Indian allies,[18] almost certainly combined with Hull's hollow proclamation to give Brock an idea when he invested Detroit the next month. In addition to parading his soldiers and Indian allies around the fort to give the false impression that they outnumbered Hull's army, he blatantly used the specter of merciless Indian warfare and clearly rattled the American general. Brock sent word to Hull that his Indian allies—led by Tecumseh himself—would be impossible to control if the siege went on very long. Only if Hull surrendered immediately could Brock insure that there would be no massacre of the civilians, including women and children, inside. The irony being that Tecumseh was one of the only Indian leaders who insisted upon humane treatment for captives. Hull, who presumably would have made a lousy card player, surrendered on August 16, 1812.[19]

The almost bloodless capture of Detroit proved a huge victory for the Anglo-Indian forces. It gave them control of much of Michigan, as well as a vital post in the chain of Great Lakes fortifications. It boosted the morale of native allies as well as soldiers and militia. Almost as gratifying for Brock and his superiors was the fact that their Indian allies had behaved "with every humanity" toward their prisoners. Britons well remembered the stinging public relations defeats inflicted by American propagandists during the Revolution (and afterward), and were keen to avoid letting their Indian allies hurt them rhetorically even as they helped militarily. Brock also understood that the Crown had not always lived up to its obligations to Indian allies. In another letter to Lord Liverpool, Brock not only spoke very highly of Tecumseh, but also seemed truly grieved by the treatment the Indians of the Northwest had received at the hands of Harrison and other American officials. Their "fictitious and ruinous pretensions," if unchecked, would eventually force Tecumseh and his brethren west of the Mississippi. "If the condition of this people could be considered in any future negotiation for Peace," he added, "it would attach them to us forever."

The Prime Minister was so pleased with both the victory and the lack of carnage that he informed Brock, "The faithful and orderly conduct of many of the Indian Tribes gives them a fair claim to protection and reward," and they were to receive ammunition as a reward. [That would seem to be a bare minimum for native allies.] With unintentional foreshadowing, he further ordered Brock to "give them every assurance that in any negotiation for peace which may be hereafter entered into with the American Government their interests will not be forgotten."[20]

Though 1812 witnessed a number of impressive British victories in the Northern theater, the Redcoats sustained a painful loss in the death of Brock at Queenstown Heights in October.[21] Brock had forged a highly effective working relationship with Tecumseh. With the general's death the British–

Indian alliance, while still terrifying to Americans, in retrospect never really recovered. Still, the inertia of American military incompetence carried into the new year. General James Winchester, in violation of (now Major General) William Henry Harrison's orders, attacked the British on the River Raisin in Michigan Territory, winning a small victory. Winchester neglected defensive measures, however, and was soon overwhelmed by a British–Indian counterattack. After the surrender, the British commander Henry Procter, who had replaced Brock, declined to leave any of his scarce Redcoats to guard the American prisoners as he withdrew. He left that task to his native allies, who promptly began killing and scalping the wounded men. Others died when they could not escape the flames of buildings the Indians set afire. It proved to be yet another propaganda victory for the Americans, and "Remember the Raisin" became a battle cry.[22]

Tennessee Congressman John Sevier, the grizzled veteran of many Indian wars, wrote of the Raisin to his compatriot James Robertson back in Knoxville. He lamented the "cruelties and barbarities" visited upon the American prisoners by the "savage" Indians. In addition to his disgust, he felt an old terror. "I fear very Much the frequent Successes of the Northern Indians will have some influence over our Southern Neighbors." The only succor, Sevier noted, was that Robertson was "so well acquainted with those people" that he would "take . . . measures accordingly."[23]

By the late summer of 1812, reports flew about the South of British and Spanish efforts to arm the Creek Indians to attack the United States. An especially persistent tale stated that a Creek, Little Warrior, a veteran of both the River Raisin and Duck River, had been given a "packet" by a British officer while the former was in Canada. The rumor—never actually confirmed—stated that the packet would secure arms for the Red Sticks once they presented it to the governor of Spanish Florida. Interestingly, the rumor was given considerable credence by American officials and settlers and was frequently repeated by both Americans (who wanted a pretext for a Creek war) and Red Sticks (who hoped it would intimidate their enemies.[24]

Completely missing (or perhaps ignoring) that the Creeks were engaged in a nasty civil war, *Wilson's Gazette* in Knoxville stated that Creek warriors were receiving British arms in Pensacola. The *Gazette* opined, "This account we believe is proof that the Creeks are friendly only until they are prepared to act otherwise." For his part, Tennessee governor Willie Blount, who had enthusiastically stumped for a war with the Creeks for years, "went as far as to dismiss reports of a Creek civil war as 'altogether fudge.'"[25]

Americans continued to insist that Britain was behind all Indian militancy, and other disruptions. Congressman John Rhea of Tennessee likely preached to the converted when he told his constituents that King George III had excited to war the tribes that defeated Harmar and St. Clair. Once more, Britain had urged Indians to war against the United States, and "helpless women and children" had been killed by the king's "savage allies." Rhea concluded with self-righteous and myopic hyperbole, Britain's "conduct has been unprovoked and atrociously inhuman and hostile," and that "Great Britain is the aggressor, and sole cause of the war against this innocent nation."[26]

Rhea's letter reads like a much less eloquent Declaration of Independence, blaming Britain for the entire quarrel and taking no responsibility for one's own actions or failings. That document's principle author would write later that year that "much however has been effected by insulating the British from their savage allies, to whom alone, and not at all to themselves they are indebted for every success they have obtained." The Indians, whom the United States had taken "such pains to save and civilize," had left the American fold and "justified extermination." The Creeks—"for whom we had done more than for any other tribe," especially irked Jefferson, though even he conceded that "not the whole of them" had attacked the Americans. Because of their *betrayal*, "they will probably submit on the condition of removing to such new settlements beyond the Mississippi as we shall assign them," he offered with smirking prophecy.[27]

Meanwhile, Americans were leading incursions into Spanish Florida, ostensibly to punish the Creeks' Seminole relatives, who raided American plantations for plunder and slaves. But Americans could not conceal their lust for Florida, for security and more. Former president Thomas Jefferson, offered his approval of one such expedition. Jefferson, the ardent expansionist and clueless agitator of Indians, praised the invading force for having "given the Spanish Creeks [i.e., Seminoles] a lesson which may be useful to them as well as to us." Yet it was "a great misfortune that you were not permitted to take possession of the whole country of Florida to point." Taking all of Florida, Jefferson offered, was a necessity of both justice and security. He then cut to the heart of the matter. Wild rumors continued to circulate that the British had brought black troops from the West Indies to Florida. (Spain did send some black troops from Cuba, primarily because they had so few regular soldiers in the region. Britain had no role at this time.) The "*colour* [emphasis added] & character of the troops they are introducing and the certainty that it will be seized by the British, made a thorn in our side during the war, & retained permanently by them afterwards."[28]

Georgia also sent an expedition after the Seminoles, and felt they had a pretext for besieging St. Augustine after an attack by "an ambuscading party of Indians, Negroes, and Spaniards from Augustine." Reports also stated that the Spanish had invited the Creeks to take up arms against the Americans, and the Seminoles had already done so. More threateningly, "Among the _____ [the editor was apparently too terrified to print the word *negroes*] particularly on the sea board, a spirit of dissatisfaction prevails. Many have taken shelter in [St.] Augustine, where they are converted into soldiers. This evil has been severely felt, and can be endured no longer." Giving some credence to white Americans' fears of black troops, the Georgians' siege of St. Augustine had been broken primarily by black militia destroying their supply train. Further ginning up fears, other papers asserted (falsely) that the governor of Florida had raised an offered bounty on American scalps to "eight dollars and a bottle of rum each." Sending a force of mounted Georgia riflemen into Florida, therefore, was "indispensable; or we shall soon see our frontier settlers flying before the uplifted tomahawk, and the murderous scalping knife reeking with the blood of our women and children."[29]

Some Red Sticks were perfectly willing to let the carnage spill outside their nation, and did target women and children. Sometime after the battle of the River Raisin, a British officer encountered a party of ten such Creeks under Little Warrior and the Tuskegee Warrior, who had fought at the battle, found them "too volatile to control, [and] had given them presents and sent them home." On their way south in February 1813, they stopped at the confluence of the Cache and Ohio Rivers, near present Mound City, Illinois. Two families, one by the name of Philips, had given the hungry warriors dinner. They then murdered both families, and left a brutal message for those who found the bodies. "The unborn baby of Mrs. Phillips had been torn from the womb and impaled on a peg; the hogs were eating the mother's intestines." According to one recent historian, "The Cache Massacre set off a chain of events that led directly to the Creek war in what is now Alabama."[30]

American opinion of the danger posed by the Red Sticks was not universal. W. C. C. Claiborne, the governor of the Louisiana Territory (and brother of American general F. L. Claiborne) could write as late as August 1813, "I do not learn that the Creeks have done much mischief." He was far more concerned with the actions of the Spanish governor at Pensacola supplying the Creeks with weapons, which he felt was "highly reprehensible." He further offered to his senatorial correspondent that the United States would be justified in capturing Pensacola, the possession of which by Americans he considered "essential to the safety of Louisiana," and an act that would "afford me the sincerest pleasure."[31]

American attitudes toward the inevitability of pan-Indian alliance proved something of a self-fulfilling prophecy, however. American agents watched the Creeks closely, if not always perceptively. They suggested the time-honored technique of recruiting other Southern nations, like the Choctaws and Chickasaws, to help forestall disaster. Newspapers as far away as Maine declared, "Strong fears are entertained that a great proportion of the Southern Indians are about joining the hostile, north western Indians in the war against the U. States."[32]

While war with the Red Sticks seemed inevitable for many Americans, the fighting actually began when American militia took it upon themselves to ambush a large party of Red Sticks at Burnt Corn Creek, some twenty miles east of the Alabama River, on July 27, 1813. Prior to Burnt Corn, the Red Sticks were apparently waiting for an opportunity to coordinate their efforts with those of Tecumseh in the North. Needing arms and ammunition to continue their internal struggle (and to eventually attack the Americans),[33] Red Sticks under the mestizo war chief Peter McQueen from Tallassee had essentially bullied the Spanish governor at Pensacola. The Spaniards gave them 1,000 lbs. of gunpowder, shot and lead, and some other trade goods, which the Red Sticks felt was a rather paltry gift. As with British–Indian relations in the Great Lakes, Americans mistook the colonial power's weakness in the face of angry Indians for a sinister desire to make Indians angry toward the United States. Upon the Red Sticks' return, 150 American militiamen ambushed them.

Though initially stunned, the Red Sticks counterattacked and drove the militia off with relative ease. While they had not expected this direct confrontation with Americans, the repulse of the attackers seemed to confirm Tecumseh's prophecy of easy victory over the United States. It also intensified their hatred of their pro-American (and primarily mestizo) cousins, who had guided the American militia to Burnt Corn. Indeed, in the aftermath, Red Sticks characterized the battle as being "between Red Sticks and mestizos," despite McQueen's own heritage. Mississippi's Governor Claiborne had a typically slanted American take on the affair. After noting that the "Creek nation of Indians have commenced Hostilities," he then admitted that the Red Sticks had in fact been "attacked by a party of militia."[34]

The very day of the Burnt Corn ambush, Agent Benjamin Hawkins wrote the governor of Georgia, noting, "that the civil war which has raged among the Creeks," [at least Hawkins recognized this part of the equation], originated with the British in Canada." Once the National Council aligned Creeks had been defeated, he added, the Red Sticks would attack friendly Indians and American settlements "without delay." When a Knoxville paper printed the above letter the next month, included were excerpts from pro-American Creek chiefs' pleas to the governor of Georgia for arms and men to defend themselves from the Red Sticks.

Throughout 1813, persistent (if inaccurate) reports circulated of British troops landing in Florida to aid the Red Sticks against the United States. One Natchez resident openly wondered if the Southern gentry possessed the necessary toughness to deal with these internal and external threats. He noted both the likelihood of a war with the Creeks and lambasted the territorial governor's failure to recruit the Choctaws against them. "You well know how little real American blood flows in the veins of most of our Cotton Bale gentry & how much aid a foreign enemy would secure from our slaves & old Tories & you well know that we have not a strong place in the whole extent of our country." An aggressively minded Kentuckian noted in a letter to his father, "Now is the time for taking Pensacola, for I think we have sufficient cause as it is evident the Creeks draw arms from the British through that quarter. I further understand that the B. have landed 600 men there to assist them."[35] The British had in fact done nothing for the Red Sticks, or any Southern Indians to this point, but the widespread belief that they had proved more than sufficient to make Americans in the region impulsive, even reckless.

After Burnt Corn, American settlers in the thinly populated Gulf Coast region *forted up*, seeking to protect themselves as best they could. In a number of places, including at the home of Samuel Mims, pro-U.S. mestizo Creeks joined them. Mims and his neighbors had thrown up a wooden palisade around his home near Lake Tensaw, dubbing the structure Fort Mims. Four hundred whites, mestizos, and pro-American Creeks, with their slaves, holed up in the protection of what they generously called a fort. Prior to August 30, 1813, the comparative quiet in the neighborhood of Fort Mims led many to believe that the worst of the war had passed by. When two slaves reported to their masters that they had seen a large body of painted Indians nearby, they were whipped for their "lies."[36]

The furious assault launched that day by 750 Red Sticks may well have had the pro-U.S. mestizos as its primary target, but by this time American settlers were unlikely to be spared. The Red Sticks were led by Hopoie Tastanangi (Far-off Warrior).[37] However, his name was difficult to spell, and thereafter Americans attributed actual leadership to his lieutenant William Weatherford, also known as Red Eagle, himself a mestizo who embodied just how complicated the Creek civil war was. Weatherford had, at least obliquely, aided Hawkins and the United States when he helped capture William Augustus Bowles and turned him over to the Spaniards. That fact would be easily overlooked after Fort Mims. By the end of the six-hour battle, at least 247 Americans and mestizo Creeks had been killed. One hundred more were prisoners, while about fifty had managed to escape in the confusion. As Joel Martin asserts, the victory was actually an exceptionally costly one for the Red Sticks. Well over three hundred of them had been killed or seriously wounded in the melee, despite the promises of their prophets that they would be unscathed. Statistically it was one of the worst days in the history of Creek war losses. Far more damaging, in the long run, were the ramifications of attacking a post holding so many Americans, especially women and children. Though Weatherford had unsuccessfully tried to stop the slaughter of noncombatants, Fort Mims, which the Americans quickly deemed a "massacre," gave the United States (especially Southerners) a long-awaited pretext, and "guaranteed that the United States would invade Muskogee."[38]

The first counterstroke to Fort Mims was a massive media assault. The September 18, 1813, *Kentucky Palladium* referred to the attack as an "AWFUL MASSACRE!" The *Charleston Courier* (SC) reported an "Indian Massacre." With unintentional irony, given the Mims' defenders refusal to believe the attack was coming, the *Courier* also noted that the intelligence "comes in a rather 'questionable shape,' being a negro's story, yet we think there is too much reason to believe it is substantially true." Even the Federalist *Columbian Centinel* (Boston) wrote of a "Great Slaughter by the Creeks," and a "dreadful massacre." Taking their story from the *National Intelligencer*, they added that they hoped that the [slightly high] description of casualties— three hundred to four hundred—was typical of the "exaggeration" of the Republican press.[39]

After years of hype about Indian wars, however, exaggeration was the order of the day. One of the early reports about Fort Mims asserted, "The Battle of Thermopylae, sustain'd by Leonidas with his little Spartan band of three hundred, for a considerable time, against two millions & a half of Perseans, is no more worthy of fame." In addition to the hyperbole, the author offered, "*many of the Northern Indians are among the Creeks and Chactaws*" [emphasis in original]. Even worse, "the Negroes have also excited considerable uneasiness, many have gone off with arms," and word was spreading that blacks, Indians, and French settlers would all fall upon American settlers.[40]

Benjamin Hawkins, who had witnessed William Bowles' worrisome efforts to liberate and recruit slaves, had also feared that the Red Sticks would inspire and utilize a slave rebellion. In the immediate aftermath of Fort Mims, he was deeply troubled that despite the large number of Muskogee-speaking blacks living in the Creek Nation, none had warned him about Fort Mims. News that some slaves had died in the battle mollified him, though only slightly. Other reports indicated that blacks inside the fort had helped cut away the pickets, while those with the Red Sticks helped rally them to renew the assault after their initial withdrawal.[41]

Military leaders on the frontier reacted swiftly and predictably to the news of Fort Mims' fall. General Ferdinand L. Claiborne at Fort Stoddert (above Mobile) observed that his orders were to "be in a state of readiness to repel any attack that may be made on any part of the Frontier of the Mississippi Territory, either by Indians, Spaniards, or the British," and further offered that the British and Spanish were actively engaged in aiding and abetting the Creeks. Noting the paradoxical weakness of the Spanish authorities, he advocated an immediate attack upon Pensacola to remove that source of supply for the Red Sticks. He added, "If I am ordered to act on the defensives only much serious injury will be done on the Frontiers. The best mode of fighting Indians is to penetrate into the heart of their Settlements and to give them battle at the threshold of their doors." Claiborne also notified Hawkins that he hoped to receive orders for an immediate invasion of the Creek Nation, and that he believed McQueen's visit to acquire arms in Pensacola had been "on orders from a British Genl. in Canada to the Governor of that place." He also received reports of Shawnees operating in McQueen's party encouraging them to make war. It was a good example of the fact and fiction that blended into belief on the frontier.[42]

CHAPTER **18**

Bleeding Pan-Indianism

Andrew Jackson had not literally jumped for joy when he learned about Fort Mims, though only because he was in no condition to do so. He was still recovering from a vicious brawl in a Nashville hotel with some of his sociopolitical rivals. Even with bullet wounds to his left arm and shoulder, he could muster the following message to his volunteer troops of Tennessee: "Brave Tennesseans! Your Frontier is threatened with invasion by the savage foe! Already do they advance towards your frontier with their scalping knives unsheathed, to butcher your wives, your children, and your helpless babes. Time is not to be lost. We must hasten to the frontier, or we will find it drenched in the blood of our fellow-citizens." Governor Blount had directed him to take two thousand men into the field "at the shortest possible day."[1]

Jackson's views and policies, particularly in light of the contemptible Indian Removal policy of his presidency, make him a tempting target for modern historians. It proves far too easy to decry his methods and lampoon his motives whenever he engaged Indians. Of course Jackson knew that leading a successful campaign against Indian enemies would reap tremendous political benefits. As a planter he certainly cast a wanton eye at Indian lands, particularly the fertile territory of the Creeks. He was also a settler, citizen, and husband who had spent his entire life immersed in stories (many of them true) about the horrors of Indian warfare on the frontier. Jackson would most likely not have understood the gender implications of Benjamin Hawkins's civilization efforts among the Creeks, and probably would not have sympathized if he had. But Jackson had heard the (true) reports of Red Stick warriors disemboweling a pregnant woman, Mrs. Philips, near the mouth of the Ohio River and impaling her fetus

215

on a stake. He was quite sincere when he condemned the Red Sticks as a "matricidal band," and he felt that fire and the sword were fitting and proper ways to deal with them.[2]

Nevertheless, by October Jackson, still weak from his Nashville wounds, had calmed down considerably. He still agreed with Claiborne and other military officers that a direct attack on the Red Sticks was necessary, but he did not feel that they would invade Tennessee soon, and was further cheered by intelligence that the Cherokees, rather than allying with the Red Sticks, would join him against them. In truth, Jackson needed the time. Despite folksongs to the contrary, most Tennesseans had been "on the verge of Indian panic" prior to Fort Mims, and the exaggerated reports of the battle did not help. Further, the years of peace since the mid-1790s had left "Tennessee volunteers, for the most part, . . . ill prepared (psychologically and physically) for the discipline of army life and the rigors of a harsh campaign." And many of them showed up for service without a firearm, or great skill in using one.[3]

As the internal Creek struggle slipped the bonds of that nation, fear that the Red Stick prophets or Tecumseh could sway other Southern tribes increased dramatically. General Claiborne and others grew alarmed when the Choctaw Chief Pushmataha, who remained in the pro-American camp with most of his nation, reported that thirty of his young warriors had joined the Creeks and planned to assault American posts. Even worse, Red Sticks had attacked his village—as they had a number of National Council Creek villages already. Though the Choctaws had been staunch American allies for decades, the public and the press were nevertheless bedeviled with the thought that they would heed the siren call of Tecumseh or the Red Stick prophets. Fortunately for the United States, the Cherokees were alarmed by the Creek civil war and its implications as well. Cherokee principal chief John Ross asked Indian agent Return Meigs, Jr., to keep him informed of the developments, and offered to send couriers with intelligence to Meigs in return.[4]

Though none could know it at the time, the Red Sticks had won their last major engagement of the war. Thousands of soldiers from Tennessee and Georgia flooded into the region and by November 1813 were conducting withering raids from which the Red Sticks had little hope of recovery. Their towns were especially vulnerable to American armies, including the town of Hillabee, which had already surrendered to Jackson. Another

American officer, who apparently had not learned of the capitulation, crushed the town, killing sixty Creeks of all ages and both sexes in what one scholar calls "the most notorious Anglo-American massacre of the war." Prior to March 1814, about seven hundred Red Sticks, including women and children, had been killed.[5] While Americans railed against the murders of white women and children, many also found pretext for behaving in kind. For both the Red Sticks and pan-Indianism, it would only get worse.

The war against Britain saw some success in 1813, but the war against Britain's Indian allies could hardly have gone better in the wake of Fort Mims. In September, Oliver Hazard Perry's stunning victory over the British fleet on Lake Erie forced a British retreat into Upper Canada. Hot on their heels was William Henry Harrison, leading an enthusiastic army of regulars, militia, and mounted Kentucky volunteers. On October 5, 1813, at the Battle of Moraviantown near the Thames River, Harrison's men stormed right through the outnumbered, demoralized Redcoats. Tecumseh and his Indians continued to fight, desperately trying to buy time for their retreating families. But when Tecumseh fell, apparently at the hands of one of the Kentuckians, his warriors drew away.[6]

Harrison's victory was somewhat marred by those same Kentuckians, who scalped and flayed some of the Indian corpses, including that thought to be Tecumseh's, to make souvenir razor strops. The sight disgusted Harrison and made it impossible for him to identify the body of his old treaty council adversary. His official report after the battle made no mention of the slain chief. A far less reserved Cincinnati paper would soon note with pride and relief not only the victory, but that "Gen. Tecumseh was among the slain."[7] The most famous pan-Indianist since Pontiac had died, and his death would prove a crippling blow to the movement, especially in Northern theater. By late 1813 Americans, perhaps in part because the rest of the war had gone so poorly, reveled in these tangible victories over their pan-Indian boogey men.

Newark New Jersey's *Centinel of Freedom* offered the following celebratory assessment of the:

Southern Indians—His Britannic majesty's tawny "Allies," who have taken up the tomahawk and scalping knife in support of the "fast anchored Isle," begin already to feel that dreadful chastisement which their folly and perfidious conduct has justly exposed them to. In addition to their late over throw at the Ten Islands, in which near 200 were killed and half that number taken prisoners, and not one escaped to tell the doleful story—they have again been surprised, and nearly *three hundred* have "bit the dust."

The piece continued, "And here we cannot but remark on the opposite policies of the American and British governments as respects the Indians." The Americans had shown "a benevolence and tenderness worthy a Christian nation," in telling the Indians to remain neutral in the war. "But the British government, as abandoned in principle, as the governing prince is notorious for debauchery, sent their prophets to prophecy lies among them. . . . The greater part of the Indians listened to the syren songs of the deceiver," the editor continued with faux lament. "They joined in the war-dance. But their dance has been the dance of death and overthrow." The Northern Indians had been "completely humbled," while those to the South were "reaping a luxuriant harvest for their perfidy." With growing confidence, the editorial concluded, "How will they curse the deceptions of the British, who have brought upon them these calamities! To use the forcible expression of Tecumseh,—may the enemies of America always be thus "thrown flat on their backs!"[8]

One of the truly fascinating aspects to Tecumseh, ably detailed by his biographer John Sugden, was how quickly (and perhaps perversely) he was incorporated into the pantheon of American heroes.[9] In the American South, he would be known as an "anti-American zealot," a view that was only encouraged by wildly inaccurate "translations" of his speeches.[10] Perhaps this reflected the even greater stakes of a "race war" in the slave-holding South. But opinion in the North was quite different. Less than six months after his death he was lionized in print. A widely reprinted piece, titled "Character of Tecumseh," shows that as early as the spring of 1814 Tecumseh's legend as a *noble savage* was rapidly eclipsing his life as a pan-Indian leader dedicated to halting American imperialism. Tecumseh was "in every respect a savage, perhaps the greatest since Pontiac," the article asserted. The fact that "It had long been a favorite object of this aspiring chief to unite the northern, western & southern Indians, for the purposes of regaining their country as far as the Ohio," was duly noted, though it seemed far less frightening with the chief dead. Yet as the war still raged, few Americans would relinquish at least the *possibility* of British machinations.

"Whether this grand idea originated in his own, or his brother's mind, or was suggested by the British, is not known; but this much is certain—he cherished the plan with enthusiasm, and actually visited the Creek Indians, to prevail on them to join in the undertaking." Americans seemed to particularly fixate on Tecumseh's opposition to the killing or torturing of prisoners, which rightly struck observers as deviating from the Indian norm. That factor may well have been the key to his *nobility* in Anglo-American eyes. With surprising frankness, the article also reported, "Some of the Kentuckians disgraced themselves by committing indignities on his dead body. He was scalped and otherwise disfigured." Tecumseh was transformed, almost overnight, from a pan-Indian nightmare to a nationalist's dream. For Americans in the North, he had become the perfect Indian—a fierce opponent whose defeat reflected glory on the republic, a gallant warrior, and a corpse.[11]

To the south, the Red Sticks continued to fight on. On March 27, 1814, Andrew Jackson and three thousand men (including five hundred Cherokees and one hundred allied Creeks) surrounded one thousand Red Sticks in their fortified village of Tohopeka. Well situated for defense, the Red Sticks had built a log wall across a narrow neck of land that formed a peninsula in a bend of the Tallapoosa River, with the river protecting the rear and flanks. American observers noted the shape and referred to it as Horseshoe Bend. The Red Sticks, perhaps three-quarters of them armed only with lances, bows, clubs or tomahawks, held against Jackson's light barrage. The general's two small fieldpieces would have had a difficult time piercing the defenses, but Jackson's Indian allies took the initiative,[12] crossed the river, and began attacking the Red Sticks from the rear. Jackson, seeing the smoke from the village, ordered a full assault, and the battle became a vicious, close quarters affair.

The Red Sticks were driven back to the river, only to find the Cherokees and Creeks had taken their canoes—and escape route—away. After the battle, in a macabre bid for accuracy, Jackson's men cut off the tips of their dead enemies' noses as they found them on the field. They tallied five hundred and fifty-seven Red Stick noses, with estimates of another two or three hundred shot in the Tallapoosa as they desperately tried to escape.

In addition, the day after the battle troops found sixteen Red Sticks hiding under a river embankment and buried them alive by collapsing their impromptu bunker. Perhaps in gruesome mimicry of the Kentuckians who killed Tecumseh, Jackson's men flayed Red Stick dead to make bridal reins. Overall, it proved a crushing defeat.[13] Despite Jackson's fears for weeks after the battle, the Red Sticks would not take the offensive again.

Jackson's writings after the battle reveal some confusion and, surprisingly, perhaps some mixed emotions as well. He never seemed able to get a precise count of the casualties or the prisoners taken. He wrote of his "Determining to exterminate them" at the beginning of the battle, and then noted in the same letter that he had taken about two hundred and fifty prisoners, "all women and children except two or three." When writing his wife Rachel, he estimated taking three hundred and fifty prisoners. He also reported the killing of sixteen Red Sticks "who had been concealed"—they were entombed in the river embankment. (When running for president, Jackson would later dispute that portion of his own report.) There was no disputing the catastrophic loss for the Red Sticks, who may have suffered nine hundred dead in the battle—the worst one-day combat loss in Native American history. He was correct however when he pronounced, "The power of the creeks is I think broken forever."[14]

For the American press and public, the battle at Horseshoe Bend was but the beginning of a love affair with Andrew Jackson. His account of the battle was widely reprinted, and spawned triumphal headlines: "Great Victory over the Creeks," graced one New York paper. The more statistically minded *Independent Chronicle* noted that it was the "Fifth victory over the Creeks," and suggested the battle had given "a death-blow" to them. *The Chronicle* had of course neglected to mention the many Creeks who had aided Jackson, but not so egregiously as the *Salem Gazette*, which reported the battle under "Exterminating the Indians." The *Georgetown Gazette*, in a piece reprinted by Boston's *The Repertory*, sarcastically inquired into the fate of "Our Red Brethren," before noting that the Creeks held about 25 million acres of land, some of which was "uncommonly fertile." "Good news from the South! The Creek War Ended!," wrote "Patriot" for the *Independent Chronicle*. The author congratulated the nation "on this signal defeat of the most powerful tribe of *British allies*. . . . Our whole Southern frontier will now be relieved from the tomahawk of the ruthless savage, nor shall we again be shocked with such horrid occurrences as the massacre at Fort Mims."[15]

William Weatherford himself had surrendered to Jackson on April 17, and Jackson soon released him with the understanding that the Red Stick captain's extended family would be spared, and that Weatherford would try to convince others to come in. Indeed, Weatherford would soon be leading attacks on Red Sticks who refused to surrender. On April 22, General Thomas Pinckney ordered Jackson's men discharged and returned to Tennessee.[16] Yet Jackson, now commissioned a Major General in the U.S. Army, realized that threats remained in the Southeast. The remnants of the Red Sticks had fled into East Florida to their Seminole relatives. A great many former slaves lived there as well, and they all felt common cause in fighting the United States and raiding slave plantations in Georgia and elsewhere. And even more dangerous foes were coming.

Americans, especially Republicans on the frontier, had castigated Britain for aiding and encouraging the Creeks to war against the United States since at least 1811–1812. The assumption of war was far from unreasonable, especially given Tecumseh's ties to both the Red Sticks and British Canada. Yet despite the flirtation of the HMS *Brazen* in the late summer of 1812, apparently "until early 1814 no high-ranking British official had been engaged in aiding the Creek Indians, and . . . all [the] supplies they had received had come from junior officials acting on their own, from private individuals, or from the Spaniards." Americans simply could not believe the lackadaisical effort to support the Red Sticks when, to them at least, the stakes were so high. Wartime evidence—the grave lack of firearms and ammunition available to the Red Sticks—only one third of the warriors carried a gun—for example, points strongly to Britain's lack of commitment to the first years of the war in the Southeast.[17]

Great Britain of course had far greater concerns in 1812 and 1813. In the midst of their fight for survival against Napoleon, they had neither wanted an American war nor devoted great resources to it. By the spring of 1814, however, Napoleon was on his heels, and Paris would soon fall to Britain and its allies. Suddenly, the British were far more willing to commit talent and resources to chastise the pesky American republic. By September 1814, 13,000 battle-hardened Redcoats had arrived in Canada, and that chronically undermanned region now had 30,000 excellent troops to throw at the Americans.[18] A diversionary attack to the south would not only facilitate their assault, but perhaps snatch some terribly valuable Gulf Coast real estate as well.

In the late spring of 1814, Whitehall called for a new commander of its North American station. He was Sir Alexander Forster Inglis Cochrane, a vice-admiral whose record and talents, even by the high standards of the Royal Navy, were impressive. His resume included combat in the Egyptian Expedition of 1801 and serving as commander in chief off the Leeward Islands from 1804 to 1814.[19] The Scotsman brought an energetic, creative leadership to the American war that had been largely missing since the death of Isaac Brock, and totally lacking in the Southern theater. His recognition of the great potential for a British-backed army of Indians and African Americans to unhinge and conquer in the thinly populated American Southeast could have wreaked havoc and drastically changed the war's outcome. Unfortunately for British-Indian arms, as had often happened during the American Revolution, the effort was at least six months too late.

CHAPTER **19**

Mistimed Alliance

From the British perspective, the Red Sticks had joined the war too early. For the Red Sticks, the British were deathly late. Vice-Admiral Cochrane and his junior officers, from May 1814 on, labored under the delusion that two thousand Indian warriors awaited merely their presence and armaments to lay waste to the American forces. The previous months had killed at least fifteen hundred of those warriors and scattered or driven off the rest. Jackson's near annihilation of the Red Sticks at Tohopeka—where the blood of the slain had supposedly dyed the river red—had certainly discouraged other Indian nations from joining the fray, at least on the British/Spanish side. Though poorly timed, British plans for the Southeast were nevertheless quite interesting.

In May 1814, Captain Hugh Pigot of the HMS *Orpheus* sent word to the "Chiefs of the Creek Nations" that he carried two thousand muskets, with ammunition and accouterments, which he would deliver to them, as well as any "other articles as they require." In this and subsequent missives, it became clear that the Admiralty sought to issue bayonets with the muskets—something Americans did not typically do with Indian allies—and fully intended to supply men to teach the Creeks basic close order drill with them. While not operating hand in glove with the Spanish, as Americans had long feared, Captain Pigot admonished his lieutenant that "In fulfilling these directions you are most particularly enjoined on no account whatever to give offence to the Spaniards in East or West Florida, but advice [*sic*] the Chiefs to this effect, as it may be the means in future of furnishing them with supplies with greater facility."[1]

Either ignorant or dismissive of the frightening death toll from Tohopeka, Cochrane's young officers continued to report enthusiastically about the potential for striking into the American interior. George Woodbine, who had been promoted to a brevet captain of the Royal Marines specifically to aid his work in recruiting auxiliaries for the Crown, was typical. He confidently asserted that he had "no doubt of several hundred American slaves, joining our standard the moment it is raised." Woodbine, it should be noted, was not a dyed-in-the-wool abolitionist. Indeed, he would spend much of his adult life as a filibuster. But he had orders to rally American slaves to the Union Jack, and knew that doing so would both terrify slave owners and materially hurt the American war effort.[2] He also had orders to rally as many Indian allies as possible.

By late May 1814, he had begun the construction of a store to house the munitions for the thousands of Indians, including Choctaws, he felt would soon flock to the British. Having met with some Indians, Woodbine reported, "the chiefs have unanimously decided, that all power to conduct operations, shall be taken out of their hands, and Lodged solely in mine, as Chief of all, as also the appointment of all Officers." Not only did Woodbine sincerely (and naively) believe that a great body of influential chiefs had ceded all war decisions to him. He insisted that he could "twist round my finger" the métis chief Perryman—a Seminole who had counted William Bowles as a son-in-law—and that they would honor a pledge to hand over all prisoners to him, and to kill only those who continued to resist. Woodbine's greatest concern seemed to be finding enough food for the great army he thought was flocking to him.[3]

A jolt of reality came when the surviving Red Sticks dictated a letter from Pensacola to the British command. They said they had been driven from their homes and had already written to the governor of Jamaica [the Duke of Manchester] for aid, but heard no reply. They did note that it "warmed their hearts" to hear that British troops were landing, and requested some desperately needed weapons and provisions. They did not mention that a significant part of their food shortage was the result of following Tecumseh's exhortations to destroy nonnative food sources, including their livestock. Nevertheless, Pigot would produce that summer a list of over 3,200 Red Sticks and Seminoles who pledged to fight the United States.[4]

Cochrane himself showed his skill in Atlantic diplomacy that July. He first wrote to the governor of Havana, assuring him that he had no intention of attacking Spanish possessions. His only motive was "to preserve the Indians from being destroyed by the United States." He added that maintaining the Indians was "the best barrier the Spanish Provinces in the Floridas can have against [American] encroachments." He even made the gesture of pledging support "in the event of Spain being at War with America." In turn, the governor of Havana went so far as to request that the British join his relief force being sent to Pensacola.[5]

Cochrane also wrote Lord Bathurst—Henry George, a member of Lord Liverpool's cabinet—to notify him that he was sending an American turtle and a box of Indian arrows for Lady Bathurst's amusement. He then asserted that Lord Melville—Henry Dundas, the Home Secretary—would "shew your Lordship what I have done with respect to the Indians." Cochrane insisted that with two thousand men he would "Give Gr. Britain the Command of that Country [meaning the Gulf Coast region]—and New Orleans." He further hoped that his Marines would "be able to bring all the Indian Tribes to Act in Concert together."[6] Had the American press read these letters they would finally have seen direct evidence of their persistent nightmares—the British military trying to foster a pan-Indian coalition to attack the United States, with the possible collusion of the Spanish.

By July, Brevet Captain Woodbine was convinced that he held tremendous sway among the Southern Indians. While that might seem ludicrous in hindsight, Jackson and the Americans had behaved with confidence bordering on hubris. They had essentially declared the Creek War over, disbanded the militia, and Jackson had begun the *negotiations* at Fort Jackson that would result in the Treaty of Fort Jackson (concluded August 9, 1814). William Henry Harrison and others had proven tough, even heavy-handed negotiators at Indian councils, but Jackson made them look genteel. The first sentence of the treaty perfectly illustrates Elise Marienstras's argument about using the imagery of Indians to forge American identity.[7] It stated: "Whereas an unprovoked, inhuman, and sanguinary war, waged by the hostile Creeks against the United States, hath been repelled, prosecuted and determined, successfully, on the part of the said States, in conformity with principles of national justice and honorable warfare."[8]

From the perspective of many—even Jackson's fellow treaty commissioners cried foul—the brazen document punished friendly Creek and Red Stick alike. It called for a cession of more than twenty million acres constituting half of the Creeks' lands—including most of their best hunting territory. As Gregory Waselkov notes, this was the largest cession forced from Native Americans up to this point in U.S. history, and it basically dared the Creeks to side with the British. Jackson, however, felt the harsh terms were necessary to prevent a future war with the Creeks. The cession he demanded would take all the Creek claims along the border with Spanish Florida, restricting Creek access to British or Spanish arms. Jackson guessed that the Creeks, pro-American and former Red Sticks, would be so wasted from two years of war that they would sign the treaty out of necessity. They did so—though at most only one Red Stick signed the treaty, the balance being allies or neutrals—under protest. The Tennessean came up with a particularly self-serving rationale for punishing the Creeks communally. He "blamed the entire Creek Nation for tolerating Tecumseh's presence among them and for the subsequent rebellion and bloodshed that had followed. According to Jackson, they should have either seized Tecumseh and sent him as a prisoner to Jackson or killed him themselves." Heads I win, tails you lose, was Jackson's negotiating framework. Upon conclusion of the "council," he did send immediate orders for food and clothing, but this was as much to keep the Indians out of the British camp as from anything approaching humanity.[9]

Meanwhile that summer Captain Woodbine complained bitterly that he could have attacked Georgia and even captured Mobile, if only he had received enough food for the vast Indian army rallying to him. Displaying some ignorance of Indian diplomacy and cordiality, he reported, "I believe I have been successful in inducing the Indians to lay aside all animosity against their fellow Countrymen, and to unite in their endeavours to oppose the common Foe." He also stated that he expected the Choctaws, Cherokees, and Chickasaws (all of whom had hundreds of warriors in the service of the United States) to soon join him. At least Woodbine tempered his optimism with a dose of realism when he assessed the situation of New Orleans. The coast from St. Marys (in Georgia) to the Mississippi, "including New Orleans, may be taken possession of without a blow," if Cochrane could only land two thousand troops. New Orleans was indeed quite vulnerable, if only the British could muster those men in time.[10]

Cochrane and the Admiralty had, by the mid- and late summer of 1814, gotten serious about equipping the Indians and blacks they hoped to recruit. Gifts of scarlet jackets, dragoon helmets, and other items of clothing were enthusiastically received by the Southern Indians, who had been poorly supplied with trade goods since the war began. The British hoped, with slowly diminishing enthusiasm, that with a stream of supplies the numerous

Choctaws—whose villages on the Mississippi made them ideal allies for an assault on New Orleans—could be swayed to join them. Young Woodbine could write at the end of July, "The Choctaws I am now convinced are ours." Lt. Col. Edward Nicolls even dreamed that four thousand Choctaws would join the British, and hoped to provide them with muskets and one thousand rounds each, plus some twenty-four-pound cannon to fortify positions.[11]

Nicolls recounted to Cochrane the story of an older Creek warrior who responded enthusiastically to his new musket and the training in the use of its bayonet. The warrior "observed that he always thought some thing was wanting, for that while the enemy was loading, and he was loading, much time was lost, that now he had a bayonet he would rush on the American, when he was sure of victory." Nicolls stated he thought, though could not be sure, that the Chickasaws, Cherokees, and some Choctaws, would join the fight. Even "messengers from the Shawanese, a people from the other side of the Ohio," said they would come "to join us right through the enemys Country." A hard dose of reality hit Nicolls, as he added, "The chiefs all believe it but it appears very improbable to me, that they could make their way so far, and through such difficulties." Nicolls also observed that the pace of enlistment for black men from the surrounding countryside was below the expected pace, "owing to the upper Creeks being in a wavering state." He felt that more could be purchased from the Creeks for British use, with 60 to 70 dollars each being a "reasonable sum." Nicolls, unlike Woodbine, was deathly serious about abolitionism, and saw his assignment on the Gulf Coast as a tremendous opportunity to not only smite the avaricious American republic, but to strike a telling blow against slavery as well.[12]

Black troops had tremendous potential as both physical and symbolic warriors. Virginians, as Alan Taylor has demonstrated, were positively terrified when the British recruited and used black troops to raid the Chesapeake. In addition to being fine and loyal combat troops, they horrified Southerners with their potential to spark slave revolts. The threat of servile insurrection expanded the schism between Southern Republicans and Northern Federalists. "Columbian," an irate Chesapeake editorialist, contrasted the patriotic response of Virginians to the "sufferings of the citizens of Boston, Concord, and Lexington," to the indifference of (anti-war) Bostonians after the deaths and scalpings at the River Raisin and the blockade of Norfolk. Even worse, Columbian lamented, "there are people in

Boston who taunt the citizens of Virginia with being the authors of their own calamity, and cherish the idea of an African insurrection!" Yet the British high command did not really hope for a widespread slave uprising through the South, as that would have wrecked the value of the region they hoped to conquer. Edward Nicolls had been chosen for his hard-charging combat record, not his antislavery beliefs, and would repeatedly exceed his authority in the name of abolition.[13]

As slavery exploded in the Deep South after the cotton gin's 1793 invention, so the always looming fear of slave rebellion had grown as well. Racial lines hardened for Americans in the South, planter and commoner alike. Indeed, many Southern Indians of means came to see common cause with white planters rather than pan-Indianists or runaway slaves. A great many Creeks, Cherokees, Choctaws, and others allied themselves with Andrew Jackson's army because they viewed British efforts to incite slave rebellion with a horror identical to their Southern white neighbors. Benjamin Hawkins, who saw five of his own slaves *stolen* by Red Sticks, would encourage allied Creeks to raid into Pensacola and to kill any blacks or whites they encountered bearing arms.[14]

Vice-Admiral Cochrane showed energy and initiative in his plans. The British assault on the southern United States—which included the successful raid that burned Washington, D.C.—could have wreaked havoc through the Southeastern states, and captured New Orleans, had the campaign been carried out a few months or even weeks earlier.[15] One can only imagine the Red Sticks' reaction to the offers of arms and munitions and troops' support, and what they might have meant had they arrived in 1813 instead of 1814. Dragoons armed with rifles, trained black troops from the Bahamas, and a growing force of runaway slaves and weapons to arm them, even 1,200 "Canadian pipe hatchets with handles"—all of these would have had a huge impact had they arrived sooner.[16]

Americans remained terribly worried about Louisiana, especially Baton Rouge, which Americans had only recently annexed,[17] much to the vexation of Spain, and the crucial city of New Orleans. One woman from St. Martin's parish noted a fear not just for her family, but for the people of Baton Rouge as well, citing the threat of invasion and the disunity of the people of New Orleans. Writing to her friend in Philadelphia, she admitted "but what I dread most is an insurrection[,] the people of colour are vastly superior in numbers to the whites and have no doubt arms will be furnish'd them by the English or Spanish government." She concluded that her sons seemed "perfectly happy and I assume [are] ignorant of the dangers that surround them." She was also aware weeks in advance that the British would mount "a serious descent" upon New Orleans, and that if General Jackson could "not muster strength enough to defeat them, I fear it will go hard with them."[18]

The British assault on New Orleans, despite having taken place after the signing of a peace accord in Ghent, might well have led to an extension of hostilities. The British had never considered New Orleans to be legitimately the property of the United States. Had General Pakenham not been defeated, the course of Gulf Coast history might well have been significantly different. Had Cochrane been able to occupy New Orleans—Andrew Jackson beat him there by a matter of days—it could have been a victorious British defense of the key city. Had the British possessed both Mobile and New Orleans, the native peoples of the Southeast would have had a far greater incentive to bring their numbers and skills to the fight and enslaved blacks a far greater reason to risk escape and revolt. As Jeremy Black asserts, a paltry number of Royal Marines, joined by Indians and escaped slaves, had waged a spirited guerilla campaign in the Southeast from Spanish territory, and their potential was probably not realized. Andrew Jackson's repeated invasions of Florida well after the war ended demonstrate in part that he still considered the multiracial warriors there a threat to American security.[19]

Americans in the Southeast were clearly terrified that continuing the conflict increased the opportunity for a race war that they would lose, and lose badly. Newspaper accounts continually noted Indians flocking to the British standard, as well as the presence of black troops encouraging slaves to join them. At least one South Carolina editor for the *City Gazette* considered the news of black troops so horrifying that he could not bring himself to print the word "negro" before "troops," and substituted ***** in its place.[20] (Perhaps this was a sorry attempt to keep literate slaves from seeing it?) For months afterward, rumors persisted that the British were bringing black troops from the West Indies to spur slave revolt and conquer the Southeast.[21] Had the War of 1812 continued through 1815, it might well have spelled disaster for the American republic.

Yet with Napoleon seemingly out of the picture in late 1814, powerful forces in the British government wanted out of the American war. British negotiators at Ghent, Belgium, did seek to include their Native American allies in the peace settlement. Their most ambitious demand came in the form of a permanent Indian homeland in the Northwest, essentially calling for a return to the 1795 Greenville Treaty's boundaries. Most of the state of Ohio would be U.S. territory, but what would become Indiana, Illinois, Michigan, and Wisconsin would be left to the region's natives as a buffer state between the United States and Upper Canada. The territory would also have allowed British traders to keep a firm hand in the Great Lakes fur trade. The roughly 100,000 whites who had settled beyond the Greenville line would have to "shift for themselves," the British insisted.[22]

The American diplomats Henry Clay and John Quincy Adams considered the proposal preposterous. When it became obvious that they would not budge on the matter, pressure from Whitehall led to the issue being dropped. Lord Liverpool, the 1st Lord of the Treasury, in particular wanted the war with America to end quickly. Even a successful war in America would be exceedingly costly, and the national debt had reached unprecedented levels while fighting Napoleon. He wanted a rapid demobilization, and was further influenced by the Duke of Wellington himself. Wellington never said the American war could not be won, but cautioned that, especially without full naval control of the Great Lakes, it would be costly and terribly difficult. By the fall of 1814, he strongly urged a peace with the United States. That peace, signed on Christmas Eve, 1814, did at least mention the Crown's Indian allies, and called for a return to the status quo of 1811, prior to Tippecanoe.[23] For Indians living east of the Mississippi River, and their pan-Indian dreams, there could be no such thing.

As unpleasant as it may seem to us in the twenty-first century, the American pre-emptive strikes at Burnt Corn Creek and Tippecanoe did in many respects accomplish the greater goals of American expansionists. Both were clumsily executed, and arose from rather flimsy evidence that would centuries later appear to have been correct. Both the Shawnee Prophet's followers and the Red Sticks were looking to eventually wage war against American encroachment, but were not fully mobilized or supplied. These engagements threw off their timing badly, and particularly in the case of Burnt Corn, disastrously. Had the Red Sticks somehow been able to avoid being drawn into a war with Andrew Jackson until the summer of 1814, when British support was available, the war in the Southeast could have taken on a completely different character. Still, by the early nineteenth century the odds for lasting pan-Indian success were so long that they probably placed an unbearable burden on good fortune. For the United States, however, pan-Indianism's failure would be celebrated as yet another sign of American exceptionalism.

For some, the dynamic of Indian war, slave insurrection, and foreign interference held too much appeal to simply abandon it with the Treaty of Ghent. Captain George Woodbine, described by historians as an "adventurer" and a "filibuster,"[24] returned to Florida in 1816, after the war. Acting as a proxy for Edward Nicolls, Woodbine was convinced he could lead his former Red Stick and black comrades in a campaign to take East Florida. Not unlike William Bowles before him, he made them believe he was an agent working with the approval of the British government. As he had played just that role so recently, it was a rather easy sell. Despite what the American press maintained, only the intervention of the governor of the Bahamas stifled his plan. According to one history of the region, "Considering the force that was available to him, there is little doubt that Woodbine would have succeeded had he not been stopped by British officials." Once officers in the Caribbean banned him from recruiting soldiers (black or white) or acquiring arms, Woodbine and fellow filibuster Gregor MacGregor could accomplish little in Florida.[25]

Despite the lack of any official British support for Woodbine, the enthusiastic support he drew from Florida Indians, in particular the Seminoles under chief Billy Bowlegs, as well as hundreds of former slaves, would bring a swift response from Americans. Bowlegs's warriors, native and black, had warred against American invaders since 1812. Though initially encouraged by the Spanish, they increasingly raided plantations in the region regardless of nationality, all the while gathering more slaves, and arming many of them.[26]

Americans in the South were furious with the raids, both for the financial damages incurred and the slave revolt they encouraged. Planters in Florida and Georgia had not forgotten the British Navy's refusal to return slaves who had flocked to their lines during the war—yet another echo of the emancipating effects of the American Revolution. The American press was predictably harsh, and repetitive, in its condemnation of the Seminoles, their black allies, and of course the "agitators" who encouraged them to mischief. Woodbine was labeled "a perfect out-law," and falsely described as working under Spanish approval. False or not, the accusation was useful for newspapermen insisting that "so long as Spain holds the Floridas, the peace of the adjacent states is at the mercy of the governors of Pensacola and St. Augustine."[27]

Woodbine drew such ire even after American forces had destroyed the "Negro Fort" at Prospect Bluff on the Apalachicola River. When Britain had evacuated the Gulf Coast after Ghent, Lt. Col. Nicolls had left behind the strong post built by British military engineers, as well as hundreds of former slaves who were now well-trained soldiers. Nicolls also left a huge cache of arms, including thousands of muskets and some cannon and ammunition. As at Horseshoe Bend, the besieging American army had a sizable contingent of friendly (and slave-owning) Creeks, led by chief William McIntosh. In July of 1816 they attacked, and quickly took the works after a lucky "hot shot" from their cannon found a powder magazine, causing a horrendous explosion in the fort. The ranking black and Seminole warriors inside were both taken wounded but alive, though the former had been blinded in the explosion. However, when the Creeks learned that an American sailor previously captured had been burned to death by the defenders, both chiefs were "scalped and shot" by the Creeks. "Nearly every soul of the den of robbers perished. The number of men, women and children amounted in all to about 300," one correspondent noted. In truth, the bulk of the black and Seminole warriors were gone, either out hunting or having fled in the days prior to the final assault. Many Americans (and Spanish officials) no doubt agreed with the sentiment, "Our only regret, notwithstanding our complete success, is that Nicolls and Woodbine, the British agents who planted this virtuous community, were not included in the explosion."[28]

The destruction of Prospect Bluff significantly reduced the munitions available to Seminole and black warriors, but it did not diminish their resolve to remain free or fight the United States. Nor did it allay the fears of Southerners or the military. Throughout 1817, headlines like "Indian Outrages—Again," ran, decrying Woodbine for having "instigated" Indians to raid American plantations. So horrifying was the thought of Woodbine emancipating black slaves that articles sometimes left the word *negroes* blank.[29]

The Scots-born Indian trader Alexander Arbuthnot, having resided for some time in Florida, wrote an editorial decrying "the arch villain Woodbine," but also calling for the just treatment of the natives. Americans ignored the condemnation of Woodbine—the editor even argued that Arbuthnot was merely Woodbine's "alias"—but would not forget the Scotsman's friendship for their Indian enemies.[30]

When Major General Edmund P. Gaines reported searching a hostile Seminole chief's home and finding a scarlet British uniform with gold epaulets, he merely confirmed the stale fears of British-Indian collusion. Adding that there were two thousand Red Sticks and Seminoles and four hundred blacks "and increasing by the addition of every runaway from Georgia able to get to them," was superfluous. A year later, estimates had the Seminoles, "with their negroes," numbering five thousand warriors.[31] Worse still, they were hard to find.

Andrew Jackson desperately wanted to hang George Woodbine and Billy Bowlegs. But Woodbine was long gone—he would die in Mexico two decades later—and Bowlegs was far too elusive. Instead, he settled for quickly trying and executing Richard Armbrister, a Nicolls protégé who had encouraged Seminole militants, and Alexander Arbuthnot, who most likely had not. The fact that Jackson had no authority to execute foreign nationals was decried outside of the American Southeast. But most Americans in the region agreed with the *Georgia Journal*'s assessment that the two Britons were obviously guilty.[32]

The Seminoles refused to be cowed, however. When General Edmund Gaines sent a letter to the chief King Hatchy, insisting that he be allowed to attack a "great many of my black people" living on the Suwannee River, the chief responded that he would "use force to stop any armed Americans from passing my towns or my lands." Further, it was he, not General Gaines, who had been wronged. Four Seminoles had been murdered by Americans while hunting, while one American had been killed trying to steal cattle. And, Hatchy noted, "I harbor no negroes."[33]

Jackson's popularity with the American public did not really wane after the Battle of New Orleans, and his rampages through Florida drew support from all but die hard Federalists. As Alan Taylor notes, the executions of Arbuthnot and Ambrister gave Jackson "even greater popularity in a nation that especially hated the British for aiding Indians and slaves."[34] Most Americans favored territorial expansion, and saw America's future as dominated by the needs and desires of its white citizenry. Jackson's heavy-handedness, and John Quincy Adams' skillful negotiations, would ultimately secure American annexation of Florida in 1819. Though annexation would go a long way toward solidifying white hegemony in the Southeast, decades of uncertainty remained.

Official correspondence and citizens' petitions from the Florida Territory in the 1820s made frequent mention of the issue of runaway slaves and their being harbored by the Seminoles. Various schemes, from unauthorized raids to purchasing them, were attempted. Creek chief William McIntosh, who had been Andrew Jackson's ally during the Creek War, and would later be executed by other Creeks for selling tribal lands, saw opportunity in Florida. In 1821, Seminole leaders complained bitterly that McIntosh and his Coweta warriors (at the behest of Jackson) had barged into their territory and "taken off a Considerable number of negroes and some Indians."[35]

Americans grew particularly concerned that the runaways were a bad influence on American slaves, as they were "in the habit of enticing them from their masters and hiding them in the thick hammocks." Even worse, the Seminoles' slaves "have by their art and Cunning the entire Controul Over their Masters," and repeatedly agitated them against the United States.[36] Despite such evidence of slaves' security threat to Americans in Florida, at least two U.S. Indian agents there were charged with official misconduct for engaging in the purchasing or smuggling of slaves.[37]

Epilogue
A Second Tecumseh?

It would be impossible to know how many razor strops the vengeful Kentucky riflemen made from Tecumseh's flesh in the aftermath of the Battle of the Thames. Undeniably, however, the chief's legend as a valiant but ultimately vanquished foe was used repeatedly to whet the image of American triumph on the frontier. The legends of Tecumseh and pan-Indianism grew in part because they were not repeated, or at least never again matched, which is not to say the fears or hopes of pan-Indianism died quickly or quietly.

From a safe distance we might opine that the hopes for a grand tribal alliance opposing American territorial pretensions died on the Thames in 1813 and the Tallapoosa in 1814. Yet nightmares do not always end so abruptly. Fears of pan-Indianism had become so embedded in the American psyche that they outweighed any rational chance for such an event. For decades after the War of 1812 ended, American officials feared pan-Indianism might rise once more. In the 1820s military leaders compared Indian affairs in Arkansas and Texas to those north of the Ohio when St. Clair's army was crushed. As late as 1827, President John Quincy Adams could note his relief that "the prospects of an extensive combination among the Indians [northwest of the Ohio] are not so menacing as had been apprehended." Still, Adams would "wait with some anxiety" until he heard General James Wilkinson's force had arrived safely at Prairie de Chien. "Invocations of Tecumseh and a comparison with the nation's greatest defeat at the hands of an organized intertribal alliance go a long way toward suggesting the era's tension and the seriousness of Indian affairs."[1]

The most direct comparisons to Tecumseh and his pan-Indian efforts surrounded one of his followers, Black Hawk, a Sauk war captain (and veteran of the River Raisin). Black Hawk had met with British agents in 1817 and requested desperately needed arms, ammunition, and blankets for his starving people. He was so taken aback by the new British policy, which allowed him only some gunpowder and tobacco, he reportedly wept in fury. The Sauks had ceded their lands in what became western Illinois in an 1804 treaty with William Henry Harrison—a cession Black Hawk and his followers insisted had been fraudulent. Black Hawk's primary rival for Sauk leadership was Keokuk, a chief who had also fought against the United States in 1812. Keokuk was the younger, more pragmatic man.

While Black Hawk spent the years after 1815 continuing to believe in the viability of British aid and military resistance to the Americans, "Keokuk and his supporters saw a need to accommodate the Americans to prevent them from destroying the people." While Keokuk added to his legitimacy in dealing with Missouri governor William Clark and leading delegations to meet U.S. officials in Washington, Black Hawk and his traditionalists grew increasingly isolated. When the U.S. insisted that the Sauks and their close relatives the Mesquakies (Foxes) leave the ceded lands in Illinois, Keokuk and his band complied. Black Hawk's band also crossed the river into what is now Iowa, but longed to return.[2]

By the late 1820s, Black Hawk sought to improve his status in part by "consulting with a half-Sauk, half-Winnebago seer named Wabokieshiek, or White Cloud." Known to whites as the Winnebago Prophet, Americans equated him with the Shawnee Prophet. While this did allow them to fall into a comfortable narrative pattern concerning Indians, especially those with pan-Indian pretensions, Wabokieshiek never approached Tenskwatawa's influence. While the Winnebago Prophet did (like Tenskwatawa) incorporate some Christian themes into his preaching, he was not nearly as militant as the Shawnee. He preached of "persistence rather than resistance," which might explain his comparatively small following. Wabokieshiek believed that if Black Hawk avoided violence, the United States would leave him be, even as he crossed the Mississippi to re-occupy his beloved village of Saukenuk. "This simply seems to have reinforced what Black Hawk already believed."[3]

Black Hawk did not seek a military confrontation with the United States, but his followers, known both derisively and ominously as the "British Band," were desperate. Despite the hope to avoid a fight, Black Hawk did seek a

EPILOGUE   237

broad coalition of Indian allies, sending messengers as far away as Arkansas and Texas. These envoys failed to bring in any interested parties. In late June 1831 the British Band crossed the Mississippi back into Illinois. They were confronted by General Edmund Gaines, who fielded not only Army regulars, but mounted Illinois militia and an armed steamboat. (As a young colonel in 1812, Gaines had advocated a preemptive invasion of Spanish Florida to suppress the Seminoles "and their corrupt British principles.")[4] As Gaines hoped, Black Hawk was intimidated by the show of force, most especially the militia, who he feared would be merciless with the band's women and children. The British Band re-crossed the Mississippi, having promised to stay there and avoid contact with British agents in return for Gaines' supplying them some much-needed corn. The Illinois militia, a generation removed from the War of 1812 but raised on tales of its glory, had been spoiling for a fight. They sneered at Gaines' agreement, calling it the "Corn Treaty."[5]

By the 1830s, with Andrew Jackson as president, U.S. policy had shifted from Jefferson's pretensions of benevolence—of harmony with Indians who agreed to be acculturated—to Jackson's hard line insistence upon Indian Removal. By now, Indians had "almost fully played [their] part as a promoter of nationalism among plain citizens . . . [and] become the emblematic sign of a remote past." In the summer of 1831 the *St. Louis Beacon*, as reprinted in the *Baltimore Patriot*, could note that the U.S. Army and Illinois militia had effected "the peaceable removal of the Indians." More importantly, the article continued, they had "dispersed a confederacy which has been forming for two years with incredible secrecy, under which the famous Sac chief BLACK HAWK, and the WINNEBAGO PROPHET, who have been endeavoring to revive the designs of the famous Shawnee Prophet and Tecumseh."[6]

The idea of swift military preemption as the ideal solution to potential Indian wars still held considerable sway. An anonymous soldier from the Jefferson Barracks in St. Louis wrote that, by calling up the military against Black Hawk, Americans might have just "prevented an extensive confederacy of the Indian tribes throughout our line of frontier, with another Tecumseh at their head." Despite such wishful thinking, Black Hawk's band returned to Illinois from Iowa in April 1832. They complained that Gaines had not provided enough corn, and the band's women had been particularly grieved to abandon their laboriously groomed cornfields in Saukenuk. They insisted upon re-occupying their village, which had already been purchased by white settlers.[7]

Black Hawk labored under the forlorn hope that other tribes would rally to him and that British supplies would flow in to feed and equip his followers. Apparently, he hoped that with a strong show of British-backed pan-Indian force, he could avoid an actual fight with the United States and simply reclaim his home. By the time he realized that it was all only pan-Indian fantasy, the army, the militia, and his old enemies the Menominees and Dakotas, were out for blood. Black Hawk's band made a desperate dash through the Wisconsin Territory, hoping to cross the Mississippi, and were caught by American gunboats and troops at the Battle of Bad Axe River. The "Black Hawk War" cost around 520 members of the British Band dead, compared to seventy-seven combined American military and civilian casualties. In a troubling homage to previous battles, some Illinois volunteers skinned the Indian corpses along the Bad Axe to make souvenir razor strops. Even worse, the Dakotas and Menominees hunted down the British Band's remnants and inflicted even more damage in the weeks after the battle.[8]

U.S. Indian agent Henry Schoolcraft, later famous for his ethnographic work, wrote from the Mackinac and St. Marys agency at Sault Ste. Marie of evidence implicating both Black Hawk's pan-Indian intentions, and the lack of enthusiasm they generated. The Sauks, Schoolcraft noted, had "taken much pains to form a league against the government." While some of the Northern tribes, like the Sioux, worried Schoolcraft by not seeming completely dismissive of Black Hawk's plans, he was cheered at their being declined by "the British band of Chippewas." The call to join the Sauks came accompanied by "a painted war club & pipe." He observed that the pipe and club were received by "Little Pine . . . a chief who cooperated with Tecumseh in the late war." Little Pine found the offer both unappealing and "equivocal," telling Schoolcraft the offer was so vague it might have meant to attack the Sioux as much as the Americans.[9]

Like the Creeks during the War of 1812, the Sauks and Mesquakies had suffered a schism over how best to deal with the encroaching Americans. Like the Red Sticks, the British Band had chosen the path of resistance. Black Hawk's followers faced even greater difficulties in gathering foreign aid and native allies. A few Winnebagos and Potawatomis had joined him, but the vast majority of natives in the upper Mississippi Valley felt joining the British Band would be futile. Some, like the Ottawa-born Potawatomi chief Shaubena—like Black Hawk a former lieutenant of Tecumseh—actively campaigned against their people's joining the British Band's struggle.[10]

From the moment Black Hawk's people crossed the Mississippi into Illinois, a great many whites simply assumed that a fight was unavoidable. As with previous attempts at pan-Indian resistance, Black Hawk's movements made the newspapers and drew a military response. Just as the Illinois volunteers hoped for an "Indian war," and some even took grisly souvenirs, so Americans recalled the great victory over Tecumseh and the Prophet by re-casting those familiar roles with Black Hawk and Wabokishiek, respectively. By defeating another "Tecumseh," this generation of frontier Americans re-quickened the heroic imagery of their forbearers. The difference was that by 1832, while the public saw the British Band as a menace, the confidence in ultimate victory was unshakeable. They utilized a "U.S. vs. Tecumseh" narrative framework in large part because they knew, and approved of, the likely outcome.

Four years after Black Hawk's surrender, and his national tour of both sympathy and curiosity, American newspapers once more carried a story about defiant Indian resistance. The *St. Augustine Herald* ran a story about a Seminole chief the whites knew as Powell. The story was re-printed as far away as New Hampshire, where the editor noted that it might prove of interest to the reader, "As he is the head of that tribe in their late and present depredations and murder." Powell was reputedly "a savage of great tact, energy of character, and bold daring." So skillfully had he thwarted the government's efforts to remove the Seminoles from the Everglades, he was entitled "to be considered as superior to Black Hawk." He was so impressive, the *Herald* noted, by right he should not even be referred to as Powell, for that "is only a nick name." His Indian name was Osceola, "and by that should be distinguished." He would be most troublesome to the government, the *Herald* continued, "if they do not act with that decision and energy that becomes the power and force of the country." Unlike the relatively weak government that had confronted McGillivray, Blue Jacket, and Dragging Canoe in the 1790s, the United States had grown up, and the citizenry expected the government to deal with Osceola quickly, before things got out of hand. With concern, if not the abject terror of previous decades, the *Herald* concluded, "The devastation and ruin that he has already caused, will not fall short of a million dollars." When the *New Hampshire Sentinel* ran the article, they reflexively gave it the headline: "A SECOND TECUMSEH."[11]

Though the actual threat of a pan-Indian coalition with foreign aid and black allies taking the offensive in the American Southeast was slim at best by the 1830s, several factors combined to make that chance seem terribly plausible. After decades of rumors and the occasional thwarted plot, Southerners confronted a true large-scale slave revolt in 1831. Nat Turner's 1831 uprising in Virginia killed dozens of whites before being put down, and its psychological impact extended far outside Virginia's borders. Turner's revolt was seen in the context of repeated threats of British-backed slave insurrection during "every war scare with the United States" in the early nineteenth century, and slaves themselves had repeatedly made reference to their hopes for British aid when in rebellion.[12]

Horrified Floridians passed resolutions calling for Federal troops to be sent among them "for the protection of the people of Florida against any insurrection of slaves or free negroes in this vicinity." Free blacks were still considered huge security risks by paranoid Southern whites. That there were so many (free) Black Seminoles as well as slaves who seemed to have considerable autonomy living with them, only made them more terrifying. Curiously, as Matthew Clavin notes, in the wake of Turner's revolt, while many American writers could romanticize about the nobly savage Seminoles, who appeared near extinction, they conflated the Virginia insurrection with blacks in Florida, and feared a repeat, or worse. "The fear of a revolutionary black army from the West Indies landing on Florida's shores was widespread during the Second Seminole War [1835–1842]." And Britain and Spain were not the only potential culprits in fomenting slave rebellion. At least one Florida officer worried that the "large number of Negroes amongst the Indians, who may be under the influence of the Abolitionists of the North, whose machinations, are now endangering our safety."[13]

The fear extended well beyond Florida. In 1836, William Laurence Poole, the military storekeeper in the Army's arsenal in Charleston, South Carolina, wrote his commanding general, Alexander Macomb, Jr., with some grave concerns. Noting that there were perhaps "20,000 able-bodied negro men slaves" within ten to twelve hours march of the fort, he felt dangerously exposed, and asked for more troops to guard the arsenal. The continuing war with the Seminoles not only diverted soldiers from protecting the arsenal, but also provided a dangerous example: "[I]f the ignorant barbarians among the Creeks, and in the far West, are influenced in their hostility by the *example* of the Seminole, why may not another race, far more intelligent and powerful (and once aroused and in arms not less brave) catch the fire of the same spirit?" Helpfully, Poole offered that if sufficient men were not sent to him, and slaves did attack the arsenal, he could always "blow up the works with my own hands."[14]

The Indian wars in the Southeast had tended to bring out the worst in Americans. Comparing Osceola to Tecumseh was relatively benign, compared to some of the other proposals encountered. In 1763, an enraged and frightened Jeffrey Amherst, in communication with his chief officers, had openly considered bringing war dogs of the type used by the Spanish during the conquest of the Americas, and turning them loose on his Indian enemies. George Washington and Henry Knox eschewed such methods, and for the nation's honor, had gone out of their way to avoid looking like Conquistadors, even as they sought to conquer. By 1836, as the Second Seminole War against Osceola's people dragged on, darker imagery became somewhat more fashionable. A Massachusetts paper ran a missive from the *Floridian*, and while they introduced it with a moral disclaimer, they printed it nevertheless.

The *Floridian* noted that proposals had been made to introduce the Cuba bloodhound, a dog bred for tracking and taking down slaves, to fight the Seminoles. Such proposals were "to be deplored," the *Floridian* intoned, but also a "necessity." Furthermore, once the Seminoles had been subdued, they would not be allowed to keep the slaves they had captured [and often adopted], and the Indians would presumably let them loose. "The country will still be infested with [black] banditti, which can hardly be exterminated by any other means." Driving the point home, the editor concluded, "We should have no scruples in calling to our aid a brute as ferocious and blood-thirsty as the enemy we have to contend with."[15] For all the beautiful rhetoric of the Revolutionary era, when it came to subduing nonwhites who threatened their economic or social order, many white Americans were strikingly similar to the Britons they reveled in despising.

Despite a series of ugly, costly wars, the United States never managed to remove all of Osceola's people from the Everglades. America's pan-Indian nightmares faded out very slowly. Up through the Civil War, the threat of British aid to a new Confederacy in the South would rekindle "long-standing concerns about Indian–European alliances." When the Dakotas went to war with Minnesota Territory in 1862, some Minnesotans claimed British fur traders were helping the natives with their uprising. The Five Civilized Tribes, the Creeks, Choctaws, Chickasaws, Cherokees, and Seminoles, had been largely removed from the Southeast to what became Oklahoma. When they sided with the Confederacy, it briefly spawned fears that a new pan-Indian alliance, this time backed by Richmond, would attack Western settlers.[16]

Whether British, Spanish, or American, officials and ordinary citizens revealed huge blind spots in recognizing Indian motivations and capabilities for unified resistance. All continually assumed that any broad coalition of Indians formed had done so at the behest of nonnative powers. They simultaneously denigrated Indian capacities while recoiling in terror from them. Southern whites utilized the additional, terribly useful tool of the chronic fear of slave rebellion—made all the more frightening when in conjunction with Indian militants—to unite and motivate the nation to fuel and rationalize territorial expansion.

The default narrative of fearing pan-Indian confederacies proved a terribly difficult crutch for Americans' national mythology to cast away. Having adversaries like a Tecumseh and a Prophet, a McGillivray, a Pontiac, or a Dragging Canoe, made conquest seem more glorious and honorable. By being skillful, worthy, but ultimately vanquished opponents, they made the perfect window dressing for the ugly business of imperialism. Having cast themselves as noble underdogs for so long, Americans balked at even the hint that they might in fact be bullies. Even when the notion of a true pan-Indian confederacy had become laughable, Americans refused to relinquish the inspiring notion that they faced great odds, and must unite to crush a rising Indian menace backed by nefarious foreign agents. In the years after 1815, tales of pan-Indianism became more like a hybrid of ghost story and patriotic fable than a dire warning.

American commentators, with the humanly ethnocentric habit of shoehorning outside phenomena into familiar categories, continually tried to place Indian leaders into boxes they felt they understood. Because the United States had ultimately survived decades of attempts at pan-Indian resistance, and foreign efforts to aid such unions, there was something oddly unifying, even comforting, about such rhetoric. Thus any Indian who sought unity and challenged American hegemony was "A Second

EPILOGUE 243

Tecumseh." But there could be only one Tecumseh, and he was gone. By thwarting pan-Indian unity from the 1790s through the War of 1812, the United States had secured its own Union in those crucial decades. As the threat of pan-Indian war grew less likely, Americans nevertheless clung to the imagery of defeating Indian enemies, while especially in the South, slave uprisings were increasingly paired with such fears, to great effect.

Repeatedly painting their opponents as "brigands" and "banditti," the people of the United States set up a default narrative whereby they could only look more virtuous, regardless of how they fought their enemies. The "anti-Indian sublime," as well as the anti-rebel slave "sublime," proved incredibly powerful and attractive imagery for white Americans looking to justify their own imperial ambitions. By recycling the stories and imagery of that triumph for years to come, Americans continually re-embraced their self-fashioned exceptionalism.

Notes

INTRODUCTION

1. Benjamin Lincoln had briefly held the title in the latter days of the Articles of Confederation.
2. Knox to Pickens, Apr. 21, 1792, Correspondence of the War Dept. Relating to Indian Affairs, Military Pensions, and Fortifications, 1791–1797, National Archives and Records Administration.
3. The Oklahoma Historical Society's online *Encyclopedia of Oklahoma History and Culture*—http://digital.library.okstate.edu/encyclopedia/entries—gives such a definition.
4. Gregory E. Dowd, *A Spirited Resistance: The North American Indian Struggle for Unity, 1745–1815* (Baltimore: Johns Hopkins University Press, 1992); Peter Silver, *Our Savage Neighbors: How Indian War Transformed Early America* (New York: W. W. Norton, 2008).
5. Paul L. Gower, ed., *Psychology of Fear* (New York: Nova Science, 2004), vii.
6. Ibid., 1, 3.
7. Ibid., 4.
8. Ibid., 12.
9. Gordon Wood, "The Paranoid Style: Causality and Deceit in the Eighteenth Century," *William and Mary Quarterly* 39, no. 3 (July 1982), 402–441.
10. Bernard Bailyn, *The Ideological Origins of the American Revolution* (Cambridge, Mass.: Belknap Press, 1967); Jill Lepore, *New York Burning: Liberty, Slavery, and Conspiracy in Eighteenth-Century Manhattan* (New York: Vintage, 2006).
11. Patrick Griffin, *American Leviathan: Empire, Nation, and Revolutionary Frontier* (New York: Hill and Wang, 2007); Richard White, *The Middle Ground: Indians, Empires and Republics in the Great Lakes Region, 1650–1815* (New York: Cambridge University Press, 1991); David Andrew Nichols, *Red Gentlemen and White Savages: Indians, Federalists, and the Search for Order on the American Frontier* (Charlottesville: University of Virginia Press, 2008); Michael N. McConnell, *A Country Between: The Upper Ohio Valley and Its Peoples, 1724–1775* (Lincoln: University of Nebraska Press, 1992); Silver, *Our Savage Neighbors*; Francis Paul Prucha, *The Sword of the*

Republic: The United States Army on the Frontier, 1783–1846 (Lincoln: University of Nebraska Press, 1987); Reginald Horsman, *Expansion and American Indian Policy, 1783–1812* (East Lansing: Michigan State University Press, 1967); Bernard Sheehan, *Seeds of Extinction: Jeffersonian Philanthropy and the American Indian* (Chapel Hill: University of North Carolina Press, 1973); Anthony F. C. Wallace, *Jefferson and the Indians: The Tragic Fate of the First Americans* (Cambridge, Mass.: Belknap Press, 1999).

12. Douglas R. Egerton, *Death or Liberty: African Americans and Revolutionary America* (New York: Oxford University Press, 2009); David P. Geggus, ed., *The Impact of the Haitian Revolution in the Atlantic World* (Columbia: University of South Carolina Press, 2001); Nathaniel Millett, *The Maroons of Prospect Bluff and Their Quest for Freedom in the Atlantic World* (Gainesville: University Press of Florida, 2013); Jim Piecuch, *Three Peoples, One King: Loyalists, Indians and Slaves in the Revolutionary South, 1775–1782* (Columbia: University of South Carolina Press, 2008); Alan Taylor, *The Internal Enemy: Slavery and War in Virginia, 1772–1832* (New York: W. W. Norton, 2013).

13. Wood, "Paranoid Style," 408–423.

14. Ibid., 410.

15. Silver, *Our Savage Neighbors*, 96.

16. Taylor, *The Internal Enemy*, 5.

17. See Joshua Piker's *Okfuskee: A Creek Indian Town in Colonial America* (Cambridge, Mass.: Harvard University Press, 2004), 3; William G. McLoughlin, *Cherokee Renascence in the New Republic* (Princeton: Princeton University Press, 1986), 17.

18. Mary Beth Norton, *In the Devil's Snare: The Salem Witchcraft Crisis of 1692* (New York: Vintage, 2003); James G. Leyburn, *The Scotch-Irish: A Social History* (Chapel Hill: University of North Carolina Press, 1962), 114, 120.

19. See Dowd, *A Spirited Resistance*, and White, *The Middle Ground*.

20. See Elise Marienstras, "The Common Man's Indian: The Image of the Indian as a Promoter of National Identity in the Early National Era," in *Native Americans and the Early Republic*, ed. Frederick E. Hoxie, Ronald Hoffman, and Peter J. Albert (Charlottesville: University of Virginia Press, 1999), 261–296.

21. Taylor, *Internal Enemy*, 213.

22. Woody Holton, *Forced Founders: Indians, Debtors, Slaves, and the Making of the American Revolution in Virginia* (Chapel Hill: University of North Carolina Press, 1999), 25.

23. See Silver, *Our Savage Neighbors*, xix, 94–117.

24. Colin G. Calloway, *The American Revolution in Indian Country: Crisis and Diversity in Native American Communities* (New York: Cambridge University Press, 1995).

1. PONTIAC AND PAN-INDIANISM

1. Daniel K. Richter, *Before the Revolution: America's Ancient Pasts* (Cambridge, Mass.: Harvard University Press, 2011), 407.

2. Cynthia J. Van Zandt, *Brothers Among Nations: The Pursuit of Intercultural Alliances in Early America, 1580–1660* (New York: Oxford University Press, 2008), 13.

3. Jill Lepore, *The Name of War: King Philip's War and the Origins of American Identity* (New York: Vintage Books, 1998), 168.

4. See Ian K. Steele, "The Shawnees and the English: Captives and War, 1753–1765," in *The Boundaries between Us: Natives and Newcomers along the Frontiers of the Old Northwest Territory, 1750–1850*, ed. Daniel P. Barr (Kent, Ohio: Kent State University Press, 2006), 7–17.

5. Morris to Shirley, Dec. 3, 1755, in *The Papers of Sir William Johnson*, vol. 2 (New York: University of the State of New York, 1921), 369–371; Johnson to William Denny, July 21, 1758, *Papers of SWJ*, vol. 2, 878.

6. Croghan to Johnson, Jan. 30, 1759, *Papers of SWJ*, vol. 10, 90–91.

7. Daniel Ingram, *Indians and British Outposts in Eighteenth-Century America* (Gainesville: University Press of Florida, 2012), 44–48.

8. Fred Anderson, *Crucible of War: The Seven Years' War and the Fate of British America, 1754–1766* (New York: Alfred A. Knopf, 2000), 460–462; David H. Corkran, *The Creek Frontier, 1540–1783* (Norman: University of Oklahoma Press, 1967), 230; Tom Hatley, *The Dividing Paths: Cherokees and South Carolinians through the Revolutionary Era* (New York: Oxford University Press, 1993), 119–146.

9. George Croghan to Johnson, winter of 1760–1761, *Papers of SWJ*, vol. 3, 337; Croghan at Ft. Pitt to Johnson, Dec. 10, 1762, *Papers of SWJ*, vol. 3, 964; Dowd, *A Spirited Resistance*, 27–30; Colin G. Calloway, *Pen and Ink Witchcraft: Treaties and Treaty Making in American Indian History* (New York: Oxford University Press, 2013), 54.

10. Anderson, *Crucible of War*, 535–537; Dowd, *A Spirited Resistance*, 27–30. In *Our Savage Neighbors*, Silver argues that the concept of Indian unity may well have predated colonial feelings of white solidarity in the Middle Colonies by decades, and that colonists might have actually borrowed the idea from Indians (177). We should note, however, that New England and the Southern colonies were already quite familiar with racial solidarity by the mid-eighteenth century.

11. Dowd, *Spirited Resistance*, 33.

12. Bill Grantham, *Creation Myths and Legends of the Creek Indians* (Gainesville: University Press of Florida, 2002), 10.

13. Theda Perdue, *"Mixed Blood" Indians: Racial Construction in the Early South* (Athens: University of Georgia Press, 2003), 2–10.

14. Ibid., 9–10; McLoughlin, *Cherokee Renascence*, 12–13.

15. First two quotes, Johnson to Gen. Jeffrey Amherst, Mar. 18, 1763, *Papers of SWJ*, vol. 10, 624; second two quotes, Fort Miamis council, Mar. 30, 1763, Minutes & Journals of Detroit Councils, vol. 1832, War Office fonds, transcripts, Mfilm C-1223, Library and Archives of Canada (LAC).

16. Quotes, including Bouquet's, in Anderson, *Crucible of War*, 537; Dowd, *War under Heaven*, 107–109.

17. *Providence* (RI) *Gazette*, June 25, 1763, and Oct. 21, 1763; Amherst to Gov. Francis Fauquier of VA, May 4, 1763, Colonial Office, Commonwealth and Foreign and Commonwealth Offices collection (hereafter CO) 5 63:105–106, National Archives of Britain.

18. See David Dixon, *Never Come to Peace Again: Pontiac's Uprising and the Fate of the British Empire in North America* (Norman: University of Oklahoma Press, 2005), 78; Amherst to Bouquet, July 25, 1762, George Croghan Papers, 1754–1808, Historical Society of Pennsylvania (HSP, hereafter George Croghan Papers).

19. Croghan to Bouquet, Mar. 19, 1763, George Croghan Papers.

20. Sir William Johnson took great pains to see Amherst removed. He saw him as dangerously incompetent in Indian affairs, and therefore a personal and financial threat. Johnson's correspondence repeatedly (and correctly) placed considerable blame on Amherst's policies for the war, and he also sent his lieutenant George Croghan to London to personally testify against the general. See Croghan to Johnson, Apr. 14, 1764, George Croghan Papers; Croghan to Johnson, July 12, 1764, George Croghan Papers; Anderson, *Crucible of War*, 552.

21. Amherst to John Stuart, June 15, 1763, CO 5 63: 293–294; Amherst to govs. of Montreal, Trois Rivieres and Quebec, June 12, 1763, CO 5 63: 233.

22. Croghan to Johnson, July 2, 1763, *Papers of SWJ*, vol. 10, 728.

23. Amherst to Colonel Forster, Aug. 23, 1763, CO 5 63: 629–635, quote on 635; Gage to Gov. Murray, Jan. 5, 1764, Thomas Gage Papers, 1754–1807, Clements Library, University of Michigan (hereafter Gage Papers); Gage to Gov. Bernard in Boston, Jan. 1, 1764, Gage Papers.

24. Stuart to Amherst, July 30, 1763, CO 5 63: 593–597. For Creek diplomacy, see Joshua A. Piker, "'White & Clean' & Contested: Creek Towns and Trading Paths in the Aftermath of the Seven Years' War," *Ethnohistory* 50, no. 2 (Spring 2003), 315–347.

25. Francis Fauquier to Amherst, Aug. 2, 1763, CO 5 63: 521–522.

26. *Providence Gazette and Country Journal*, July 2, 1763—extract of a letter from a Gentleman at Albany to his friend in Boston, dated June 16, 1763.

27. Dowd, *War under Heaven*, 189–190, 211; Elizabeth A. Fenn, *Pox Americana: The Great Smallpox Epidemic of 1775–82* (New York: Hill and Wang, 2001), 88–89.

28. Johnson's memo concerning Indians, Nov. 10, 1763, *Papers of SWJ*, vol. 4, 235; Plan for the Future Management of Indian Affairs, July 10, 1764, CO 5 65: 683–705. See also David Dixon, "'We Speak as One People': Native Unity and the Pontiac Indian Uprising," in Barr, *The Boundaries between Us*, esp. 57–60; Tyler Boulware, *Deconstructing the Cherokee Nation: Town, Region, and Nation among Eighteenth-Century Cherokees* (Gainesville: University Press of Florida, 2011), 137.

29. Stuart to Johnson, *Papers of SWJ*, vol. 10, 950–951; James R. Atkinson, *Splendid Land, Splendid People: The Chickasaw Indians to Removal* (Tuscaloosa: University of Alabama Press, 2004), 88–91.For Catawbas, see James M. Merrell, *The Indians' New World: The Catawbas and their Neighbors from European Contact through the Era of Removal* (New York: W. W. Norton, 1991). For Choctaws, see James Taylor Carson, *Searching for the Bright Path: The Mississippi Choctaws from Prehistory to Removal* (Lincoln: University of Nebraska Press, 1999).

30. Stuart to Johnson, *Papers of SWJ*, vol. 10, 950–951. For Gun Merchant, see Corkran, *Creek Frontier*, 230–233; Piker, *Okfuskee*, 52–65.

31. Gage to Johnson, Jan. 12, 1764, *Papers of SWJ*, vol. 4, 304. He repeated these sentiments in a Jan. 27, 1764, letter to John Stuart, in Gage Papers. Corkran, *Creek Frontier*, 236–237. David Hackett Fischer discusses Gage's humanity in *Paul Revere's Ride* (New York: Oxford University Press, 1994).

32. Loftus to Gage, Apr. 19, 1764, Gage Papers; Farmar to Sec. of War Ellis, Jan. 24, 1764, in *Mississippi Provincial Archives, 1763–1766*, vol. 1, *English Dominion*, ed. Dunbar Rowland (Charleston, S.C.: Nabu Press, 2011 [1911]), 17.

33. Dowd, *War under Heaven*, 106–113.

34. Silver, *Our Savage Neighbors*, 98.

2. DUELING DIPLOMACIES

1. Gage to Stuart in Mobile, June 19, 1764, Gage Papers.

2. Capt. Gavin Cochran to Gage, Jan. 3, 1765, Gage Papers. For more conspiratorial reports involving the French and Spaniards, see Guy Johnson to Gage, July 5, 1768, in *Papers of SWJ*, vol. 12, 543.

3. Lettre de M. de Reclerc au Ministre Appel en faveur des nations Sauvage nos allies Difficultes que presente l'Estasement des Anglais dans la Colonies, No 335 Nouvelle Orleans à 2 May 1763, Mississippi Provincial Archives, 1612–1763, French Dominion, reel 1026, Mississippi Department of Archives.

4. Conseils aux Sauvages sur la Cession de la Colonie aux Anglais, Nov. 14, 1763, ibid. For Choctaw dissuasion, see John Richard Alden, *John Stuart and the Southern Colonial Frontier* (New York: Gordian Press, 1966), 195.

5. Journal of the Augusta Conference, CO 5 65: 515–566; Atkinson, *Splendid Land*, 89; Carson, *Searching for the Bright Path*, 35; Greg O'Brien, "Protecting Trade through War: Choctaw Elites and the British Occupation of the Floridas," in *Empire and Others: British Encounters with Indigenous Peoples, 1600–1850*, ed. Martin Daunton and Rick Halpern (Philadelphia: University of Pennsylvania Press, 1999), 149–166.

6. Jack M. Sosin, *Whitehall and the Wilderness: The Middle West in British Colonial Policy* (Lincoln: University of Nebraska Press, 1961), 39–43; *Providence Gazette and Country Journal* (Charles Town, S.C.), July 23, 1763, printed a preliminary proclamation by King George III, received by the governor of South Carolina in Dec. 1761, banning Western settlement by colonists, and further evacuating settled lands claimed by Indians.

7. Celia Barnes, *Native American Power in the United States, 1783–1795* (London: Fairleigh Dickinson University Press, 2003), 37; Holton, *Forced Founders*, 7–8.

8. Gregory E. Dowd, "Thinking outside the Circle: Tecumseh's 1811 Mission," in *Tohopeka: Rethinking the Creek War and the War of 1812*, ed. Katherine E. Holland Braund (Tuscaloosa: University of Alabama Press, 2012), 30; Holton, *Forced Founders*, 16–18; Croghan to Johnson, May 10, 1770, *Papers of SWJ*, vol. 7, 652.

9. Croghan to Johnson, May 10, 1770, *Papers of SWJ*, vol. 7, 652–653.

10. *Boston Gazette*, Apr. 23, 1764; *Georgia Gazette*, June 28, 1764.

11. Holton, *Forced Founders*, 18.

12. First two quotes, John Stuart to Earl of Halifax, Apr. 6, 1765, CO 5 66: 61–66; third quote, Geo. Johnstone to Stuart, June 3, 1766, CO 5 67: 61. See also Patricia Galloway, "'So Many Little Republics': British Negotiations with the Choctaw Confederacy, 1765," *Ethnohistory* 41, no. 4 (Autumn 1994), 513–537.

13. John Stuart to Gov. Wm. Tryon, May 28th, 1766, Charleston, in *The Correspondence of William Tryon and Other Selected Papers*, vol. 1, *1758–1767*, ed. William S. Powell (Raleigh: Division of Archives and History, 1980), 295–296 (hereafter *Correspondence of Tryon*); Boulware, *Deconstructing the Cherokee*, 147.

14. Stuart to Gov. Tryon, May 28, 1766, in *Correspondence of Tryon* 1, 295–296.

15. Fintan O'Toole, *White Savage: William Johnson and the Invention of America* (New York: Farrar, Straus and Giroux, 2005), 264.

16. Ibid., 319.

17. Gage to Stuart, Aug. 30, 1766, CO 5 67: 229–231.

18. O'Toole, *White Savage*, 276; Holton, *Forced Founders*, 10; Calloway, *Pen and Ink Witchcraft*, 79.

19. Alan Taylor, *The Divided Ground: Indians, Settlers, and the Northern Borderland of the American Revolution* (New York: Alfred A. Knopf, 2006), 42–45.

20. Eric Hinderaker, *Elusive Empires: Constructing Colonialism in the Ohio Valley, 1673–1800* (New York: Cambridge University Press, 1999), 166–167; Hinderaker further notes that Bayton, Wharton, and Morgan lost tens of thousands of pounds in an ill-advised plot to corner the Indian trade in Illinois. Croghan quote, Calloway, *Pen and Ink Witchcraft*, 58.

21. Holton, *Forced Founders*, 9.

22. Taylor, *Divided Ground*, 40–45; Holton, *Forced Founders*, xix.

23. Jerry E. Clark, *The Shawnee* (Lexington: University Press of Kentucky, 1993), 40–41.

24. Hinderaker, *Elusive Empires*, 169; George Morgan to Baynton and Wharton, Apr. 5, 1768, George Morgan Letterbook, 109–115, HSP.

25. Hinderaker, *Elusive Empires*, 169.

26. O'Toole, *White Savage*, 276.

27. McConnell, *A Country Between*, 256–257; Johnson quoted in Boulware, *Deconstructing the Cherokee*, 144; Calloway, *Pen and Ink Witchcraft*, 86.

28. Holton, *Forced Founders*, 26. Parliament ultimately rejected the petition in late 1769.

29. Stuart to Lord Hillsborough, Feb. 12, 1769, CO 5 70: 249–254.

30. Holton, *Forced Founders*, 26–26, quote on 27; Calloway, *Pen and Ink Witchcraft*, 86.

31. Dowd, *A Spirited Resistance*, 43.

32. First and third quotes, Stuart to Hillsborough, Oct. 3, 1769, CO 5 70: 583–585; second quote, Trader George Munro in the Creek Nation to Stuart, May 31, 1769, CO 5 70: 517–518.

33. Stuart in Charles Town to Botetourt, Aug. 3, 1769, CO 5 70: 587–588.

34. Talk from the Headmen and Warriors of the Cherokee Nation to Stuart, July 29, 1769, CO 5 70: 595–596.

35. Stuart to Lord Hillsborough, Jan. 20, 1770, CO 5 71: 103–106; Alden, *John Stuart*, 276–277.
36. Stuart to Lord Botetourt, Jan. 13, 1770, CO 5 71: 121–124.
37. Hillsborough to Stuart, June 12, 1770, CO 5 71: 258; Hillsborough to Stuart, July 31, 1770, CO 5 71: 289–290.
38. Holton, *Forced Founders*, 28–30, quote on 28.

3. STUART BESIEGED

1. Croghan to Gage, Jan. 1, 1770, George Croghan Papers.
2. Gage to Johnson, May 20, 1770, in *Papers of SWJ*, vol. 12, 822; Gage to Johnson, June 10, 1770, in *Papers of SWJ*, vol. 7, 733; quote, Gage to Johnson, Oct. 8, 1770, in *Papers of SWJ*, vol. 12, 873; Holton, *Forced Founders*, 31.
3. Holton, *Forced Founders*, 23–24, quote on 24.
4. Johnson to Gage, Jan 4., 1771, in *Papers of SWJ*, vol. 12, 881–882; Calloway, *Pen and Ink Witchcraft*, 88.
5. O'Toole, *White Savage*, 319.
6. McConnell, *A Country Between*, 266; Dunmore quoted in James Corbett David, *Dunmore's New World: The Extraordinary Life of a Royal Governor in Revolutionary America—with Jacobites, Counterfeiters, Land Schemes, Shipwrecks, Scalping, Indian Politics, Runaway Slaves, and Two Illegal Royal Weddings* (Charlottesville: University of Virginia Press, 2013), 76.
7. Stuart to Hillsborough, Apr. 27, 1771, CO 5 72: 421.
8. Quote, Stuart to Hillsborough, June 12, 1772, CO 5 73: 323–333; Hillsborough to Stuart, Aug. 7, 1772, CO 5 73: 467–468; Lord Dartmouth to Stuart, Dec. 9, 1772, CO 5 73: 907–912; Dartmouth to Stuart, May 5, 1773, CO 5 74: 139; see Alden, *John Stuart*, 329–333.
9. Quotes, A Talk from the Cherokee Nation to Alexander Cameron, July 21, 1772, CO 5 73: 831–834.
10. Stuart to Dartmouth, Jan. 4, 1773, CO 5 74: 39–40.
11. Stuart to Dartmouth, June 21, 1773, CO 5 74: 291–296; Dartmouth to Stuart, Mar. 3, 1774, CO 5 74: 63.
12. Stuart to Dartmouth, June 21, 1773, CO 5 74: 291–296; Boulware, *Deconstructing the Cherokee*, 149–150.
13. Stuart to Dartmouth, June 21, 1773, CO 5 74: 291–296.
14. Stuart to Dartmouth, Aug. 2, 1774, CO 5 75: 329–332.

4. DUNMORE'S FLEETING VICTORY

1. Affidavits of Thomas Sharp and Isaac Thomas from Fincastle County, Va., Feb. 12–Feb. 20, 1774, CO 5 75: 335–337.
2. Lord Dunmore in Williamsburg to Stuart, Apr. 30, 1774, CO 5 75: 339–340.
3. David, *Dunmore's New World*, 63.

4. John R. Finger, *Tennessee Frontiers: Three Regions in Transition* (Bloomington: Indiana University Press, 2001), 47–48.

5. Ibid.; Finger, *Tennessee Frontiers*, 47–48; Hatley, *Dividing Paths*, 217–219.

6. Griffin, *American Leviathan*, 104.

7. Some have argued that the murders were a deliberate attempt to goad the Shawnees and Mingos into a war, which would presumably end with their defeat and more land cessions. See Holton, *Forced Founders*, 33–34.

8. White, *The Middle Ground*, 361.

9. Calloway, *Pen and Ink Witchcraft*, 90.

10. Silver, *Our Savage Neighbors*, xix, argues convincingly that the fear of Indian war was sometimes used by "provincial leaders and publicists" to form their own coalitions.

11. McConnell, *A Country Between*, 276.

12. White, *Middle Ground*, 361–363, Dunmore quote, 362; first two quotes, McConnell, *A Country Between*, 276–277; Meredith Mason Brown, *Frontiersman: Daniel Boone and the Making of America* (Baton Rouge: Louisiana State University Press, 2008), 58. For Shawnee population estimate, see James H. Howard, *Shawnee! The Ceremonialism of a Native American Tribe and Its Cultural Background* (Athens: Ohio University Press, 1981), 32. For Cherokees, see Peter H. Wood, "The Changing Population of the Colonial South: An Overview by Race and Region, 1685–1790," in *Powhatan's Mantle: Indians in the Colonial Southeast*, ed. Gregory Waselkov, Peter H. Wood, and Tom Hatley, rev. ed. (Lincoln: University of Nebraska Press, 2006), 60.

13. Josiah Martin in New Bern (N.C.) to Stuart, July 21, 1774, CO 5 75: 387. Joshua Piker argues that the Southern frontier was not especially prone to Indian–white violence in the years before the Revolution. See his "Colonists and Creeks: Rethinking the Pre-Revolutionary Southern Backcountry," *The Journal of Southern History* 70, no. 3 (Aug. 2004), 503–540.

14. *SWJ Papers*, vol. 12, 1045–1047; Johnson to Haldimand, Mar. 19, 1774, *SWJ Papers*, vol. 12, 1085; Larry L. Nelson, *A Man of Distinction among Them: Alexander McKee and British-Indian Affairs along the Ohio Country Frontier, 1754–1799* (Kent: Kent State University Press, 1999), 24–28.

15. McKee to Johnson, Apr. 16, 1774, in *SWJ Papers*, vol. 12, 1088–1090.

16. Haldimand in N.Y. to WJ, Feb. 24, 1774, in *SWJ Papers*, vol. 8, 1044.

17. Johnson to Dartmouth, in *SWJ Papers*, vol. 8, 1142–1143.

18. White, *Middle Ground*, 357–358; Reuben Gold Thwaites and Louise Phelps Kellogg, eds., *Documentary History of Dunmore's War 1774* (Madison: Wisconsin State Historical Society, 1905), 15–17.

19. Johnson to Dartmouth, June 20, 1774, CO 5 75: 277.

20. Ibid.; Taylor, *The Divided Ground*, 70–71.

21. See Wilbur R. Jacobs, *Francis Parkman, Historian as Hero: The Formative Years* (Austin: University of Texas Press, 1991), esp. 59–67.

22. See Guy Johnson to Gage, July 26, 1774, Aug. 11, 1774, and Aug. 19, 1774, Gage to Guy Johnson, Aug. 21, 1774, and Sept. 18, 1774, in *SWJ Papers*, vol. 13, 641–679; Stuart to Dartmouth, Sept. 12, 1774, CO 5 75: 439–440.

NOTES TO PAGES 56–63

23. Stuart to Gage, Oct. 6, 1774, Gage Papers; Gage to Haldimand, July 23, 1774, Gage Papers.

24. Paul W. Mapp, *The Elusive West and the Contest for Empire, 1713–1763* (Chapel Hill: University of North Carolina Press, 2011), 416–423.

25. Finger, *Tennessee Frontiers*, 48–49; Patrick Griffin, *American Leviathan*, 92; Matthew C. Ward, "The Indians Our Real Friends: The British Army and the Ohio Indians, 1758–1772," in Barr, *The Boundaries between Us*, 79; White, *Middle Ground*, 362–363, quotes on 363; Gage to John Stuart, Oct. 3, 1774, Gage Papers; Fischer, *Paul Revere's Ride*, 42–43.

26. Among the Shawnee dead was the war chief Puckeshinwau, father of the future pan-Indian leader Tecumseh. See John Sugden, *Tecumseh: A Life* (New York: Henry Holt, 1998), 28. See also Thwaites and Kellogg, *Documentary History of Dunmore's War*.

27. Robert S. Allen, *His Majesty's Indian Allies: British Indian Policy in the Defence of Canada, 1774–1815* (Toronto: Dundurn Press, 1992), 41–42.

28. White, *Middle Ground*, 364.

29. Gage to Stuart, Nov. 14, 1774, Gage Papers; Stuart to Gage, Nov. 19, 1774, Gage Papers; Gage to Stuart, Nov. 26, 1774, Gage Papers.

5. REVOLUTION AND REALIGNMENT

1. Gage to Stuart, Dec. 28, 1774, Gage Papers; Stuart to Gage (private) Jan. 18, 1775, Gage Papers. See also Joseph T. Glatthaar and James Kirby Martin, *Forgotten Allies: The Oneida Indians and the American Revolution* (New York: Hill and Wang, 2006), 69–101.

2. Stuart to Gage, Jan. 28, 1775, Gage Papers.

3. Stuart to Gage, May 26, 1775, Gage Papers.

4. William Campbell in Charles Town to Gage, July 1, 1775, Gage Papers; Stuart to Gage, July 9, 1775, St. Augustine, Gage Papers. Stuart to Dartmouth, July 21, 1775, CO 5 76: 307; Holton, *Forced Founders*, 144–148, convention quoted on 144; Jemmy quote in extract of a Sept. 12, 1775, letter from Charleston, S.C., in *Connecticut Journal*, Oct. 25, 1775.

5. Taylor, *Internal Enemy*, 25–26. Taylor argues that the proclamation itself was a bluff by Dunmore (23).

6. Stuart to Gage, July 20, 1775, Gage Papers; Piecuch, *Three Peoples, One King*, 34.

7. Commonplace Book of Dr. George Gilmer (1743–1795) of Albemarle, Va., Mss 5: 5 G4213:1 Virginia Historical Society Library, 75–77.

8. Dartmouth to Guy Johnson, July 24, 1775, CO5 76: 247; Gage to Stuart, Sept. 12, 1775, Gage Papers; Gage to McKee, Sept. 12, 1775, Gage Papers.

9. Glatthaar and Martin, *Forgotten Allies*, 108–112.

10. Brown, *Daniel Boone*, 68–70.

11. Ibid., 70–71. See Martin's Feb. 10, 1775, proclamation in *The Colonial Records of North Carolina*, vol. 9, *1771–1775*, ed. William L. Saunders (New York: AMS Press, 1968 [1888]), 1122–1125.

12. Robert J. Conley, *The Cherokee Nation: A History* (Albuquerque: University of New Mexico Press, 2005), 58. See also the Apr. 15, 1777, deposition of Samuel Wildon in *Calendar of Virginia State Papers and Other Manuscripts* (hereafter *CVSP*) vol. 1, *1652–1781*, William P. Palmer, ed. (New York: Knaus Reprint Corporation, 1968 [1875]), 283; Wm. Christian to Patrick Henry, Oct. 23, 1776, and Dowd quote, in Dowd, *Spirited Resistance*, 49.

13. Stephen Aron, *How the West Was Lost: The Transformation of Kentucky from Daniel Boone to Henry Clay* (Baltimore: Johns Hopkins University Press, 1996), 38–39.

14. *Pennsylvania Journal*, printed in *Essex Journal and New Hampshire Packet*, Apr. 5, 1776; Silver, *Our Savage Neighbors*, 94.

15. Taylor, *Internal Enemy*, 10.

16. First quote, Wm. Christian in Fincastel Town to Col. Wm. Preston in Smithfield, June 8th, 1776, Draper Mss 4 QQ 49 transcripts in Arthur Campbell Papers, Mss A C 187, FHS; second quote, Pres. Page of Va. to N.C. Council of Safety, Aug. 1, 1776, *The Colonial Records of North Carolina*, vol. 10, *1775–1776*, 730; Dixon and Hunter's *Virginia Gazette*, Aug. 3, 1776.

17. *Virginia Gazette*, Aug. 17, 1776, Sept. 14, 1776, and Nov. 1, 1776; William Dell, A Journal of the Motions of the Continental Army, Commanded by the Honble. Griffifth Rutherford, Esqr. Brigadier Generall against the Cherokee Indians, Aug. 29–Sept. 30, 1776, FHS; Corkran, *The Creek Frontier*, 298–299.

18. Carleton to Lords of the Treasury, Nov. 25, 1776, HM Treasury collection (hereafter T1) 520: 185, National Archives of Britain.

19. William Knox's extract of Stuart to Lord Germaine, Mar. 10, 1777, in T1 535: 269–270.

20. Ibid.

21. John Steele Papers, 689 Series 1 corr., folder 4, UNC, contains a copy of the May 20, 1777, treaty, which was later enclosed in Wm. Blount's May 5, 1789, letter to Steele.

22. Hatley, *The Dividing Paths*, 224–225.

23. Dixon and Hunter's *Virginia Gazette*, May 30, 1777.

6. BRITAIN'S PAN-INDIAN GAMBLE

1. Haldimand to Lord Germaine, Sept. 20, 1777, in T1 528: 126; Stuart to John Robinson and Lords Treasurers, Feb. 4, 1778, in T1 540: 35.

2. See Joseph Martin at Ft. Patrick Henry to Col. Arthur Campbell, Sept. 9, 1778, in Arthur Campbell Papers; Stuart to John Robinson, Aug. 24, 1778, in T1 540: 28.

3. John Wereat to Lincoln, Aug. 18, 1779, Augusta, in Benjamin Lincoln Papers, 1778–1804, David M. Rubenstein Rare Book and Manuscript Library, Duke University; Edward J. Cashin, "'But Brothers, It Is Our Land We Are Talking About': Winners and Losers in the Georgia Backcountry," in *An Uncivil War: The Southern Backcountry during the American Revolution*, ed. Ronald Hoffman, Thad W. Tate, and Peter J. Albert (Charlottesville: University Press of Virginia, 1985), 240–275.

4. Dowd, *Spirited Resistance*, 57.

5. Griffin, *American Leviathan*, 146–147.

6. Dowd, *Spirited Resistance*, 58.

7. For McCrea's murder, see Linda Colley, *Captives* (New York: Pantheon Books, 2002), 225–230, and June Namias, *White Captives: Gender and Ethnicity on the American Frontier* (Chapel Hill: University of North Carolina Press, 1993), 117–120. Silver, *Our Savage Neighbors*, 243–248.

8. Troy Bickham, *Savages within the Empire: Representations of American Indians in Eighteenth-Century Britain* (New York: Oxford University Press, 2005), 246–268, quotes on 246, 255, 268; Namias, *White Captives*, 117–120; Piecuch, *Three Peoples*, 119–120. Burke's three-hour speech did receive brief notice in America, though the only coverage I could find was in the Loyalist *Royal Pennsylvania Gazette*'s May 15, 1778, issue.

9. Twet,ha,rech,té (Cayuga speaker) addressing Col. Guy Johnson, Nov. 3, 1779, Minutes & Journals of the Detroit Councils, vol. 1832, War Office fonds, LAC, 55. For the campaign, see Glenn F. Williams, *Year of the Hangman: George Washington's Campaign against the Iroquois* (Yardley, Pa.: Westholme, 2005).

10. Quote, Dowd, *Spirited Resistance*, 58; Proceedings of a General Meeting with the Chief of the Six Nations, Mar. 20, 1780, Niagara, Superintendent of Indian Affairs in the Northern District of North America fonds, Mfilm 2943 Series 1, Lot 686, LAC, 8; Extract of a letter, Major DePeyster in Detroit to Commissary of Indian Affairs with the Upper Cherokees, Apr. 5, 1780, PRO 30 11 78: 352.

11. Capt. Henry Bird to Maj. Arent De Peyster, July 1, 1780, in "Haldimand Papers," *Historical Collections*, vol. XIX (Lansing: Michigan Pioneer and Historical Society, 1911), 538–539; White, *Middle Ground*, 407; Nelson, *Man of Distinction*, 114–117.

12. Piecuch, *Three Peoples*, 11.

13. Cameron to Lord Germaine, Sept. 20, 1780, CO 5 82: 176–178; Bethune to Cameron, Aug. 27, 1780, enclosed, CO 5 82: 190–191.

14. Bethune to Cameron, Sept. 4, 1780, CO 5 82: 190–191; Cameron to Maj. Gen. John Campbell in Pensacola, Sept. 18, 1780, CO 5 82: 196–197; Campbell to Cameron, Sept. 18, 1780, CO 5 82: 204, 209–210; Williams (dictated letter—he was illiterate) to Lincoln, Mar. 7, 1780, in Benjamin Lincoln Papers.

15. Thomas Brown, Lt. Col. Commanding King's Rangers, to Cornwallis, Dec. 17, 1780, PRO 30 11 4: 345; quotes, Edward J. Cashin, "Winners and Losers in the Georgia Backcountry," in Hoffman, Tate, and Albert, *An Uncivil War*, 264.

16. Campbell to Jefferson, Feb. 28, 1781, *CVSP*, vol. 1, *1652–1781*, 548; Campbell to Jefferson Mar. 28, 1781, ibid., 602; Piecuch, *Three Peoples*, 207–208.

17. *Papers of Nathanael Greene*, vol. 7, *26 Dec., 1780–29 Mar. 1781*, ed. Dennis M. Conrad (Chapel Hill: University of North Carolina Press, 2002), 351; Lanier to Greene, Apr. 19, 1781, Nathanael Greene Papers, David M. Rubenstein Rare Book and Manuscript Library, Duke University; Lanier to Greene, May 27, 1781, in Conrad, *Papers of Greene*, vol. 8, 317.

18. Haldimand to Germaine, T1 578: 50–51.

19. Floyd to May, Apr. 8, 1782, *CVSP*, vol. 1, *1652–1781*, 122.

20. Campbell to Davies, Apr. 25, 1782, ibid., 138.

21. Martin to Anthony Wayne, Mar. 23, 1782, Anthony Wayne Papers, vol. 15, 115, HSP; Read to Wayne, Apr. 29, 1782, Anthony Wayne Papers, vol. 16, 99; Wayne, blank pass, July 16, 1782, Anthony Wayne Papers, vol. 18, 20; Greene to Wayne, Mar. 7, 1783, Anthony Wayne Papers, vol. 19, 16.

22. Wayne to Moore, May 10, 1782, Anthony Wayne Papers, vol. 16, 125.

23. Wayne to Greene, May 23, 1783, Anthony Wayne Papers, vol. 19, 20.

24. Wayne to Greene, June 24, 1782, in Conrad, *Papers of Greene*, vol. 11, 365; Wayne to Greene, July 28, 1782, Anthony Wayne Papers; Fishbourn to Greene, June 24, 1782, Anthony Wayne Papers, vol. 17, 92.

25. John Bowman in Lincoln County, Va., to Gov. Harrison, Aug. 30, 1782, *CVSP*, vol. 3, *1782–1784*, 277; Martin to Gov. of North Carolina, Sept. 18, 1782, ibid., 318; talk of the Chickasaws to the commanders of every American station between the Chickasaws and the Ohio, July 9, 1782, in Tennessee Papers, Draper Manuscripts, 1XX50, 19.

26. A. Campbell in Wash County to Col. Wm. Davies, Oct. 3, 1782, *CVSP*, vol. 3, *1782–1784*, 337. In April, Campbell could tell Benjamin Harrison with great relief that the Northern tribes' emissaries "had failed in stirring up a general war against the whites." See ibid., 464.

27. Martin to Harrison, Feb. 2, 1783, *CVSP*, vol. 2, *1652–1781*, 426–427; Greene to B. Lincoln, Feb. 2, 1783, Conrad, *Papers of Greene*, vol. 12, *Oct. 1, 1782–May 21, 1783*, 403.

28. White, *Middle Ground*, 407; Raven quoted in Cashin, "Winners and Losers in the Georgia Backcountry," 273; see also Allen, *His Majesty's Indian Allies*, 53–55.

7. A NEW NATION WITH OLD FEARS

1. *Pennsylvania Journal*, Jan. 21, 1784, quoting the Assembly from Dec. 2, 1783.
2. Ibid.
3. *Pennsylvania Journal*, Jan. 24, 1784; Peale to George Weedon, Jan. 20–Feb. 10, 1784, in *The Selected Papers of Charles Willson Peale and His Family*, vol. 1, *Charles Willson Peale: Artist in Revolutionary America, 1735–1791*, ed. Lillian B. Miller (New Haven:

Yale University Press, 1983), 405–406. Silver also notes this tragic occurrence in *Our Savage Neighbors*, 262.

4. While there was a certain rationale for ceding the lands west of the Appalachians to the United States, François Furstenberg argues that Britain "almost certainly could have" left the western lands, especially north of the Ohio, to their Indian allies in 1783, significantly crimping Americans' opportunities for expansion. See Furstenberg, "The Significance of the Trans-Appalachian Frontier in Atlantic History," *American Historical Review* 113, no. 3 (June 2008), 647–677, quote on 675.

5. Timothy D. Willig, *Restoring the Chain of Friendship: British Policy and the Indians of the Great Lakes, 1783–1815* (Lincoln: University of Nebraska Press, 2008), 12–13.

6. Haldimand in Quebec to Sir John Johnston, Feb. 6, 1783, Haldimand Papers, Mfilm A-686, LAC.

7. T1 578: 42; Germain to Lords of Treasury, PRO T1 578: 44; McKee's enumeration of Indians residing in the district of Detroit for the year 1782, in Superintendent of Indian Affairs in the Northern District of North America (1756–1829), Mfilm H-2943, MG 19, F-35, Series 1, Lot 704, 1–2, LAC; Nelson, *Man of Distinction among Them*, 149–152.

8. Taylor, *Divided Ground*, 112.

9. I follow Taylor's excellent discussion from *The Divided Ground*, 112–115. See also Colley's *Captives*, which argues that in many respects eighteenth-century Britons were held "captive" by their colonial entanglements.

10. Council held at Lower Sandusky, Sept. 6, 1783, Minutes & Journals of Detroit Councils, vol. 1832, War Office fonds. For McKee's career, see Nelson, *Man of Distinction*.

11. Willig, *Restoring the Chain of Friendship*, 14–15.

12. Remarks on the Management of Indians in North America, Nov. 22, 1782, Haldimand Papers, Mfilm A-686; Glatthaar and Martin, *Forgotten Allies*, 296–298.

13. Meeting held by the Six Nations and a Deputation from the Shawanese, Delawares & Cherokees at Niagara on the 2–4th & 6th of Oct. 1783, Superintendent of Indian Affairs Collection, Mfilm Series 1, Lot 708, 1–6, LAC; for Brant, see Isabel Thompson Kelsay, *Joseph Brant, 1743–1807, Man of Two Worlds* (Syracuse: Syracuse University Press, 1984).

14. Joseph Brant's answer to Gen. Schuyler's speech at Saratoga, July 29, 1783—given at Loyal Village, Oct. 22, 1783, Superintendent of Indian Affairs Collection, Mfilm Series 1, lot 708, 1, LAC.

15. Furstenberg, "Significance of the Trans-Appalachian Frontier," 663.

16. Calloway, *American Revolution in Indian Country*; Marienstras, "The Common Man's Indian," in Hoxie, Hoffman, and Albert, *Native Americans and the Early Republic*, 261–296, quote on 261.

17. Pickens to Gov. Guerard [S.C.], Apr. 13, 1784, Indian Affairs, case 4, box 14, folder 6, HSP; Pickens to Guerard, May 9, 1784, Indian Affairs (under Pickens), case 4, box 14, folder 6, HSP.

18. Kevin T. Barksdale, *The Lost State of Franklin: America's First Secession* (Lexington: University Press of Kentucky, 2009).

19. Richard Caswell to Evan Shelby, May 31, 1787, King's Mountain Papers, Draper Manuscripts, 11DD3–5.

20. Martin in Chotee to Gov. Caswell, Sept. 19, 1785, Cherokee Collection, Mfilm 815, Tennessee State Archives; talk of the Old Tassel in Chota to the governors of Va. & N.C., Sept. 19, 1785, Cherokee Collection, Mfilm 815.

21. Theda Perdue, *Cherokee Women: Gender and Culture Change, 1700–1835* (Lincoln: University of Nebraska Press, 1998), 92; Stanley W. Hoig, *The Cherokees and Their Chiefs: In the Wake of Empire* (Fayetteville: University of Arkansas Press, 1998), 60, 64; Cynthia Cumfer, *Separate Peoples, One Land: The Minds of Cherokees, Blacks, and Whites on the Tennessee Frontier* (Chapel Hill: University of North Carolina Press, 2007), 27–36.

22. *Pennsylvania Mercury*, Feb. 17, 1786.

23. Samuel McDowell to Gov. Henry, Apr. 18, 1786, Bullitt Family Papers, FHS; Saunders' July 24, 1786, report to Finney in N.Y., rec. Oct. 21, 1786, printed in *New-Hampshire Spy* (Portsmouth), Nov. 10, 1786 and in *Salem Mercury* (Salem, Mass.) Nov. 25, 1786, offered, "A Mr. Schoff from Upper Cohas . . . [states] 'There is no room to doubt but the Savages here mentioned act from the same motives with those in the Ohio country—urged on and supported by Britain.'"

24. *Middlesex Gazette*, Dec. 18, 1786; *Connecticut Courant and Weekly Intelligencer* (Hartford), Jan. 15, 1787.

25. Extract of a Letter from Alexander M. Gillivray [*sic*], Chief of the Creek Indians. "Little Tallassee," June 30, 1787, in *City Gazette and Daily Advertiser* (Charleston, South Carolina), Dec. 8, 1787; Campbell to John Brown, Dec. 29, 1787, Arthur Campbell Papers. See also Robbie Ethridge, *Creek Country: The Creek Indians and Their World* (Chapel Hill: University of North Carolina Press, 2003), 11.

26. See Peter S. Onuf, *Statehood and Union: A History of the Northwest Ordinance* (Bloomington: Indiana University Press, 1992).

27. Knox had served as secretary of war under the Articles of Confederation in the 1780s.

28. Boulware, *Deconstructing the Cherokee*, 165.

29. Arthur Campbell to Henry Knox, [illegible month] day 29, 1789, Arthur Campbell Papers; Washington's diary entry for Mar. 11, 1790, in *The Diaries of George Washington 1748–1799*, vol. 4, *1789–1799*, ed. John C. Fitzpatrick (Boston: Houghton Mifflin, 1925), 99–102.

30. Knox to Washington, June 15, 1789, Henry Knox Papers II, Massachusetts Historical Society (MHS); for Indian-hating, see Nichols, *Red Gentlemen, White Savages*.

31. Knox to Washington, June 15, 1789, Henry Knox Papers II.

32. Ibid.

33. Ibid.

34. Ibid.; Taylor, *Divided Ground*, 238.

NOTES TO PAGES 98–104   259

35. Jon Parmenter, "Dragging Canoe (Tsi'yu-gûnsi'ni), Chickamauga Cherokee Patriot," in *The Human Tradition in the American Revolution*, ed. Nancy L. Rhoden and Ian K. Steele (Wilmington: Scholarly Resources, Inc., 1999), 130–131.

8. THE TALENTED MR. MCGILLIVRAY

1. Report of Knox to Washington, July 6, 1789, "Relating to the Southern Indians," *American State Papers: Indian Affairs, Class II* (hereafter *ASPIA*), vol. 1, 15.
2. Ibid. Also discussed in Caughey, *McGillivray*; Ethridge, *Creek Country*, 11; David J. Weber, *The Spanish Empire in North America* (New Haven: Yale University Press, 1992), 283–284.
3. Report of Knox to Washington, July 6, 1789, "Relating to the Southern Indians," *ASPIA*, vol. 1, 15.
4. Wayne to Aedaneus Burke, June 4, 1789, Anthony Wayne Papers, vol. 19, 81.
5. Report of Knox to Washington, July 6, 1789, "Relating to the Southern Indians," *ASPIA*, vol. 1, 15; Nichols, *Red Gentlemen*, 114–119.
6. Nichols, *Red Gentlemen*, 112.
7. Caughey, *McGillivray*, 43. Indeed, Knox sent Caleb Swan, deputy agent to the Creeks, to escort McGillivray all the way home from the Treaty of New York, partly as a gesture of hospitality, and partly for the intelligence he would be able to gather. Knox's report on Creek military strength was based largely on the "Report of Caleb Swan to Henry Knox, May 2, 1791," MssB.B284.d., vol. 32, American Philosophical Society Library.
8. Caughey, *McGillivray*, 44–45; Weber, *Spanish Frontier*, 284–285.
9. Jackson quoted in Caughey, *McGillivray*, 45.
10. Susan Richbourgh Parker, "So in Fear of Both the Indians and the Americans," in *America's Hundred Years' War: Expansion to the Gulf Coast and the Fate of the Seminole, 1763–1858*, ed. William S. Belko (Gainesville: University Press of Florida, 2011), 36.
11. He lost, though he would be popularly elected as a U.S. Congressman in 1791. See Wayne to [Ga. legislature?], Nov. 1, 1788, Anthony Wayne Papers, vol. 19, 70; See also David A. Nichols, "Land, Republicanism, and Indians," *Georgia Historical Quarterly* 85 (Summer 2001), 199–226; for Stono and Florida, see *NY Weekly Journal*, Apr. 28, 1740, and *Boston Evening Post*, May 12, 1740.
12. Butler to Roger Parker Saunders, Aug. 26, 1790, Pierce Butler (1744–1822) Papers, South Caroliniana Library, University of South Carolina (hereafter Pierce Butler Papers); Butler to John Houstoun, Sept. 27, 1790, ibid.; Barnes, *Native American Power*, 90; Anthony Wayne to Gen. James Jackson, Dec. 2, 1790, Anthony Wayne Papers, vol. 19, 109.
13. Caughey, *McGillivray*, 47–52; Knoxville report printed in *Dunlap's American Daily Advertiser*, Nov. 1, 1792.
14. Carondelet to O'Neill, Mar. 30, 1792, AGI legajo 18, Papeles de Cuba.
15. Knox to Gov. Edward Telfair of Georgia, Aug. 31, 1792, in *ASPIA*, vol. 1, 259.

16. As Michael Beatty pointed out at the 2009 Mid-America History conference, there is little if any evidence that the United States actually made these secret payments to McGillivray and the other mico signers. See also Ethridge, *Creek Country*, 199–202.

17. Furstenberg, "Significance of the Trans-Appalachian Frontier," 664–665.

18. Nichols, *Red Gentlemen*, 49.

19. Perdue, *Cherokee Women*, 52.

20. Washington to Lafayette, Aug. 11, 1790, *Writings of George Washington*, vol. 31, 87.

9. OHIO CONFEDERATES TRIUMPHANT

1. John Sugden, *Blue Jacket: Warrior of the Shawnees* (Lincoln: University of Nebraska Press, 2000); Reginald Horsman, *Matthew Elliott, British Indian Agent* (Detroit: Wayne State University Press, 1964), 62–63, 66–69.

2. Wiley Sword, *President Washington's Indian War: The Struggle for the Old Northwest, 1790–1795* (Norman: University of Oklahoma Press, 1985), 202–204; Richard C. Knopf, "Anthony Wayne: The Man and the Myth," *Northwest Ohio Quarterly* 64, no. 2 (Spring 1992), 35–42.

3. Extract of a Letter from Gen. Chapen. in the Genesee Country to His Son in This City Dated Canodoque [Canandaigua], May 9, 1791, *Vermont Gazette*, May 30, 1791; *Pennsylvania Mercury*, July 16, 1791.

4. *Pennsylvania Journal and Weekly Advertiser* (Philadelphia) hereafter *PAJWA*, Dec. 14 and Dec. 21, 1791; Benjamin Rush commonplace book, 1792–1813, B R89c, APS, 79.

5. Hammond to Lord Grenville, Dec. 10, 1791, FO 116/1: 27, NAB; Hammond to Grenville, Jan. 9, 1792, FO 116/1: 70–72; *New Hampshire Gazette* (Portsmouth), Apr. 4, 1792.

6. Butler to Robert Goodloe Harper, Feb. 18, 1792, Pierce Butler Papers; Butler to Peter Freneau in Charleston, Nov. 25, 1792, Pierce Butler Papers.

7. Hamilton to Dundas, Apr. 18, 1791, CO 37 43: 9.

8. Extract of Hamilton to George Hammond, Jan. 13, 1792, CO 37 43: 222; Hamilton to Dundas, Jan. 20, 1792, CO 37 43: 217.

9. Extract of Hamilton to Hammond, Jan. 13, 1792, CO 37 43: 222.

10. Ibid., 222–223.

11. Simcoe to Dundas, Feb. 16, 1792, CO 42 316: 76; Dundas in Whitehall to Simcoe, May 5, 1792, CO 42 316: 116.

12. As David A. Nichols notes, generally Britons who lived closer to Indian country proved more belligerent towards the United States than those at a distance; see Nichols, *Red Gentlemen*, 150. Quote, Willig, *Restoring the Chain of Friendship*, 28.

13. Grenville to Hammond, Sept. 1, 1791, in *The Correspondence of Lieut. Governor John Graves Simcoe, with Allied Documents relating to his administration of the*

government of Upper Canada (hereafter *Correspondence of Simcoe*), vol. 1, ed. E. A. Cruikshank (Toronto: Ontario Historical Society, 1923–1931), 58; Simcoe to Dundas, June 30, 1791, ibid., 30; Dundas to Robert Prescott, Sept. 1, 1791, in Robert Prescott fonds MG 23, G II 17, Series 1, vol. 6, Mfilm H-2532, 2, LAC.

14. Col. Butler at Niagara to Sir John Johnston, June 29, 1791, Superintendent of Indian Affairs in the Northern District of North America fonds, MG 19, F-35, Series 2, lot 690, 1, Mfilm H-2944; Taylor, *Divided Ground*, 241–242, 254, 275; Simcoe to Dundas, June 30, 1791, *Correspondence of Simcoe*, vol. 1, 30.

15. Simcoe in Quebec to Dundas, Apr. 28, 1792, *Correspondence of Simcoe*, vol. 1, 142; last quote, Barnes, *Native American Power*, 145.

16. Stevenson to Simcoe, May 8, 1792, *Correspondence of Simcoe*, vol. 1, 156. Stevenson is listed as a trader from Montreal in the *Correspondence of Simcoe*, but identified as an agent and army officer by Alan Taylor in *The Civil War of 1812: American Citizens, British Subjects, Irish Rebels, and Indian Allies* (New York: Alfred A. Knopf, 2010), 49.

17. Simcoe to McKee, Sept. 24, 1792, Daniel Claus and family fonds, vol. 5, *1792–1793*, Mfilm C-1479, LAC; Nelson, *Man of Distinction*, 160–165.

18. Capt. Joseph Brant to John Johnson, Aug. 14, 1791, Superintendent of Indian Affairs in the Northern District of North America fonds, MG 19, F-35, Series 2, lot 693, Mfilm H-2944, 1, LAC; Barnes, *Native American Power*, 186. In *Divided Ground*, Taylor notes that the emissaries were killed because they had bypassed the diplomatic "back door" to the confederacy, which ran through British forts on the lakes, and had taken a more direct route, which happened to be a warpath (268).

19. *PAJWA*, June 22, 1791; Knox to Brant, June 27, 1792, in Native American Collections, Clements Library, University of Michigan; Journal of mission to the Indians by Hendrick Aupaumut, 1791, Am .573, HSP.

20. Daniel Claus and family fonds, vol. 5, *1792–1793*, Mfilm C-1479, 84–88. The Northwestern confederacy's suggestion for paying settlers is found in Colin G. Calloway, ed., *The World Turned Upside Down: Indian Voices from Early America* (New York: Bedford St. Martin's, 1994), 181–183. Horsman, *Matthew Elliott*, 70–91.

21. See Hammond to Simcoe, July 11, 1792, *Correspondence of Simcoe*, vol. 1, 176; Simcoe to McKee and Butler, June 22, 1793, Daniel Claus and family fonds, vol. 5, *1792–1793*, Mfilm C-1479, 158; Henry Dundas in Whitehall to Lt. Gov. Clarke, Mar. 16, 1792, CO 42 89: 101–103; Dundas to Simcoe, May 5, 1792, CO 42 316: 116–117; Hammond to Lord Grenville, July 3, 1792, FO 4 16: 1.

22. Henry Mots [Lord Dorchester's secretary] to Lt. Col. Beckwith, Feb. 10, 1791, CO 42 73: 135; Horsman, *Matthew Elliott*, 70–91.

23. Extract of a letter from McKee in Detroit to Sir John Johnston, Apr. 1, 1791, CO 42 73: 285.

24. Simcoe's speech to the Western Indians, June 22, 1793, in *Correspondence of Simcoe*, vol. 1, 364.

25. Dorchester to Seven Nations, Feb. 18, 1794, Superintendent of Indian Affairs in the Northern district of North America (1756–1829), Mfilm H-2944, MG 19, F7, LAC; Taylor, *Civil War of 1812*, 54.

10. HENRY KNOX'S NIGHTMARE

1. Butler to Gunn, Oct. 2, 1793, Pierce Butler Papers; Butler to John Houstoun, Nov. 5, 1793, Pierce Butler Papers.

2. *PAJWA*, Aug. 12, 1789, Sept. 9, 1789, and Nov. 11, 1789; Wayne to Aedanus Burke, Oct. 7, 1788, Wayne Family Papers, William L. Clements Library, University of Michigan.

3. David Brion Davis, "Impact of the French and Haitian Revolutions," in Geggus, *Impact of the Haitian Revolution*, 7; Egerton, *Death or Liberty*, 259.

4. Lachance, "Repercussions of the Haitian Revolution in Louisiana," in Geggus, *The Impact of the Haitian Revolution*, 209–210; Jack D. L. Holmes, "The Abortive Slave Revolt at Pointe Coupée, Louisiana, 1795," *Louisiana History: The Journal of the Louisiana Historical Association* 11, no. 4 (Autumn, 1970), 341–362, 352.

5. Robert Alderson, "Charleston's Rumored Slave Revolt of 1793," in Geggus, *Impact of the Haitian Revolution*, 94.

6. "Foreign Intelligence from French papers—dateline Paris," Mar. 3, 1793, *Massachusetts Mercury* (Boston), May 20, 1793.

7. Robert J. Alderson, Jr., *This Bright Era of Happy Revolutions: French Consul Michel-Ange-Bernard Mangourit and International Republicanism in Charleston, 1792–1794* (Columbia: University of South Carolina Press, 2008), xi, 103, 142–143, 161.

8. Alderson, "Charleston's Rumored Slave Revolt," in Geggus, *Impact of the Haitian Revolution*, 103; Newman, "American Political Culture and the French and Haitian Revolutions," in Geggus, *Impact of the Haitian Revolution*, 80.

9. Blount to James Robertson, Jan. 2, 1792, James Robertson Papers, box 1, folder 7.

10. Jon Parmenter, "Dragging Canoe," 131.

11. Blount to Robertson, Apr. 1, 1792, James Robertson Papers, box 1, folder 7; Oct. 17, 1792, James Robertson Papers, box 1, folder 7; Blount to Robertson, May 20, 1792, James Robertson Papers, box 1, folder 7; McLoughlin, *Cherokee Renascence*, 25.

12. Knox to Blount, Nov. 26, 1792, Correspondence of the War Dept. Relating to Indian Affairs, Military Pensions, and Fortification, 1791–1797, M1062, roll 1 (NARA).

13. Knox to McGillivray, Feb. 17, 1792, in *ASPIA*, vol. 1, 246–247; Charles A. Weeks, *Paths to a Middle Ground: The Diplomacy of Natchez, Boukfouka, Nogales and San Fernando de las Barrancas, 1791–1795* (Tuscaloosa: University of Alabama Press, 2005), 85.

14. In *Dividing Paths*, Hatley notes that the Cherokees were so impressed with Pickens as an adversary that they called him *Skiagusta*, or "Warrior" (231).

15. Knox to Andrew Pickens, Apr. 21, 1792, *ASPIA*, vol. 1, 251–252; Pickens to Knox, Sept. 13, 1792, *ASPIA*, vol. 1, 316; Knox to Gov. of Virginia, May 16, 1792, *CVSP*, vol. 5, *1790–1792*, 545.

16. Parmenter, "Dragging Canoe," 131.

17. Knox to Gov. Lee of Virginia, May 16, 1792, *CVSP*, vol. 5, 545.

18. Parmenter, "Dragging Canoe," 132; McLoughlin, *Cherokee Renascence*, 25, 40; Boulware, *Deconstructing the Cherokee*, 165–166.

19. Extract of Minutes of information given to Blount from James Carey, sent to Sec. of War by Blount, Nov. 8, 1792, William Blount Miscellaneous Papers, FHS; McLoughlin, *Cherokee Renascence*, 40.

20. Carondelet in New Orleans to O'Neill, June 13, 1792, AGI, legajo 18, Papeles de Cuba; Weber, *Spanish Frontier*, 284–285; "hypocrisy," in *PAJWA*, Nov. 7, 1792.

21. Henry Knox, "Statement Relative to the Frontiers Northwest of the Ohio," Dec. 26, 1791, *ASPIA*, vol. 1, 197.

22. Knopf, "Anthony Wayne," 37. In *ASPIA*, vol. 1, 466, Piomingo, the pro-U.S. Chickasaw chief, chided James Robertson on June 17, 1793, saying, "My brother, I hardly know what you mean by treating with tribes that are always at war with you, and will be, until you whip them." On the other hand, a Shawnee man speaking to John Heckwelder in the late 1780s had criticized the American symbol of the eagle holding arrows and olive branches. The eagle, the Shawnee insisted, was overly proud and "the enemy of all the birds." Misreading the cultural significance of the olive branches, he saw them as "switches," seeing the bird's entire depiction as hostile. Quoted in Elizabeth Perkins, *Borderlands: Experience and Memory in the Revolutionary Ohio Valley* (Chapel Hill: University of North Carolina Press, 1998), 66.

23. Washington to House and Senate, Nov. 6, 1792, Dec. 3, 1793, in *American State Papers: Foreign Relations, Class I*, vol. 1 (Washington, D.C.: Gales and Seaton, 1833), 19–22; Knox to Pickens, Sept. 5, 1793, *ASPIA*, vol. 1, 365; quote about Jackson in Cumfer, *Separate Peoples, One Land*, 68.

24. See Wayne to James Wilson, July 4, 1789, Wayne Family Papers; Wayne to Henry Knox (private), May 5, 1790, Wayne Family Papers.

25. Extract of Hammond to Simcoe, Apr. 21, 1792, CO 42 316: 264–265; William Eaton in Pittsburgh to Stephen Jacobs, Apr. 15, 1793, Native American collections, Clements Library.

26. Furstenberg, "The Significance of the Trans-Appalachian Frontier," 664; Cayton quoted in ibid.

27. Marienstras, "The Common Man's Indian," 280.

28. Perdue, *Cherokee Women*, 88; quotes, Barnes, *Native American Power*, 118.

29. Blount to Knox, Nov. 8, 1792, *ASPIA*, vol. 1, 325–330; extracts from the deposition of Michael Cupps and Nancy Smith, taken by Elihu Lyman, justice of the peace for Greene County [Southwest Territory], Apr. 23, 1793, *ASPIA*, vol. 1, 369.

30. Campbell to Steele, Mar. 28, 1792, Arthur Campbell Papers.

31. Seagrove to Barnard, Feb. 24, 1793, in *ASPIA*, vol. 1, 377–378; Seagrove to Knox, Apr. 19, 1793, ibid., 378; Barnard to Seagrove, June 20, 1793, ibid., 394.

32. Campbell to Gov. Lee, Apr. 24, 1793, in *CVSP*, vol. 6, *1792–93*, 351; Lewis at Ft. Lee to Gov. Lee, June 26, 1793, ibid., 412.

11. BOWLES, PART ONE

1. Confidential, Luis de las Casas in Havana to the Count of Aranda, Dec. 3, 1792, AGI Legajo 9, no. 26 (Estado, Santo Domingo).
2. Baron de Carondelet in New Orleans to Don Luis de las Casas, Nov. 20, 1792, AGI Legajo 9, no. 26 (Estado, Santo Domingo).
3. Washington to Congress, Dec. 16, 1793, in *American State Papers: Foreign Relations, Class I*, vol. 1, 247; see also Hammond to Grenville, Nov. 6, 1792, and Hammond to Grenville, Dec. 4, 1792, in FO 116 3: 14–20.
4. Manuel Gayoso de Lemos in Natchez to Carondelet, Apr. 11, 1793; de Lemos in Natchez to Carondelet, May 10, 1793; Gayoso de Lemos in Natchez to Carondelet, May 11, 1793; de Lemos in Natchez to Carondelet, June 17, 1793; de Lemos in Natchez to Carondelet, Dec. 22, 1793, all in AGI legajo 2353, Papeles de Cuba.
5. McKee at Detroit, May 10, 1794, Daniel Claus and family fonds, vol. 6, *1793–1794*, Mfilm C-1479, 137; Lawrence Kinnaird, "Spanish Treaties with Indian Tribes," *The Western Historical Quarterly* 10, no. 1 (Jan. 1979), 39–48.
6. Weber, *Spanish Frontier*, 288–291.
7. Maj. John Smith, 5th Regt.'s report to Capt. Le Maistre, Military Secretary, enclosed with Lord Dorchester to Grenville, Jan 23. 1791, CO 42 73: 37–50, quote on 50.
8. Wright, *Bowles*, 1–13. In "The Cherokee Frontiers, the French Revolution, and William Augustus Bowles," in Duane H. King, ed., *The Cherokee Indian Nation: A Troubled History* (Knoxville: University of Tennessee Press, 1979), William C. Sturtevant, points out that even English newspapers sometimes misidentified Bowles' origins as British rather than colonial (78).
9. Wright, *Bowles*, 15–25; Benjamin Baynton, *Authentic Memoirs of William Augustus Bowles, Esquire, Ambassador for the United nations of Creeks and Cherokees, to the Court of London* (New York: Gale, 2010 [1791]), 36–40.
10. Wright, *Bowles*, 26; Caughey, *McGillivray of the Creeks*, 24–25.
11. Wright, *Bowles*, 26–27.
12. *PAJWA*, Feb. 4, 1789.
13. Gilbert C. Din, *War on the Gulf Coast: The Spanish Fight against William Augustus Bowles* (Gainesville: University Press of Florida, 2012), 64.
14. David, *Dunmore's New World*, 159–160; Wright, *Bowles*, 27–29.
15. Wright, *Bowles*, 29–30, quote on 29.
16. Ibid., 31–32.
17. As Din notes in *War on the Gulf Coast*, Bowles asserted his leadership over Creeks and Cherokees "without the slightest authority. . . . [and] vastly embellished their strength" (36).
18. Wright, *Bowles*, 37–42; Barnes, *Native American Power*, 157.

19. Stanley Elkins and Eric McKitrick, *The Age of Federalism: The Early American Republic, 1788–1800* (New York: Oxford University Press, 1993), 212–223; Weber, *Spanish Frontier*, 285–286.

20. Wright, *Bowles*, 44–50; Din, *War on the Gulf Coast*, 36.

21. Sturtevant, "William Augustus Bowles," 84.

22. First quote, *Concord Herald* (New Hampshire) Apr. 27, 1791, from London, Powderham-Castle, Feb. 6; Baynton, *Authentic Memoirs*, 56, 63.

23. First quotes, Wright, *Bowles*, 56–57; *Gazette of the United States* (Philadelphia), Sept. 7, 1791; Sturtevant, "William Augustus Bowles," 85; last quote, Bowles to a gentleman in Halifax, dated Aug. 31, 1791, *PAJWA*, Apr. 11, 1792.

24. Wright, *Bowles*, 58.

25. Ibid., 59–61; Din, *War on the Gulf Coast*, 36–37.

26. Wright, *Bowles*, 62–63.

27. Wayne to Major John Berrien, Dec. 5, 1791, Wayne Family Papers; *PAJWA*, Dec. 9 and Dec. 14, 1791; third quote, *PAJWA*, Jan. 4, 1792.

28. Wright, *Bowles*, 38, 62–63; *Dunlap's American Daily Advertiser* (Philadelphia), Mar. 8, 1792; *Freeman's Journal* (Philadelphia), Dec. 7, 1791.

29. Arthur Campbell to ?, Jan. 13, 1792, Arthur Campbell Papers; Samuel Newall to Campbell, Feb. 1, 1792, King's Mountain Papers, Draper Manuscripts, 9DD67.

30. Wright, *Bowles*, 62–63; first quote, Chinabee, at Conference of Cherokee (and other) chiefs with the Sec. of War, Jan. 9, 1792, in *ASPIA*, vol. 1, 205; Knox to McGillivray, Feb. 17, 1792, ibid., 246; Knox to Seagrove, Feb. 20, 1792, ibid., 250; *Kentucky Gazette*, Apr. 28, 1792; *Federal Gazette* (Philadelphia), Mar. 10, 1792.

31. Wright, *Bowles*, 65–79; Nichols, *Red Gentlemen*, 109; Barnes, *Native American Power*, 158–159; *Kentucky Gazette*, May 26, 1792; *Herald of the United States* (Warren, Rhode Island), May 12, 1792; *PAJWA*, May 2, 1792.

32. Knox to Henry Lee, *ASPIA*, vol. 1, 255; Knox to Seagrove, Apr. 29, 1792, ibid., 254–255; McGillivray to Seagrove, Apr. 8, 1792, ibid., 296; Seagrove to Pres. Washington, July 5, 1792, ibid., 305–306.

33. Knox to McGillivray, Aug. 11, 1792, *ASPIA*, vol. 1, 256–257; Seagrove to Creek Nation, Apr. 14, 1793, ibid., 381–382; Nathaniel Pendelton in Savannah, to James Iredell, June 22, 1792, James Iredell, Sr. and Jr., Papers, 1724–1890, David M. Rubenstein Rare Books and Manuscripts Library, Duke University; Seagrove to President, July 27, 1792, Henry Knox Miscellaneous Papers, FHS.

12. PAN-INDIANISM CRESTS

1. *PAJWA*, July 10, 1793.

2. Ockillissa Chopka—Principal Chief and Speaker, Houthlie opoi Mico, or Great far off— War King, and Tustuniccal Opoi, or Great far off—Warrior—at Cowetah Old Town, April 12, 1793, to Col. A McKee, Alexander and Thomas McKee collection, MG 19 F16, LAC (hereafter McKee Collection).

3. Simcoe to Alured Clarke, July 29, 1793, in *Correspondence of Simcoe*, vol. 1, 392–393.

4. Ockillissa Chopka—Principal Chief and Speaker, Houthlie opoi Mico, or Great far off—War King, and Tustuniccal Opoi, or Great far off—Warrior—at Cowetah Old Town, April 12, 1793, to Col. A McKee, McKee Collection.

5. *PAJWA*, Apr. 24, 1793, May 29, 1793, June 5, 1793, July 3, 1793.

6. Robertson to Shelby, May 26, 1793, Tennessee Papers, Draper Manuscripts, 4XX15; Shelby to James Wilkinson, June 1793 [no date], Wayne Papers, vol. 27, 46; Blount to Sevier, Aug. 28, 1793, Tennessee Papers, Draper Manuscripts, 4XX33 (Tennessee Papers), 59.

7. Simcoe to Allured Clark, July 29, 1793, *Correspondence of Simcoe*, vol. 1, 392–393; Nelson, *Man of Distinction*, 165; Wayne to Knox, July 10, 1793, Wayne Papers, vol. 27, 105.

8. Weber, *Spanish Frontier*, 284.

9. John McDonald at Cherokees to A. McKee, Apr. 10, 1794, McKee Collection.

10. Nichols, *Red Gentlemen*, 6–10, 112–114; Arrell M. Gibson, *The Chickasaws* (Norman: University of Oklahoma Press, 1971), 58–79; Atkinson, *Splendid Land, Splendid People*, 111–137.

11. Campbell to Knox, [illegible month] 29th day, 1789, Arthur Campbell Papers; Campbell to Washington, May 10, 1789, Arthur Campbell Papers.

12. Blount to Robertson, Oct. 17, 1792, James Robertson Papers, box 1, folder 7; Blount to Robertson, Dec. 2, 1792, James Robertson Papers, box 1, folder 7.

13. Blount to Bloody Fellow, Sept. 13, 1792, James Robertson Papers, box 1, folder 7; Blount to Robertson, Jan. 8, 1793, James Robertson Papers, box 1, folder 8; Mar. 28, 1793, James Robertson Papers, box 1, folder 8.

14. Tatham to Gov. Lee, Apr. 28, 1793, *CVSP*, vol. 6, *1792–1793*, 354; Campbell to Gov. Lee, May 31, 1793, ibid., 392.

15. René Chartrand, *Louis XIV's Army* (New York: Osprey Publishing Ltd., 1988), 41; Ian K. Steele, *Warpaths: Invasions of North America* (New York: Oxford University Press, 1995), 53.

16. Carondelet to Robertson, May 21, 1793, James Robertson Papers, box 2, folder 1; Chickasaws to Robertson, Feb. 13, 1793, Wayne Papers, vol. 26, 87.

17. See "Account of the Men, Women, and Children Belonging to the Chickasaw Nation Assembled . . . at the Chickasaw Bluffs for the Purpose of Receiving Their Annuities," Oct. 9, 1810, Misc. Accounts of the Chickasaw Bluffs Trading House, Entry 39, Records of the Office of Indian Trade, RG 75 [thanks to David A. Nichols for this source]; Wood, "The Changing Population of the Colonial South," 95; Wayne to Clark, June 18, 1793, Wayne Papers, vol. 27, 48.

18. Knox to Wayne, Apr. 27, 1793, James Robertson Papers, box 3, folder 11; Carondelet to Messrs. Jos. Jaudenes and Jos. Viar, Oct. 28, 1793, in *American State Papers: Foreign Relations, Class I*, vol. 1, 306.

19. Nichols, *Red Gentlemen*, 76.

20. Blount himself later presented a petition in the House of Representatives from Hanging Maw's widow "praying for redress of injuries sustained contrary to law, in the year 1793, from a party of whites, commanded by Beard." See *Federal Gazette* (Baltimore), Jan. 12, 1797.

21. Smith to Robertson, June 19, 1793, James Robertson Papers, box 3, folder 4.

22. Gov. Isaac Shelby to Henry Knox, Feb. 10, 1794, Henry Knox Miscellaneous Papers; Lewis in Fort Lee to Gov. Lee, Feb. 17, 1794, *CVSP*, vol. 7, *1794–1795*, 32.

23. Wayne to Knox, Oct. 17, 1794, Wayne Papers, vol. 37, 91.

24. Francis Preston to Johnny Preston, Dec. 1793, Robert Preston Family Papers—Joyes Collection, Mss A .P937j1, FHS; Jan. 1, 1794, Robert Preston Family Papers—Joyes Collection.

25. Copy of the report of the Committee on Indian Affairs received at Knoxville Apr. 11th 1794, James Robertson Papers, box 3, folder 11.

26. *Annals of Congress* vol. IV, *1793–1795* (1849), 831, 837, 1251–1256, 1263–1270, 1400–1402.

27. *Dunlap's American Daily Advertiser* (Philadelphia), July 8, 1794; *Western Star* (Stockbridge, Mass.), Aug. 5, 1794; Blount in Knoxville to Robertson, Aug. 6th, 1794, James Robertson Papers, box 1, folder 10; Piomingo to Robertson, June 17, 1793, Wayne Papers, vol. 27, 47.

28. For Fallen Timbers and its aftermath, see Sword, *President Washington's Indian War*, and Alan D. Gaff, *Bayonets in the Wilderness: Anthony Wayne's Legion in the Old Northwest* (Norman: University of Oklahoma Press, 2008).

29. Simcoe to Dundas, Mar. 2, 1794, CO 42 22: 129.

30. Campbell to Gov., May 22, 1795, in *CVSP*, vol. 8, *1795–1798*, 241.

31. Vigo to Wayne, Oct. 12, 1794, Wayne Papers, vol. 37, 80; Major Doyle at Fort Massac to Thomas Postel, Feb. 8, 1795, Wayne Papers, vol. 39, 53; Pickering to Wayne, Apr. 15, 1795, Wayne Papers, vol. 40, 50; Hamtramck to Wayne, May 8, 1795, Wayne Papers, vol. 40, 102.

32. Wayne to O'Hara, Feb. 3, 1795, Wayne Papers, vol. 39, 44; Wayne to Capt. Pasteur, June 11, 1795, Wayne Papers, vol. 41, 59; Wayne to Pickering, June 17, 1795, Wayne Papers, vol. 41, 82.

33. Wayne to Gov. St. Clair, June 5, 1795, Wayne Papers, vol. 41, 49.

34. Wayne to Pickering, Sept. 3, 1795, Wayne Papers, vol. 42, 88; Wayne to Clark, Sept. 10, 1795, Wayne Papers, vol. 42, 106; Wayne to Clark (private and confidential), Sept. 10, 1795, Wayne Papers, vol. 42, 107.

35. Wayne to Pickering, Nov. 12, 1795, Wayne Papers, vol. 43, 44; quote, Weber, *Spanish Frontier in North America*, 289; Kinnaird, "Spanish Treaties with Indian Tribes," 48.

36. Colin G. Calloway, *Crown and Calumet: British-Indian Relations, 1783–1815* (Norman: University of Oklahoma Press, 1987), 195.

37. Barnes, *Native American Power*, 175.

38. Robertson to Blount, Jan. 10, 1795, James Robertson Papers, box 1, folder 10; Blount to Robertson, Jan. 20, 1795, James Robertson Papers, box 1, folder 10; Atkinson, *Splendid Land*, 170–171.

39. Furstenberg, "Significance of the Trans-Appalachian Frontier," 667–670; Alderson, *Bright Era of Happy Revolutions*, 179–180.

40. Carondelet's talk to Mad Dog of the Tuckabatchees, Mar. 25, 1795, James Robertson Papers, box 2, folder 1.

41. On Dec. 30, 1796, according to the *Annals of Congress*, vol. 5, 4th Congress, 2nd session, p. 1741, Congressman Andrew Jackson presented a petition from George Colbert of the Chickasaws, asking for remuneration because they fed and housed a Colonel Mansker and forty-six men for sixty days. The men had marched (without orders) to help the Chickasaws against the Creeks.

42. Blount to Robertson, May 4, 1795, James Robertson Papers, box 1, folder 10; Blount to Robertson, May 31, 1795, James Robertson Papers, box 1, folder 10; Pickering to Robertson, May 9, 1795, James Robertson Papers, box 3, folder 13; Blount to Robertson, Aug. 11, 1795, James Robertson Papers, box 1, folder 12.

43. Blount to Robertson, Aug. 11, 1795, James Robertson Papers, box 1, folder 12; Blount to Robertson, Nov. 11, 1795, James Robertson Papers, box 1, folder 12; Blount to Robertson, Nov. 15, 1795, James Robertson Papers, box 1, folder 12. In *Splendid Land*, Atkinson concludes that the lack of subsequent reference to the cannon in the documents means they were probably returned to Nashville, though that would not explain why Robertson suddenly lost his militia commission (167).

44. Furstenberg, "Significance of the Trans-Appalachian Frontier," 657–658.

45. Ibid., 667–668. See William R. Nester, *George Rogers Clark: I Glory in War* (Norman: University of Oklahoma Press, 2012); *Centinel of the North-Western Territory*, Jan. 24, 1794.

13. THE FEAR REMAINS THE SAME

1. Now in northern West Virginia.

2. John Connell in Brooke County to the governor, Mar. 25, 1797, *CVSP*, vol. 8, *1795–1798*, 426–427.

3. Sevier to Cocke, July 6, 1797, Gov. John Sevier Papers, 1796–1801 (First Series of Administrations), TSA.

4. *Kentucke* [sic] *Gazette*, Oct. 11, 1797, and Nov. 8, 1797.

5. Samuel J. Cabell of Virginia, Mar. 7, 1796, in *Circular Letters of Congressmen to Their Constituents 1789–1829, vol. 1, First Congress–Ninth Congress 1789–1807*, ed. Noble E. Cunningham, Jr. (Chapel Hill: University of North Carolina Press, 1978), 40.

6. In fact, Cox was arrested soon after this article appeared, though eventually exonerated. *Encyclopedia of Alabama* (online).

7. *Kentucke Gazette*, Aug. 8, 1798.

NOTES TO PAGES 167–175   269

8. Wm. C. C. Claiborne in Knoxville to J. Dayton, Aug. 22, 1798, Indian Affairs, case 1, box 34, HSP.
9. Samuel Mitchell in the Lower Choctaw Towns to Col. Henley, Jan. 17, 1800, David Henley Papers, David M. Rubenstein Rare Books and Manuscripts Library, Duke University.
10. *Dictionary of Canadian Biography Online*, vol. 5.
11. Mr. President Peter Russell, Military Secretary's Office #24, to Duke of Portland, Feb. 3, 1799, MG 23 HI 2, vol. 2, 4-11, LAC; Mr. President Peter Russell, Military Secretary's Office #24, to Jos. Baby et al., Feb. 10, 1799, MG 23 HI 2, vol. 2, 4–11; last quote, Taylor, *Civil War of 1812*, 83; Nelson, *Man of Distinction*, 183–185; Horsman, *Matthew Elliott*, 143–147.
12. Peter Selby to Russell, Jan. 23, 1799, Letters from Mr. President Peter Russell, Military Secretary's Office #24, MG 23 HI 2 vol. 2, 22, LAC; and Russell to Gen. Prescott, Apr. 4, 1799, in Letters from Mr. President Peter Russell, Military Secretary's Office #24, MG 23 HI 2 vol. 2, 50; *Dictionary of Canadian Biography Online*, vol. 5.
13. See Wallace, *Jefferson and the Indians* and Sheehan, *Seeds of Extinction*.
14. *Western Spy and Hamilton Gazette* (Cincinnati), Aug. 6, 1799.
15. Furstenberg, "Significance of the Trans-Appalachian Frontier," 668–670, quotes on 670. For fear of black French army and "seriously considered," see Egerton, *Death or Liberty*, 266.
16. Quotes from Lachance, "Repercussions of the Haitian Revolution," in Geggus, *Impact of the Haitian Revolution*, 210; *Diary, or Loudon's Register* (N.Y.), Oct. 7, 1793, extract of a letter from Charleston, Aug. 25, 1793. In *This Bright Era*, Alderson, argues that had the French-backed invasion of Florida succeeded in the mid-1790s, Napoleon might not have abandoned St. Domingue so quickly (179).
17. Jefferson to Harrison, Feb. 27, 1803, in *The Papers of William Henry Harrison, 1800–1815*, ed. Douglas E. Clanin (Indianapolis: Indiana Historical Society, 1999), hereafter *Papers of WHH*.
18. *Connecticut Journal*, Jan. 20, 1803; *United States Chronicle* (Providence, Rhode Island), Apr. 7, 1803.
19. Marienstras, "The Common Man's Indian," 272.
20. Jefferson to "The Special Envoy to France" (Madison), Jan. 13, 1803, in *Thomas Jefferson: Writings*, ed. Merrill D. Peterson (New York: Literary Classics of the United States, Inc., 1984), 1113; quote, Furstenberg, "Significance of the Trans-Appalachian Frontier," 674.

14. BOWLES, PART TWO

1. *PAJWA*, Sept. 5, 1792; Ockillissa Chopka—Principal Chief and Speaker, Houthlie opoi Mico, or Great far off—War King, and Tustuniccal Opoi, or Great far off—Warrior—at Cowetah Old Town, April 12, 1793, to Col. A. McKee, Manuscripts, McKee Collection.

2. David, *Dunmore's New World*, 169.
3. Reprinted in the *Mercantile Advertiser* (N.Y.), May 4, 1799.
4. *The General Aurora Advertiser* (Philadelphia), May 3, 1799.
5. Isaac Joslin Cox, "Hispanic-American Phases of the 'Burr Conspiracy,'" *The Hispanic American Historical Review* 12, no. 2 (May 1932), 145–175.
6. Taylor, *Civil War of 1812*, 56.
7. Din, *War on the Gulf Coast*, 114.
8. *The Philadelphia Gazette*, Sept. 3, 1799; *Columbian Museum* (Savannah, Georgia), Nov. 12, 1799.
9. Bowles to Little Prince of Coweta, Nov. 30, 1799, Simon Gratz Collection, case 4, box 4, HSP.
10. Hawkins to Jackson, July 18, 1800, reprinted in the Sept. 1, 1800, *Kentucky Gazette*.
11. Din, *War on the Gulf Coast*, 115–124.
12. Ibid., 144–147.
13. *Philadelphia Gazette*, June 4, 1802; *Salem Register* (Mass.), July 5, 1802.
14. Din, *War on the Gulf Coast*, 168, 175; Taylor, *Internal Enemy*, 97–103.
15. Wright, *Bowles*, 160–171; Benjamin W. Griffith, Jr., *McIntosh and Weatherford, Creek Indian Leaders* (Tuscaloosa: University of Alabama Press, 1988), 52; Din, *War on the Gulf Coast*, 199–210.
16. Din, *War on the Gulf Coast*, 212–215.

15. INDIANS AND THE JEFFERSONIAN MIND

1. *Boston Gazette*, Jan. 23, 1806; Furstenberg, "Significance of the Trans-Appalachian Frontier," 674; Weber, *Spanish Frontier in North America*, 291–292.
2. Mead to Pytchlin, June 23, 1806, Indian Affairs (under C. Mead), case 3, box 2, folder 60, HSP.
3. *The Argus of Western America* (Frankfort, Ky.) Sept. 3, 1808, FHS.
4. For the Prophet and his movement, see R. David Edmunds, *The Shawnee Prophet* (Lincoln: University of Nebraska Press, 1983); Sugden, *Tecumseh*; Dowd, *Spirited Resistance*.
5. Harrison to Dearborn, May 23, 1807, in Clanin, *Papers of WHH*; Harrison to Henry Dearborn, July 11, 1807, ibid.
6. Spencer C. Tucker and Frank T. Reuter, *Injured Honor: The Chesapeake–Leopard Affair, June 22, 1807* (Annapolis: Naval Institute Press, 1996).
7. Harrison to legislature, Aug. 17, 1807, in Clanin, *Papers of WHH*, repr. in the *Vincennes Western Sun*, Aug. 22, 1807.
8. Silver, *Our Savage Neighbors*, 94.
9. Marienstras, "Common Man's Indian," 265, 268–275, quote on 270.
10. Rachel Hope Cleves, *The Reign of Terror in America: Visions of Violence from Anti-Jacobinism to Anti-Slavery* (New York: Cambridge University Press, 2009), 164.

Some, like Mary Rowlandson's captivity narrative, *The Sovereignty and Goodness of God* (Cambridge, 1682) had been quite popular and were rarely, if ever, out of print. Others were more obscure, but compensated with graphic and gruesome titles, like Archibald Loudon's *A Selection of the Most Interesting Narratives of Outrages Committed by the Indians in Their Wars with the White People* (Carlisle, Penn., 1808). See also Taylor, *Civil War of 1812*, 136–137.

11. The *Trenton Federalist*, June 20, 1808, carried a report of a Creek attack in Tennessee, but noted, "The democrat papers ascribe this conduct of the Indians to the British—although these Indians live very remote from any English settlement or possessions."

12. Marienstras, "Common Man's Indian," 286. For the "cynical war" argument, see Taylor, *Civil War of 1812*, 136–137, and Joel W. Martin, *Sacred Revolt: The Muskogees' Struggle for a New World* (Boston: Beacon Press, 1991), 153–154. For dread of Indian warfare, see Taylor, *Civil War of 1812*, 204–210.

13. *Western Spy and Hamilton Gazette*, Sept. 14, 1807.

14. Harrison to HD, Aug. 13, 1807, in Clanin, *Papers of WHH*; extract of a letter from an Officer at Ft. Michilimackinac to his brother, July 24, 1807, in *Alexandria Daily Advertiser* (Virginia), Oct. 9, 1807. "Carver's Travels" referred to Jonathan Carver's *Travels through the Interior Parts of North America in the Years 1766, 1767, and 1768*, the narrative of a militiaman from Massachusetts who had traveled through the early West in the years of his service in the French and Indian War. Carver's was one of the first successful travelogues of North America, with at least twenty-one editions in several languages by 1813. See *The Journals of Jonathan Carver and Related Documents, 1766–1770*, ed. John Parker (Minneapolis: Minnesota Historical Society Press, 1976), 228.

15. McKee Collection, 10–12; Horsman, *Matthew Elliott*, 170.

16. The United States was equally unprepared, though the Secretary of War did try to recruit a spy to view Canadian defenses up close; see Dearborn to M. Bailly, Nov. 27, 1807, in Correspondence RG 107.2.1, Records of the Office of the Secretary of War, 1791–1947, NARA; Horsman, *Elliott*, 171–173.

17. Sugden, *Tecumseh*, 187; Gore in York, Upper Canada, Mar. 28, 1808 (Private) to "Dear Cooke," in CO 42 348: 32.

18. Harrison to Eustis, June 26, 1810, in Clanin, *Papers of WHH*.

19. Ibid.; Gregory E. Dowd, "Thinking and Believing: Nativism and Unity in the Ages of Pontiac and Tecumseh," *American Indian Quarterly*, vol. 16, no. 3 (Summer, 1992), 309–335.

20. Elliott to Dep. Lt. Gen. William Claus, Oct. 16, 1810, CO 42 351: 36; Elliott to Claus, Nov. 10, 1810, CO 42 351: 40; Christopher Densmore, *Red Jacket: Iroquois Diplomat and Orator* (Syracuse: Syracuse University Press, 1999), 78–79; Horsman, *Elliott*, 179–182.

21. Elliott to Claus, Nov. 10, 1810, CO 42 351: 40.

22. Ibid., 40–43; Gore to Earl of Liverpool, Mar. 1, 1811, ibid., 30.

23. Harrison to Eustis, July 10, 1811, quoted in Dowd, "Thinking outside the Circle," 38.

24. Harrison to Eustis, Aug. 6, 1811, in Clanin, *Papers of WHH*. For Tecumseh's journey, see John Sugden, "Early Pan-Indianism: Tecumseh's Tour of the Indian Country, 1811–1812," *American Indian Quarterly* 10, no. 4 (Autumn, 1986), 273–304.

25. Harrison to Eustis, Aug. 7, 1811, in Clanin, *Papers of WHH*.

16. FEAR'S RESURGENCE

1. Eustis to Johnston, Feb. 18, 1811, and Circular Letter of Apr. 15, 1811, to Indian Agents, both in Records of the Office of the Secretary of War, Letters Sent, Indian Office Letter Book C, NARA.

2. *Louisiana Gazette and New Orleans Daily Advertiser*, Aug. 20, 1811.

3. Extract of a letter from a young man in Gov. Harrison's army, dated Sept. 26, 1811, reprinted in *The Enquirer* (Richmond, Va.), Nov. 11, 1811.

4. See Sugden, *Tecumseh*, 231–236; Robert M. Owens, *Mr. Jefferson's Hammer: William Henry Harrison and the Origins of American Indian Policy* (Norman: University of Oklahoma Press, 2007), 217–222.

5. *Columbian Centinel*, Dec. 7, 1811.

6. Ethridge, *Creek Country*, 12. See also Angela Pulley Hudson, *Creek Paths and Federal Roads: Indians, Settlers, and Slaves and the Making of the American South* (Chapel Hill: University of North Carolina Press, 2010).

7. Kappler, *Indian Treaties*, 85; McKee to Monroe, Sept. 11, 1811, State Department Territorial Papers, Florida series, 1777–1824, vol. 1, *Oct. 13, 1777–Dec. 1811*, NARA, Florida State Archives; Griffiths, *McIntosh and Weatherford*, 64–70.

8. *Vincennes Western Sun*, Dec. 14, 1811. The author, "American Statesman," might have been Harrison himself. Frank Lawrence Owsley, Jr., *Struggle for the Gulf Borderlands: The Creek War and the Battle of New Orleans, 1812–1815* (Gainesville: University Press of Florida, 1981), 10.

9. *National Intelligencer*, Dec. 16, 1811.

10. See Martin, *Sacred Revolt*, 133–149; Sugden, *Tecumseh*, 237–251; Sugden, "Early Pan-Indianism," 273–304; Dowd, "Thinking outside the Circle," 36. Kathryn E. Braund definitively demonstrates that the Red Sticks were named for their painted clubs, rather than counting sticks. See "Red Sticks," in Braund, *Tohopeka*, 86.

11. Wells to Harrison, Mar. 1, 1812, in Clanin, *Papers of WHH*; Eustis to WHH, Jan. 17, 1812, ibid.

12. Hawkins to Nathanel Greene, June 25, 1785, Nathanael Greene Papers.

13. Robertson to David Henley, June 19, 1797, David Henley Papers; Hawkins to Henley, July 28, 1797, David Henley Papers.

14. See Claudio Saunt, "'Domestic . . . Quiet Being Broke': Gender Conflict among Creek Indians in the Eighteenth Century," in *Contact Points: American Frontiers from the Mohawk Valley to the Mississippi, 1750–1830*, ed. Andrew R. L. Cayton and Frederika Teute, (Chapel Hill: University of North Carolina Press, 1998), 151–174; Ethridge, *Creek Country*, 12–18; quote, Braund, *Tohopeka*, 1.

15. Florette Henri, *The Southern Indians and Benjamin Hawkins, 1796–1816* (Norman: University of Oklahoma Press, 1986), 107–109, 212, 280; Martin, *Sacred Revolt*, 133–135.

16. Shanks to Eustis, July 12, 1810, State Department Territorial Papers, Florida, 1777–1824, vol. 1, *Oct. 13, 1777–Dec. 1811*, NARA, Florida State Archives; James G. Cusick, *The Other War of 1812: The Patriot War and the American Invasion of Spanish East Florida* (Athens: University of Georgia Press, 2003); Ethridge, *Creek Country*, 15–18.

17. Claiborne to Jefferson, Sept. 29, 1803, in *Territorial Papers of the United States*, vol. 9, *The Territory of Orleans, 1803–1812*, ed. Clarence E. Carter (Washington, D.C.: U.S. Government Printing Office, 1940), 59.

18. Wilkinson to Sec. of War Dearborn, Dec. 21, 1803, ibid., 139.

19. John Graham to Sec. of State, Sept. 9, 1805, ibid., 499; statement of Stephen, a free negro, Jan. 29, 1806, ibid., 575–576.

20. James H. Dormon, "The Persistent Specter: Slave Rebellion in Territorial Louisiana," *Louisiana History: The Journal of the Louisiana Historical Association* 18, no. 4 (Autumn, 1977), 389–404, quotes on 391, 393; Gabriel's plot quote in Taylor, *Internal Enemy*, 97.

21. Thomas Marshall Thompson, "National Newspaper and Legislative Reactions to Louisiana's Deslondes Slave Revolt of 1811," *Louisiana History: The Journal of the Louisiana Historical Association* 33, no. 1 (Winter 1992), 5–8.

22. Ibid., 8–9.

23. Ibid., 11–21, quotes on 11 and 21.

24. Thompson, "National Newspaper and Legislative Reactions," 23–25, quotes on 23, 25, 26; for "brigands" and "banditti," see Dormon, "Persistent Specter," 400, and "Extract of a Letter from Mr. Andry, Father, to His Excellency Governor Claiborne," Jan. 11, 1811, in *The Sentinel of Freedom* (Newark, N.J.), Feb. 19, 1811.

25. *Vincennes Western Sun*, May 26, June 30, and Aug. 4, 1812.

17. DEATH BY THE RIVER'S SIDE

1. Tom Kanon, "The Kidnapping of Martha Crawley and Settler–Indian Relations prior to the War of 1812," *Tennessee Historical Quarterly* 64, no. 1 (Spring 2005), 3–23, quote on 3.

2. Ibid., 12, 15; the *Nashville Clarion* (as reprinted in the *Vincennes Western Sun*, Aug. 4, 1812) insisted that the war party had full support among influential Creek leaders and that there were no efforts to punish the guilty. As Kanon notes, both assertions were false, but nevertheless widely believed by Westerners.

3. In June 1812, shortly before the American declaration of war against Britain, the War Department unceremoniously dumped James Neely as the Chickasaw Agent, noting that the hostile disposition of the Indian tribes made it "expedient" for the government to "avail itself of General James Robertson's Services."

See Sec. of War to Neely, June 4, 1812, in Records of the Office of the Secretary of War, Letters Sent, Indian Office Letter Book C, NARA.

4. Robertson to Sevier, Oct. 26, 1812, in King's Mountain Papers, Draper Manuscripts, 16DD43.

5. Nathaniel Millett, *The Maroons of Prospect Bluff and Their Quest for Freedom in the Atlantic World* (Gainesville: University Press of Florida, 2013), 78.

6. Tom Kanon, "Before Horseshoe: Andrew Jackson's Campaigns in the Creek War Prior to Horseshoe Bend," in Braund, *Tohopeka*, 106, 118.

7. Jackson quoted in Kanon, "Kidnapping of Crawley," 5; Martin, *Sacred Revolt*, 154–156.

8. As Rachel Hope Cleves reminds us, 40 percent of the Congress voted against the war, including a close Senate vote of 19 to 13 in favor. See *The Reign of Terror in America*, 156.

9. A matching letter from Jackson to Winchester has not been found, though the sentiments and phrasing, especially the writer's "impatience" with the "war minister," and begging for the order to attack the Creeks, evokes Jackson.

10. *Vincennes Western Sun*, Sept. 22, 1812, and Sept. 29, 1812; Owsley, Jr., *Struggle for the Gulf Borderlands*, 19.

11. *Vincennes Western Sun*, Sept. 19, 1812; *National Intelligencer*, Nov. 14, 1812.

12. Adam Rothman, *Slave Country: American Expansion and the Origins of the Deep South* (Cambridge, Mass.: Harvard University Press, 2005), 119.

13. CO 42 352: 55.

14. Ibid., 56.

15. Ibid., 107; Taylor, *Civil War of 1812*, 149–159.

16. CO 42 352: 124.

17. Taylor, *Civil War of 1812*, 136–137, 204–206. See also Silver, *Our Savage Neighbors*, and Perkins, *Border Life*.

18. As Colin G. Calloway reminds us in *Crown and Calumet*, even after victory there the British remained suspicious that their Indian allies would turn on them (216).

19. Taylor, *Civil War of 1812*, 161–169; Sugden, *Tecumseh*, 299–306, 326–327, 334–338.

20. Brock to Gen. Prevost, Aug. 17, 1812, CO 42 352: 105–106; Brock to Lord Liverpool, Aug. 29, 1812, CO 42 352: 127; Lord Liverpool to Brock, Nov. 16, 1812, CO 42 352: 144.

21. Taylor, *Civil War of 1812*, 188.

22. Sugden, *Tecumseh*, 321–323; Taylor, *Civil War of 1812*, 210–212.

23. Sevier to Robertson, Feb. 25, 1813, James Robertson Papers, box 4, folder 2.

24. Robert P. Collins, "'A Packet from Canada': Telling Conspiracy Stories on the 1813 Creek Frontier," in Braund, *Tohopeka*, 54–62.

25. *Wilson's Gazette*, Aug. 31, 1812, TSA; Martin, *Sacred Revolt*, 151; quote about Blount in John Grenier, "'We Bleed Our Enemies in Such Cases to Give Them Their Senses': Americans' Unrelenting Wars on the Indians of the Trans-Appalachian West, 1810–1814," in Braund, *Tohopeka*, 176.

26. Feb. 8, 1813, in *Circular Letters of Congressmen to Their Constituents 1789–1829*, vol. 2, 803–809.

27. Jefferson to David Bailie, Dec. 29, 1813, in *The Papers of Thomas Jefferson, Retirement Series*, vol. 7, ed. J. Jefferson Looney (Princeton: Princeton University Press, 2011), 91.

28. Jefferson to William Cocke, Apr. 17, 1813, *The Papers of Thomas Jefferson*, vol. 6, 67–68; Frank Lawrence Owsley, Jr., and Gene A. Smith, *Filibusters and Expansionists: Jeffersonian Manifest Destiny, 1800–1821* (Tuscaloosa: University of Alabama Press, 1997), 77.

29. *The Courier* (Washington, D.C.), Oct. 24, 1812; *The Enquirer* (Richmond, Va.), Oct. 30, 1812; Owsley and Smith, *Filibusters and Expansionists*, 79.

30. Gillum Ferguson, *Illinois in the War of 1812* (Urbana: University of Illinois Press, 2012), 119–120.

31. W. C. C. Claiborne to Sen. James Brown, Aug. 25, 1813, Mississippi Territory Papers—Governor's Correspondence SG3114, Alabama Department of Archives and History (ADAH).

32. John Pitchlynn to Robertson, Apr. 27, 1813, James Robertson Papers, box 3, folder 14; *American Advocate* (Hallowell, Maine), Aug. 21, 1813.

33. In *A New Order of Things*, Claudio Saunt notes that Spanish documents make this Red Stick intention perfectly clear (262).

34. Gregory A. Waselkov, *A Conquering Spirit: Fort Mims and the Redstick War of 1813–1814* (Tuscaloosa: University of Alabama Press, 2006), 99–101; quote, Saunt, *New Order of Things*, 262. Robert G. Thrower offers, "The Battle of Burnt Corn did not cause the Creek War, since the Indians were already bringing in arms with which to fight a war; however, it no doubt motivated many of those who were unaffected to join the hostiles"; see Thrower, "Causalities and Consequences of the Creek War: A Modern Perspective," in Braund, *Tohopeka*, 16. Claiborne to Jefferson, Aug. 14, 1813, *The Papers of Thomas Jefferson*, vol. 7, 389. Claiborne wrote this letter eleven days before his letter to Senator Brown, stating that the Creeks had not done much mischief.

35. Hawkins to David Mitchell, July 27, 1813, in *Letters, Journals and Writings of Benjamin Hawkins*, vol. 2, *1802–1816*, ed. C. L. Grant (Savannah, Ga.: Beehive Press, 1980), 651–652. Reprinted in *Wilson's Gazette* (Knoxville), Aug. 30, 1813, under the headline "Indian War!!"; P.A. Foote in Adams County, Kentucky, to his father William, in Dumfries, Virginia, Sept. 13, 1813, Foote Family Papers, Mss A F 688, FHS; Samuel Brown, Natchez, to Col. John C. Bartlett, Ft. Meigs, Sept. 13, 1813, Sanders Family Papers, S215 fl. 5, FHS.

36. H. W. Brands, *Andrew Jackson: His Life and Times* (New York: Doubleday, 2005), 194.

37. Waselkov, *Conquering Spirit*, 127.

38. Waselkov, *Conquering Spirit*, 226; Martin, *Sacred Revolt*, 156–158, quote on 157; Waselkov, "Fort Jackson and Its Aftermath," in Braund, *Tohopeka*, 160.

39. *Charleston Courier*, Oct. 1, 1813; *Columbian Centinel*, Oct. 6, 1813.

40. W. C. Mead to F. L. Claiborne, Sept. 20, 1813, Claiborne (J. F. H.) Collection: Book F, Letters and Papers Relating to the Indian Wars, 1812–1816 (hereafter Claiborne Collection: Indian Wars), Mississippi Department of Archives (MDA).

41. Waselkov, *Conquering Spirit*, 148; Saunt, *New Order of Things*, 263.

42. Claiborne to J. W. Bowyer, Aug. 9, 1813, Claiborne Collection: Indian Wars; Claiborne to Gov. of Georgia, Aug. 14, 1813, Claiborne Collection: Indian Wars; Claiborne to Hawkins, Aug. 14, 1813, Claiborne Collection: Indian Wars; Capt. James B. Wilkinson in Mobile to General F. L. Claiborne, Aug. 4, 1813, Claiborne (J. F. H.) Collection, Book F, Letters and Papers Relating to the Fort Mims Massacre, MDA.

18. BLEEDING PAN-INDIANISM

1. Jackson to the Tennessee Volunteers, Sept. 24, 1813, in *Papers of Andrew Jackson*, vol. 2, ed. Harold D. Moser, et al. (Knoxville: University of Tennessee Press, 1980–2013), 428.

2. Saunt, *New Order of Things*, 266, 268, Jackson quoted on 268.

3. John Strother to Jackson, Oct. 5, 1813, Moser, *Papers of Andrew Jackson*, vol. 2, 433–435; Jackson to John Coffee, Oct. 7, 1813, ibid.; Brands, *Andrew Jackson*, 196; quotes, Kanon, "Before Horseshoe," 107–110.

4. F. L. Claiborne to H. Toulmin, Sept. 12, 1813, Claiborne Collection: Indian Wars; *The Repertory* (Boston), Oct. 9, 1813; Ross to Meigs, July 30, 1813, in *The Papers of Chief John Ross*, vol. 1, *1807–1839*, ed. Gary E. Moulton (Norman: University of Oklahoma Press, 1985), 19.

5. Martin, *Sacred Revolt*, 158–159, quote on 158; Saunt, *New Order of Things*, 270.

6. Sugden, *Tecumseh*, 368–380.

7. *Western Spy and Miami Gazette*, Oct. 16, 1813; Sugden, *Tecumseh*, 374–380; Owens, *Mr. Jefferson's Hammer*, 229–230.

8. *Centinel of Freedom* (Newark), Dec. 7, 1813.

9. Sugden, *Tecumseh*, 383–401. See also Gordon M. Sayre's *The Indian Chief as Tragic Hero: Native Resistance and the Literatures of America from Moctezuma to Tecumseh* (Chapel Hill: University of North Carolina Press, 2005), 268–302.

10. Gregory E. Dowd, "Thinking outside the Circle," in Braund, *Tohopeka*, 45. Tecumseh is often attributed to have talked of destroying all "the whites," when his intent was to stop the United States, not the British, Spanish, or French. These accounts can usually be traced to Victorian-era histories with little if any sourcing.

11. *New Jersey Journal* (Elizabethtown), Mar. 29, 1814; Sugden, *Tecumseh*, 383–401; Mariensas, "Common Man's Indian," 268–269.

12. Brands, *Andrew Jackson*, 215–222; American policy had kept Jackson's Indian allies as poorly armed as the Red Sticks. See Braund, "Red Sticks," in Braund, *Tohopeka*, 98.

13. Susan M. Abram, "Cherokees in the Creek War: A Band of Brothers," in Braund, *Tohopeka*, 135; Thrower, "Causalities and Consequences," ibid., 24.

14. For Jackson's disputing the report, see Moser et al., *The Papers of Andrew Jackson*, vol. 3, *1814–1815*, 53. See Jackson to Pinckney, Mar. 28, 1814, ibid., 52–54; Jackson to Rachel Jackson, Apr. 1, 1814, ibid., 54–55. For casualties, see Kanon, "Before Horseshoe," in Braund, *Tohopeka*, 105.

15. *New York Gazette*, Apr. 20, 1814; *Independent Chronicle* (Boston), Apr. 21, 1814; *Salem Chronicle*, Apr. 22, 1814; *The Repertory*, May 7, 1814; *Independent Chronicle* (Boston), May 19, 1814.

16. Moser et al., *Papers of Jackson*, vol. 3, 433–434; Waselkov, "Fort Jackson and the Aftermath," in Braund, *Tohopeka*, 161; Millett, *Maroons of Prospect Bluff*, 48.

17. Owsley, *Struggle for the Gulf Borderlands*, 28–29.

18. Donald R. Hickey, *The War of 1812: A Forgotten Conflict* (Urbana: University of Illinois Press, 1989), 183. See also J. C. A. Stagg, *The War of 1812: Conflict for a Continent* (New York: Cambridge University Press, 2012); Jeremy Black, *The War of 1812 in the Age of Napoleon* (Norman: University of Oklahoma Press, 2009); Troy Bickham, *The Weight of Vengeance: The United States, the British Empire, and the War of 1812* (New York: Oxford University Press, 2012).

19. Printed guide to Cochrane Papers, National Library of Scotland, Edinburgh.

19. MISTIMED ALLIANCE

1. Pigot to Lt. Woodbine, May 10, 1814, Cochrane Papers, MS 2328, North American Station, Southern Indians, National Library of Scotland, 5–6.

2. Woodbine at Prospect Bluff to Capt. Pigot, May 25, 1814, in Cochrane Papers, 14; Millet, *Maroons of Prospect Bluff*, 28.

3. Woodbine to Pigot, May 25, 1814, Cochrane Papers, 14–15; May 31, 1814, Cochrane Papers, 14–15; Edward J. Cashin, *The King's Ranger: Thomas Brown and the American Revolution on the Southern Frontier* (New York: Fordham University Press, 1999), 184.

4. Letter dictated by the Red Sticks at Pensacola, June 9, 1814, Cochrane Papers, 28; Thrower, "Causalities and Consequences," in Braund, *Tohopeka*, 15; Millett, *Maroons of Prospect Bluff*, 45.

5. Cochrane to governor of Havana, July 4, 1814, Cochrane Papers, 30; Lt. D. Hope of HMS *Shelburne* to Gov. Cameron (Bahamas), July 29, 1814, ibid., 41.

6. Alexander Cochrane in Bermuda to Lord Bathurst, July 14, 1814, War Office, Armed Forces, Judge Advocate General, and related bodies collection (hereafter WO) 1 141: 9–10, National Archives of Britain.

7. Marienstras, "Common Man's Indian," 270–278, 286.

8. Charles Kappler, ed., *Indian Treaties, 1778–1883* (Mattituck, N.Y.: Amereon House, 1972 [1904]), 107.

9. Saunt, *New Order of Things*, 270–272; Kappler, *Indian Treaties, 1778–1883*, 107; Brands, *Jackson*, 231–235; Owsley, *Struggle for the Gulf*, 86–92; Waselkov, "Fort Jackson

and the Aftermath," in Braund, *Tohopeka*, 163; Thrower, "Causalities and Consequences," in Braund, *Tohopeka*, 25–26, quote on 25. As Colin G. Calloway notes in *Crown and Calumet*, British agents convinced many Red Sticks that the Treaty of Ghent would return the land to them (246–247).

10. Woodbine to Cochrane, July 25, 1814, Cochrane Papers, 35. For Britain's overly optimistic dreams for Creek capabilities, see Calloway, *Crown and Calumet*, 204–205.

11. Woodbine to Gov. Cameron, July 26, 1814, Cochrane Papers, 37–52; Woodbine to Capt. Lockyer, July 30, 1814, Cochrane Papers, 37–52; Woodbine to Cameron, Aug. 9, 1814, Cochrane Papers, 37–52; Nicolls to Cameron, Aug. 4, 1814, Cochrane Papers, 37–52, quote on 39.

12. Millet, *The Maroons of Prospect Bluff*, 22–30; Nicolls to Cochrane, Aug. 12, 1814, Cochrane Papers, 59–60.

13. Taylor, *Internal Enemy*, 121, 132, 138; *Republican Star*, Mar. 30, 1813; e-mail conversation with Daniel Millett, Jan. 19, 2014.

14. Millett, *Maroons of Prospect Bluff*, 72–82; Rothman, *Slave Country*.

15. See Owsley's excellent discussion in *Struggle for the Gulf Borderlands*, 95–132.

16. Cochrane to Lord Bathurst (private), Aug. 18, 1814, in Cochrane Papers, 27–30; "Return of Articles to Complete the Supply of Presents for the Indian Campaign to the Southward Shipped on Board the Norfolk Transport," Sept. 1, 1814, WO 1 142: 33.

17. Owsley and Smith, *Filibusters and Expansionists*, 63.

18. Emily Trist to Catherine Wistar Bache, Aug. 22, 1814, Catherine Wistar Bache Papers, Mss B.B124, American Philosophical Society Library; Trist to Bache, Dec. 21, 1814, Catherine Wistar Bache Papers, .

19. Owsley, *Struggle for the Gulf Borderlands*, 188–195; Robert V. Remini, *The Battle of New Orleans: Andrew Jackson and America's First Military Victory* (New York: Penguin Books, 1999), 42–55; Hickey, *War of 1812*, 206–208; Black, *The War of 1812 in the Age of Napoleon*, 194. As Waselkov notes, it can be argued that the Red Sticks and their descendants continued to resist until 1858. See Waselkov, "Fort Jackson and the Aftermath," in Braund, *Tohopeka*, 167.

20. *Enquirer*, Jan. 7, 1815; *City Gazette*, Jan. 23, 1815.

21. Taylor, *Internal Enemy*, 346.

22. Quote, Hickey, *War of 1812*, 290.

23. Black, *War of 1812*, 205–211.

24. Owsley and Smith, *Filibusters and Expansionists*, 146; Joe Knetsch, *Florida's Seminole Wars, 1817–1858* (Charleston, S.C.: Arcadia Publishing, 2003), 19.

25. Owsley and Smith, *Filibusters and Expansionists*, 147; Millett, *Maroons of Prospect Bluff*, 236.

26. Owsley and Smith, *Filibusters and Expansionists*, 177.

27. Paul E. Hoffman, *Florida's Frontiers* (Bloomington: Indiana University Press, 2002), 267; *American Watchman* (Wilmington, Del.), July 23, 1817.

28. Owsley and Smith, *Filibusters and Expansionists*, 104–105, 110; Extract of a Letter to a Gentleman in this City, dated Camp Crawford, August 5, in the *Commercial Advertiser* (N.Y.C.), Sept. 3, 1816. See also William S. Belko, "Epilogue to the War of 1812: The First Monroe Administration, American Anglophobia, and the first Seminole War," in Belko, *America's Hundred Years' War*, 54–102; Millett, *Maroons of Prospect Bluff*, 227–233.

29. *National Intelligencer*, Washington, D.C., May 1, 1817.

30. *The American Beacon and Commercial Diary* (Norfolk, Va.), July 3, 1817.

31. *The Reflector* (Milledgeville, Ga.), Dec. 2, 1817; "Richmond, March 23. Important from the Army! Extract of a Letter from an Officer in Gen. Gaines' Army," in *The American Beacon and Commercial Diary*, Mar. 26, 1818.

32. Owsley and Smith, *Filibusters and Expansionists*, 145, 157, 159; printed in the *City of Washington Gazette*, June 6, 1818.

33. *Connecticut Journal*, Dec. 22, 1818.

34. Taylor, *Internal Enemy*, 347.

35. John R. Bell to Sec. of War Calhoun, July 17, 1821, in *Territorial Papers of the U.S., Vol. XXII—Florida Territory 1821–1824*, ed. C. E. Carter (1956), 126; Millett, *Maroons of Prospect Bluff*, 250.

36. Gov. DuVal to Thomas McKenney, Mar. 2, 1826, in *Territorial Papers of the U.S., Vol. XXIII—Florida Territory, 1824–1828*, ed. C. E. Carter (1958), 454.

37. *Territorial Papers of the U.S., Vol. XXIV—Florida Territory, 1828–1834*, ed. C. E. Carter (1959), 114, 230.

EPILOGUE

1. Adams quotes, Adams to Sec. of War James Barbour, Aug. 22, 1827, James Barbour Papers, 1792–1842, New York Public Library (NYPL); last quote, Stephen Rockwell, *Indian Affairs and the Administrative State in the Nineteenth Century* (New York: Cambridge University Press, 2010), 138.

2. Thomas J. Lappas, "A Perfect Apollo: Keokuk and Sac Leadership during the Removal Era," in Barr, *The Boundaries between Us*, 221.

3. Patrick J. Jung, *The Black Hawk War of 1832* (Norman: University of Oklahoma Press, 2007), 56–57.

4. Gates to a gentleman in Washington, D.C., in *City Gazette and Daily Advertiser* (Charleston, S.C.), Dec. 10, 1812.

5. Jung, *Black Hawk War*, 59–65; John W. Hall, *Uncommon Defense: Indian Allies in the Black Hawk War* (Cambridge, Mass.: Harvard University Press, 2009), 107.

6. First quote, Marienstras, "The Common Man's Indian," 296; *Baltimore Patriot*, July 21, 1831.

7. *St. Louis Beacon*, reprinted by the *Pittsfield Sun*, Aug. 4, 1831; Jung, *Black Hawk War*, 72.

8. Jung, *Black Hawk War*, 172; Hall, *Uncommon Defense*, 181. For the impact of the Black Hawk War on future generations, see Michael J. Sherfy, "A Persistent Removal: Black Hawk, Commemoration, and Historic Sites in Illinois," *Journal of the Illinois State Historical Society*, 100, no. 3 (Fall 2007), 240–267.

9. Schoolcraft to George B. Porter, Aug. 15, 1832, in *The Black Hawk War, 1831–1832*, vol. 2, Letters and Papers, part 2, June 24, 1832–October 14, 1834, ed. Ellen M. Whitney (Springfield: Illinois State Historical Library, 1975), 1008.

10. Hall, *Uncommon Defense*, 128.

11. *New Hampshire Sentinel* (Keene, N.H.) Feb. 11, 1836.

12. Taylor, *Internal Enemy*, 348–349.

13. Carter, *Territorial Papers of the United States, vol. XXIV, Florida 1828–1834*, 581, 619, 643; Matthew Clavin, "'It Is a Negro, Not an Indian War': Southampton, St. Domingo, and the Second Seminole War," in Belko, *America's Hundred Years' War*, 182–199, quote on 199; Brig. Gen. Hernandez to Gov. Eaton, Oct. 26, 1835, in Carter, *Territorial Papers of the United States, vol. XXV—Florida 1834–1839*, 190.

14. Poole to Macomb, June 16, 1836, in Charleston arsenal letterbook of William Laurence Poole, Feb. 25, 1836–May 5, 1838, MssCol 3655, NYPL. [Thanks to Mike Conlin.]

15. Printed in the *New Bedford Mercury*, Jun. 17, 1836.

16. Rockwell, *Indian Affairs and the Administrative State*, 222–223.

Bibliography

ARCHIVAL SOURCES

Alabama Department of Archives and History, Montgomery, Ala. (ADAH)
    Mississippi Territory Papers—Governor's Correspondence
American Philosophical Society Library, Philadelphia, Penn.
    Benjamin Rush's commonplace book, 1792–1813
    Caleb Swan Journal extracts, 1790–1791
    Catherine Wistar Bache Papers
Archivo General de Indias (AGI) [copies in Illinois History Room, University of Illinois Library, Urbana, Ill.]
    Papeles de Cuba
David M. Rubenstein Rare Book and Manuscript Library, Duke University
    Benjamin Lincoln Papers, 1778–1804
    Nathanael Greene Papers
    James Iredell, Sr. and Jr., Papers, 1724–1890
    David Henley Papers
Filson Historical Society Library, Louisville, Ken. (FHS)
    C. B. William Blount Letters
    Arthur Campbell Papers
    William Dell Journal, 1776
    C. K. Henry Knox and Instructions, 1787–1793
    Robert Preston Papers—Joyes Collection
    Foote Family Papers
    Sanders Family Papers
    Bullitt Family Papers
Historical Society of Pennsylvania (HSP), Philadelphia, Penn.
    Anthony Wayne Papers
    Butler Papers
    George Croghan Papers, 1754–1808
    George Morgan Letterbook, 1767–1768

Simon Gratz Collection
Indian Affairs collection
Library and Archives of Canada (LAC) Ottawa, Canada
Daniel Claus and family fonds
War Office fonds, transcripts
Alexander and Thomas McKee Collection
Superintendent of Indian Affairs of the Northern District of North America fonds
Haldimand Papers
Robert Prescott fonds
MG23 HI 2, vol. 2: Letterbook transcriptions from Mr. President Peter Russell, Military Secretary's Office Number 24
Massachusetts Historical Society Library (MHS), Boston, Mass.
Henry Knox Papers II
Mississippi Department of Archives (MDA), Jackson, Miss.
Mississippi Provincial Archives, 1612–1763, French dominion
Claiborne (J. F. H.) Collection
National Archives and Records Administration (NARA), Washington, D.C.
Records of the Office of the Secretary of War, 1791–1948
Records of the Office of the Secretary of War, Letters Sent
Indian Office Letter Book C
Records of the Bureau of Indian Affairs, 1793–1999
State Department Territorial Papers, Florida, 1777–1824
National Archives of Britain (NAB), Kew, U.K.
Colonial Office, Commonwealth and Foreign and Commonwealth Offices collections
HM Treasury collection
War Office, Armed Forces, Judge Advocate General, and related bodies collection
Foreign Office (FO) collections
National Library of Scotland (NLS), Edinburgh, U.K.
Cochrane (Thomas John) Papers
New York Public Library, Schwarzman Building
Charleston arsenal letterbook of William Laurence Poole, Feb. 25, 1836– May 5, 1838
James Barbour correspondence, 1792–1848
South Caroliniana Library (SCL), Columbia, S.C.
Pierce Butler Papers, 1744–1822
Wisconsin Historical Society, Madison
The Draper Manuscripts
King's Mountain Papers
Tennessee Papers
Tennessee State Library and Archives (TSA), Nashville, Tenn.
Cherokee Collection

James Robertson Papers, 1784–1814
Gov. John Sevier Papers, 1796–1801 (First Series of Administrations)
Southern Historical Collection at the Louis Round Wilson Special Collections Library, University of North Carolina, Chapel Hill, N.C.
John Steele Papers, 1716–1846
Virginia Historical Society Library, Richmond, Va.
Commonplace Book of Dr. George Gilmer (1743–1795) of Albemarle, Va.
William L. Clements Library, University of Michigan, Ann Arbor, Mich.
Thomas Gage papers, 1754–1807
Anthony Wayne Family Papers, 1681–1913
Native American Collections

PUBLISHED PRIMARY SOURCES

American State Papers: Foreign Relations, Class I. Vol. 1. Washington, D.C.: Gales and Seaton, 1831.
American State Papers: Indian Affairs, Class II. Vol. I. Washington, D.C.: Gales and Seaton, 1831.
Annals of Congress. 24 vols. Washington, D.C.: Gales and Seaton, 1851–1853.
Baynton, Benjamin. *Authentic Memoirs of William Augustus Bowles, Esquire, Ambassador for the United nations of Creeks and Cherokees, to the Court of London.* New York: Gale, 2010 [1791].
Boyd, Julian P., ed. *The Papers of Thomas Jefferson.* 20 vols. Princeton: Princeton University Press, 1952.
Calloway, Colin G., ed. *The World Turned Upside Down: Indian Voices from Early America.* New York: Bedford/St. Martin's, 1994.
Carter, Clarence Edwin, ed. *The Territorial Papers of the United States.* Washington, D.C.: The United States Government Printing Office.
   Vol. IX The Territory of Orleans, 1803–1812 [1940]
   Vol. XXII Florida Territory, 1821–1824 [1956]
   Vol. XXIII Florida Territory, 1824–1828 [1958]
   Vol. XXIV Florida Territory, 1828–1834 [1959]
   Vol. XXV Florida Territory, 1834–1839 [1960]
Clanin, Douglas E., ed. *The Papers of William Henry Harrison, 1800–1815.* Microfilm. Indianapolis: Indiana Historical Society, 1999.
Clark, Walter, ed. *The State Records of North Carolina.* Vol. 11, *1776.* New York: AMS Press, 1968.
Conrad, Dennis M., Roger N. Parks, Martha J. King, and Richard K. Showman, eds. *The Papers of Nathanael Greene, 1776–1783.* 13 vols. Chapel Hill: University of North Carolina Press, 1983–2001.
Cunningham, Noble E., Jr. *Circular Letters of Congressmen to Their Constituents, 1789–1829.* 2 vols. Chapel Hill: University of North Carolina Press, 1978.

Cruikshank, E. A., ed. *The Correspondence of Lieut. Governor John Graves Simcoe, with Allied Documents Relating to His Administration of the Government of Upper Canada.* 5 vols. Toronto: Ontario Historical Society, 1923–1931.

Davis, K. G., ed. *Documents of the American Revolution, 1778–1783.* 21 vols. Dublin: Irish Academic Press, 1998.

Encyclopedia of Alabama (online).

Fitzpatrick, John C., ed. *The Diaries of George Washington, 1748–1799.* 4 vols. Boston: Houghton Mifflin, 1925.

———. *The Writings of George Washington from the Original Manuscript Sources, 1745–1799.* 39 vols. Washington, D.C.: U.S. Government Printing Office, 1931–1944.

Grant, C. L., ed. *Letters, Journals and Writings of Benjamin Hawkins.* Vol. 2, *1802–1816.* Savannah, Ga.: Beehive Press, 1980.

"Haldimand Papers." In *Historical Collections.* Vol. 19. Lansing: Michigan Pioneer and Historical Society, 1911.

Kappler, Charles C., ed. *Indian Treaties, 1778–1883.* Mattituck, N.Y.: Amereon House, 1972 [1904].

Looney, J. Jefferson. *The Papers of Thomas Jefferson, Retirement Series.* 11 vols. Princeton: Princeton University Press, 2004–2015.

Miller, Lillian B., ed. *The Selected Papers of Charles Willson Peale and His Family.* 5 vols. New Haven, Conn.: Yale University Press, 1983–2000.

Moulton, Gary, ed. *The Papers of Chief John Ross.* Vol. 1, *1807–1839.* Norman: University of Oklahoma Press, 1985.

Moser, Harold D., et al., eds. *The Papers of Andrew Jackson.* 9 vols. Knoxville: University of Tennessee Press, 1980–2013.

Palmer, William P., Sherwin McRae, Raleigh Edward Colston, R. F. Walker, and H. W. Flournoy, eds. *Calendar of Virginia State Papers and Other Manuscripts.* 9 vols. New York: Knaus Reprint Corp., 1968 [1875].

Parker, John, ed. *The Journals of Jonathan Carver and Related Documents, 1766–1770.* Minneapolis: Minnesota Historical Society Press, 1976.

Peterson, Merrill D., ed. *Thomas Jefferson: Writings.* New York: Literary Classics of the United States, Inc., 1984.

Powell, William S., ed. *The Correspondence of William Tryon and Other Selected Papers.* 2 vols. Raleigh: Division of Archives and History, Department of Cultural Resources, 1980.

Rowland, Dunbar, ed. *Mississippi Provincial Archives, 1763–1766.* Vol. 1, *English Dominion.* Charleston, S.C.: Nabu Press, 2011 [1911].

Saunders, William L., ed. *The Colonial Records of North Carolina.* 8 vols. New York: AMS Press, 1968–1978 [1888–1890].

Sullivan, James, and Alexander C. Flick, eds. *The Papers of Sir William Johnson.* 13 vols. New York: University of the State of New York, 1921–1951.

Thwaites, Reuben Gold, and Louise Phelps Kellogg, eds. *Documentary History of Dunmore's War, 1774.* Madison: Wisconsin Historical Society, 1905.

Whitney, Ellen M., ed. *The Black Hawk War, 1831–1832.* Vol. 2, *Letters and Papers,* part 2, June 24, 1832–October 14, 1834. Springfield: Illinois State Historical Library, 1975.

NEWSPAPERS

Argus of Western America (Frankfort, Ken.)
Dixon & Hunter's *Virginia Gazette*
Dunlap's American Daily Advertiser (Philadelphia)
Enquirer (Richmond, Va.)
Kentucky Gazette (Frankfort)
Kentucky Palladium (Frankfort)
Louisiana Gazette and New-Orleans Daily Advertiser
Pennsylvania Journal
Pennsylvania Journal and Weekly Advertiser
Providence Gazette and Country Journal (Charles Town, S.C.)
Vincennes (Ind.) *Western Sun*
Virginia Gazette (Williamsburg)
National Intelligencer (Washington, D.C.)
Western Spy and Hamilton Gazette (Cincinnati)
Western Spy and Miami Gazette (Cincinnati)
Western Star (Stockbridge, Mass.)
Wilson's Gazette (Knoxville)

Online newspaper databases

ProQuest

Connecticut Courant and Weekly Intelligencer

Readex Newspapers—Early American Newspapers Series 1–3, 1690–1922

CONNECTICUT

Connecticut Current and Weekly Intelligencer
Connecticut Gazette (New London)
Connecticut Mirror
Middlesex Gazette (Middletown)
New-Haven Gazette
Norwich Packet

DELAWARE

American Watchman (Wilmington)

GEORGIA

Columbian Museum (Savannah)
Georgia Gazette (Savannah)
Reflector (Milledgeville)

MARYLAND

Federal Gazette (Baltimore)
Republican Star (Easton)

MAINE

American Advocate (Hallowell)

MASSACHUSETTS

Boston Evening-Post
Boston Gazette
Boston Post-Boy
Columbian Centinel (Boston)
Independent Chronicle (Boston)
Massachusetts Spy (Boston)
New Bedford Mercury
Pittsfield Sun
Repertory (Boston)
Salem Mercury

NEW HAMPSHIRE

Concord Herald (New Hampshire)
New Hampshire Gazette (Portsmouth)
New Hampshire Spy (Portsmouth)

NEW JERSEY

Centinel of Freedom (Newark)
New Jersey Journal (Elizabethtown)
Trenton Federalist

NEW YORK

Albany Daily Advertiser
Commercial Advertiser (N.Y.C.)
Mercantile Advertiser (N.Y.C.)
New York Gazette (N.Y.C.)
New York Weekly Journal (N.Y.C.)
Otsego Herald (Cooperstown)

PENNSYLVANIA

Dunlap's Daily Advertiser (Philadelphia)
Federal Gazette (Philadelphia)
Freeman's Journal (Philadelphia)
Gazette of the United States (Philadelphia)
General Aurora Advertiser (Philadelphia)

Pennsylvania Mercury (Philadelphia)
Pennsylvania Packet (Philadelphia)
Philadelphia Gazette and Universal Daily Advertiser (Philadelphia)
Royal Pennsylvania Gazette (Philadelphia)

RHODE ISLAND

Herald of the United States (Warrenton)
Providence Gazette

SOUTH CAROLINA

City Gazette and Daily Advertiser (Charleston)
The Southern Patriot (Charleston)

VERMONT

Vermont Gazette (Bennington)

VIRGINIA

Alexandria Gazette and Daily Advertiser
American Beacon and Commercial Diary (Norfolk)
Enquirer (Richmond)

WASHINGTON, D.C.

City of Washington Gazette
Courier
Daily National Intelligencer

BOOKS, ARTICLES, AND ESSAYS

Alden, John Richard. *John Stuart and the Southern Colonial Frontier: A Study of Indian Relations, War, Trade, and Land Problems in the Southern Wilderness, 1754–1775*. New York: Gordian Press, 1966.

Alderson, Robert J., Jr. *This Bright Era of Happy Revolutions: French Consul Michel-Ange-Bernard Mangourit and International Republicanism in Charleston, 1792–1794*. Columbia: University of South Carolina Press, 2008.

———. "Charleston's Rumored Slave Revolt of 1793." In *The Impact of the Haitian Revolution in the Atlantic World*, edited by David P. Geggus. Columbia: University of South Carolina Press, 2001.

Allen, Robert S. *His Majesty's Indian Allies: British Indian Policy in the Defence of Canada, 1774–1815*. Toronto: Dundurn Press, 1992.

Anderson, Fred. *Crucible of War: The Seven Years' War and the Fate of British North America, 1754–1766*. New York: Alfred A. Knopf, 2000.

Aron, Stephen. *How the West Was Lost: The Transformation of Kentucky from Daniel Boone to Henry Clay*. Baltimore: Johns Hopkins University Press, 1996.

Atkinson, James R. *Splendid Land, Splendid People: The Chickasaw Indians to Removal.* Tuscaloosa: University of Alabama Press, 2004.

Bailyn, Bernard. *The Ideological Origins of the American Revolution.* Cambridge, Mass.: Belknap Press, 1967.

Barksdale, Kevin T. *The Lost State of Franklin: America's First Secession.* Lexington: University Press of Kentucky, 2009.

Barr, Daniel P., ed. *The Boundaries between Us: Natives and Newcomers along the Frontiers of the Old Northwest Territory, 1750–1850.* Kent, Ohio: Kent State University Press, 2006.

Barnes, Celia. *Native American Power in the United States, 1783–1795.* London: Fairleigh Dickinson University Press, 2003.

Bickham, Troy. *Savages within the Empire: Representations of American Indians in Eighteenth-Century Britain.* New York: Oxford University Press, 2005.

———. *The Weight of Vengeance: The United States, the British Empire, and the War of 1812.* New York: Oxford University Press, 2012.

Black, Jeremy. *The War of 1812 in the Age of Napoleon.* Norman: University of Oklahoma Press, 2009.

Boulware, Tyler. *Deconstructing the Cherokee Nation: Town, Region, and Nation among Eighteenth-Century Cherokees.* Gainesville: University Press of Florida, 2011.

Brands, H. W. *Andrew Jackson: His Life and Times.* New York: Doubleday, 2005.

Braund, Katherine E., ed. *Tohopeka: Rethinking the Creek War and the War of 1812.* Tuscaloosa: University of Alabama Press, 2012.

Brown, Meredith Mason. *Frontiersman: Daniel Boone and the Making of America.* Baton Rouge: Louisiana State University Press, 2008.

Calloway, Colin G. *The American Revolution in Indian Country: Crisis and Diversity in Native American Communities.* New York: Cambridge University Press, 1995.

———. *Crown and Calumet: British-Indian Relations, 1783–1815.* Norman: University of Oklahoma Press, 1987.

———. *Pen and Ink Witchcraft: Treaties and Treaty Making in American Indian History.* New York: Oxford University Press, 2013.

Campbell, William J. *Speculators in Empire: Iroquoia and the 1768 Treaty of Fort Stanwix.* Norman: University of Oklahoma Press, 2012.

Carson, James Taylor. *Searching for the Bright Path: The Mississippi Choctaws from Prehistory to Removal.* Lincoln: University of Nebraska Press, 1999.

Cashin, Edward J. "'But Brothers, It Is Our Land We Are Talking About': Winners and Losers in the Georgia Backcountry." In *An Uncivil War: The Southern Backcountry during the American Revolution,* edited by Ronald Hoffman, Thad W. Tate, and Peter J. Albert. Charlottesville: University of Virginia Press, 1985.

———. *The King's Ranger: Thomas Brown and the American Revolution on the Southern Frontier.* New York: Fordham University Press, 1999.

Caughey, John Walton. *McGillivray of the Creeks.* Norman: University of Oklahoma Press, 1959.

Cayton, Andrew, and Frederika Teute, eds. *Contact Points: American Frontiers from the Mohawk Valley to the Mississippi, 1750–1830*. Chapel Hill: University of North Carolina Press, 1998.

Chartrand, René. *Louis XIV's Army*. New York: Osprey Publishing Ltd., 1988.

Clark, Jerry E. *The Shawnee*. Lexington: University Press of Kentucky, 1993.

Clavin, Matthew. "'It Is a Negro, Not an Indian War': Southampton, St. Domingo, and the Second Seminole War." In *America's Hundred Years' War: U.S. Expansions to the Gulf Coast and the Fate of the Seminole, 1763–1858*, edited by William S. Belko. Gainesville: University Press of Florida, 2011.

Cleves, Rachel Hope. *The Reign of Terror in America: Visions of Violence from Anti-Jacobinism to Anti-Slavery*. New York: Cambridge University Press, 2009.

Colley, Linda. *Captives*. New York: Pantheon Books, 2002.

Conley, Robert J. *The Cherokee Nation: A History*. Albuquerque: University of New Mexico Press, 2005.

Corkran, David H. *The Creek Frontier, 1540–1783*. Norman: University of Oklahoma Press, 1967.

Cox, Isaac Joslin. "Hispanic-American Phases of the 'Burr Conspiracy.'" *The Hispanic American Historical Review* 12, no. 2 (May 1932): 145–175.

Cumfer, Cynthia. *Separate Peoples, One Land: The Minds of Cherokees, Blacks, and Whites on the Tennessee Frontier*. Chapel Hill: University of North Carolina Press, 2007.

Cusick, James G. *The Other War of 1812: The Patriot War and the American Invasion of Spanish East Florida*. Athens: University of Georgia Press, 2003.

David, James Corbett. *Dunmore's New World: The Extraordinary Life of a Royal Governor in Revolutionary America—with Jacobites, Counterfeiters, Land Schemes, Shipwrecks, Scalping, Indian Politics, Runaway Slaves, and Two Illegal Royal Weddings*. Charlottesville: University of Virginia Press, 2013.

Davis, David Brion. "Impact of the French and Haitian Revolutions." In *The Impact of the Haitian Revolution in the Atlantic World*, edited by David P. Geggus. Columbia: University of South Carolina Press, 2001.

Daunton, Martin, and Rick Halpern, eds. *Empire and Others: British Encounters with Indigenous Peoples, 1600–1850*. Philadelphia: University of Pennsylvania Press, 1999.

Densmore, Christopher. *Red Jacket: Iroquois Diplomat and Orator*. Syracuse: Syracuse University Press, 1999.

Dictionary of Canadian Biography (online).

Din, Gilbert C. *War on the Gulf Coast: The Spanish Fight against William Augustus Bowles*. Gainesville: University Press of Florida, 2012.

Dixon, David. "'We Speak as One People': Native Unity and the Pontiac Indian Uprising." In *The Boundaries between Us: Natives and Newcomers along the Frontiers of the Old Northwest Territory, 1750–1850*, edited by Daniel P. Barr. Kent, Ohio: Kent State University Press, 2006.

Dormon, James H. "The Persistent Spectre: Slave Rebellion in Territorial Louisiana." *Louisiana History: The Journal of the Louisiana Historical Association* 18, no. 4 (Autumn 1777): 389–404.

Dowd, Gregory E. *A Spirited Resistance: The North American Indian Struggle for Unity, 1745–1815*. Baltimore: Johns Hopkins University Press, 1992.
———. "Thinking and Believing: Nativism and Unity in the Ages of Pontiac and Tecumseh." *American Indian Quarterly* 16, no. 3 (Summer 1992): 309–335.
———. *War under Heaven: Pontiac, the Indian Nations and the British Empire*. Baltimore: Johns Hopkins University Press, 2002.
Edmunds, R. David. *The Shawnee Prophet*. Lincoln: University of Nebraska Press, 1983.
Egerton, Douglas R. *Death or Liberty: African Americans and Revolutionary America*. New York: Oxford University Press, 2009.
Elkins, Stanley, and Eric McKitrick. *The Age of Federalism: The Early American Republic, 1788–1800*. New York: Oxford University Press, 1993.
Encyclopedia of Alabama (online).
Ethridge, Robbie. *Creek Country: The Creek Indians and their World*. Chapel Hill: University of North Carolina Press, 2003.
Fenn, Elizabeth A. *Pox Americana: The Great Smallpox Epidemic of 1775–82*. New York: Hill and Wang, 2001.
Ferguson, Gillum. *Illinois in the War of 1812*. Urbana: University of Illinois Press, 2012.
Finger, John R. *Tennessee Frontiers: Three Regions in Transition*. Bloomington: Indiana University Press, 2001.
Fischer, David Hackett. *Paul Revere's Ride*. New York: Oxford University Press, 1995.
Furstenberg, François. "The Significance of the Trans-Appalachian Frontier in Atlantic History." *American Historical Review* 113, no. 3 (June 2008): 647–677.
Gaff, Alan D. *Bayonets in the Wilderness: Anthony Wayne's Legion in the Old Northwest*. Norman: University of Oklahoma Press, 2008.
Galloway, Patricia. "'So Many Little Republics': British Negotiations with the Choctaw Confederacy, 1765." *Ethnohistory* 41, no. 4 (Autumn 1994): 513–537.
Geggus, David P., ed. *The Impact of the Haitian Revolution in the Atlantic World*. Columbia: University of South Carolina Press, 2001.
Gibson, Arrell M. *The Chickasaws*. Norman: University of Oklahoma Press, 1971.
Glatthaar, Joseph T., and James Kirby Martin. *Forgotten Allies: The Oneida Indians and the American Revolution*. New York: Hill and Wang, 2006.
Gower, Paul. L., ed. *Psychology of Fear*. New York: Nova Science, 2004.
Grantham, Bill. *Creation Myths and Legends of the Creek Indians*. Gainesville: University Press of Florida, 2002.
Griffin, Patrick. *American Leviathan: Empire, Nation, and Revolutionary Frontier*. New York: Hill and Wang, 2007.
Griffith, Benjamin W., Jr. *McIntosh and Weatherford, Creek Indian Leaders*. Tuscaloosa: University of Alabama Press, 1988.
Hall, John W. *Uncommon Defense: Indian Allies in the Black Hawk War*. Cambridge, Mass.: Harvard University Press, 2009.
Hatley, Tom. *The Dividing Paths: Cherokees and South Carolinians through the Revolutionary Era*. New York: Oxford University Press, 1993.
Henri, Florette. *The Southern Indians and Benjamin Hawkins, 1796–1816*. Norman: University of Oklahoma Press, 1986.

Hickey, Donald R. *The War of 1812: A Forgotten Conflict.* Urbana: University of Illinois Press, 1989.
Hinderaker, Eric. *Elusive Empires: Constructing Colonialism in the Ohio Valley, 1673–1800.* New York: Cambridge University Press, 1997.
Hoffman, Paul E. *Florida's Frontiers.* Bloomington: Indiana University Press, 2002.
Hoffman, Ronald W., Thad W. Tate, and Peter J. Albert, eds. *An Uncivil War: The Southern Backcountry during the American Revolution.* Charlottesville: University of Virginia Press, 1985.
Hoig, Stanley W. *The Cherokees and Their Chiefs: In the Wake of Empire.* Fayetteville: University of Arkansas Press, 1998.
Holmes, Jack D. L. "The Abortive Slave Revolt at Pointe Coupée, Louisiana, 1795." *Louisiana History: The Journal of the Louisiana Historical Association* 11, no. 4 (Autumn 1970): 341–362.
Holton, Woody. *Forced Founders: Indians, Debtors, Slaves, and the Making of the American Revolution in Virginia.* Chapel Hill: University of North Carolina Press, 1999.
Horsman, Reginald. *Expansion and American Indian Policy, 1783–1812.* East Lansing: Michigan State University Press, 1967.
———. *Matthew Elliott, British Indian Agent.* Detroit: Wayne State University Press, 1964.
Hoxie, Frederick E., Ronald Hoffman, and Peter J. Albert, eds. *Native Americans and the Early Republic.* Charlottesville: University of Virginia Press, 1999.
Howard, James H. *Shawnee! The Ceremonialism of a Native American Tribe and its Cultural Background.* Athens: Ohio University Press, 1981.
Hudson, Angela Pulley. *Creek Paths, and Federal Roads: Indians, Settlers, and Slaves and the Making of the American South.* Chapel Hill: University of North Carolina Press, 2010.
Ingram, Daniel. *Indians and British Outposts in Eighteenth-Century America.* Gainesville: University Press of Florida, 2012.
Jacobs, Wilbur R. *Francis Parkman: Historian as Hero; The Formative Years.* Austin: University of Texas Press, 1991.
Jung, Patrick J. *The Black Hawk War of 1832.* Norman: University of Oklahoma Press, 2007.
Juricek, John T. *Colonial Georgia and the Creeks: Anglo-Indian Diplomacy on the Southern Frontier, 1733–1763.* Gainesville: University Press of Florida, 2010.
Kanon, Tom. "Before Horseshoe: Andrew Jackson's Campaigns in the Creek War Prior to Horseshoe Bend." In *Tohopeka: Rethinking the Creek War and the War of 1812,* edited by Katherine E. Braund. Tuscaloosa: University of Alabama Press, 2012.
———. "The Kidnapping of Martha Crawley and Settler-Indian Relations Prior to the War of 1812." *Tennessee Historical Quarterly* 64, no. 1 (Spring 2005): 3–23.
Kelsay, Isabel Thompson. *Joseph Brant 1743–1807, Man of Two Worlds.* Syracuse: Syracuse University Press, 1984.
King, Duane H., ed. *The Cherokee Indian Nation: A Troubled History.* Knoxville: University of Tennessee Press, 1979.

Kinnaird, Lawrence. "Spanish Treaties with Indian Tribes." *The Western Historical Quarterly* 10, no. 1 (Jan. 1979): 39–48.
Knetsch, Joe. *Florida's Seminole Wars, 1817–1858*. Charleston, S.C.: Arcadia, 2003.
Knopf, Richard C. "Anthony Wayne: The Man and the Myth." *Northwest Ohio Quarterly* 64, no. 2 (Spring 1992): 35–42.
Lachance, Paul. "Repercussions of the Haitian Revolution in Louisiana." In *The Impact of the Haitian Revolution in the Atlantic World*, edited by David P. Geggus. Columbia: University of South Carolina Press, 2001.
Landers, Jane. *Black Society in Spanish Florida*. Urbana: University of Illinois Press, 1999.
Lappas, Thomas J. "A Perfect Apollo: Keokuk and Sac Leadership during the Removal Era." In *The Boundaries between Us: Natives and Newcomers along the Frontiers of the Old Northwest Territory, 1750–1850*, edited by Daniel P. Barr. Kent, Ohio: Kent State University Press, 2006.
Lepore, Jill. *New York Burning: Liberty, Slavery, and Conspiracy in Eighteenth-Century Manhattan*. New York: Vintage, 2006.
———. *The Name of War: King Philip's War and the Origins of American Identity*. New York: Knopf, 1998.
Leyburn, James G. *The Scotch-Irish: A Social History*. Chapel Hill: University of North Carolina Press, 1962.
Littlefield, Daniel F., Jr. *Africans and Creeks: From the Colonial Period to the Civil War*. New York: Praeger, 1979.
Mapp, Paul W. *The Elusive West and the Contest for Empire, 1713–1763*. Chapel Hill: University of North Carolina Press, 2011.
Marienstras, Elise. "The Common Man's Indian: The Image of the Indian as a Promoter of National Identity in the Early National Era." In *Native Americans and the Early Republic*, edited by Frederick E. Hoxie, Ronald Hoffman, and Peter J. Albert. Charlottesville: University of Virginia Press.
Martin, Joel W. *Sacred Revolt: The Muskogees' Struggle for a New World*. Boston: Beacon Press, 1991.
McConnell, Michael N. *A Country Between: The Upper Ohio Valley and Its Peoples, 1724–1775*. Lincoln: University of Nebraska Press, 1992.
McLoughlin, William G. *Cherokee Renascence in the New Republic*. Princeton, N.J.: Princeton University Press, 1986.
Merrell, James M. *The Indians' New World: The Catawbas and Their Neighbors from European Contact through the Era of Removal*. New York: W. W. Norton, 1991.
Millett, Nathaniel. *The Maroons of Prospect Bluff and Their Quest for Freedom in the Atlantic World*. Gainesville: University Press of Florida, 2013.
Namias, June. *White Captives: Gender and Ethnicity on the American Frontier*. Chapel Hill: University of North Carolina Press, 1993.
Nelson, Larry L. *A Man of Distinction among Them: Alexander McKee and British-Indian Affairs along the Ohio Country Frontier, 1754–1799*. Kent, Ohio: Kent State University Press, 1999.

Nester, William R. *George Rogers Clark: I Glory in War.* Norman: University of Oklahoma Press, 2012.

Newman, Simon P. "American Political Culture and the French and Haitian Revolutions." In *The Impact of the Haitian Revolution in the Atlantic World*, edited by David P. Geggus. Columbia: University of South Carolina Press, 2001.

Nichols, David A. "Land, Republicanism, and Indians." *Georgia Historical Quarterly* 85 (Summer 2001): 199–226.

———. *Red Gentlemen and White Savages: Indians, Federalists, and the Search for Order on the American Frontier.* Charlottesville: University of Virginia Press, 2008.

Norton, Mary Beth. *In the Devil's Snare: The Salem Witchcraft Crisis of 1692.* New York: Vintage, 2003.

O'Brien, Greg. "Protecting Trade through War: Choctaw Elites and the British Occupation of the Floridas." In *Empire and Others: British Encounters with Indigenous Peoples, 1600–1850*, edited by Martin Daunton and Rick Halpern. Philadelphia: University of Pennsylvania Press, 1999.

Onuf, Peter S. *Statehood and Union: A History of the Northwest Ordinance.* Bloomington: Indiana University Press, 1992.

O'Toole, Fintan. *White Savage: William Johnson and the Invention of America.* New York: Farrar, Straus and Giroux, 2005.

Owens, Robert M. "Jean Baptiste Ducoigne, the Kaskaskias, and the Limits of Thomas Jefferson's Friendship." *Journal of Illinois History* 5 (Summer 2002): 109–136.

———. *Mr. Jefferson's Hammer: William Henry Harrison and the Origins of American Indian Policy.* Norman: University of Oklahoma Press, 2007.

Owsley, Frank Lawrence, Jr. *Struggle for the Gulf Borderlands: The Creek War and the Battle of New Orleans, 1812–1815.* Gainesville: University of Press of Florida, 1981.

Owsley, Frank Lawrence, Jr., and Gene A. Smith. *Filibusters and Expansionists: Jeffersonian Manifest Destiny, 1800–1821.* Tuscaloosa: University of Alabama Press, 1997.

Parmenter, Jon. "Dragging Canoe (Tsi'yu-gûnsi'ni), Chickamauga Cherokee Patriot." In *The Human Tradition in the American Revolution*, edited by Nancy L. Rhoden and Ian K. Steele. Wilmington, Del.: Scholarly Resources, 1999.

Perdue, Theda. *Cherokee Women: Gender and Culture Change, 1700–1835.* Lincoln: University of Nebraska Press, 1998.

———. *"Mixed Blood" Indians: Racial Construction in the Early South.* Athens: University of Georgia Press, 2003.

Perkins, Elizabeth. *Borderlands: Experience and Memory in the Revolutionary Ohio Valley.* Chapel Hill: University of North Carolina Press, 1998.

Piecuch, Jim. *Three Peoples, One King: Loyalists, Indians and Slaves in the Revolutionary South, 1775–1782.* Columbia: University of South Carolina Press, 2008.

Piker, Joshua A. "Colonists and Creeks: Rethinking the Pre-Revolutionary Southern Backcountry." *The Journal of Southern History* 70, no. 3 (August 2004): 503–540.

———. *Okfuskee: A Creek Indian Town in Colonial America.* Cambridge, Mass.: Harvard University Press, 2004.

———. "'White and Clean' and Contested: Creek Towns and Trading Paths in the Aftermath of the Seven Years' War." *Ethnohistory* 50, no. 2 (Spring 2003): 315–347.

Prucha, Francis Paul. *The Sword of the Republic: The United States Army on the Frontier, 1783–1846*. Lincoln: University of Nebraska Press, 1987.

Remini, Robert V. *The Battle of New Orleans: Andrew Jackson and America's First Military Victory*. New York: Penguin Books, 1999.

Rhoden, Nancy L., and Ian K. Steele, eds. *The Human Tradition in the American Revolution*. Wilmington, Del.: Scholarly Resources, 1999.

Richter, Daniel K. *Before the Revolution: America's Ancient Pasts*. Cambridge, Mass.: Harvard University Press, 2011.

Rockwell, Stephen J. *Indian Affairs and the Administrative State in the Nineteenth Century*. New York: Cambridge University Press, 2010.

Rodriguez, Junius P. "Always 'En Garde': The Effects of Slave Insurrection upon the Louisiana Mentality, 1811–1815." *Louisiana History: The Journal of the Louisiana Historical Association* 33, no. 4 (Autumn 1992): 399–416.

Rothman, Adam. *Slave Country: American Expansionism and the Origins of the Deep South*. Cambridge, Mass.: Harvard University Press, 2005.

Saunt, Claudio. "'Domestic . . . Quiet Being Broke': Gender Conflict among Creek Indians in the Eighteenth Century." In *Contact Points: American Frontiers from the Mohawk Valley to the Mississippi, 1750–1830*, edited by Andrew Cayton and Frederika Teute. Chapel Hill: University of North Carolina Press, 1998.

———. *A New Order of Things: Property, Power, and the Transformation of the Creek Indians, 1733–1816*. New York: Cambridge University Press, 1999.

Sayre, Gordon M. *The Indian Chief as Tragic Hero: Native Resistance and the Literatures of America from Moctezuma to Tecumseh*. Chapel Hill: University of North Carolina Press, 2005.

Sheehan, Bernard H. *Seeds of Extinction: Jeffersonian Philanthropy and the American Indian*. Chapel Hill: University of North Carolina Press, 1973.

Sherfy, Michael J. "A Persistent Removal: Black Hawk, Commemoration, and Historic Sites in Illinois." *Journal of the Illinois State Historical Society* 100, no. 3 (Fall 2007): 240–267.

Silver, Peter. *Our Savage Neighbors: How Indian War Transformed Early America*. New York: W. W. Norton, 2008.

Sosin, Jack M. *Whitehall and the Wilderness: The Middle West in British Colonial Policy*. Lincoln: University of Nebraska Press, 1961.

Spencer, C. Tucker, and Frank T. Reuter. *Injured Honor: The Chesapeake–Leopard Affair, June 22, 1807*. Annapolis: Naval Institute Press, 1996.

Stagg, J. C. A. *The War of 1812: Conflict for a Continent*. New York: Cambridge University Press, 2012.

Steele, Ian K. *Warpaths: Invasions of North America*. New York: Oxford University Press, 1995.

———. "The Shawnees and the English: Captives and War, 1753–1765." In *The Boundaries between Us: Natives and Newcomers along the Frontiers of the Old Northwest Territory, 1750–1850*, edited by Daniel P. Barr. Kent, Ohio: Kent State University Press, 2006.

Sturtevant, William C. "The Cherokee Frontiers, the French Revolution, and William Augustus Bowles." In *The Cherokee Indian Nation: A Troubled History*, edited by Duane H. King, ed. Knoxville: University of Tennessee Press, 1979.

Sugden, John. *Blue Jacket: Warrior of the Shawnees*. Lincoln: University of Nebraska Press, 2000.

———. "Early Pan-Indianism: Tecumseh's Tour of the Indian Country, 1811–1812." *American Indian Quarterly* 10, no. 4 (Autumn 1986): 273–304.

———. *Tecumseh: A Life*. New York: Henry Holt, 1998.

Sweet, Julie Anne. *Negotiating for Georgia: British-Creek Relations in the Trustee Era, 1733–1752*. Athens: University of Georgia Press, 2005.

Sword, Wiley. *President Washington's Indian War: The Struggle for the Old Northwest, 1790–1795*. Norman: University of Oklahoma Press, 1985.

Taylor, Alan. *The Civil War of 1812: American Citizens, British Subjects, Irish Rebels, and Indian Allies*. New York: Alfred A. Knopf, 2010.

———. *The Divided Ground: Indians, Settlers, and the Northern Borderland of the American Revolution*. New York: Alfred A. Knopf, 2006.

———. *The Internal Enemy: Slavery and War in Virginia, 1772–1832*. New York: W. W. Norton, 2013.

Thompson, Thomas Marshall. "National Newspaper and Legislative Reactions to Louisiana's Deslondes Slave Revolt of 1811." *Louisiana History: The Journal of the Louisiana Historical Association* 33, no. 1 (Winter 1992): 5–29.

Van Zandt, Cynthia J. *Brothers among Nations: The Pursuit of Intercultural Alliances in Early America, 1580–1660*. New York: Oxford University Press, 2008.

Wallace, Anthony F. C. *Jefferson and the Indians: The Tragic Fate of the First Americans*. Cambridge, Mass.: Belknap Press, 1999.

Ward, Matthew C. "The Indians Our Real Friends: The British Army and the Ohio Indians, 1758–1772." In *The Boundaries between Us: Natives and Newcomers along the Frontiers of the Old Northwest Territory, 1750–1850*, edited by Daniel P. Barr. Kent, Ohio: Kent State University Press, 2006.

Waselkov, Gregory A. *A Conquering Spirit: Fort Mims and the Redstick War of 1813–1814*. Tuscaloosa: University of Alabama Press, 2006.

Waselkov, Gregory A., Peter H. Wood, and Tom Hatley, eds. *Powhatan's Mantle: Indians in the Colonial Southeast*. Rev. ed. Lincoln: University of Nebraska Press, 2006.

Weber, David J. *The Spanish Empire in North America*. New Haven, Conn.: Yale University Press, 1992.

Weeks, Charles A. *Paths to a Middle Ground: The Diplomacy of Natchez, Boukfouka, Nogales, and San Fernando De Las Barrancas, 1791–1795*. Tuscaloosa: University of Alabama Press, 2005.

White, Richard. *The Middle Ground: Indians, Empires and Republics in the Great Lakes Region 1650–1815*. New York: Cambridge University Press, 1991.

Williams, Glenn F. *Year of the Hangman: George Washington's Campaign against the Iroquois*. Yardley, Penn.: Westholme, 2005.

Willig, Timothy D. *Restoring the Chain of Friendship: British Policy and the Indians of the Great Lakes, 1783–1815*. Lincoln: University of Nebraska Press, 2008.

Wood, Gordon. "The Paranoid Style: Causality and Deceit in the Eighteenth Century." *William and Mary Quarterly* 39, no. 3 (July 1982): 402–441.

Wood, Peter H. "The Changing Population of the Colonial South: An Overview by Race and Region, 1685–1790." In *Powhatan's Mantle: Indians in the Colonial Southeast* [rev. ed.], edited by Gregory A. Waselkov, Peter H. Wood, and Tom Hatley. Lincoln: University of Nebraska Press, 2006.

Wright, J. Leitch, Jr. *William Augustus Bowles: Director General of the Creek Nation*. Athens: University of Georgia Press, 2010.

Index

References to illustrations are in italic type.

Abenakis, 79
Adams, John, 118
Adams, John Quincy, 169, 230, 233, 235
Alderson, Robert, 120, 269n16
Amherst, Sir Jeffrey, 24, 25, 26, 31, 241, 248n20
Arbuthnot, Alexander, 233
Armbrister, James, 233
Aron, Stephen, 65
Attakullakulla (Little Carpenter, Cherokee chief), 21, 34, 47, 48, 50, 64
Augusta, Georgia, 79
Aupaumut, Capt. Hendrick, 114

Bacon's Rebellion, 20
Bailyn, Bernard, 6
Barnes, Celia, 103
Beard, John, 155–156, 267n20
Bickham, Troy, 76
biological warfare against Indians, 27
Bird, Capt. Henry, 77
black drink, 22, 23
Black Hawk, 14, *135*, 235–239
Black Hawk War, 236–239
black soldiers, fear of, 40, 170, 179, 229
Bloody Fellow (Cherokee chief), 153
Blount, William (governor of Southwestern Territory), 120–121, 123, 126, 138, 151, 153, 156–157, 162–163, 267n20

Blount, Willie (governor of Tennessee), 202; dismisses Creek civil war, 208
Blue Jacket, 107, 111, 239
Blue Licks, battle of, 83
Boone, Daniel, 63, 65, 83
Boone, Jemima, 65
Botetourt, Governor (Virginia), 41, 42
Boulware, Tyler, 95, 122
Bouquet, Henry, 24, 30
Bowlegs, Billy (Seminole chief), 231
Bowles, William Augustus, 101, 120–121, 127, *130*, 137, 139–149, 158, 175–176, 199, 212, 224, 264n8, 264n17; Arthur Campbell's assessment of, 146; captured by Spanish, 147; death of, 180–181; liberates slaves, 177–179, 231; and war with Spanish, 144
Brant, Joseph (Mohawk chief), 80, 89, 93, 114, 156, 168; insists upon Fort Miami, 113
Braund, Katherine, 196, 272n10
British influence on Indians, 101, 105, 117, 137, 151, 182, 185, 188, 196, 203, 208, 211, 214, 219, 221–226, 233, 241, 258n23
Brock, Gen. Sir Isaac, 204, 222; death of, 206; and Tecumseh, 205–206
Brown, Thomas, 79
Burgoyne, Gen. John, Saratoga campaign of, 73, 75

Burke, Edmund, 76, 77, 255n8
Burnt Corn Creek, battle of, 210, 212, 230
Burr, Aaron, conspiracy of, 126, 177, 198
Butler, Col. John, 89, 112
Butler, Sen. Pierce, 102–103, 109, 117

Cache River Massacre, 209–210
Calloway, Colin, 12, 274n18, 278n9
Cameron, Alexander, 4, 78
Campbell, Arthur, 49, 79, 81, 83, 94, 95, 125, 127–128, 152–154, 158, 256n26
Carleton, Sir Guy, 66; becomes Lord Dorchester, 111, 116, 139
Carondelet, Gov. Baron de, 103–104, 123, 137, 155, 161–163; opposes giving artillery to Chickasaws, 154, 163
Catawbas, 20, 24, 27, 28, 32, 37
Catholic-Indian conspiracy, fear of, 30, 54
Cayton, Andrew R. L., 125
Cherokees, 21, 22, 23, 24, 27, 28, 29, 31, 32, 35, 36, 43, 46, 48, 49, 50, 52, 53, 56, 58, 64, 67–68, 73–74, 76, 79, 80, 83–84, 87–88, 91–92, 95, 101, 105, 110, 117, 120, 123–124, 126, 128, 139, 142–143, 151–152, 154, 156, 158–159, 162, 165, 179, 194–195, 226–228; as ally of Andrew Jackson, 219–220, 225; Cherokee War of 1760, 25, 34, 66; and Fort Stanwix, 37–42, 47; receive gunpowder from Transylvania Co., 63; and Shawnees, 65; visit Williamsburg, 69
Chesapeake-Leopard Affair, 183, 186
Chickamaugas, 64–65, 77, 78, 81, 83, 92–93, 95, 97, 120–121, 123, 127, 142, 155
Chickasaws, 24, 27, 29, 32, 35, 36, 41, 45, 46, 47, 48, 59, 67, 74, 76, 78, 79, 84, 91, 98, 108, 121–122, 128, 138, 143, 150–157, 160–163, 226–227, 268n41; ask for artillery, 154, 163, 171, 179; war with Creeks, 100, 268n41
Chickasaw Bluffs, Spanish fort at, 160–161
Chippewas, 39, 43, 74, 77, 186, 238
Choctaws, 28, 29, 31, 32, 36, 40, 42, 46, 48, 53, 56, 59, 61, 67, 77, 78, 84, 91, 119, 128, 138, 140, 152–153, 158, 160, 162–163, 171, 181–182, 187, 189, 194, 196, 226–228
Claiborne, Gen. F. L., 213–214, 216
Claiborne, W. C. C., 167, 197, 210–211, 275n34
Clark, George Rogers, 80–81, 93, 109, 138, 152, 163–164; disrupts pan-Indianism, 74–75, 77
Clark, William, 155, 160, 192, 236
Clay, Henry, 193, 230
Cleves, Rachel Hope, 274n8
Cochrane, Vice Adm. Alexander, 222–226, 228
Cocke, Sen. William, 165
confederacies, 42, 44, 45, 46, 47; pro-British, 67, 74, 107
conflation of Indians and foreigners, 75, 208
Constitution, U.S., 94
Crawley, Martha, 200–202
Creeks, 3, 9, 12, 22, 23, 24, 28, 29, 32, 33, 34, 35, 36, 37, 39, 40, 41, 42, 43, 45, 46, 48, 52, 53, 56, 59, 60, 61, 66–67, 73, 77, 79, 82, 84, 87–88, 91, 94, 99, 117–122, 124–125, 128, 138–140, 142–143, 145–146, 149–152, 155–156, 158–162, 171, 176, 178–179, 182, 187, 189, 193, 196, 204, 208, 212, 214, 228, 232, 241; and accusations of matricide, 216; American roads through territory of, 193–194; civil war, 195, 201, 208; diplomacy with U.S., 95,

103–104; meet with Northern Indians, 4, 47, 93, 114; and Red Sticks, 195, 196, 200–203, 207, 209–217, 219–223, 228, 230–233, 272n10, 278n19
Croghan, George, 4, 21, 25, 26, 33, 35, 37, 43, 248n20
"crying blood," 23
Cumberland settlement, 143, 154

Dartmouth, Lord, 45, 46, 47, 54, 62, 66
decapitation, practiced on rebel slaves, 61, 119, 198
Delawares, 22, 23, 31, 33, 34, 41, 43, 49, 51, 74, 77, 83, 88, 182, 188
De Lemos, Gov. Gayoso, 137, 151
Deslondes Revolt, 198–199, 203
Detroit, Mich., 25, 26, 39, 43, 74, 77, 79, 80, 84, 89, 97, 120, 204; Gen. Hull surrenders, 205–206
Dixon, David, 25
dogs, use of: against former slaves, 241; against Indians, 27, 241
Dowd, Gregory, 4, 7, 22, 29, 64, 188, 194
Dragging Canoe (Chickamauga chief), 64, 68, 97, 98, 120, 122–123, 142, 158, 239, 242
Duck River, Tenn., Red Stick raid on, 200–203
Dunmore, Lord, 48, 49, 50, 55, 57, 62, 63, 101, 141, 149, 175; arms Shawnee hostages, 60; Dunmore's War, 52, 57, 65, 225n7; emancipation proclamation of, 61, 199

Ecuyer, Simeon, 27
Elliott, Matthew (agent), 188, 189
Egerton, Douglas, 7
Emistisiguo (Creek chief), 47; death of, 82–83
Enlightenment, 6, 8, 29
exceptionalism, American, 242–243

Fallen Timbers, battle of, 158; remembered, 186
Fauquier, Francis (governor of Virginia), 34
fear, 6; of armed free blacks, 197–199, 204, 209, 226, 227–229, 231–232; of Indian-slave collusion, 8, 9, 60, 102; of slave insurrection, 6, 7, 71, 101, 118–120, 177, 197–200, 203–204, 211, 213, 228–229, 243
Federalists, criticize pro-war Jeffersonians, 191, 193, 196, 227
Florida, 14, 28, 119, 162, 177–179, 194, 196, 198, 202–203, 207–211, 221, 223–226, 237, 269n16; slave raids and, 82, 231–234
Fort De Chartres, 56
Fort Loudoun, 21
Fort Miami, 158
Fort Mims massacre, 212–217, 220; media coverage of, 213
Fort Pitt, 25, 30, 56, 62
Franklin (frontier state), 91
Franklin, Benjamin, 37
free blacks, fear of armed, 197–199, 204, 209, 226, 227–229, 231–232
French, influence among Indians, 24, 26, 28, 29, 30, 32, 54, 162, 166, 170–171
Furstenberg, François, 90, 257n4

Gage, Gen. Thomas, 4, 26, 27, 29, 31, 35, 36, 43, 56, 57, 58, 59, 62, 152
Gaines, Gen. Edmund, 233, 237
Gates, Gen. Horatio, 76
Geggus, David, 7
"general Indian war," 6, 7, 12, 59
George III (king), 12, 36, 41, 55, 60, 88, 139, 142–143
Georgia, 48, 82, 104
Germaine, Lord George, 66, 76, 80
Girty, James, 189
Girty, Simon, 88

Gore, Francis, 187, 189
Greene, Gen. Nathanael, 79, 82, 84
Grenville, Lord William, 111
Griffin, Patrick, 7, 50
Gun Merchant (Creek chief), 28
Gunn, Rep. James, 102–103, 117

Haiti. *See* Saint Domingue
Haldimand, Gen. Frederick, 53, 56, 73, 80, 81, 87, 89
Hamilton, Alexander, 113, 191
Hamilton, Henry, 74, 109–111, 141; plans for Indian homeland of, 110
Hammond, George, 108, 110, 146; as mediator between U.S. and Northwestern Confederacy, 111, 115, 125
Hampton, Gen. Wade, 198–199
Hanging Maw (Cherokee chief), 142, 155–156, 158
Harmar, Gen. Josiah, 106–109, 115, 139, 208
Harrison, William Henry, 171, 174, 182–183, 185, 187–190, 192–193, 195, 206–207, 217, 236, 272n8
Hawkins, Benjamin, 100, 178, 195–196, 202, 211, 228; civilization program with Creeks, 215; disruption of Indian gender roles, 196
Henderson, Richard, and Transylvania Co., 60, 63–65
Hillabee massacre, 216–217
Hillsborough, Lord, 39, 40, 41, 42, 45
Hinderaker, Eric, 37, 250n20
Holston River, 60, 68, 81, 177
Holton, Woody, 42, 43
Horseshoe Bend (Tohopeka), *133*; battle of, 219–221, 223, 232
Horsman, Reginald, 7
Hull, Gen. William, 205–206; proclamation of, 204
Hurons, 20, 43, 88

Illinois Company, 38
Indian buffer state, 115, 230
Indian diplomacy, European influence on gender roles in, 92
"Indian-hating," 8, 35; and Americans' self-image, 90
Indian-slave collusion, fear of, 8, 9, 60, 102
Indian trade goods, necessity of, 61, 66, 74, 87
intertribal warfare, encouraged to forestall pan-Indianism, 27, 29, 44, 48, 161–162
Iroquois League, 20, 21, 22, 33, 34, 36, 37, 40, 46, 52, 55, 58, 76, 77, 89–90, 93, 110, 113; divided in Revolutionary War, 63

Jackson, Andrew, 13, 14, 124, *134*, 138, 173–174, 215–216, 219–221, 225–226, 228–230, 237, 267n41, 274n9; hangs British nationals, 233–234; motives for Creek war, 202–203
Jackson, Sen. James, 102, 178
Jay, John, 125, 158
Jefferson, Thomas, 13, 79, 115, 118–119, 169, 171, 179, 183, 208
Johnson, Sir Guy, 56, 62
Johnson, Sir William, 4, 21, 25, 27, 28, 35, 36, 43, 116, *129*, 248n20; death of, 55–56; and Lord Dunmore's War, 52; and Treaty of Fort Stanwix, 37–41, 44, 46, 54, 89

Kanon, Tom, 201, 273n2
Kaské, Charlot (Shawnee beloved man), 33
Kentucky, 38, 39, 40, 42, 46, 51, 57, 63, 64, 77, 81, 96, 101
Keokuk (Winnebago Prophet), 236
Kickapoos, 47, 57, 186
King Philip's War, 20, 61

INDEX

Kings Mountain, battle of, 79
Knox, Henry, 3, 4, 105–106, 115, 121, 123–124, 128, *131*, 146–147, 152, 154, 162, 191, 241, 258n27, 259n7; estimates cost of conquest of Indians, 97; report on Indian Affairs, 95–97, 157; seeks to appease Creeks, 99–101, 121; and struggle between national honor and land acquisition, 94

Lachance, Paul, 118
Lafayette, Marquis de, 105
land speculation, 37–38, 41–42, 60–63
Las Casas, Gov. Luis de, 137
Lepore, Jill, 6
Little Turkey (Cherokee chief), 142
Little Turtle (Miami chief), 107
Logan, John (Mingo chief), 51
Louisiana, 28, 118, 170, 172, 176, 181, 197–199, 210
Louverture, Toussaint, 118

Madison, James, 172, 187, 193
Mangourit, Michel, 119–120
Mapp, Paul W., 56
Marienstras, Elise, 184, 225
maroons, 173
Martin, Joel, 212
Martin, Joseph, 91
Martin, Josiah (governor of North Carolina), 63
McConnell, Michael N., 7, 45
McCrea, Jane, 75–76, 184, 255n7
McGillivray, Alexander (Creek chief), 93, 99, 101, 103, 118, 120–121, 140–142, 144–146, 148–149, 179, 239, 242, 259n7; death of, 122, 149, 158
McIntosh, William (Creek chief), 232, 234
McKee, Alexander, 52, 53, 62, 87, 88, 113, 115, 120, 138, 149, 175, 188; death of, 168–169

McKee, Thomas, 186
McQueen, Peter (Red Stick chief), 210, 214
Melville, Lord, 109–111, 115, 225
Menominees, 169, 238
Mesquakies (Foxes), 236–237
Metacom (King Philip), 10
Miamis, 24, 39, 47, 52, 57, 74, 106, 114
Millett, Nathaniel, 7, 278n13
Mingos, 51, 77, 88
Miró, Gov. Esteban, 98, 154
Mobile, Ala., 29, 31, 67 171, 179, 193, 203, 226, 229
Moraviantown, battle of, 217
Morgan, George, 37
Mortar (Upper Creek chief), 28, 35, 47, 59

Napoleon, 170–172, 182, 189, 221, 229
"Nasty Plot," 6, 10
Neolin, 22
Newman, Simon P., 120
New Orleans, 31, 40, 171, 197–199, 225, 228, 229
Nichols, David A., 7, 155, 258n30, 260n12
Nickajack, 123
Nicolls, Lt. Edward, 227–228; emancipation efforts of, 231–232
Nootka Sound crisis, 142–143
Northern Indians, 12, 28, 29, 31, 42, 43, 44, 47
Northwest Confederacy, 107, 113, 114, 120, 124, 127, 137, 151, 158, 161, 260n20
Norton, Mary B., 10

Occonostotah (Cherokee chief), 42, 47
Ohio Indians, 28
Old Tassel (Cherokee chief), 84, 91; murder of, 95
Oneidas, 33, 93; fear Indian alliance against, 62–63

O'Neill, Gov. Arturo, 103, 104, 123
Ordinance of 1785, 94
Ordinance of 1787, 94, 96, 102
Osages, 45, 189
Osceola (Seminole chief), *136*, 239–241; compared to Tecumseh, 240
Ottawas, 39, 43, 64

Pakenham, Gen. Edward, 229
pan-American union, proposed, 62
pan-Indianism, 12, 13, 14, 20, 21, 30, 39, 114–115; British support for, 116; defined, 4; as encouraging white unity, 57
Panton & Leslie, 99, 101, 140, 144, 147
Parkman, Francis, 8, 55
Peale, Charles Willson, 85–86
Pensacola, 34, 138–140, 203–204, 207, 210–211, 214, 224–225, 228, 232
Philadelphia, celebrates Treaty of Paris, 85–86
Philatuche (Afro-Creek chief), 141
Pia Matta (Chickasaw chief), 32
Pickens, Gen. Andrew, 90–91, 118, 122, 150, 262n14
Pickering, Timothy, 159, 162–163
Piecuch, Jim, 7, 77
Pigot, Capt. Hugh, 223–224
Piker, Joshua, 28, 252n13
Piomingo (Mountain Leader, Chickasaw chief), 83, 100, 108, 122, 155, 157, 160, 263n22
Point Pleasant (battle of), 57–58
Pontiac (Ottawa chief), 5, 10, 12, 17, 23, 24, 28, 32, 33, 71
Pontiac's War, 19, 26, 27, 29; influence of, 52, 88, 105, 159, 186, 189, 217, 242
Potawatomis, 39, 43, 74, 238
Proclamation of 1763, violations of, 32, 39, 42, 47, 50, 63, 249n6
Procter, Gen. Henry, 207

Prospect Bluff, fort at, 232
Prucha, Francis P., 7

Raven of Chota (Cherokee chief), 84
Red Jacket (Seneca chief), 188
Red Sticks. *See* Creeks
Republicans, Jeffersonian, 185, 191–193, 196, 202–203, 227
Revolution, American, 12, 71
Revolution, French, 72, 103, 138, 163
Revolution, Haitian. *See* Saint Domingue
River Raisin, massacre at, 207, 209, 227
Robertson, James, 50, 63, 149, 154, 157–158, 161, 162–163, 196, 201–202, 207, 263n22, 268n43, 273n3
Roosevelt, Theodore, 8
Rothman, Adam, 204
Running Water, 123
Russell, Peter, 168–169

Saint Augustine, Florida, 60, 82, 84, 102, 141, 203, 209, 230
Saint Domingue, 13, 118–119, 170–172, 176, 179, 197–198, 269n16
Sauks, 14, 186, 236, 237–238; British Band of, 236–238
Scioto Confederacy, 38, 43, 53
Scots-Irish, 10
Seagrove, James (agent), 127–128, 147–148, 150
Seminoles, 141, 178–179, 202, 208, 221, 224, 231–233, 237, 239–241; black Seminoles, 233; Second Seminole War, 239–241
Senecas, 22, 24, 33, 43, 52, 53, 74, 108
Sevier, John, 50, 63, 79, 165, 201, 207
Shawnees, 3, 20, 21, 26, 45; diplomacy of, 22, 23, 24, 31, 33, 36, 43, 45, 46, 47, 48, 50, 56, 58, 61, 63–65, 74, 76–77, 87–88, 93, 98, 101, 105, 121–122, 127, 149, 151, 171, 183, 186, 191, 214, 227; and Lord Dunmore's War,

52–53, 57; and Treaty of Fort Stanwix, 38, 41, 51
Sheehan, Bernard, 7
Shelby, Isaac, 149, 156
Silver, Peter, 7, 8, 12, 30, 65, 247n10, 257n3; anti-Indian sublime hypothesis of, 65, 72, 126, 243; and literary anti-Indianism, 75, 183–184
Simcoe, Lt. Gov. John Graves, 112–113, 116, 151, 158, 168, 176–177
Sioux, 77, 169, 238, 242
Slaves: British emancipation efforts, 81–82, 226–229, 240; fear of insurrection by, 6, 7, 71, 101, 118–120, 177, 197–200, 203–204, 211, 213, 228–229, 243; in New York City, 10; raids from Florida, 141; recovery of by owners, 68, 82, 117, 231–234
South Carolina, 33, 36
Southern Indians, 12, 13, 21, 26, 27, 28, 29, 30, 31, 43, 44, 47, 189, 191; culture of, 23
Spanish, influence among Indians, 26, 28, 40, 45, 60, 71, 78, 98, 101, 104, 105, 117–119, 123, 128, 137, 139, 148, 150, 153–154, 160, 166–168, 178, 181, 196–199, 203, 209–211, 214, 229, 232
St. Clair, Arthur: British euphoria at defeat of, 109; defeat of by Northwestern Confederacy, 107–111, 120, 123, 125, 127, 145, 147, 192; legacy of, 208, 235; recommendation of to reconcile Indians, 97
Steele, John, 117, 127
Stevenson, Charles, 112–113, 261n16
Stono Rebellion, 102
Stuart, Charles, 34
Stuart, John, 4, 24, 25, 26, 27, 28, 29, 31, 32, 33, 35, 40, 45, 46, 48, 49, 53, 57, 59, 66–67, 69, 73, 127; encourages intertribal warfare, 48, 56; flees Charles Town, 60; opposes Fort Stanwix cession, 44, 46–47; seeks Sir William Johnson's job, 56
Sugden, John, 218

Tagaia (Cayuga chief), 89
Taylor, Alan, 7, 9, 227, 233, 257n9, 260n16, 260n18
Tecumseh, 13, 14, *132*, 173, 186–190, 192–196, 203, 205–206, 210–211, 216–217, 252n26, 276n10; death of, 217; legacy, 217–219, 235, 237–243
Tenskwatawa (Shawnee Prophet), 173, 182, 185, 187–190, 192–194, 204, 230, 236–237, 242
Thomas, John, 45
Thrower, Robert G., 275n34
Tippecanoe, battle of, 187, 192, 195, 201, 204, 230
tomahawk and scalping knife, rhetoric of, 183, 191, 220
Treaty of Dewett's Corner, 67–68
Treaty of Fort Harmar, 102
Treaty of Fort Jackson, 225–226
Treaty of Fort McIntosh, 102
Treaty of Fort Stanwix, 37–42, 44, 46–47, 51, 54–55; cited as protecting Indian lands, 116
Treaty of French Broad, 117
Treaty of Greenville, 158–159, 161, 165, 230
Treaty of Hard Labor, 38
Treaty of Long Island, 68
Treaty of New York, 100–104, 145–146
Treaty of Nogales, 151
Treaty of Paris (1783), 13, 85; terms, 86
Treaty of Rock Landing, 145
Treaty of San Ildefonso, 161
Treaty of San Lorenzo, 161
Turner, Nat, revolt of, 240

Van Zandt, Cynthia, 20
Vincennes, 74
Virginia, 35, 36, 39, 40, 41, 43, 48, 51, 58

Wallace, Anthony F. C., 7
war belts, pan-Indian, 77, 182, 186
Ward, Nancy (Cherokee beloved woman), 92
Warrior's Path, 65, 68
Waselkov, Gregory, 225, 278n19
Washington, George, 3, 13, 63, 76, 80, 85, 99, 107, 118, 162, 195; administration of confronts pan-Indianism, 116; fears black troops encouraging slave revolts, 170; fears Western secession, 105; seeks to avoid war with Southern nations, 101–102, 124, 148, 156–157; struggle between national honor and land acquisition of, 94–95
Watauga Association, 50, 63, 65, 78, 79
Watts, John (Cherokee chief), 122

Wayne, Gen. Anthony, 82–83, 100, 102, 118, 124, 145, 150–151, 155–161, 191–193, 259n11; and Legion of the U.S., 125; on multi-ethnic British forces, 82
Weatherford, William (Red Eagle, Red Stick chief), *134*, 179, 212, 221
West Florida, 40
White, Richard, 7, 57, 84
Whitesides, William, 159
Wilkinson, Gen. James, 140, 160, 197, 235
Willig, Timothy, 87
Winamac (Potawatomi chief), 187
Wood, Gordon, 6, 8
Woodbine, George, 224–227, 231–233
Wyandots, 39, 74, 77, 91, 101

www.ingramcontent.com/pod-product-compliance
Lightning Source LLC
Chambersburg PA
CBHW022104150426
43195CB00008B/264